The Thing about Museums

The Thing about Museums constitutes a unique, highly diverse collection of essays unprecedented in existing books in either museum and heritage studies or material culture studies. Taking varied perspectives and presenting a range of case studies, the chapters all address objects in the context of museums, galleries and/ or the heritage sector more broadly. Specifically, the book deals with how objects are constructed in museums, the ways in which visitors may directly experience those objects, how objects are utilised within particular representational strategies and forms, and the challenges and opportunities presented by using objects to communicate difficult and contested matters. Topics and approaches examined in the book are diverse, but include the objectification of natural history specimens and museum registers; materiality, immateriality, transience and absence; subject/ object boundaries; sensory, phenomenological perspectives; the museumisation of objects and collections; and the dangers inherent in assuming that objects, interpretation and heritage are 'good' for us.

Sandra Dudley is Senior Lecturer in the School of Museum Studies, University of Leicester, UK. Recent books include *Materialising Exile: material culture and embodied experience among Karenni refugees in Thailand* (2010) and *Museum Materialities* (Routledge 2010).

Amy Jane Barnes has recently completed doctoral research on the collection, interpretation and display of visual culture of the Chinese Cultural Revolution in contemporary British museums (University of Leicester 2009).

Jennifer Binnie, University of Leicester, UK, is looking at the impact which art within museums and galleries may have upon well-being.

Julia Petrov, University of Leicester, UK. Her current project traces the development of dress exhibitions in museums in England and North America over the twentieth century.

Jennifer Walklate, University of Leicester, UK. Her Arts and Humanities Research Council-funded research explores and compares the production of temporal experiences in museums and works of literature.

The Thing about Museums

Objects and Experience, Representation and Contestation

Essays in Honour of Professor Susan M. Pearce

Edited by Sandra Dudley, Amy Jane Barnes, Jennifer Binnie, Julia Petrov and Jennifer Walklate

LONDON AND NEW YORK

First published 2012
by Routledge
2 Park Square, Milton Park, Abingdon, Oxon OX14 4RN

Simultaneously published in the USA and Canada
by Routledge
711 Third Avenue, New York, NY 10017

Routledge is an imprint of the Taylor & Francis Group, an informa business

British Library Cataloguing in Publication Data
A catalogue record for this book is available from the British Library

Library of Congress Cataloging in Publication Data
The thing about museums : objects and experience, representation and contestation : essays in honour of professor Susan M. Pearce / edited by Sandra Dudley . . . [*et al.*].
    p. cm.
    Includes bibliographical references and index.
    1. Museum exhibits–Case studies.   2. Museum techniques–Case studies.
    3. Museums–Philosophy.   I. Dudley, Sandra H.   II. Pearce, Susan M.
    AM151.T55 2011
    069'.5–dc22

                                                                          2011011489

ISBN: 978-0-415-67904-6 (hbk)
ISBN: 978-0-203-80352-3 (ebk)

Typeset in 10/12pt Baskerville
by Graphicraft Limited, Hong Kong

Printed and bound in Great Britain by
CPI Antony Rowe, Chippenham, Wiltshire

For Susan Pearce

Contents

ILLUSTRATIONS

Contributors

Amy Jane Barnes has recently completed doctoral research on the collection, interpretation and display of visual culture of the Chinese Cultural Revolution in contemporary British museums (University of Leicester 2009). Prior to this she was employed as Curatorial Assistant at the Percival David Foundation of Chinese Art (SOAS).

Caroline Bergeron has worked in public relations, particularly within the corporation social responsibility area. She was also responsible for the exhibitions sector of the National Public Library of Quebec. She is currently doing her PhD in Museum Studies and working for Université de Montréal, Canada.

Jennifer Binnie is currently a PhD student at University of Leicester, UK, looking at the impact which art within museums and galleries may have upon wellbeing. She is funded by AHRC and The Art Fund. She has come from a background in psychology, with particular interest in colour and contour prefer-ence, and children's drawing.

Beverley Butler is Senior Lecturer in Cultural Heritage Studies in the Institute of Archaeology, University College London, UK. Her research interests include cultural memory, heritage as wellbeing/illbeing, archival imaginations and ethno-graphic methods. She has conducted long-term research in Egypt and Palestine and is author of *Return to Alexandria: an ethnography of cultural heritage revivalism and museum memory* (Left Coast Press).

Hannah-Lee Chalk is currently undertaking a PhD at the University of Man-chester's Department of Social Anthropology, UK. Her research aims to extend material culture theory to collections of natural objects, in order to under-stand how natural objects are attributed value. She has a degree in Geography/ Geology (University of Manchester) and an MSc in Museum Studies (University of Leicester), and has worked in the museum sector and with geological collec-tions for a number of years.

Shirley Chubb's visual practice focuses on critical interventions within museum collections and archives. She is Senior Lecturer in Fine Art at the University of

Chichester, UK, and in 2007 was awarded a practice-based PhD by publication at the School of Arts and Communication, University of Brighton.

Nikki Clayton holds a PhD in Museum Studies from the University of Leicester. She works as a Project Officer for Leicestershire's Open Museum; a service that loans objects, artworks and touring museum displays. She established the Moving Objects loans scheme, and specialises in supporting local service providers and hard-to-reach community groups to use the loans collections as inspiration for creative writing and arts initiatives. She is co-editor of *Words & Things: writing creatively from objects and art.*

Chris Dorsett is a long established artist-curator with public outputs ranging from published essays to solo exhibitions. He is presently Reader in Art School Practices in the School of Arts and Social Sciences (A&SS), Northumbria University. He has published, presented and exhibited widely in the UK and abroad, with a particular focus on installations in museums and a special interest in the practices, objects and interpretations of museums.

Sandra Dudley is a social anthropologist and currently Senior Lecturer in the School of Museum Studies, University of Leicester, UK. Her research interests encompass material culture, materiality, dress, museums, art, exile, displacement, Southeast Asia and ethnography. Recent books include *Materialising Exile: material culture and embodied experience among Karenni refugees in Thailand* (Berghahn 2010) and *Museum Materialities* (ed., Routledge 2010).

Mark Goodwin works as a community poet in the East Midlands, UK, including with Leicestershire's Open Museum for over eight years. He co-wrote *Words & Things: writing creatively from objects and art*, published as part of the Write:Muse initiative. He received an Eric Gregory Award from The Society of Authors in 1998. Mark has published three full-length poetry collections: *Else* (Shearsman, 2008); *Back of A Vast* (Shearsman, 2010); *Shod* (Nine Arches Press, 2010).

Despina Kalessopoulou works as an archaeologist-museologist at the National Archaeological Museum in Athens, Greece, where she is involved in museum communication, education and exhibition design. Her major areas of interest and published work are on issues of museum education and interpretation. She is currently completing her PhD at the University of Thessaly, researching the scope and development of child-centred museum spaces.

Meighen S. Katz has a background in museum and film and has worked as a staff curator and a curatorial researcher on a number of historical exhibitions, most recently an in-exhibition theatrette in *The Melbourne Story* (Melbourne Museum). She is a faculty member, in the School of Applied Media and Social Science, Monash University, Australia.

Michael Katzberg, a museologist, cultural critic and occasional exhibition lighting designer and museum consultant, is a guest researcher based at the Amsterdam School for Cultural Analysis (ASCA), University of Amsterdam. His interests include the history and theory of museum lighting and the role played by advancements in technology; the history and theory of the display of Bio-Art; and the relationship between museum theory and cultural practice from a cultural analytic perspective.

Malika Kraamer is currently Curator of World Cultures at New Walk Museum and Art Gallery, Leicester, UK. She publishes on African textiles and did a PhD at the School of Oriental and African Studies, London, on Ewe cloth. She has taught several university courses on African Art and worked in different museums in the UK and the Netherlands.

Marlen Mouliou holds a PhD in Museum Studies from the University of Leicester. She works for the Hellenic Ministry of Culture and Tourism (Directorate of Museums, Exhibitions and Educational Programmes), where she has been involved in developing and redisplaying archaeological museums. She is also adjunct lecturer in museology at the Universities of Thessaly and Athens, and a founding member of the Editorial Board of the Greek scientific journal *Tetradia Mouseiologias* [*Museological Notebooks*].

Maria Lucia de Niemeyer Matheus Loureiro attained a degree in Museology from Museu Histórico Nacional (Brazil) in 1976 and completed a doctorate in Information Science at Universidade Federal do Rio de Janeiro. She researches information in art, and musealisation processes in art and science. Her professional experience includes museums of art, science and technology, a historic house and a botanic garden. Currently, she works at Museu de Astronomia e Ciências Afins.

Julia Petrov is a PhD student at the School of Museum Studies at the University of Leicester, UK. Her project traces the development of dress exhibitions in museums in England and North America over the twentieth century. Having previously worked with collections of dress, textiles and social history, she is a member of the Costume Society of America and the Costume Society of Great Britain.

Helen Rees Leahy is Director of the Centre for Museology and Director of the Art Gallery and Museum Studies programme at the University of Manchester, UK. She formerly worked as a curator and museum director, and has organised numerous exhibitions of fine art and design. Helen has published on topics relating to heritage, art collecting, the art market and art criticism, and the visitor's embodied encounter with the museum or exhibition.

Roger Sansi is Lecturer in Anthropology at Goldsmith's College, University of London. He has worked extensively on Afro-Brazilian art and material culture and on contemporary art in Spain. His publications include *Fetishes and Monuments: Afro-Brazilian art and culture in the 20th century* (Berghahn 2007) and 'The hidden life of stones: historicity, materiality and the value of Candomblé objects in Bahia' (*Journal of Material Culture*, Alfred Gell prize 2005).

Helen Saunderson is an exhibiting visual artist subsequent to a BA in Fine Art and Psychology (University of Reading). She is currently researching for a cross-disciplinary PhD in the School of Psychology at the University of Leicester, investigating how art experts and novices perceive contemporary art. She formerly worked as a schoolteacher.

Alice Semedo is Assistant Professor and Director for the MA Museology Studies at University of Porto, Portugal. A former doctoral student of Susan Pearce she has published on topics relating to her research interests such as museological narratives and discourses, professional museological identity, and contemporary missions for museums. She has also organized several publications which include *Museums, Discourses and Representations* (2005) and *University Museums with Science Collections* (2005).

Geoffrey N. Swinney, until the end of 2009, was for over 30 years Principal Curator of Lower Vertebrates in National Museums Scotland (NMS). In 2010, he was Research Curator in Natural Sciences, charged with collating material on the history of the institution. He continues his researches in this area as an Honorary Research Associate of NMS and for a PhD on an historical geography of the Museum.

Wing Yan Vivian Ting teaches Art Administration and Curatorship in the Academy of Visual Arts, Hong Kong Baptist University. She has a PhD in Museum Studies from the University of Leicester and her research interests focus on object–visitor communication and the display and interpretation of different cultures. She gained extensive curatorial experience with Chinese ceramic collections during placements at the Museum of East Asian Art in Bath and the Bristol City Museum and Art Gallery.

Marijke Van Eeckhaut is a research assistant in modern and contemporary visual arts at Ghent University, Belgium. Her current PhD research concerns the reconciliation of constructivism and the museum of contemporary art. Prior to this she has worked for the Museum of Contemporary Art in Antwerp and has taught at the Royal Academy of Fine Arts in the same city. Her interests include contemporary art, interpretation and museum education.

Marzia Varutti is currently a research fellow at the School of Museum Studies, University of Leicester, UK. Her doctoral dissertation, based on ten months' fieldwork in China, investigated the representation of the nation in museums in Beijing, Shanghai, and Jiangsu, Zhejiang, Sichuan and Yunnan Provinces. Her interests are the representation of cultural diversity in Chinese and Taiwanese museums, and cultural representation in European ethnographic museums.

Jennifer Walklate is a PhD student in the School of Museum Studies at the University of Leicester, UK. Her Arts and Humanities Research Council funded research explores and compares the production of temporal experiences in museums and works of literature, with the intention of developing current museological practice in spatial and exhibition design.

Claire Warrior is Senior Exhibitions Curator at the National Maritime Museum, Greenwich. She is currently a doctoral student at the Scott Polar Research Institute, University of Cambridge, in collaboration with the National Maritime Museum, working on the museum's Polar collections. Her research is supported by the Arts and Humanities Research Council.

Klaus Wehner is a practising artist working with photography and installation. He is the founder of the *Museum Clausum* in which he acts as 'collector' and 'curator', often aiming to work in collaboration with other museums as host institutions. Current and past work can be seen at www.museumclausum.org. The museum is also the subject of his current practice-based PhD research in Visual Arts at Goldsmiths, University of London, examining the relationship between photography and objects staged for exhibition.

Linda Young is a historian who teaches aspects of cultural heritage and museum studies at Deakin University, Melbourne. She has worked as a curator in museums and historic houses in Sydney, Perth and Adelaide. Her PhD led to the book *Middle Class Culture in the Nineteenth Century: America, Australia, Britain* (Palgrave, 2003). She has researched and written on houses, furnishings and jewellery; and is currently working on a book on the history of historic houses as a species of museum.

Preface

The chapters in this book originated as some of the papers presented at the international *Material Worlds* conference, hosted by the School of Museum Studies in December 2008 at the University of Leicester. I convened that conference in order to celebrate the long and distinguished contribution of Professor Susan M. Pearce to material culture studies, museum studies and archaeology. This book is, however, neither conference proceedings nor a simple *Festschrift*. All the papers to be found here have been significantly developed and revised since they were presented at the conference. They also represent only a proportion of all those submitted to the conference and for possible publication.

Numerous articles written by authors with no connections to Susan Pearce are presented alongside contributions from former students and colleagues. Some chapters mark the continuing importance of the methodological and theoretical approaches with which Susan Pearce's work has been associated. Many, conversely or in addition, identify and explore new agenda in their studies of material culture, museums and heritage. In keeping with Professor Pearce's own interdisciplinarity, chapters come from those working with objects not only in archaeology, anthropology and museum studies, but also a wide range of other subjects. The book has considerable international scope too, with authors from North and South America, Australia and numerous European countries, as well as the UK. As a result, we hope this book presents a genuinely rich diversity of perspectives on theoretical and practical aspects of things in museum and heritage settings.

Sandra Dudley
Leicester, 25 February 2011

1 Introduction
Museums and things

Sandra Dudley

Museums are about things. At least, museums hold things; and from most viewpoints objects and collections continue – some post-museums notwithstanding, perhaps – conventionally to define the museum and distinguish it from other cultural, epistemological and pedagogical establishments. This is not to say, of course, that museums are *only* about things or that objects are all that matters in the museum: much of the museological literature of the past twenty years at least, has been devoted to demonstrating precisely the opposite, showing the extent to which museums are about people, not just collections. Nevertheless, for most institutions and most observers it is objects, and the collection, preservation, storage, documentation, research and display thereof, that most easily characterise museums in contrast to other sorts of publicly oriented organisations which may also have goals of keeping and expanding knowledge, and educating and entertaining people.[1] Explorations of museums and heritage settings that begin from and focus on things, can thus illuminate the changing social and political dynamics in how and why objects come to, and then are experienced and utilised within, the museum. Ultimately, these object-focused studies can also give us further theoretical and practical insight into the museum institution itself, as many of the chapters in this book demonstrate.

At the same time, the kinds of museum- and heritage-based, object-focused studies found on the pages that follow, represent an opportunity both to apply approaches from wider material culture studies to museum contexts and to develop and extend thinking about objects through work done in museum settings. Museums are not, it is generally assumed, 'real life' in the sense of the life the objects within them lived before they entered its walls: a ritual libation cup on display in an ethnographic museum is no longer used in the religious ceremonies in which it was once so central; instead of moving from hand to hand, mouth to mouth, being filled with ceremonial liquid, drunk dry and refilled once more, the cup sits motionless, empty, permanently parched, viewed passively through the glass of its display case, untouched, unused, unblessed and unmoved. Hence, it is a commonplace to think of museum objects as not only decontextualised – because of their removal from their original contexts – but also 'dead'.[2] But if one can move away from this limited view, as an increasing number of object theorists as well as museum specialists are beginning to do, one sees that while objects may no longer be in their original contexts they are still in a setting that is none-theless real – they have been *re-* rather than *de-*contextualised – and they are still 'alive' in the sense of being experienced and engaged with by human subjects. Museum objects continue to participate in socialised relationships and interactions and to be attributed particular – and changing – meanings and values as a result. This, together with the museum space's particularity, because of its use of objects, as on one level at least a material space *par excellence* (albeit a problematic one), implies some interesting possibilities for researching and theorising people–object engagements and their implications – a good reason for museums and their objects to come back towards the centre of material culture studies.

Indeed, pushing museum studies of objects back towards a central place in material culture studies is part of a wider effort to re-engage the museum at the centre of object theory: a place it has not properly held since the late nineteenth century. It is an agenda that has recently been taken further forward by some edited collections of various kinds (e.g. Edwards, Gosden and Phillips 2006, Knell 2007a, Dudley 2010a). However, fundamental to and central within the late twentieth century efforts that began – or perhaps more properly, reignited – this agenda, is the work of Susan Pearce, in whose honour the essays in this book have been written and collected (e.g. Pearce 1989, 1990, 1992). Pearce's post-structuralist perspectives and her analyses of and insights into the semiotics and multiple interpretations attributable to museum objects and collections by differ-ent visitors, curators and others have had a lasting influence that continues today. Indeed, it is an influence that resonates throughout this very volume, directly (e.g. the semiotic model utilised by artist and academic Shirley Chubb as part of her analysis of two of her exhibitions in Chapter 14) and indirectly (e.g. the creative, subjective, poetic interpretations of objects discussed by Nikki Clayton and Mark Goodwin in Chapter 13).

The resurgence of interest in material culture studies and theory which began in anthropology and cognate disciplines in the 1980s and 1990s through the work of Susan Pearce and others (e.g. Miller 1985, Hodder 1987)[3] has now spread, to differing degrees and with varying effects, throughout the humanities and social sciences. It is not, therefore, unusual to find a primary focus on objects in fields as apparently distinct as human geography, cultural history, social anthropology or science technology studies. What form that primary focus might take, however, differs widely. In previous decades, for example, material culture studies have concentrated on the sociohistorical trajectories of things, on how objects make and change meanings and values, and on the embeddedness of material culture in social relationships (e.g. Appadurai 1986, Kopytoff 1986, Pearce 1995, Hosk-ins 1998; on similar themes in relation to colonial exchange see Thomas 1991, 1994). Processes of consumption have been a particularly important focus of much extant work (e.g. Miller 1987) although, as Ingold (2007) has pointed out, there has hardly been an equivalent emphasis on production [although there are some notable exceptions, particularly in the fields of the anthropology of art (e.g. Morphy 1991; various in Coote and Shelton 1992) and textiles (e.g. Barnes 1989; various in Weiner and Schneider 1989, Ahmed 2002)]. Some debates have focused on the notion of agency and whether or not objects can be said to have it in some form (e.g. Gell 1998, Dant 1999, Gosden 2005, Tilley 2007). Recently, there has also been increased interest in sensory perception and the potential contribution of anthropological insights, in particular into the culturally constituted nature of the senses (or at least, of our interpretations of the data we obtain from our physical senses; e.g. Howes 2003, 2005), and in phenomenologically informed approaches that stress, in different ways, the embodied nature of experience (e.g. Ingold 2000, Tilley 2004).

Some of these material culture emphases have been more influential than others on museum and heritage-based studies in recent years. The biographical and social life approaches to objects, and economic anthropology more broadly, have had significant influence on directly or indirectly stimulating studies of object trajectories and exchange in relation to collection and institutional histories (Clifford 1988, Price 1989, Kirshenblatt-Gimblett 1998, Gosden and Knowles 2001; see also Ames 1992), as has actor-network theory (e.g. Gosden, Larson and Petch 2007) and narratology (e.g. Bal 1994). The biographical and social life approach is also that taken by Marlen Mouliou and Despina Kalessopoulou in Chapter 4 of this volume, in which they explore aspects of the lives of emblematic objects in the National Archaeological Museum of Athens, 'itself a biographical object of a nation', as they explain. This approach also in some ways underlies, although indirectly, Linda Young's chapter (Chapter 10) on heroes' house museums – at least in so far as the 'magic' and affective power of these places lie in the degree to which their interpretation emphasises the authenticity of their biography as objects. Caroline Bergeron's chapter on museums and collectors (Chapter 17), on the other hand, while it relates to biography in its emphasis on the collection as extension – and, indeed, creation – of the self (cf. Bourdieu 1990), draws heavily too on economic anthropology, particularly classical gift-exchange theory, to explore the relationships between collector-donors and museum-recipients. Claire Warrior (Chapter 19) also examines the contribution of collections to both personal histories and emergent and solidifying identities – in her case, national and individual identities and the narratives and meanings that have developed around Polar artefacts now in the UK National Maritime Museum.

Sense-focused and related material cultural approaches have also begun to be explored in relation to museums (e.g. Classen 2005; various in Edwards *et al.* 2006, Candlin 2007, Dudley 2010a), and again this is a theme elaborated upon by some of the chapters in this volume. The influence on the museum experience and on our responses to museum objects of the different sensory modalities that are able to operate in a particular gallery environment are considered in Chapter 11 by Helen Saunderson, who brings empirical psychological data to bear on her reflections on visiting an exhibition. In the following chapter, Wing Yan Vivian Ting also examines aspects of sensory and wider bodily experience in museums, this time drawing particularly on both Chinese philosophy of art and Western phenomenological approaches, especially that of Merleau-Ponty. Julia Petrov too (Chapter 16) addresses embodiment, materiality and the senses – especially the relationship between the visual and the (imagined) haptic – in museums, in an exploration that focuses particularly on the display of dress. One may not necessarily agree with her description of curatorial practice as 'highly haptic' (except by comparison to the average museum visitor's experience), but her introductory scoping of the museum as a place that emphasises ideas rather than things is an important reminder of a emergent theme in some of the literature in recent years, in which the museum's problematic relationships to objects and the fundamental ways in which people and objects interact, are beginning to be more fully investigated.

Some of the extant and important museum studies – as opposed to material culture studies – literature has examined the museum as an important part of our visual culture or indeed as a 'way of seeing' in its own right (e.g. Alpers 1991, Hooper-Greenhill 2000). Many chapters in this book focus not on the senses broadly or on their interrelationships, but on the visual in particular – albeit on differing levels. In Chapter 6, Klaus Wehner, a practising artist, develops an analogy between the 'posed' object on display and the photograph, drawing on Barthes' notion of *punctum*. Display is the focus too of Michael Katzberg's chapter (Chapter 9) on the power of lighting in developing exhibition narrative – which, like Wehner, Dorsett, Rees Leahy and others, usefully reminds us of the importance of the overall context in which objects are displayed and of the materiality and sensory qualities of that context, as well of exhibited objects individually. Like Wehner, Meighen Katz also focuses on photographs (Chapter 23), in her case American images of the Great Depression in the 1930s. Her discussion brings our attention not only to the power of the visual per se, but also to the materiality of the photograph as object (cf. Edwards and Hart 2004, Edwards 2009, 2010). Roger Sansi (Chapter 15) addresses the visual too, but in the context of the notion of 'spectacle' and its possible forms – as the building and blockbuster exhibition, as the museum archive, as relational aesthetics within the gallery space – in contemporary art settings.

Some published work has looked at the very notion of the 'museum object', examining the subjective, shifting and often problematic means by which things in interpretive settings are used to represent wider stories or pieces of reality (e.g. Pearce 1992, Knell 2007b). Geoffrey Swinney's chapter (Chapter 3) extends notions of what constitutes a 'museum object' to museum registers and exposes them as shifting, situated and contingent constructions of meaning and knowledge no less than any other kind of material culture. Maria Lucia de Niemeyer Matheus Loureiro also seeks to examine fundamental questions about the idea of the museum object (Chapter 5), particularly in the context of art, with her philosophical discussion of the 'musealisation' processes (selection, documentation, display) by which something becomes a museum piece. Other work has discussed objects in the context of topics at the core of wider museum studies – rather than material culture studies – focusing on visitors, for instance. Marijke Van Eeckhaut takes such an approach in her exploration of whether paintings can have certain qualities that make them appeal to particular groups (Chapter 8).

Terminology more generally has been the subject of much writing by material culture scholars. The phrase 'material culture' is now viewed differently in some contexts than formerly: natural history and geology specimens, for instance, would once have been thought of simply as 'specimens' – that is, as natural objects rather than artefacts, they would not have been considered 'material culture'. Yet now – indeed, since Pearce (1992, 1994a) – we understand that the moment such objects are removed from the ground, the moment they are selected and collected, they become material culture. As such, the study of them can tell us as much, if not more, than we might learn from an aristocrat's art collection or a mission-ary ethnography collection; 'they exemplify', as Hannah-Lee Chalk suggests in Chapter 2, after Prown (1982), 'unintentional expressions of culture'. Fossils, shells or dead butterflies are 'as much social constructs as spears or typewriters, and as susceptible to social analysis' (Pearce 1994b: 10).

'Materiality' too, is a contentious term. In a 2007 debate between Ingold, Tilley and others, for example, Ingold argued, with some considerable justifica-tion, that most of those who talk and write about 'materiality' seem 'to have hardly anything to say about materials' (2007: 1) and claimed that 'the concept of materiality, whatever it might mean, has become a real obstacle to sensible enquiry into materials, their transformations and affordances' (2007: 2). Tilley, meanwhile, considered that Ingold had misunderstood or oversimplified the potential meanings of the term 'materiality', and in the process had risked sound-ing as if he were making a call for material culture studies to return to much earlier, conservative, culturally unaware approaches (Tilley 2007). Whatever their respective nuances of 'materiality', both Ingold and Tilley have been particularly sensitive in their own work to the reality and physical, social and cultural significances of the material characteristics of the objects – the material culture – about which they write. They have paid careful attention to such qualities as form, colour, texture, surface, material, physical change over time or under certain conditions, and the relationship between an object and its surrounding medium – as well as, of course, the relationships between an object and a per-ceiving subject (responding to the object's sensible qualities), and the environment and sociocultural contexts in which the object and subject exist. This focus on the material realities that objects present, as well as on the wider social, cultural, economic and political exchanges and networks within which they are embedded and important, is a laudable and surely essential component in a rounded study of material culture. Yet, as Ingold and others have pointed out (e.g. Willumson 2004, Ingold 2007, Dudley 2010b, 2011), a surprisingly considerable proportion of the material culture studies literature actually has no such material emphasis at all.

Of course, not all studies can include such a detailed examination of the physical stuff of which objects are made or of the qualities that are particularly important for people's sensory experience of them. In museum-based studies of material culture in particular, however, it is perhaps especially remarkable that more work has not focused on the physical and sensory attributes of objects and their implications for the uniqueness, actual and potential, of the museum expe-rience. But more studies with that level of analysis, with a real concentration on weight, temperature, smell, three-dimensionality, textural qualities, taste, movement, colour, are needed. Some of the chapters in this book take this approach, at least in part (e.g. those by Saunderson, Ting, Petrov, Dorsett). Helen Rees Leahy, conversely, focuses on what at first sight may appear to be the very opposite of materiality: the absence of objects in the museum. Yet her exploration, and the questions its raises about authenticity, not only provides a contrast that enables greater reflection on the meanings of physicality in museum spaces, but also leaves us with an almost palpable sense of the *presence* that absence itself can come to have (Chapter 18). Presence, in this case material presence, and the interpretive implications of its occasional troubling removal or disturbance, is the key theme of artist-curator Chris Dorsett's chapter (Chapter 7), beginning with the tale of a collapsing sculpture and connecting to Klaus Wehner's explorations of Barthes's *punctum* in relation to material objects (Chapter 6).

Much of the material culture studies and museum studies literature alike reminds us that neither objects nor museums and heritage settings exist in a political vacuum; indeed, they are inherently political, given both their origins and development, and their past, present and potential relationships with communities (e.g. Karp and Lavine 1991, Karp *et al.* 1992, Bennett 1995, Peers and Brown 2003, Watson 2007). Such political and contentious contexts are well explored through several case studies in this volume, including Malika Kraamer's account of an apparently Nigerian *kente* cloth under her curatorial care about which she received a strongly worded complaint from a museum visitor certain it was, like them, Ghanaian (Chapter 20). She uses her experience to challenge museums to do more to highlight the multiple and contested interpretations and histories of objects. Marzia Varutti too looks at problematic cultural representations in museums, in particular the complex and problematic articulation of ethnic minority cultural difference and national identity in China (Chapter 21). Amy Jane Barnes continues the broad theme (Chapter 22), arguing how extensively the particularly visual culture of the Chinese Cultural Revolution has influenced Western perceptions of the People' Republic of China (PRC) and demonstrating how problematic UK museum collection and interpretation of that visual culture has been. The political aesthetics and aesthetical politics of representation are further explored in the last two chapters of the book, broadening out into objects of heritage and their meanings and values for different people in Alice Semedo's moving account of a museum set up to memorialise Aldeia da Luz, a lost village in southern Portugal (Chapter 24) and Beverley Butler's powerful analysis of heritage in Egyptian and Palestinian contexts, in which she problematises the notion of heritage as healing or curative (Chapter 25).

Structure of the book

The diverse essays brought together in this book in honour of Susan Pearce all in some way address objects in the context of the museum, gallery and heritage sectors. As the book progresses, it moves through explorations of how objects are constructed in museums, the multiple possibilities of direct object experience, how objects are utilised within particular representational strategies and forms, and the challenges and opportunities presented by using objects to communicate difficult and contested issues. Between them, and from different perspectives, the chapters deal with some fundamental questions related to the ontological and political status and power, and phenomenological and representational qualities, of objects in museums and other heritage settings. Topics and approaches examined in the pages that follow are diverse, but include the objectification of natural history specimens and museum registers; materiality, immateriality, transience and absence; subject–object boundaries; sensory, phenomenological perspectives; the museumisation of objects and collections; and the dangers inherent in assuming that objects, interpretation and heritage are 'good' for us. Case studies throughout the book cover a wide range of objects, collections, institutions and contexts – and in so doing, we hope do some justice to Susan Pearce's own expansive academic interests. Subjects range across geology, Chinese ceramics, Greek archaeology, contemporary art and its museums, African *kente* cloth, heroes' house museums, historic costume collections, photographs, museum–collector relationships, Chinese folk and propagandistic memorabilia, Arctic collections, contemporary Egyptian and Palestinian heritage in political context, poetry and even an entire Portuguese village.

With the exception of the Afterword, the chapters that follow are grouped into the book's four main parts, each of which begins with its own introduction but is briefly outlined here. The first part of the book, *Objects and their creation in the museum*, includes explorations of the nature of objects in museums and of how museum processes – selection, documentation, display and so on – transform physical things into *objects* and involve different discourses. Objects are shown to be diverse in nature, and are understood as active and powerful in their own right in the displays and representations in which they take part. Some of the chapters in this part of the book draw on models such as actor-network theory to explore the processes by which the meanings and values of things, and the discourses that are woven around them, are created, enacted and transformed in museum and gallery spaces.

The remainder of the book looks more specifically at how objects work in museum and heritage settings. In the second part, *Visitors' engagements with museum objects*, chapters focus particularly on how objects are encountered, the ways in which things and people mutually interact, and the possibilities for exploiting these interactions creatively. Authors look at a variety of ways in which exhibitionary contexts contribute to the experience of, engagement with and creative possibilities of objects, and examine the multiple meanings and understandings that can result. Moving on to its third part, *The uses of objects in museum representations*, the book continues to emphasise the role of objects within exhibitionary settings, but now with a series of chapters that, rather than the previous section's focus on how visitors experience and respond to objects as material things, explore the different strategies and forms through which museums do, or could use objects to make representations and tell stories. In its final part, *Objects and difficult subjects*, the book considers the use of objects to represent difficult or disputed subjects and, ultimately, the contested nature of the notion of 'heritage' itself. The authors in this section challenge the epistemology of the museum and raise questions about how knowledge around objects is created and represented. In different ways, all confront the legacies of political regimes and representations through the material culture of museum collections. The book then concludes with an Afterword based on an interview with Susan Pearce. Major instigator of and witness to the radical changes in the academic study of material culture and museums in the UK and internationally over the last fifty years, Pearce is well-placed to put these – and thus, indirectly, the chapters in this book – into context and to speculate on what the future might bring to the field. But the Afterword also allows Susan Pearce, inspiration to the *Material Worlds* conference and to this book, her own voice.

Acknowledgements

For help with this chapter, particularly for notes relating to the specific parts of this book, I am grateful to my co-editors. In relation to the book more generally, all the editors, but especially I, owe a great debt of gratitude first and foremost to our authors – we thank them for their patience and hard work. We are also deeply appreciative of the effort put in by all those who contributed to the original conference, even those whose papers have not been published here. The 2008 *Material Worlds* meeting would not have been what it was without the very valuable input of all its speakers, attendees, helpers and, particularly, Howard Morphy of the Australian National University, who led the summing up. We thank all our peer reviewers and Routledge's reviewers of the book. We also thank colleagues and students at the University of Leicester for support and assistance, both at the original conference and during later preparation for publication – they are too many to list in entirety, but we are especially grateful to Ceri Jones, Simon Knell, Barbara Lloyd, Geun-Tae Park, Jim Roberts and Richard Sandell. Gratitude goes too to Klaus Wehner for his help with the image for the front cover of the book. And of course we are deeply appreciative of the work, support and inspiration of Susan Pearce.

Notes

1 This is true of traditional Western notions of the museum at least, but does not hold true universally (cf. Kreps 2003, 2006, Stanley 2007).
2 Others use different, and less harsh, analogies. Fiona Kerlogue, for example, interestingly compares museum objects to actors – some get to 'star' in more 'shows' than others; some (those in store) are 'resting' for a very long time! I find this analogy engaging and constructive but still problematic: I would not say, for example, that objects 'rest' when not on display; they may still be experienced and interacted with by museum staff and researchers. Similarly, in my view objects' lives in museums are not less 'real' than their pre-museum lives; neither are they synchronously juxtaposed to the 'real' in the way that actors' stage performances and real lives are (Kerlogue 2004, Dudley 2005).
3 Indeed, the interests began much earlier in an influential article by Peter Ucko (1969).

Bibliography

Ahmed, M. (2002) *Living Fabric: weaving among the nomads of Ladakh Himalaya*, Bangkok: Orchid Press.

Alpers, S. (1991) 'The museum as a way of seeing', in I. Karp and S. Lavine (eds) *Exhibiting Cultures: the poetics and politics of museum display*, Washington, DC: Smithsonian Institution Press, pp. 25–32.

Ames, M. (1992) *Cannibal Tours and Glass Boxes: the anthropology of museums*, Vancouver: University of British Columbia Press.

Appadurai, A. (ed.) (1986) *The Social Life of Things: commodities in cultural perspective*, Cambridge: Cambridge University Press.

Bal, M. (1994) 'Telling objects: a narrative perspective on collecting', in J. Elsner and R. Cardinal (eds) *The Cultures of Collecting*, Carlton: Melbourne University Press, pp. 97–115.

Barnes, R. (1989) *The Ikat Textiles of Lamalera: a study of an Eastern Indonesian weaving tradition*. Leiden: E.J. Brill.

Bennett, T. (1995) *The Birth of the Museum: history, theory, politics*, London: Routledge.

Bourdieu, P. (1990) *In Other Words: essays towards a reflexive sociology*, Stanford: Stanford University Press.

Candlin, F. (2007) '"Don't touch! Hands off!" Art, blindness and the conservation of expertise', in E. Pye (ed.) *The Power of Touch: handling objects in museum and heritage contexts*, Walnut Creek, CA: Left Coast Press, pp. 89–106.

Classen, C. (2005) 'Touch in the museum', in C. Classen (ed.) *The Book of Touch*, Oxford: Berg, pp. 275–86.

Clifford, J. (1988) *The Predicament of Culture*, Cambridge, MA: Harvard University Press.

Coote, J. and A. Shelton (eds) (1992) *Anthropology, Art and Aesthetics*, Oxford: Clarendon.

Dant, T. (1999) *Material Culture in the Social World: values, activities, lifestyles*, Buckingham: Open University Press.

Dudley, S. (2005) 'Review of Fiona Kerlogue (ed.), *Performing Objects: Museums, Material Culture and Performance in Southeast Asia*', *International Institute for Asian Studies Newsletter*, 39: 24.

Dudley, S. (ed.) (2010a) *Museum Materialities: objects, engagements, interpretations*, London: Routledge.

Dudley, S. (2010b) 'Museum materialities: objects, sense and feeling', in S. Dudley (ed.) *Museum Materialities: objects, engagements, interpretations*, London: Routledge, pp. 1–17.

Dudley, S. (2011) 'Material visions: dress and textiles', in J. Ruby and M. Banks (eds) *Made to Be Seen: perspectives on the history of visual anthropology*, Chicago: University of Chicago Press, pp. 45–73.

Edwards, E. (2009) 'Thinking photography beyond the visual', in J.J. Long, A. Noble and E. Welch (eds) *Photography: theoretical snapshots*, London: Routledge, pp. 31–48.

Edwards, E. (2010) 'Photographs and history: emotion and materiality', in S. Dudley (ed.) *Museum Materialities: objects, engagements, interpretations*, London: Routledge, pp. 21–38.

Edwards, E. and J. Hart (eds) (2004) *Photographs, Objects, Histories: on the materiality of images*, London: Routledge.

Edwards, E., C. Gosden and R. Phillips (2006) (eds) *Sensible Objects: colonialism, museums and material culture*, Oxford: Berg.

Gell, A. (1998) *Art and Agency: an anthropological theory*, Oxford: Oxford University Press.

Gosden, C. (2005) 'What do objects want?', *Journal of Archaeological Method and Theory*, 12: 193–211.

Gosden, C. and C. Knowles (2001) *Collecting Colonialism: material culture and colonial change*, Oxford: Berg.

Gosden, C., F. Larson and A. Petch (2007) *Knowing Things: exploring the collections at the Pitt Rivers Museum 1884–1945*, Oxford: Oxford University Press.

Hodder, I. (ed.) (1987) *The Archaeology of Contextual Meanings*, Cambridge: Cambridge University Press.

Hooper-Greenhill, E. (2000) *Museums and the Interpretation of Visual Culture*, London: Routledge.

Hoskins, J. (1998) *Biographical Objects: how things tell the stories of people's lives*, London: Routledge.

Howes, D. (2003) *Sensual Relations: engaging the senses in culture and social theory*, Ann Arbor: University of Michigan Press.

Howes, D. (ed.) (2005) *Empire of the Senses: the sensual culture reader*, Oxford: Berg.

Ingold, T. (2000) *The Perception of the Environment: essays on livelihood, dwelling and skill*, London: Routledge.

Ingold, T. (2007) 'Materials against materiality', *Archaeological Dialogues*, 14: 1–16.

Karp, I. and S.D. Lavine (eds) (1991) *Exhibiting Cultures: the poetics and politics of museum display*, Washington, DC: Smithsonian Institution Press.

Karp, I., C.M. Kreamer and S. Lavine (eds) (1992) *Museums and Communities: the politics of public culture*, Washington, DC: Smithsonian Institution Press.

Kerlogue, F. (ed.) (2004) *Performing Objects: museums, material culture and performance in Southeast Asia*, London: The Horniman Museum.

Kirshenblatt-Gimblett, B. (1998) *Destination Culture: tourism, museums and heritage*, Berkeley: University of California Press.

Knell, S. (ed.) (2007a) *Museums in the Material World*, London: Routledge.

Knell, S. (2007b) 'Museums, reality and the material world', in S. Knell (ed.) *Museums in the Material World*, London: Routledge, pp. 1–28.

Kopytoff, I. (1986) 'The cultural biography of things: commoditization as process', in A. Appadurai (ed.) *The Social Life of Things: commodities in cultural perspective*, Cambridge: Cambridge University Press, pp. 64–92.

Kreps, C. (2003) *Liberating Culture: cross-cultural perspectives on museums, curation, and heritage preservation*, London: Routledge.

Kreps, C. (2006) 'Non-Western models of museums and curation in cross-cultural perspective', in S. Macdonald (ed.) *Blackwell Companion in Museum Studies*, London: Blackwell, pp. 457–73.

Miller, D. (1985) *Artefacts as Categories: a study of ceramic variability in central India*, Cambridge: Cambridge University Press.

Miller, D. (1987) *Material Culture and Mass Consumption*, Oxford: Blackwell.

Morphy, H. (1991) *Ancestral Connections: art and an Aboriginal system of knowledge*, Chicago: University of Chicago Press.

Pearce, S.M. (ed.) (1989) *Museum Studies in Material Culture*, Leicester: Leicester University Press.

Pearce, S.M. (1990) *New Research in Museum Studies: objects of knowledge*, London: Athlone.

Pearce, S.M. (ed.) (1992) *Museums, Objects and Collections: a cultural study*, Leicester: Leicester University Press.

Pearce, S.M. (1994a) 'Introduction', in S.M. Pearce (ed.) *Interpreting Objects and Collections*, London: Routledge, pp. 1–6.

Pearce, S.M. (1994b) 'Museum objects', in S.M. Pearce (ed.) *Interpreting Objects and Collections*, London: Routledge, pp. 9–11.

Pearce, S.M. (1995) *On Collecting: an investigation into collecting in the European tradition*, London: Routledge.

Peers, L.L. and A.K. Brown (eds) (2003) *Museums and Source Communities: a Routledge reader*, London: Routledge.

Price, S. (1989) *Primitive Art in Civilized Places*, Chicago: University of Chicago Press.

Prown, J.D. (1982) 'Mind in matter: an introduction to material culture theory and method', *Winterthur Portfolio*, 17: 1–19.

Stanley, N. (ed.) (2007) *The Future of Indigenous Museums*, Oxford: Berghahn.

Thomas, N. (1991) *Entangled Objects: exchange, material culture and colonialism in the Pacific*, Cambridge, MA: Harvard University Press.

Thomas, N. (1994) *Colonialism's Culture: anthropology, travel, government*, Princeton: Princeton University Press.

Tilley, C. (2004) *The Materiality of Stone: explorations in landscape phenomenology*, Oxford: Berg.

Tilley, C. (2007) 'Materiality in materials', *Archaeological Dialogues*, 14: 16–20.

Ucko, P. (1969) 'Penis sheaths: a comparative study', *Proceedings of the Royal Anthropological Institute*, 1969: 24–66.

Watson, S. (ed.) (2007) *Museums and their Communities*, London: Routledge.

Weiner, A.B. and J. Schneider (eds) (1989) *Cloth and Human Experience*, Washington, DC: Smithsonian Institution Press.

Willumson, G. (2004) 'Making meaning: displaced materiality in the library and the art museum', in E. Edwards and J. Hart (eds) *Photographs, Objects, Histories: on the materiality of images*, London: Routledge, pp. 62–80.

Part I

Objects and their creation in the museum

Introduction

Jennifer Walklate

In the beginning, there is creation. Before the rest of the book raises its questions about the ways in which objects are perceived, displayed and politically articulated, it is necessary that some time be spent reflecting upon the objects themselves, their diverse natures, the manifold ways in which they come to be formed and the various factors involved in the production of their 'thinginess'.

It seems only appropriate therefore, that the initial chapters in this book of 'things' focus upon the occurrences through which these things come to be. Indeed, it is worth raising the question of what, in fact, constitutes an 'object', and where such categorical boundaries lie. 'Things' are not simple, either materially or conceptually, and nor are they homogeneous. Their generation is equally intricate. The diversity of object-entities necessitates the acknowledgement of the equally heterogeneous processes of creation which accompany the musealisation of 'things'. Neither are acts of creation straightforward, for they are not simply material, but complex metaphysical formulations and transformations which create and refigure the identities of objects throughout the entire course of their lives.

The following five chapters embroil themselves in such epistomological speculation. A number question standard opinions regarding the natures of objects, taking as their 'things' of study such marginalised entities as rocks and registers, alongside the more conventional and the obviously emblematic. Some deal with the processes of objectification, using frameworks such as actor-network theory and meaning mapping to illustrate the actions that accord an object its culturally symbolic value. Each chapter, however, confirms that, from the most neglected to the most applauded, all objects, and the acts performed upon them, are equally deserving of recognition for their intricacies. All the authors encourage, if not explicitly call for, a new conceptualisation of what we mean by 'objects', how we go about their creation and thereafter how we go about using them.

Hannah-Lee Chalk's chapter focuses upon the primary processes of acquisition. Using actor-network theory, Chalk expands upon the conventionally brief narratives that accompany the collection of earth science specimens, and generates a three-step plan by which she identifies the sub-processes of selection, removal and inscription. By attending primarily to the conceptual creation of objects, she very explicitly picks up a thread that runs throughout this volume: the more intangible paratexts which surround and give meanings to the physical 'thing'. Responding to Pearce's call for a more cultural approach to nature, she blurs the boundaries between 'cultural' and 'natural' objects, and questions why such distinctions have been made. In doing so, she not only addresses a lacuna in museological theory, but also challenges the discourses of scientific objectivity. It is thus that she shows us the value of 'romancing the stones'.

Romancing the unloved is a theme picked up in the following chapter. Like Chalk, Geoffrey Swinney seeks to address a gap in museological study, although his focus lies upon the documentary record as a hitherto neglected object. A slight shift in processual chronology and the angle of actor-network theory allows the chapter both to speak to and move beyond many of the issues raised by Chalk. At the centre of this discussion is the uniquely positioned museum register, at once an object and a description of objectification, a collection of collections and collecting, the ultimate meta-object. Teasing out the themes of inscription and reinscription, Swinney invites his reader into a world of palimpsests, in which both document and object are shown to be consistently mutable, and in which 'creation' is not deemed an act with a defined beginning and end, but rather an encouragement to enter upon new and multiple paths of becoming.

Mutability and multiplicity are central themes for Mouliou and Kalessopoulou. Their essay moves further along the journey of object-making by examining the ways in which objects develop and extend their biographies, specifically in regard to re-imaginings of ancient items in contemporary contexts, the role of modes of display and the evocation of wonder. Their objects are much more visible, being emblematic artefacts housed in the National Archaeological Museum of Athens. This public character allows the authors to examine the polyvocality of meaning-making, which they suggest occurs in three discourses: of epistemology, of intervention and of the public. This diversity of voices and layering suggests that the visualisation of object-creation processes is equally diverse, and this idea is extended in the authors' use of mindmapping, rather than standard textual documentation, as a way of recording meaning-making. The chapter, however, retains that ontological questioning of the nature of objecthood, so central a theme of this part of the book, by situating museum–visitor–object in a mutually generative network in which the location of creative power becomes obscured.

De Niemeyer Matheus Loureiro brings many complexities of creation to the fore. Here, the networks of agents highlighted in the preceding chapter become a central focus, and she questions the relationships between contemporary art and the museum in a world in which much art is site-specific, external and ephemeral. Is it, the chapter asks, the physical inclusion of a work in a museum that makes it a work of art, or is its status as art that which affords it a position in a museum? The choice of the author to focus on art-objects is one that brings with it a unique set of issues. By their very nature, deliberately created works of art, valued initially for their aesthetics rather than their use-value, are of a different ontological character from many other artefacts, and are less likely to have suffered a metaphysical schism through removal from an originatory context. Whilst many objects can be seen as symbols for what they once were, the artwork often remains precisely what it was, for art, as Pomian and Heidegger are used to show, is already a symbol, a self-negation.

Symbolism, negation and artifice arise, too, in the chapter by Klaus Wehner. In his exploration of the mediating action of museum photography, the institutions themselves are turned into images, into objects. Photography as a mode of recording speaks directly to the chapters by Chalk and Swinney, with their calls for innovative approaches to documentation. The selectivity to which Chalk accorded so much importance is made plain in the framing and posing to which photographs are subject, and, like Swinney's register, the photographic record is shown to be a recursive, reflexive meta-object. Wehner also picks up on the central theme of the palimpsest and, by engaging with the Barthsian concepts of *studium* and *punctum*, he draws out the importance of recognising the value of subjectivity and the power which it can provide. In illustrating these concepts, the chapter recalls not only Mouliou and Kalessopoulou's contribution, but a central concern of both this part of the book and the volume as a whole. Furthermore, the processes of imagification, the flattening of meaning and self-negation which come to the fore in the preceding chapter are drawn out in Wehner's analysis of the act and product of photography itself. This complex discussion brings together many of the threads raised in the foregoing chapters, and provides a springboard into the rest of the book.

These five chapters can be seen as the genesis of discussions that recur throughout the volume. Threaded throughout the text shall be found discussions of the ontological nature of object-entities, of the recording and visualisation of their objectification, and of the agents and acts involved in their creation. There is a joy in a beginning, for it intimates a future, and in the journey towards this is to be found great promise. Here, the potential is for an acknowledgement of polyvocality, subjectivity and complexity, and the need and possibilities for innovation which this provides. It is time to begin.

2 Romancing the stones

Earth science objects as material culture

Hannah-Lee Chalk

Introduction

The word romance has numerous different meanings of which I want to focus on just two: romance as 'a strong, sometimes short-lived attachment, fascination or enthusiasm for something', and meaning 'a mysterious or fascinating quality or appeal, as of something adventurous, heroic or strangely beautiful' (*American Heritage Dictionary of the English Language* 2004). I hope to demonstrate that the collection of scientific objects by earth scientists is a romantic activity; fieldwork remains a heroic and adventurous pursuit.[1] But also, for the collector, this romance with the stones is in fact short-lived; a fleeting encounter, but a passionate one nonetheless. Detailed consideration of the 'coming into being' of three rock specimens will suggest that even the most apparently mundane of scientific objects, when reunited with accounts of their collection, can become fascinating pieces of material culture which have the potential to shed light on the both the cultures of the earth sciences, and the processes and practices of scientific field collecting.

The primary content of this chapter is necessarily limited by the particular case study on which it is based, and therefore focuses on rocks, the processes and practices involved in their collection, and the university context within which this takes place. However, in focusing on this particular scientific practice, I hope to shed light on and contribute to the overall 'bigger picture' (Shapin 2005: 241) which, in this case, relates to the scope and application of material culture studies, and the nature and meanings of natural scientific objects. That the specimens at the centre of this micro study were collected for use in an academic institution is particularly significant because such objects are valued first and foremost as functional scientific specimens – it was never intended that they should become expressions of culture. Indeed, if, as Prown suggests, it is those objects that 'express culture unconsciously [that] are more useful as objective cultural indexes' (1982: 2), then it follows that university earth science collections provide an ideal subject for material culture analysis as they exemplify unintentional expressions of culture. Therefore, in treating these earth science objects as material culture, I hope to present the academic earth sciences as a form of culture.[2]

Before I continue, it is useful to clarify briefly the meanings of a number of terms that appear throughout this chapter. In focusing on university collections in particular, it has become increasingly apparent that there are inconsistencies in the terminology used by universities with reference to academic disciplines, and that which museums use to describe the subject matter of collections. Indeed, this problem reflects the fundamentally complex and interconnected histories of the natural sciences and the changing relationships between disciplines such as natural history and geology, throughout their development and evolution.[3] These are messy terms and it is not appropriate to dwell on this matter here; however, in order to avoid confusion, I will briefly define three key terms that I have adopted. Throughout this chapter, I use 'natural science' as an umbrella term for those scientific disciplines and collections concerned with nature; both biological and physical. Within the natural sciences, I use the term 'earth sciences' (which, in academia, has replaced the more traditional term 'geology') to refer to collections of rocks, minerals and fossils as well as their corresponding disciplines of petrology, mineralogy and palaeontology, and 'natural history' to describe collections of both zoological and botanical objects and the corresponding academic biological sciences.[4]

In order to contextualise what follows, it is also useful to introduce briefly the recent developments in both museology and material culture studies that underpin the research from which this chapter draws. To begin with, 'material culture' is a particularly problematic term due to its variable meanings and connotations; however, for the purposes of this chapter, I will use the term to reflect my interest in the relations and connections between objects and people as a way of exploring the values that are attributed to objects.[5] Of particular significance to my research has been the encroachment of natural objects into the previously unyielding field of material culture studies. Traditionally, it was the very 'naturalness' of natural objects that led to their exclusion; after all, a prerequisite for the 'material' of material culture studies was that the objects were made or modified by man (Prown 1982: 2). That the acceptance of these 'natural' objects into the remit of material culture studies has flourished in museology should be of no surprise; considered in the context of the museum, there is little theoretical difference between museum objects because all objects in collections – whether cultural or natural, artistic or scientific – are similarly selected, partial and modified and these attributes constitute material culture. Such developments have helped to clear a path for new ways of thinking about natural objects, the significance of which is marked by the emergence of a 'natural museology'.[6]

While natural museology is becoming an increasingly multidisciplinary endeavour,[7] there is a strong preference in the literature towards natural history objects and collections, particularly on the processes and practices of taxidermy and the creation of dioramas.[8] In contrast, earth science collections have not received such attention and, with the exception of a handful of authors, of whom Simon Knell is exemplary, these collections remain largely untheorised.[9] Why have earth science collections failed to generate the level of interest given to other types of natural and cultural material? Is it because the processes and practices involved in their collection and preparation are less cultural than those for natural history or cultural collections? I believe not; earth science objects are, to use

Susan Pearce's words, 'as much social constructs as spears or typewriters, and as susceptible to social analysis' (Pearce 1992: 6).

In order to make my point, this chapter takes as its focus three rock specimens belonging to a university teaching collection. The earth sciences rely upon the authenticity of their objects, and the belief that they remain 'the same' as they were in nature (Bernasconi, Maerker and Pickert 2007: 3, Dahlbom 2009: 67). In spite of their ability to function in a variety of different roles throughout their academic careers, the specimens contained in university earth science collections – especially those used for research purposes – appear to function as objective, impartial scientific evidence: literally 'hard facts' (Knell 2007a: 10). For Baker, this apparent detachment of earth scientists from their objects of study reflects 'the ingrained habit of modern scientists to view Earth as a totally mindless, inanimate object' (2000: 8), which he relates to the common assumption that the earth sciences (and other historical sciences) are reducible to the laboratory sciences, in particular, physics. In this sense, the material that is collected and used by earth scientists for both teaching and research activities may, at first sight, appear to be devoid of culture; perhaps the least likely suspects for treatment as material culture. However, I intend to demonstrate that, by retracing the processes and practices enacted upon scientific specimens during their collection, an alternative perspective emerges.

In talking of creation, of coming into being, I am not suggesting that these scientific objects have been created from scratch; that these things exist materially prior to becoming scientific objects is undeniable. To talk of coming into being is, rather, to emphasise the ways in which scientific attention transforms these things: 'The participle "in the becoming" . . . captures the distinctively generative, processual sense of the reality of scientific objects, as opposed to the quotidian objects that simply are' (Daston 2000: 13). This chapter focuses on the creation of earth science objects; the activity known in the museum sector as active or primary acquisition, in which an object is transferred from its field occurrence into an artificial context for the first time. For the purposes of this chapter, this process refers to the removal of rock specimens from their *in situ* field occurrence in Ireland, and their transfer into the artificial context of a university teaching collection.[10]

The coming into being of scientific objects

Three specimens of sillimanite schist (a metamorphic rock) were collected from a field site in Connemara, Ireland, during an Easter field course for second year undergraduate students. The decision to collect the material had been made prior to the trip, and as a result, the collector had planned ahead, ensuring that appropriate equipment was available. The collector also knew exactly what type of material to collect, where to find it and how much was required, so successfully removed three pieces of rock from three different exposures at the collecting site. These specimens were labelled and taken back to the department, where they were subsequently incorporated into a teaching collection.[11]

According to the school curator's initial description, the collection of the sillimanite schist was relatively straightforward and simple. However, if we follow

Latour and 'look at the type of aggregates thus assembled and at the ways they are connected to one another' (Latour 2005: 22), we are suddenly faced with an altogether more complex situation; one in which the collecting process unravels into a tangled web of relations. In order to provide a more thorough analysis of the processes and practices through which these objects came into being, it is necessary to explore in more detail the reasons for collecting the specimens, their intended use and the collector's experiences in the field.[12]

The teaching collections used in undergraduate practical sessions combine material from a variety of sources, ranging from purchased specimens to material collected during research projects. Due to the size of the department's collections, teaching staff are encouraged to make use of the existing collections rather than acquiring additional specimens. However, if members of staff require material that is not available in the existing collections, and 'if a suitable opportunity arises' (Finch 2008), they may be given permission to collect additional samples for use in practical teaching sessions.

The material in question was collected in order to 'garnish' (Finch 2008) an existing teaching collection used in practical sessions for a second year course unit in sedimentary and metamorphic petrology. Students use the teaching sets (a combination of hand specimens, thin sections and additional resources such as maps) in order to determine both the relationships between a suite of rocks and the processes leading to their formation. An increase in the number of students taking this course had required the creation of additional sets of material; however, it soon became apparent that no further samples of one particular component – sillimanite schist – existed in the department's collections,[13] preventing further sets from being made up. In order for further teaching sets to be created, it was agreed that additional samples of sillimanite schist should be acquired.

In its teaching context, the function of the sillimanite schist is to display a distinct schistose fabric and clustering of the minerals sillimanite and mica – faserkiesel – allowing students to observe both the fabric and mineralogical content of the rock (using hand specimens and thin sections, respectively). Because the function of the sillimanite schist relies on the presence of a particular fabric and mineralogy, and because these features result from particular conditions of formation (rather than being location-specific), the collection of new material was not limited to the exact site from which the original material came. It was therefore decided that additional material would be collected during the annual field course in Connemara, where similar rocks were known to exist.

The need to collect material containing sillimanite was the main influence directing the selection process; however, factors such as specimen size and the amount of material required were also taken into consideration. Thus, it would be necessary to collect sufficient material to enhance the existing teaching sets, but also to take into account the possibility that some of the material may not, in fact, be similar enough to the original material to be of use.

The decision to collect material from a particular location was influenced by the collector's knowledge of the relative abundance of sillimanite schist in the

Connemara area, and of the existence of outcrops next to a road; the accessibility of the exposure was therefore a vital factor. Previous visits to the site meant that the collector knew that there were plenty of sizable exposures from which to obtain material – all of which outcropped at an accessible height; increasing the chances of selecting appropriate material for collection.

Having identified some appropriate material, the collector was required to remove samples from the outcrop. The availability of large enough hammers, chisels, safety glasses, newspaper, sacks and permanent markers – 'collecting paraphernalia' (Finch 2008) which were taken on the field course for the purpose of collecting this material – also influenced the collection process, allowing the effective and safe removal of sufficient material, and its subsequent labelling, wrapping and removal from the site.

Having selected and removed the specimens, knowledge of their intended function also influenced both the labelling and recording of the specimens; for example, the strike and dip were not marked on the specimen because their particular function did not require the material to be oriented. While observation of the specimens in the field suggested that the material was appropriate for its intended purpose, it was understood that more detailed investigation of the material (in thin section) back at the department would be required in order to confirm this. Therefore, with this in mind, the three specimens were assigned individual reference numbers consisting of the initials of the locality and a consecutive number, which were written directly onto the specimen with permanent ink. Additional information, including the date of collection, locality, rock type and intended use, were recorded in a field-collecting notebook.

While the collector's knowledge and understanding of the reasons for collecting material provided him with a rational framework within which to work, the decision to collect particular pieces cannot be considered without acknowledging the situated and transient nature of the field. The particular pieces of sillimanite schist that were collected were therefore equally the result of the conditions experienced in the field; the fact that the outcrops 'were situated in a peat bog and that it was raining at the time' (Finch 2008). Furthermore, the hardness of the rock meant that both strength and persistence were required in order to break material away from the outcrop.

This account is far more revealing than the initial explanation as it acknowledges the complexities, the negotiations and the compromises that had been overlooked in the original version. Equipped with this example, I will now address the processes and practices involved in the coming into being of scientific objects in more general terms. Due to the complexity of the matter, I have devised a 'three-step plan' which divides the collecting process into stages of selection, removal and inscription.

Step 1: selection

It is clear that the acquisition of a natural history specimen involves selection . . . This process turns a 'natural object' into a humanly-defined piece, and means that natural history objects and collections . . . can also be treated as material culture and discussed in these terms.

(Pearce 1992: 5–6)

Selection lies at the heart of the collecting process, providing an important distinction between collecting and hoarding.[14] In terms of collecting in the natural sciences, Daston and Galison highlight the selection process as a specific stage in the creation of scientific objects, explaining that: 'No science can do without such standardized working objects, for unrefined natural objects are too quirkily particular to cooperate in generalizations and comparisons' (Daston and Galison 2007: 19, 22). While collecting in the field ranges from the planned to the fortuitous, it remains an activity involving some degree of intentionality as it is ultimately the result of a conscious decision to remove a particular piece of material from its field context. In searching for an appropriate sample, the collector is weighing up a complex set of factors that must be taken into account, and these necessarily shape the scientific object that is created. While the selection process may be a conceptual stage, it operates on two different levels relating to what is collected and why.

The reasons for collecting material can be understood as forming a collecting context, whereas the particular material that results from the collecting process relates to pragmatics. On one level, the creation of a scientific object reflects a particular context in which the collecting process occurs. For the sillimanite schist, the collecting context combined institutional factors, such as the increase in class size and the department's collecting policy; disciplinary factors including the content of the course unit, the use of teaching sets and the convention of recording associated information in a field notebook; and personal factors, ranging from the choice of collecting site, to the fitness and strength of the collector and his determination and skill at hammering.

While the collecting context provides the intentions and rationale for collecting material, the immediate conditions experienced in the field also influence the selection and collection of particular objects.[15] These factors, over which the collector has little or no control, are the pragmatics of collecting. It therefore follows that the selection of a sample is an act of negotiation; a compromise between the intended function of a specimen and the immediate conditions experienced in attempting to collect it. In the case described above, the pragmatic factors included the rainy weather, the presence of a peat bog (itself a product of landscape, climate, vegetation cover and relief), visibility, the spatial distribution of outcrops and the hardness of the rock.

Step 2: removal

The decision to collect a particular piece of material is also subject to the potential difficulties associated with its removal. The most appropriate sample may not be the easiest to reach, retrieve or remove; and while the right tools are often essential, so too are the skills and strength of the collector. As Henning

(2006: 59) has described; 'The very act of collecting is a transformative act, a surgical operation of excision which violates that which it leaves behind'.

Whether simply by picking up loose material, or by physically hammering a piece of rock from an outcrop, the removal of material from its *in situ* environment transforms a natural object into something else, both physically and conceptually. Physically, moving or removing the object may expose fresh surfaces, changing the appearance of the object; previously hidden features may be revealed as all three dimensions of the rock become visible. Removal by more physical means will also modify both the dimensions and mass of the object, reshaping and resizing it. Conceptually, this is a transformative process whereby a natural object has either been selected, or singled out by a human, and wrenched from its *in situ* environment with a view to entering a different realm, to performing a function, to meeting a need.

It is no longer a piece of something; landscape, outcrop, exposure, deposit, feature, debris, scree or talus; it is something in its own right. It is no longer natural; it has become something to do something with – a tool with a function of displaying features, proving hypothesis, representing outcrops or supplying data. If, for example, the object is discarded at this point, it may return to the natural realm; however, its involvement with the collector who picked it up or hammered it out would perhaps mean that it returns as an artefact, albeit a fleeting one, rather than a piece of nature. By physically moving or reshaping the object, the collector has changed it; the object has been denaturalised and decontextualised, but while it is no longer natural, it has not yet become a scientific object.

Step 3: inscription

The final stage in the creation of scientific objects can be understood as inscription. Again, this may change the object physically, as when an object is marked with dip and strike, younging direction, top and bottom, or any other numbers, symbols or words that a collector may feel the need to impress onto it. In addition, detailed records of the object *in situ* – its position, location, associations and horizon – are made in the field notebook; linking an object to its unique data set. Conceptually, the object has been overprinted with data, observations and records, the precise details and style of which are strongly influenced by institutional, disciplinary and personal factors, such as particular conventions, expectations, requirements and preferences.

The extracted and inscribed object becomes a tangible vessel for the associated information that its number represents, and thus also for the original natural object *in situ*. By combining object, inscription and associated information, the collector is able to bring a piece of the field into the lab. As Latour (1999: 46) notes; 'samples will remain attached to their original context solely by the fragile link of the numbers inscribed in black felt-tip pen on the little transparent bags'. At this point, having been selected, removed and inscribed, the object has become something else; no longer part of outside nature, the object has become a scientific specimen.

Romance or affair?

The creation of earth science objects through field collecting is an activity that remains poorly understood. On one level, this reflects the complexity of the process, and as Pearce explains:

> The impulses against which this selective structuring is done, and from which collections result, are complex. They embrace both traditional social notions about what constitutes 'proper' or 'valuable' or 'prestigious' material collections, and obscure but compelling movements in each individual's heart and mind which leads each one to collect.
>
> (Pearce 1995b: 18)

The processes and practices of field collecting are also, however, rarely documented or formally acknowledged, reflecting both the situated nature of fieldwork and the conventions of scientific reporting.

The lack of formal accounts of field collecting can be partly explained by the tacit and embodied nature of field practice (Lorimer 2003: 292). Because fieldwork activities are subject to the immediate, uncontrollable and often unpredictable conditions experienced in a specific place at a particular time, field collecting requires a combination of the rigor of standard protocols and the flexibility of instinct and intuition. Frodeman, for example, likens this to Merleau-Ponty's concept of motor-intentionality, in which 'the directed state of action/perception . . . operates before we consciously posit an object for examination' (Frodeman 2004: 155). Thus, the collector may not even be aware of the ways in which the pragmatics of collecting have affected the processes and practices enacted on an object during its collection.

A further reason for the lack of acknowledgement of the fieldwork experience has been identified by Clifford (1997: 57), who describes the process of writing up fieldwork as 'the translation of ongoing experience and entangled relationship into something distanced and representable'. Thus, details of the selection, removal and inscription practices involved in the collection process are effectively lost in translation but this sterilisation of objects renders them functional in the scientific world. Thus, any romance with the stones taking place during collection is likely to vanish as a result of both the 'implicit [and] non-propositional' (Frodeman 2004: 155) nature of field collecting, and the 'impersonal, formal and formulaic' (Fortey 2000: xvi) conventions of scientific reporting. As a result, the coming into being of scientific objects is shrouded in mystery, as it remains unimportant in the functional lives of objects. The example on which this chapter has focused illustrates this particularly well: in contrast to the curator's detailed account of the collecting process, for the students who examine the material in their petrology practical there is no mention of how the object came into being (Finch 2008); its previous context has been deleted; it has been purified. What may have been a romance at the time must be written off as a meaningless affair in order for scientific objects to function.

Conclusions

The specimens contained in university earth science collections provide unlikely candidates for treatment as material culture; however, by exploring the processes and practices involved in their creation, it is clear that they offer a valuable source of inquiry. While much of the romance of fieldwork remains either overlooked or hidden during the scientific career of an object, the contexts and relations through which specimens come into being can be teased out from personal accounts and associated information recorded at the time of collection. By re-uniting specimens with a detailed account of their collection it has become clear that associated information (both recorded and remembered) has the potential to add further dimensions and meanings to both individual objects and the larger collections to which they belong: indeed, such details are often retained alongside archived research collections or as appendices to theses.

On one level, then, the act of collecting can be understood as affecting all objects in the same way; blurring the lines that have traditionally been drawn between natural and cultural objects. Thus, while they may have started out as natural entities, the objects contained in university earth science collections are artefacts due to human intervention in both their coming into being and sub-sequent existence, and the changes (physical and conceptual) arising from being selected, removed and inscribed through the collecting process.[16] For example, just as a piece of rock may be selectively removed from its *in situ* environment in order to create an artefact such as an arrowhead, it may also be collected by a scientist as a source of raw material for the purpose of creating hand specimens for teaching purposes. Thus, on one level there is very little difference between arrowheads and hand specimens because, by acknowledging both the romantic and personal nature of the collecting process, it is clear that these objects con-stitute material culture and can be studied as such.

However, while it cannot be denied that human involvement significantly affects the meanings of any collected object, to simply classify university earth science collections alongside 'spears and typewriters' risks oversimplifying the situation. Thus, on another level, these objects are different from man-made artefacts, and it seems to me that what sets them apart is their purpose; these things are collected because the collector believes in their ability to generate knowledge and understanding about nature. Indeed, what earth scientists are trying to capture when they collect samples is exactly this naturalness, and this is not the same as collecting a stone because of its hardness, colour, shape or indeed any one of the multitude of qualities that may turn it into a raw material from which to create something else like an arrowhead. In this way, a piece of rock in a university earth science collection cannot be understood in the same way as a piece of rock in an archaeology collection, and neither would they be treated in the same way.

In considering the coming into being of these natural scientific objects, it has become apparent that in the earth sciences a complex relationship exists between objects and collectors, and this is particularly apparent from the associated information that is collected alongside an object. While the information that is recorded during the collection process – its nature, quantity and level of detail – necessarily reflects the intended use of a particular object, it is clear from the case described above that in reality, both the tangible (field notebook) and intangible (verbal account of memories) records of the collecting event far exceed that which is required in order for the object to function in academia. This attention to (surplus) detail demonstrates a certain degree of attachment and interest that goes beyond that which is expected of the collector within the conventions of the earth sciences, and in this sense, the relationship between collector and object can be understood as romantic in nature. However, while field collecting requires the collector to participate actively in the creation of earth science objects, at the same time there remains a distance between them as the collector also fulfils the role of passive scrutator. This is clearly no normal romance!

In using the notion of romance to investigate the coming into being of three rock specimens, this chapter has demonstrated that the social analysis of university earth science collections is a fruitful endeavour. Indeed, the value of understanding in detail the processes and practices involved in collecting scientific objects lies in enhancing our existing knowledge of the content, development, history and uses of collections and using this to make informed decisions about their uses, treatment and status in the future. This, in turn, has much larger implications; the importance of understanding the cultures of the earth sciences cannot be overstated, considering their central role in our understanding of and responses to the changing planet on which we live. There is clearly much scope for further research into earth science objects and the complex and changing relationships in which they are embroiled; in particular, the fascinating manner in which earth scientists are simultaneously detached from – and engaged with – their objects of study (c.f. Candea 2010). While questions surrounding the extent to which this relationship exists elsewhere in the natural sciences, and whether it is restricted to academia, also remain unanswered, this chapter has responded to Pearce's call for a more cultural understanding of natural objects (1994: 1), and it is hoped will provide a starting point for further debate in the future.

Acknowledgements

I would like to thank Bob Finch for contributing both his time and knowledge during the interview, and also the two anonymous referees for providing valuable and insightful feedback. Further thanks are due to Dr Sam Alberti and Dr Nick Merriman for their continued support, encouragement and advice.

Notes

1 Noah Heringman (2003, 2004) considers in detail the connections between geology and Romantic literature.
2 This chapter is based on doctoral research carried out at the University of Manchester's Department of Social Anthropology in which university earth science collections form the focus of an investigation into the ways in which natural objects are attributed value.

3 For a detailed consideration of the historical development of the geological sciences, see Guntau (1996) and Rudwick (1996), amongst others. A more modern study is provided by Cato (1994), who attempted to quantify the extent to which these terminological ambiguities have permeated the museum sector in the USA, concluding that there was a lack of consensus on the meaning of terms such as natural history and natural science.

4 While this distinction is, to some extent, artificial, it does reflect a very real division of the natural sciences within the UK museum sector. This is exemplified by the distinction between the Geological Curators' Group, which is concerned with earth science collections, and the Natural Science Collections Association (previously the Biology Curator's Group), whose remit is natural history collections.

5 In the museological literature, see Alberti (2008) and Knell (2007a), amongst others. Also, the category of material culture has recently been the subject of an interesting debate between Ingold (2007a,b) and Tilley (2007).

6 Alberti provides an introduction to natural museology, and defines its scope in terms of 'the practices of collecting, preservation, and displaying certain things – animals, plants, fossils and rocks – and the conceptual and exhibitionary frameworks in which they are set' (2008: 74).

7 For an example of the multidisciplinary nature of natural museology see Alberti (2008), Ellis (2008), Patchett and Foster (2008), Poliquin (2008) and Rader and Cain (2008).

8 For a thorough review of such work see Alberti (2008).

9 For work considering fossils, see, for example, Rudwick (1976), Knell (2000, 2007b) and Carneiro (2005). Pickert (2007) offers a rare contribution with her consideration of rocks and petrology collections.

10 The particular example that I use in this chapter originates from fieldwork carried out at the University of Leeds' School of Earth and Environment during 2008. The information is taken from an interview (Finch 2008) about the use of specimens for teaching. In what follows, I focus explicitly on the coming into being of these objects. However, this is merely one aspect of a larger trajectory which extends to their use and circulation, and the potential of these objects to function in a variety of roles and contexts; elements of my research that are beyond the scope of this chapter, but which will form the basis of future work.

11 This account paraphrases the school curator's initial description of the sillimanite schist, made during the interview (Finch 2008).

12 The information that follows paraphrases the school curator's description of the collecting process during the interview (Finch 2008).

13 The original material originated from a research project, and was subsequently transferred into the teaching collection.

14 On 'selection' see Pearce (1992: 7, 1995a: 23). For the distinction between collecting and hoarding, see, for example, Belk *et al.* (1988: 548).

15 See, for example, Kuklick and Kohler (1996), Driver (2000), Dewsbury and Naylor (2002), Kohler (2002) and Livingstone (2003). The predominance of biological and geographical fieldwork in these examples reflects a trend that is representative of the wider literature on this subject.

16 This distinction between degrees of naturalness and artefactuality is addressed by Siipi who explains that: 'The lines between natural and unnatural may be drawn differently from the ones between artefacts and non-artefacts' (2003: 420).

Bibliography

Alberti, S.J.M.M. (2008) 'Constructing nature behind glass', *Museum and Society*, 6: 73–97.

American Heritage Dictionary of the English Language, 4th edn (2004) Houghton Mifflin Company [Online]. Available at: http://dictionary.reference.com/browse/romance (Accessed: 24 August 2009).

Baker, V.R. (2000) 'Conversing with the Earth: the geological approach to understanding', in R. Frodeman (ed.) *Earth Matters: the earth sciences, philosophy and the claims of community*, Upper Saddle River, NJ: Prentice Hall.

Belk, R.W., M. Wallendorf, J. Sherry, M. Holbrook and S. Roberts (1988) 'Collectors and collecting', *Advances in Consumer Research*, 15: 548–53.

Bernasconi, G., A. Maerker and S. Pickert (2007) 'Objects in transition', in G. Bernasconi, A. Maerker and S. Pickert (eds) *Objects in Transition: an exhibition at the Max Planck Institute for the History of Science*, Berlin: Max Planck Institute.

Candea, M. (2010) ' "I fell in love with Carlos the meerkat": engagement and detachment in human–animal relations', *American Ethnologist*, 37: 241–58.

Carneiro, A. (2005) 'The museum of the Geological Survey of Portugal: the role of the "Bilobites" collection in the 19th-century palaeoichnological controversy', in M. Beretta (ed.) *From Private to Public: natural collections in museums*, Sagamore Beach, MA: Watson Publishing International.

Cato, P. (1994) 'Variation in operational definitions of natural history in a sample of natural history-oriented museums', *Museum Management and Curatorship*, 1994(13): 251–63.

Clifford, J. (1997) *Routes: travel and translation in the late twentieth century*, Cambridge, MA: Harvard University Press.

Dahlbom, T. (2009) 'Matter of fact: biographies of zoological specimens', *Museum History Journal*, 2: 51–72.

Daston, L. (2000) 'Introduction: The coming into being of scientific objects', in L. Daston (ed.) *Biographies of Scientific Objects*, Chicago: University of Chicago Press.

Daston, L. and P. Galison (2007) *Objectivity*, New York: Zone Books.

Dewsbury, J.D. and S. Naylor (2002) 'Practicing geographical knowledge: fields, bodies and dissemination', *Area*, 34: 253–60.

Driver, F. (2000) 'Editorial: field-work in geography', *Transactions of the Institute of British Geography*, 25: 267–8.

Ellis, R. (2008) 'Rethinking the value of biological specimens: laboratories, museums and the Barcoding of Life Initiative', *Museum and Society*, 6: 172–91.

Finch, R. (2008) *Earth science teaching collections at the University of Leeds.* [Interview], Interview at The University of Leeds with H. Chalk, 6 May 2008.

Fortey, R. (2000) 'Introduction', in P.J. Wybrow (ed.) *Travels with the Fossil Hunters*, Cambridge: The Natural History Museum and Cambridge University Press.

Frodeman, R. (2004) 'Philosophy in the field', in B.V. Foltz and R. Frodeman (eds) *Rethinking Nature: essays in environmental philosophy*, Bloomington: Indiana University Press.

Guntau, M. (1996) 'The natural history of the earth', in N. Jardine, J.A. Secord and E.C. Spary (eds) *Cultures of Natural History*, Cambridge: Cambridge University Press.

Henning, M. (2006) *Museums, Media and Cultural Theory*, Maidenhead: Open University Press.

Heringman, N. (ed.) (2003) *Romantic Science: the literary forms of natural history*, Albany: State University of New York Press.

Heringman, N. (2004) *Romantic Rocks, Aesthetic Geology*, Ithaca, NY: Cornell University Press.

Ingold, T. (2007a) 'Materials against materiality', *Archaeological Dialogues*, 14: 1–16.

Ingold, T. (2007b) 'Writing texts, reading materials: a response to my critics', *Archaeological Dialogues*, 14: 31–8.

Knell, S.J. (2000) *The Culture of English Geology, 1815–1851: a science revealed through its collecting*, Aldershot: Ashgate.

Knell, S.J. (2007a) 'Museums, reality and the material world', in S.J. Knell (ed.) *Museums in the Material World*, London: Routledge.

Knell, S.J. (2007b) 'Consuming fossils and museums in early nineteenth-century England', in S.J. Knell (ed.) *Museums in the Material World*, London: Routledge.

Kohler, R.E. (2002) *Landscapes and Labscapes: exploring the lab-field border in biology*, Chicago: University of Chicago Press.

Kuklick, H. and R.E. Kohler (eds) (1996) 'Science in the field special issue', *Osiris*, 11.

Latour, B. (1999) *Pandora's Hope: essays on the reality of science studies*, Cambridge, MA: Harvard University Press.

Latour, B. (2005) *Reassembling the Social: an introduction to actor-network-theory*, Oxford: Oxford University Press.

Livingstone, D. (2003) *Putting Science in its Place: geographies of scientific knowledge*, Chicago: University of Chicago Press.

Lorimer, H. (2003) 'The geographical field course as active archive', *Cultural Geographies*, 10: 278–308.

Patchett, M. and K. Foster (2008) 'Repair work: surfacing the geographies of dead animals', *Museum and Society*, 6: 98–122.

Pearce, S.M. (1992) *Museums, Objects and Collections: a cultural study*, London: Leicester University Press.

Pearce, S.M. (1994) 'Introduction', in S.M. Pearce (ed.) *Interpreting Objects and Collections*, London: Routledge.

Pearce, S.M. (1995a) *On Collecting: an investigation into collecting in the European tradition*, London: Routledge.

Pearce, S.M. (1995b) 'Collecting as medium and message', in E. Hooper-Greenhill (ed.) *Museum, Media, Message*, London: Routledge.

Pickert, S. (2007) 'Building blocks of the earth', in G. Bernasconi, A. Maerker and S. Pickert (eds) *Objects in Transition: an exhibition at the Max Planck Institute for the History of Science*, Berlin: Max Planck Institute.

Poliquin, R. (2008) 'The matter and meaning of museum taxidermy', *Museum and Society*, 6: 123–34.

Prown, J.D. (1982) 'Mind in matter: an introduction to material culture theory and method', *Winterthur Portfolio*, 17: 1–19.

Rader, K.A. and V.E.M. Cain (2008) 'From natural history to science: display and the transformation of American museums of science and nature', *Museum and Society*, 6: 152–71.

Rudwick, M.J.S. (1976) *The Meaning of Fossils: episodes in the history of palaeontology*, 2nd edn, Chicago: University of Chicago Press.

Rudwick, M.J.S. (1996) 'Minerals, strata and fossils', in N. Jardine, J.A. Secord and E.C. Spary (eds) *Cultures of Natural History*, Cambridge: Cambridge University Press.

Shapin, S. (2005) 'Hyperprofessionalism and the crisis of readership in the history of science', *Isis*, 96(2): 238–43.

Siipi, H. (2003) 'Artefacts and living artefacts', *Environmental Values*, 12: 413–30.

Tilley, C. (2007) 'Materiality in materials', *Archaeological Dialogues*, 14: 16–20.

3 What do we know about what we know? The museum 'register' as museum object

Geoffrey N. Swinney

Introduction

> Museums are very familiar with exploring the past on behalf of others or for the benefit of the objects in their care, but rarely examine their own history. Lack of time and [other] resources frequently mean that archives relating to the history of these institutions are not treated with the same diligence that is assigned to records about objects.
>
> (Pearson 2005: 29)

This essay addresses, in part, the issue to which Cathy Pearson signals by considering museum registers. By registers I mean those documents and textual practices that construct collections and that record the career trajectories, or biographies, of objects, and the networks of actors and actants (*sensu* Latour 2005a) – including makers, users, collectors, agents, dealers, conservators, shippers, preparators, curators, tools, machines, preservatives, inks, paints, packing materials and collecting apparatus of all kinds – with which they engage, in their pre-museum and intra-museum careers (Kopytoff 1986, Latour 1988, 1992, Alberti 2005). As for any biographical study, be it of people or things, to use Susan Sontag's aphorism, '[o]ne cannot use the life to interpret the work. But one can use the work to interpret the life' (Sontag 1996: 111). The 'work', the register, provides access to its 'life', the practices of its creation, intended use and its materiality. As the title suggests, this essay considers how registers provide knowledges about collections, and challenges prevailing perceptions that registers are an unproblematic resource. To do this I adopt the epistemological position that registers are themselves museum objects – 'meta-objects', collections of records about collections, an archive of an archive.

Situating the register in this way is to conceptualise it as both a museum object and a working tool. This duality seemingly challenges Susan Pearce's characterisation of a museum object as something 'set-aside', 'sacred' (Pearce 1995: 406). Rather, the register has a unique status as a 'boundary object' – characterised by Susan Leigh Star and James Griesemer (1989) as a scientific object that inhabits more than one social world whilst satisfying the informational requirements of each of those worlds. This essay, written in honour of Susan Pearce, is an opportunity to prompt and promote critical discussion of the register's unique status.

For museum staff, the register is a mundane object, familiar and unproblematic. As *a working tool* it is largely treated uncritically, as a naturalised technology or a 'black box' – a technology the functioning of which is unquestioned and taken for granted (Latour 1987: 2). The register as a *museum object* is similarly generally considered a primary, unproblematic, authentic and authoritative source of knowledge. Rarely do we apply to the register the sort of critical scrutiny to which we subject other objects in a museum. To suggest such scrutiny is my project here. What knowledges do the register permit? How, and to what extent can the practices of a museum be reconstituted through its register or registers? What might such reconstitution reveal about the changing meaning and value of material objects (including the register itself)? In short, what do we know about what we know?

'Register': noun and verb

The museum register is a material object, be that object a ledger or spreadsheet. It is also a technology, by and through which the museum is constructed and constituted, its collections disciplined and its objects arrayed. The verb 'to register' denotes registration as a process. It is the performance of those rituals that confers a museum identity upon an object thereby removing it from the 'outside world' and assimilating it into the museum. Registration is, therefore, a form of 'rite of passage' (van Gennep 1984). It is a complex of actions which have changed over time. Generally, it is associated with aspects of accountability for expenditure and/or accountability for the 'stock' of items. Registration enacts and records a change of ownership (for an overview of recent and historic practice see Stone 1992). The register assembles (other) objects to form an archive. Unlike the collections themselves, the register records not only items retained by a museum, but also provides a trace of those objects that, through decay, damage, theft or deaccession and disposal, are no longer materially present. Many, maybe most, museum objects are mundane and derive distinction (and are distinguishable) only through association with extrinsic sources with which they are 'in register' (for a brief discussion see Swinney, in press). One consequence is that embodied in the 'textual practices' of registration and the register are matters of authority and credibility (Alberti 2008). As in other archives, which for Charles Withers (2002: 304) are 'topological site and nomological space', the making of knowledge depends upon 'principles of credibility', themselves matters of 'interpretation, implication and trust' (Osbourne 1999: 53). I contend that an assessment of the authority and credibility of the registers, and an ability to interpret these objects, depends upon knowledge of the process of their production.

I should make clear that here I use the term 'registers' in a broad sense to include the various documentary records of the (other) objects that constitute the museum. These include not only the original or primary inscriptions which form part of the ritual of accession and assimilation, but also subsequent annotations to them. The latter may be made in the same document or in associated documentary spaces, such as 'catalogues', 'loan books', 'location indexes', 'disposal books', computerised databases and so forth. Such inscriptions accrue in layers, or strata, as objects and knowledge move in, about and through the physical and epistemic spaces of the museum. To use Michel Foucault's metaphor, the inscriptions and the knowledges that they represent have an archaeology (Foucault 2002). Meanings and values of objects, within the museum as elsewhere, are dynamic and unstable, situated and contingent (Alberti 2005, Swinney 2006, Knell, MacLeod and Watson 2007). These are generally matters of how objects were understood, how they were intended to be used and how they *were* used. Thus, the inscriptions that the registers and associated documents contain relate to processes of mobility and to the flow of objects and knowledges into, around and sometimes out of a museum.

The register is far from being an unproblematic source. The strata of inscriptions not only accumulate, they may also erode, as documents are lost, discarded or transcribed and translated. As Bruno Latour reminds us, transcription from one medium to another is rarely (if ever) a simple copying process or translocation (Latour 1987). Re-inscription is a process of translation, a re-contextualisation which changes meanings and values. Translation, as Gayatri Chakravorty Spivak counsels, is an act of violence which involves tearing material out of the cultural context, the idiom, of its production (Spivak 2000). Inevitably things are lost in translation. Changing language or medium (and concomitant acts of reparation) inflicts or imposes new meanings. Thus, the inscriptions of museum, like other objects in a museum, are subject to the violence of the 'museum effect', by which an object is 'dislocated from its point of origin' (Alberti 2007: 373). The museum effect, I contend, applies not only to specimens, but also to the material inscriptions that represent them.

As noted by Samuel Alberti, 'museum scientists [and other museum staff] operates [*sic*] within the cultural space carved out by their predecessors' (Alberti 2008: 84). In other words, knowledge of the meanings of the register's inscriptions is a major component of the *habitus* (Pierre Bourdieu's term which roughly equates to a 'comfort zone' in relation to a repertoire of action) of those who serve as guides to, and facilitators of, collections (Bourdieu 1977). Such gatekeepers to the knowledges about and embodied within, collections – in roles conceptualised in the 'old museology' as a monologue and in post-modern terms of the 'new museology' as dialogic – operate within their *habitus* (for an introduction to the changing epistemology of museums see Hooper-Greenhill 1992). Historically, much of this knowledge was substantially tacit, embodied in the curator (for discussion of the nature of tacit knowledge see Polayni 1967, Baumard 1999). Thus, it is substantially extrinsic to the inscriptions themselves. Such extrinsic knowledge is constructed through working with the collections and particularly with the registers. It may, therefore, be considered as 'experiencing the registers'. Yet such embodied knowledge is fragile and slippery. It depends on the vagaries of individual memory, the selective and the often distorting processes of absorption into corporate or collective memory. All too frequently, in this transfer from individual to corporate memory, myth tends to be hegemonic. In recent decades computers have offered the potential to enable registers to be assembled in virtual space. They have presented also the enticing prospect of disembodying, capturing and controlling tacit knowledges. Yet both the transfer of inscriptions from ledger to electronic media, and attempts to capture and corral the tacit knowledges about the nature of the registers, are translations. The capture of tacit knowledges is a particularly complex task, for it may be so slippery as to be 'untranslatable'. How are meanings of inscriptions made in the age of the quill altered in the cyberspace of 'spreadsheet accountability'? (Knell 2004: 10).

Registers, along with object labels, are often conceptualised as constituting the primary record of what we know about collections – but to what extent are they primary? Daniel Montello and Paul Sutton (2006) provide a working distinction between primary sources from secondary sources. For them, the former were 'data collected specifically for the purpose of a researcher's particular study'; the latter 'data collected . . . for another research or non-research purpose'. Given that those data inscribed into registers have often been culled from enterprises other than public collection-building, in this model registers may seem to fall under the category of secondary sources. However, recent scholarship has challenged a rigid dichotomy between 'the field' and collection and, therefore, between primary and secondary sources. For museum studies the material sites of the museum and its documentation are themselves 'a field site' (see, for example, Herle 2000, 2001). Considered thus, the museum becomes a primary location for study and its registers primary data. Such approaches to registers are similar to those taken by auditors of commercial accounts as discussed by Alain Desrosieres, who noted that, for auditors:

> '[R]eality' is nothing more than the database to which they have access. Normally, such users do not want to (or cannot) know what happened before the data entered the base. They want to be able to trust the 'source' (here the database) as blindly as possible to make their arguments – backed by that source – as convincing as possible.
>
> (Desrosieres 2001: 346)

Just as a collection is the product of processes of selection and discrimination, so too the archive of that archive is itself never 'raw' data (Lynch 1999: 67). The representation of each specimen in documentary form is itself the product of processes of selection and manipulation and is but one of a multiplicity of sets of data that could have been selected to describe and delineate that object. The register constructs the museum in a particular way. As a consequence, the material setting of the museum and that of its register are spaces that blur and problematise the primary–secondary dichotomy.

Materialising and re-materialising the register

Registers are more than the inscriptions they hold. They are themselves material objects. The inscriptions in the registers are revealing of power relations, such as who had the right to write these documents, and of protocols and practices. Such evidence might be intrinsic, such as signatures or initials, or extrinsic, such as the subsequent identification of individual writers through recognition of their handwriting. Whilst intrinsic evidence is reasonably robust, extrinsic evidence is fugitive and particularly liable to loss in translation.

The migration and translation of registers from one paper-based medium to another, and from hard-copy to digital media, either by transcription, photography or digitisation, changes their materiality. At each translation the register is re-materialised. Things are lost in these translations: not only may information be lost but so too might other qualities related to the 'thingness' of the 'document' – recent scholarship has made a similar point about the materiality of photographs (see, for example, Edwards and Hart 2004). Lost are the feel of paper becoming increasingly brittle and discoloured with age, the handwriting and the textural qualities of quill, pencil or other implements used to inscribe or annotate an entry, the colours of inks used, the feel of leather and board bindings, the smell of these materials, and the traces of powdery decay transferred to those who handle them. Similarly lost may be the particular clack of the keyboard, the distinctive glow of characters on a particular computer screen, the insubstantial feel of the eight-inch or four-and-a-half inch floppy discs, the imperfections in the mirrored surface of a particular CD, and the act of faith that each of those individual discs or a particular hard-drive or silicon chip will regurgitate and return those data consigned to it. Lost too is the haptic memory, that 'corporeal way of knowing', embodied in the materiality of the register – memories destroyed and made anew at each translation (O'Neill 2001). Each layer of translation embodied (and embodies) an act of curatorial practice, and subsequent engagement with the register is an act of the sort that for Caitlin DeSilvey constitutes 'a moment of mimetic labour [which] opened up a channel of communication that tracked along former networks of relation and resonance' (2007: 41). Thus, in DeSilvey's terminology, working with the register, thereby experiencing a register as an object, presents the potential for embodied 'practical remembrance' of past curatorial actions – encounters that are at once both intimate and alien, a recovered yet a borrowed experience. DeSilvey's work reinforces the point that such remembrance is contingent upon an appreciation of the context of the production of the sources, matters that generally are not intrinsic to the sources themselves.

Intrinsic and extrinsic knowledge

With this in mind, in the remainder of this essay I seek to unpack the 'black box' that is the register. This raises questions of to what extent are these primary, original, authentic inscriptions: or to express it differently, 'what do we know about what we "know" about the collections'? The study examines the boundaries and spaces of interaction between documented and tacit knowledge. It takes as a case study the registers of National Museums Scotland (NMS),[1] and in particular those of that component of that body which was the former Royal Scottish Museum (RSM) and its predecessor institutions: the Industrial Museum of Scotland (inclusive of the Natural History Museum, Edinburgh) and the Edinburgh Museum of Science and Art (for a history of the institution see Allan

1954, Waterston 1997, Swinney and Shaw 1998).[2] For simplicity I refer to this institution simply as RSM.

The registers of the RSM, as objects, allow at least a partial reconstitution of its registration practices. These pre-date the establishment of a government-funded national museum in Edinburgh in 1854 and have a genealogy that can be traced back into the Natural History Museum of the Toun College of Edinburgh, later the University of Edinburgh. Intrinsic to that museum's documentation, much of it now deposited in NMS, is an account of the origin of those documentary practices. This reveals that formalised recording of the contents of the Museum began in the academic year 1812–13 when King George III granted monies from 'Our Revenues arising in Scotland applicable to the uses of our civil government' specifically for the acquisition of specimens. An annual sum, not exceeding £100, was made payable against a declaration of expenses incurred. This payment was conditional upon:

> [T]he Professor should lodge with this Court an accurate Inventory or List of all the Articles of Natural History at present in the Museum the property of the Public, And that he annually afterwards make a Report to us of the State of the Museum and additions made to it in the course of the year, that in the event of a less active or zealous professor succeeding to the chair, the proposed allowance for expenses may not be improperly applied.
>
> (King's Warrant 1812)

The inventory took the form of a ledger, bearing the title *Catalogue &c The Museum of the College of Edinb'*. It contained a case-by-case listing of the contents of the Museum preceded by transcripts of parts of the correspondence with the Barons of the Exchequer which intimated the circumstances of the list's production. Thereafter, each May an annual report was written into the ledger briefly describing acquisitions made during the year (the reporting-year was subsequently changed to begin 1 July). Generally, each lot entered in the ledger was there allocated a running number. Preceded by the year of its details being recorded in the ledger, these numbers provided a unique reference between object and its documentary representation. The numbers were of the form 1825–1826.14. They were not attached to, or otherwise directly associated with, the objects that they represented. Thus, they were a means of accounting for expenditure rather than of accounting for objects. The existence of two series of notebooks, the Daily Report Book and the Weekly Report Book, suggests that the compilation of the annual list was a protracted process involving inscriptions transferred from other documents – from label, to a Daily Report Book, to a Weekly Report Book, thence to the 'Catalogue'.[3] These documents contain different levels of detail about the specimens and their provenance.

With the establishment of the government-funded Industrial Museum of Scotland in 1854, the Natural History Museum was placed under the administration of the South Kensington-based Science and Art Department of the Committee of Council on Education. Under this administration it was incorporated into the new endeavour to establish industrial collections. This change of ownership of the Natural History Museum was associated with new systems of accountability. The numbers allocated in the 'Catalogue' were associated with the specimens to which they referred by being written onto the specimen labels or directly onto the specimens themselves. In this way each specimen was brought *into register* with the 'Catalogue' entry that represented it. Future volumes of the ledger were titled 'Register' rather than 'Catalogue'.

In 1855, a new register was established for the industrial collections: the natural history register continued as previously, except that the reporting year was changed to the calendar year in 1856 (the first calendar year report being for 1857). Initially, the numbering practices in the newly created industrial register differed from those used in the natural history registers. In the industrial register entries formed one continuous numbered series. Beginning in October 1855, by the end of December 1864 the series had reached number 1182. Thereafter, the industrial collecting stream adopted the same practice as the natural history stream, resetting the number sequence at the beginning of each year. The two registers then operated in parallel, constructing parallel textual spaces of 'museological science' (Pickstone 1994).

The disciplining of objects, as industrial or natural history, was enacted both through their allocation to the material spaces of the museum building, and through their allocation to the documentary spaces of the registers. Registers do not merely record collections, they construct them: documentary practices are part of a technology through which collections are made and delineated. A few examples of the disciplining of objects, based on understanding of the use and meaning of an item, not (necessarily) on its material form, serve to illustrate the role of the Museum's documentary practices in shaping collections. The acquisition of wet-preserved specimens of the West African electric catfish *Malapterurus beninensis* by both the industrial and the natural history collections illustrates how materially similar objects had different meanings in the different material and documentary spaces. In the natural history collections, specimens of this fish was given meaning as part of the fauna of the rivers of West Africa, and as an element in the construction of the taxon siluriformes – the batch of specimens 1855.27 included part of the syntypic series (those specimens examined by the author of the specific name) for *M. beninensis* (Murray 1855, Swinney 1990, Eschmeyer 1998). In the industrial collections, a specimen (1858.308) was acquired as an example of a medical technology, an electro-therapy 'machine', used in a particular geographical and cultural context (Wilson 1857). Similarly, the registers reveal that both the natural history and the industrial collections acquired rock samples – in natural history they illustrated the fabric of the earth; in the industrial collections they were examples of building stones, ores or coals. They further reveal that, whilst the natural history collections did not acquire botanical specimens, the industrial stream acquired extensive economic botany collections, although these were de-accessioned and transferred to the Royal Botanic Garden, Edinburgh in 1938 (Royal Scottish Museum 1939).

As the collections of the RSM grew and developed they were further disciplined. In 1901, the industrial collections were classified into separate technological and art and ethnography collections, and six years later a separate geological section (later a department) was carved out of the Natural History Department leaving a rump of the former natural history collection as a zoology department in all but name. The creation of these new departments was enacted through re-classification of the material objects, the specimens, in the collections. Classification (and re-classification) always involves degrees of physical movement and epistemic relocation. The proliferation of registers shows that the re-classifications were performed substantially through the documentary practices of the Museum. Material objects were partitioned into these new departments and new registers assembled by transcribing (translating) existing records into new ledgers. The stationers' marks in some of the ledgers used for the registers reveal the history of their production and show that the inscriptions they contain were not necessarily contemporary with the accession event that they recorded (Table 3.1).

Table 3.1 Royal Scottish Museum Natural History Department 'permanent' registers.

Period	Title of volume (spine title)	Stationer's code
1812/13– 1852/53	Catalogue and Additions	[none]
1853/54–1869	Catalogue and Additions	[none]
1870–1878	Register of/Museum/ Specimens/1870/to/1878	[none]
1878–1885	[spine damaged]	[none]
1886–1890	Register of/Museum/ Specimens/1886 to [ms] 1890	M&G Ltd – 1 bk 300 lvs – 6-03
1890–1893	Register/of Museum/Specimens &c/Natural History/Department	M&G Ltd – 1 bk 300 lvs – 7-03
1894–1896	Register/of Museum/Specimens &c/Natural History/Department	M&G Ltd – 1 bk 300 lvs – 7-03 3 bks 300 lvs – 8-03
1896–1898	Register/of Museum/Specimens &c/Natural History/Department	M&G Ltd – 1 bk 300 lvs – 7-03 3 bks 300 lvs – 8-03
1899–1900	Register/of Museum/Specimens &c/Natural History/Department	M&G Ltd – 1 bk 300 lvs – 7-03 3 bks 300 lvs – 8-03
1901–1904	Register/of Museum/Specimens &c/Natural History/Department	M&G Ltd – 1 bk 300 lvs – 7-03 1 bk 300 lvs – 11-03
1904–1907	Register/of Museum/Specimens &c/Natural History/Department	(1044) Wt 3432-8 1 bk 300 lvs 2/12 M&G Ltd
1907–1911	Register/of Museum/Specimens &c/Natural History/Department	(207) Wt 3384-7 1 bk 360 lvs 2/12 M&G Ltd (1866) Wt 4023-14 2 bks 300 lvs 4/12
1911–1915	Register/of Museum/Specimens &c/Natural History/Department	(207) Wt 3384-7 1 bk 360 lvs 2/12 M&G Ltd (1866) Wt 4023-14 2 bks 300 lvs 4/12
1915–1921	Register/of Museum/Specimens &c/Natural History/Department	[none]
1921–1927	Register/of Museum/Specimens &c/Natural History/Department	[none]
1927–1949	Register/of Museum/Specimens &c/Natural History/Department	[none]

Taking the natural history registers as an example, it seems that M&G Ltd produced a number of ledgers in 1903 which were used to construct a record of specimens acquired in the period 1886–1904, indicating that the primary record of registration was made in some other document and subsequently transferred.

This examination of the registers, as objects, reveals that the enactment of the documentary rituals of accessioning therefore occurred in diverse documentary sites and at different times. The creation of new departments through the establishment of new documents and documentary practices resulted in a proliferation of registers. The new 'departmental' registers, which came to be termed 'scroll registers', were created using a smaller format ledger than those used previously. These scroll registers operated in parallel with the already established, larger format, natural history and industrial collections registers. The latter were, in some of the RSM's documentation referred to as the 'permanent' registers, a rhetoric that assigned subaltern status to the scroll registers. Despite this rhetoric, the complex of registration practices became a matter of concern for the Museum's administers. At the close of the nineteenth century, the Museum had been transferred to the administration of the Scotch (later Scottish) Education Department. In 1912, responding to governmental concerns about accountability for objects in national museums in Britain generally (Committee of Public Accounts 1912), this department issued instructions about the conduct of the RSM. In a minute to the Keepers of the four department, headed 'Registration of Acquisitions', the RSM Director required that:

The Secretary [of the Scotch Education Department] has instructed that a Report be made to him on the state of the Museum Registers of Acquisition at the end of every six months (June and December). The first Report will be called for on the 31st. December next.

The Secretary has also instructed that attention be given to the following points:

1   The method of Registration to be uniform throughout the Departments, simple in its working, and in the result capable of satisfying the requirements of an Audit officer at any moment.
2   On the receipt of a specimen the appropriate entry, whenever possible, to be made at once in the permanent Register.
3   If, as is sometimes inevitable, time is wanted to identify and describe the object, or otherwise complete the information to be put on record, the transcription from a Scroll Register into the permanent Register to be done as speedily as possible, so as to leave the smallest amount of room for error or omission.
4   The books used for the permanent Register to be of a durable nature in respect to paper and binding.
5   The permanent Registers to be kept in a fire-proof chamber, and, when removed for reference, to be returned to this chamber every night.

6   Printed lists of acquisitions are not to be regarded as part of a registration system or as in any way taking the place of the permanent
Register, which is the only record that will be held valid by the Audit
officer.[4]

A broadly similarly worded set of requirements was included in a printed
General Instructions issued in about 1912.[5] However, this and subsequent efforts to
regulate documentary practices proved only partially effective and throughout
much of the twentieth century the relationship between the scroll registers and
the permanent registers remained confused, as is clear in the following extract from
a memorandum sent by the Central Reprographics Service of Her Majesty's
Stationary Office in 1972:

[B]ecause of the remoteness of the master record (located in a strongroom
in the basement), each of the Museum's four departments is keeping its own
duplicate records and, as invariably happens in such a situation, the master
record suffers. Our understanding is that the master relating to the Technology
Department has not been updated since 1952 and that the Geology Department keeps its own record in first-class order but that their contribution to
the master record, although up-to-date, is incomplete.[6]

The writer referred to the departmental registers as 'duplicate records', apparently believing the inscriptions they contained to be faithfully reproduced in the
permanent or master record. However, examination of these documents reveals
that this was not so. At different times in the history of each department either
the scroll register or the permanent register had been the site of the rituals of
accession. Over the years the production histories of these various 'copies' of the
registers had been forgotten, and in consequence subsequent annotations were
made inconsistently (and perhaps indiscriminately) into either the scroll or the
permanent register (and only occasionally into both). This resulted in a complex
legacy of documents that are not identical and which include different versions
and translations of earlier documents – a 'cascade of inscriptions' (Latour 1987:
241). It was this complex that was subsequently used to generate the finding aids
to the collections – the location books, loans books, case-contents lists, computerised databases, and so on. For example, in the 1930s a procedure was adopted
whereby the registers of the Art and Ethnographical Department were translated
into typescript. The technology of typewriting required that the entries were
typed onto loose sheets and these were then bound (presumably at the end of
the year) to form a Year Book. These Year Books were annotated as further
information was acquired about an object. The manuscript annotations were of
two kinds: those that extended the description of the form of the object were
added beneath the original entry; those relating to its subsequent history – its
disposal, citation in a publication, or conservation – were added opposite the
original entry (i.e. on the right-hand page in volume). The Year Books form
part of the cascade of inscriptions of the curatorial department which for much

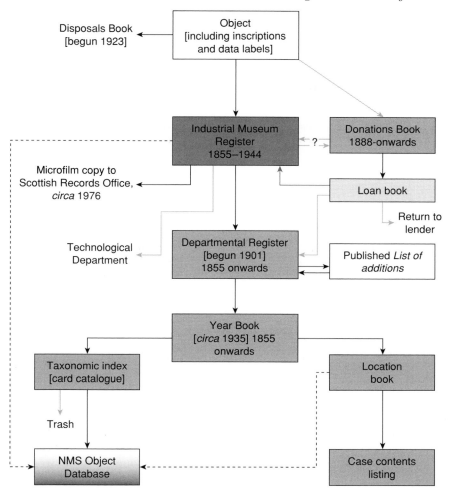

Figure 3.1 Cascade of inscriptions in the Royal Scottish Museum's Department of Art and Ethnography. Grey arrows indicate partial flows. The dotted arrows indicate a project to capture data in an electronic database.

of the twentieth century was called the Department of Art and Ethnography (Figure 3.1).[7]

Similarly, the Geological Department began typing its registers in about 1960. As in other instances of register creation this retrospective data recording involved translation. For example, the entry in the Natural History 'permanent' register for 1897.94 reads: 'Specimen of Scoria from the Island of Tanna, New Hebrides.'[8] The typed register, presumably following re-examination of the specimen, re-interprets or translates it as: 'Lava, with anorthite phenocrysts, from Island of Tanna, New Hebrides, OCEANIA'.[9]

To sum up then, the Museum's register is a 'cascade of inscriptions' made at different times, and in different material and epistemic spaces. It is this cascade, or parts of it, that has been translated, with slippages and dislocations, from notebooks to ledgers and, more recently, from ledgers to spreadsheets and databases.

Postscript: an afterthought about a forethought

Over the years staff changes caused embodied tacit knowledge of the nature of the registers to be lost from the RSM. In consequence, the distinctions between the scroll registers and the permanent registers were unappreciated. As noted above, at different times, and in different curatorial departments, either one functioned as the primary site of registration and subsequent annotations were added apparently indiscriminately to either, or to other documentary sources such as the Year Books. With initiatives to capture the information held in the various ledgers in computerised form, a project which I led in the late 1970s (Clarke 1983), the distinction between the different registers was not appreciated. As a result, the scroll registers and the large-format registers were treated as unproblematic copies of each other (Figure 3.1). They were used uncritically and indiscriminately to construct the computerised database and, whichever 'version' of the register was used, it was subjected to a simple 'intrinsic' reading, without sensitivity to the context of its production. The present study's focus on the registers as objects has reconstituted some of the messy complexity of past documentary practices and enabled a more critical assessment of their contents. In so doing it raises issues about the authority and credibility of the computerised translations of the earlier documents. Knowledge of the register, as museum object, is not merely of historical or academic interest. It impinges on the day-to-day operation of the museum and on its planning for the future.

Computers made their entry into museums as tools for managing large amounts of information which pre-existed in printed or written form. However, as my colleague Angus Kneale insightfully observed (personal communication, 17 September 2008), once inside museums they frequently were re-invented into a source, or *the* source, of information. They created, effectively, a new site of registration in virtual space. As such they were used as tools for management and procedural control, and increasingly came to connect objects (including registers and the inscriptions they contain) in global flows of information through cyberspace, variously theorised as constructing, 'object-orientated democracies', 'digital heritages' or the 'network society' (Castells 2004, Latour 2005b, Cameron 2008a). As Fiona Cameron has suggested, within such networks documentation 'is a node in a much larger and more complex public space for the circulation of object meaning and significance' (2008b: unpaginated). With this ability to detach objects and collections information from their fixed place in time and space so that they circulate as multiples and reproductions via online collections interfaces, an understanding of the nature of that object which is the museum register becomes increasingly vital. As Kneale observed of museum documentation generally, and computerised records in particular, '[a]ssumptions are made about it in present-day terms which can not be substantiated because its history is yet to catch up with it' (personal communication, 17 September 2008). In other words, before (and whilst) reading the register, be it a ledger or presented on computer screen, it is necessary to be sensitive to the contexts of its production and also to that of our reading. Registers do not simply record collections, they construct them. Registers are themselves material objects, which have a unique status within museums, disciplining collections and bringing (other) objects into register with their archival record. Yet the registers themselves are material objects. Our understanding of the register and *the nature of the register* shapes our understanding of our collections which, in turn, shapes our material worlds. So, in conclusion, I contend that, in engaging with the register, we must be alert to the need to critically assess what we know about what we know. For as the former US Secretary of State, Donald Rumsfeld, observed:

> As we know, there are known knowns; there are things we know we know. We also know there are known unknowns; that is to say we know there are some things we do not know. But there are also unknown unknowns – the ones we don't know we don't know.
>
> (Rumsfeld, quoted in Seely 2003)

Disclaimer

Comments and opinions contained in this paper are those of the author and do not necessarily reflect those of the institutions to which he is affiliated.

Acknowledgements

I am grateful to Angus Kneale for permission to cite his insightful comment. I also express gratitude to Sandra Dudley, Nick Fraser, Bob McGowan, Rose Watban, Charles Withers and the staff of NMS Library for assistance in various ways in the preparation of this paper. I am indebted to Wun Chan for allowing access to his unpublished critical appraisal of the relative status of primary and secondary data: 'From discourse analysis, deconstruction and archives', unpublished paper to ESRC/RSGS Advanced Research Training in Human Geography, Kindrogan, September 2008. I also thank two anonymous reviewers whose constructive criticism helped improve the quality of the essay.

Notes

1 The National Museums of Scotland (NMS) was created by the National Heritage (Scotland) Act 1985. Following a re-branding exercise in 2006, the Museum adopted the operating name National Museums Scotland, although for all statutory purposes it retains the title as given in the Act.
2 With the enactment of the National Heritage (Scotland) Act 1985 the Royal Scottish Museum ceased to exist. Its collections were vested in NMS and its former buildings renamed the Royal Museum of Scotland, which in about 1995 was abbreviated to the Royal Museum.

3 The Daily and Weekly Report Books maintained by William Macgillivray, whilst assistant to Professor Robert Jameson, are in NMS, Library Archive.
4 [Royal Scottish Museum] Minute Book, 5 June 1912, NMS, Library Archive, pp. 248–9.
5 [Royal Scottish Museum] General Instructions, NMS, Library Archive.
6 Cooper to Tebble, SA 169/6, 30 March 1972. NMS Library, current files.
7 I am indebted to Rose Watban for her description of the documentation practices in the Art and Ethnography Department (R. Watban, personal communication, 19 March 2008).
8 'RSM N.H. Dept Vol V.' (small format or 'scroll' register). NMS, Natural History Archive.
9 The Museum's Object Database record was entered from the Geology Department typed scroll register.

Bibliography

Alberti, S.J.M.M. (2005) 'Objects and the museum', *Isis*, 96: 559–71.

Alberti, S.J.M.M. (2007) 'The museum affect: visiting collections of anatomy and natural history', in A. Fyfe and B. Lightman (eds) *Science in the Marketplace: nineteenth-century sights and experiences*, Chicago: University of Chicago Press, pp. 371–403.

Alberti, S.J.M.M. (2008) 'Constructing nature behind glass', *Museum and Society*, 6: 73–97.

Allan, D.A. (ed.) (1954) *The Royal Scottish Museum 1854–1954*, Edinburgh: Oliver and Boyd.

Baumard, P. (1999) *Tacit Knowledge in Organisations*, London: Sage.

Bourdieu, P. (1977) *Outline of a Theory of Practice*, Cambridge: Cambridge University Press.

Castells, M. (2004) 'Informationalism, networks, and the network society: a theoretical blueprint', in M. Castells (ed.) *The Network Society: a cross-cultural perspective*, Northampton, MA: Edward Elgar, pp. 3–45.

Cameron, F.R. (2008a) 'Object-oriented democracies: conceptualising museum collections in networks', *Museum Management and Curatorship*, 23: 229–43.

Cameron, F.R. (2008b) 'Object-orientated democracies: contradictions, challenges and opportunities', *Museums and the Web 2008*. Available at: http://www.archimuse.com/mw2008/papers/cameron/cameron.html (Accessed 10 May 2010).

Clarke, A.S. (1983) 'Department of Natural History', in N. Tebble and D. Heppell (eds) *Royal Scottish Museum Triennial Report 1980-81-82*, Edinburgh: Royal Scottish Museum, pp. 44–9.

Committee of Public Accounts (1912) 'First, second and third reports of the Committee of Public Accounts', *Parliamentary Papers (House of Commons Sessional Papers)*, Session 1912–13, 57, 199, 156, VI: i–xxxiv, 1–289 [21–343].

DeSilvey, C. (2007) 'Practical remembrance: material and method in a recycled archive', in E. Gagen, H. Lorimer and A. Vasudevan (eds) 'Practicing the archive: reflections on method and practice in historical geography', *Historical Geography Research Series*, 40: 37–45.

Desrosieres, A. (2001) 'How real are statistics? Four possible attitudes', *Social Research*, 68: 339–55.

Edwards, E. and J. Hart (eds) (2004) *Photographs Objects Histories: on the materiality of images*, London: Routledge.

Eschmeyer, W.N. (ed.) (1998) *Catalog of Fishes*, electronic version (updated 26 August 2010). Available at: http://research.calacademy.org/ichthyology/catalog/fishcatmain.asp (Accessed 12 October 2010).

Foucault, M. (2002) *The Archaeology of Knowledge*, London: Routledge.

Herle, A. (2000) 'Torres Strait Islanders stories from an exhibition', *Ethnos*, 65: 253–74.

Herle, A. (2001) 'Exhibition and representation: stories from the Torres Strait Islanders exhibition', *Museum International*, 53: 8–18.

Hooper-Greenhill, E. (1992) *Museums and the Shaping of Knowledge*, London: Routledge.

King's Warrant [Transcript] (23 October 1812) *Catalogue &c The Museum of the College of Edinb'* Vol. 1, NMS, Natural History Archive.

Knell, S.J. (2004) 'Altered values: searching for a new collecting', in S.J. Knell (ed.) *Museums and the Future of Collecting* (2nd edn), Aldershot: Ashgate, pp. 1–46.

Knell, S.J., S. MacLeod and S. Watson (2007) 'Introduction', in S.J. Knell, S. MacLeod and S. Watson (eds) *Museum Revolutions: how museums change and are changed*, London: Routledge, pp. xix–xxvi.

Kopytoff, I. (1986) 'The cultural biography of things: commoditization as a process', in A. Appadurai (ed.) *The Social Life of Things: commodities in a cultural perspective*, Cambridge: Cambridge University Press, pp. 64–94.

Latour, B. (1987) *Science in Action: how to follow scientists and engineers through society*, Philadelphia, PA: Open University Press.

Latour, B. (1988) 'Mixing humans and nonhumans together: the sociology of a door-closer', *Social Problems*, 35: 298–310.

Latour, B. (1992) 'Where are the missing masses? The sociology of a few mundane artifacts', in W.E. Bijker and J. Law (eds) *Shaping Technology / Building Society: studies in sociotechnical change*, Cambridge, MA: MIT Press, pp. 151–80.

Latour, B. (2005a) *Reassembling the Social: an introduction to actor-network-theory*. Oxford: Oxford University Press.

Latour B. (2005b) 'From realpolitik to dingpolitik or how to make things public', in B. Latour and P. Weibel (eds) *Making Things Public: atmospheres of democracy*, Cambridge, MA: MIT Press, pp. 1–31.

Lynch, M. (1999) 'Archives in formation: privileged spaces, popular archives and paper trails', *History of Human Sciences*, 12: 65–88.

Montello, D.R. and P.C. Sutton (2006) *An Introduction to Scientific Research Methods in Geography*, London: Sage.

Murray, A. (1855) 'On electrical fishes; with a description of a new species of *Malapterurus* from Old Calabar, received from the Rev. Hope W. Waddell, missionary there', *Proceedings of the Royal Physical Society of Edinburgh*, 1: 20–1.

O'Neill, M.E. (2001) 'Corporeal experience: a haptic way of knowing', *Journal of Architectural Education*, 55: 3–12.

Osbourne, T. (1999) 'The ordinariness of the archive', *History of Human Sciences*, 12: 51–64.

Pearce. S. (1995) *On Collecting: an investigation into collecting in the European tradition*, London: Routledge.

Pearson, C. (2005) 'Museum archives: gateway to the past', *Museums Journal*, February 2005: 29.

Pickstone, J.V. (1994) 'Museological science? The place of the analytical/comparative in nineteenth-century science, technology and medicine', *History of Science*, 32: 111–38.

Polayni, M. (1967) *The Tacit Dimension*, New York: Doubleday and Company.

Royal Scottish Museum (1939) *Report on the Royal Scottish Museum for the Year 1938*, Edinburgh: His Majesty's Stationery Office.

Seely, H. (2003) 'The poetry of D.H. Rumsfeld: recent works by the Secretary of Defense', *Slate*, 2 April 2003. Availble at: http://www.slate.com/id/2081042/ (Accessed 18 September 2008).

Sontag, S. (1996) 'Under the sign of Saturn', in S. Sontag *Under the Sign of Saturn*, London: Vintage, pp. 109–34.

Spivak, G.C. (2000) 'Translation as culture', *Parallax*, 6: 13–24.

Star S.L. and J. Griesemer (1989) 'Institutional ecology, "translations" and boundary objects: amateurs and professionals in Berkeley's Museum of Vertebrate Zoology, 1907–39', *Social Studies in Science*, 19: 387–420.

Stone, S.M. (1992) 'Documenting collections', in J.M.A. Thompson (ed.) *Manual of Curatorship: a guide to museum practice*, London: Butterworth Heinemann, pp. 213–28.

Swinney, G.N. (1990) 'Actinopterygii', in J.S. Herman, R.Y. McGowan and G.N. Swinney (eds) *Catalogue of the Type Specimens of Recent Vertebrates in the National Museums of Scotland*, Edinburgh: National Museums of Scotland, pp. 1–5.

Swinney, G.N. (2006) 'Reconstructed visions: the philosophies that shaped part of the Scottish national collections', *Museum Management and Curatorship*, 21: 128–42.

Swinney, G.N. (in press) 'Afterword' in S.J.M.M. Alberti (ed.) *Afterlives of Animals: a museum menagerie*, Charlottesville, VA: University of Virginia Press.

Swinney, G.N. and M.R. Shaw (1998) 'History of the zoological collections of the National Museums of Scotland', *Bush Telegraph*, 27: 23–32.

van Gennep, A. (1984) *The Rites of Passage*, London: Routledge.

Waterston, C.D. (1997) *Collections in Context: the museum of the Royal Society of Edinburgh and the inception of a national museum for Scotland*, Edinburgh: NMS Publishing.

Wilson, G. (1857) 'On the electric fishes as the earliest electric machines employed by mankind', *Edinburgh New Philosophical Journal* (new series), 6: 267–88.

Withers, C.W.J. (2002) 'Constructing "the geographical archive"', *Area*, 34: 303–11.

4 Emblematic museum objects of national significance

In search of their multiple meanings and values

Marlen Mouliou and Despina Kalessopoulou

Objects bring together thought and feeling

(Turkle 2007: 9)

Museum objects and 'gazing' visitors: introductory notes

Years ago in his book *Eccentric Spaces*, Robert Harbison approached museums as spaces 'full of verbiage' and 'incessantly of babbling objects' (Harbison 2000: 31) immobilised and secluded in graveyard-like environments. Indeed, museums have often been viewed as 'materialistic enterprises' that aimed to 'immortalize the spirit of civilizations past by replacing persons with objects, extracting their life and thought' (Hein 2000: 51). However, as Susan Pearce has shown in her seminal work, the basis of museum objects' intense interest is their ability to be both signifiers and signified, that is simultaneously carriers of a real part of the past into the present and bearers of perpetual symbolic re-interpretations (Pearce 1992: 27). Like people, objects have a social life and a career, all the more so in a great national museum where art objects populate the galleries and demanding crowds never cease to pass by, look, ponder, admire, learn or even appropriate by instantaneously capturing the materiality of the artworks in their camera lenses.

Museums shape to a large extent the lives of objects found in their collections but these objects also correspondingly shape the history of their host museums by their material presence, their signification and the infinite dialogues they instigate with the visiting public. This is a dialectical and recursive relationship which has often been emphasised by museum theorists and practitioners. Thus, in this chapter, because we consider the relationship between museums, objects and persons truly intriguing, we attempt to explore the cultural biography of emblematic objects in the context of a large national museum of ancient art, itself a biographical object of a nation, by drawing on material culture theories[1] on the social lives and agency of things.

Emblematic museum objects of national significance and the tracing of their social lives: research methodology

We chose the National Archaeological Museum of Athens as a platform for this investigation because it is one of the most iconic objects of the Greek nation, with a central position in the museum history of the country. Although it officially opened its doors to visitors in 1889, the foundation of a central archaeological museum for Greece was conceived much earlier, in 1829. The Museum houses collections dating from the prehistoric to the Roman period, from various parts of Greece. Since its inception, it has been considered a national shrine of Greek art in which the nation's unbroken continuity is manifest in the exhibition of antiquities, as is still the case in many other Greek archaeological museums.[2]

The organisational logic of its displays has remained more or less unchanged, being based on the material classification and linear chronological continuity of its collections: i.e. Vases, Bronzes, and Sculpture plus Prehistoric and Anatolian Antiquities.[3] In the aftermath of the Second World War, for the duration of which the Museum closed down and all its collections were buried underground for protection, the re-opening of just three of its many galleries in 1948 was greeted by intellectuals and the print media alike with delight. Although at the time the nation was still embroiled in a devastating civil war, some voices assigned an allegorical significance to this re-opening, corresponding to the desire for a national resurgence and strengthening of the nation's collective consciousness and unity (Mouliou 2008: 84–9).

Almost six decades later, in the Olympic summer of 2004, the re-opening of the Museum after yet another structural transformation and re-organisation of exhibitions, was greeted with similarly enthusiastic newspaper headlines, such as 'the jewel of Athens', 'the jewel of our civilization', 'our national treasure', 'one of our best weapons for the Olympic Games of 2004', 'the ark of ancient Greek art' or 'the window on ancient Greek civilization'.[4] A careful study of the Museum visitors' book also confirms the public's strong perceptions of the symbolic nature of the Museum. In the visitors' comments, the Museum is characterised mainly as 'beautiful', a characterisation associated both with the beauty of its exhibits, but also with the aesthetic interpretive approach that prevails in this Museum. Greek visitors state that they are proud of being Greek, while foreigners recognise the uniqueness of its collections and their capacity to represent one of the greatest civilisations of Europe and of humanity.[5]

However, national museums of ancient art tend to consolidate their basic narratives, which seem to become frozen in time; any substantial move away from epistemological traditions is often regarded as challenging and most likely rejected as being too risky. In fact, the post-war 1950s re-display, which has been characterised as 'the greatest archaeological undertaking of this era in Greece' (Petrakos 1995: 110), still defines the rationale of the major part of the Museum's most recent renovation, carried out between 2002 and 2008. Christos Karouzos, the then director of the Museum and author of its first post-war re-display had claimed that 'a Museum of the History of Art has as its *main* objective not to serve history *tout court* but the History of Art' (Karouzos 1981: 137–8). The current director of the National Archaeological Museum, Nikolaos Kaltsas, asserts that the philosophy of the exhibits' presentation has not changed (Kontrarou-Rassia 2004: 14; see also Kaltsas 2007b: 46). The principles of classical purity and chronological order prevail. Although numerous thematic units have been added throughout the exhibitions in order to illustrate different aspects of the ancient Greek world, the National Archaeological Museum is basically a Museum of Art, and it is characterised by austerity and economy in its exhibition media.

If all this is borne in mind, a biographical account of museum collections, tested on the ground in a large national museum, can open up constructive ways of seeing and appreciating objects as entities in motion within an otherwise static museum environment. Thus, the idea of a project was born; this project was not intended to be audience research[6] but rather an experimental attempt to trace the social biographies[7] of some of the most iconic objects of the National Archaeological Museum. We determined that the objects' lives could be traced in the context of three generic discourses:[8] the *epistemological*, the *intervening* and the *public* one.

1   *The epistemological discourse*[9] is the prevailing formal museum narrative on the material and immaterial significations of the selected emblematic objects, which can be investigated through the textual information available to visitors (such as panels and captions, official museum guide books and website entries), as well as the current mind sets of the museum curators responsible for the displays investigated.

2   *The intervening discourse* is formulated by the extremely diverse voices that speak to potential museum visitors in direct or indirect ways and shape their personal object appropriations. This discourse is created on different platforms and channelled through various pathways (guides and guide books, TV documentaries, tour operators, personal readings of history and fiction and so on).

3   *The public discourse*[10] is naturally the most diverse and difficult of all to map. However, it can be the most revealing. Agentive changes in social theory have led theorists to talk in new ways about the agency of objects and how museum objects can be seen as empty vessels without the agency of museum visitors and their sensory and cognitive interactions with museum things.

In an attempt to chart and understand the unknown territory of visitors' 'enchanted' and imaginative minds vis-à-vis the emblematic material world of the Museum, we conducted our research in four stages.

First of all, we tried to delimit the term 'emblematic' in order to construct an interpretive model for analysing the features of the museum objects under investigation. We came up with a model that was designed as a mind map (Figure 4.1),[11] as we thought this was an efficient tool to record the various dimensions of emblematic objects as well as to explore their possible interconnections. The model was devised based on information gathered from different sources, such as dictionary definitions of the words 'emblem', 'icon' and 'emblematic',[12] and features of the concept 'icon', as provided by the UK's Department of Culture, Media and Sport in its online project *Icons*.[13]

We then set out to select the most emblematic objects to focus on. Although our archaeological knowledge together with information from sources representing

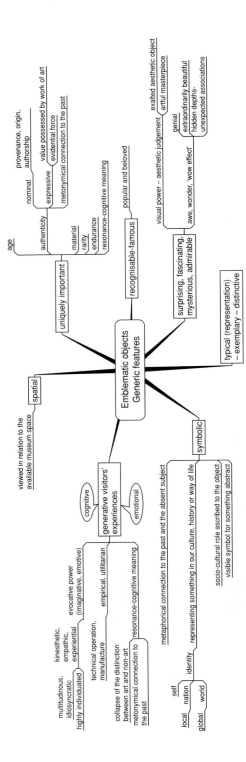

Figure 4.1 Our model of analysis for emblematic museum objects; a mind map of their various generic elements.

the *intervening discourse*[14] might have been sufficient for this selection process, we also wanted to explore the question based on the visitors' own choices. Therefore we analysed hundreds of comments recorded in the visitors' book[15] and at the same time we conducted two small-scale surveys[16] of visitors entering and leaving the Museum, in order to assess their views on the matter before and after the museum visit. The 'stars' of the entry survey proved to be the classical bronze statue of Zeus or Poseidon (Figure 4.2a), a Mycenaean golden funerary mask (the so-called Mask of Agamemnon; Figure 4.2c) and the marble sculpture collection in general (with no preference for a specific statue), while in the exit survey, the Zeus/Poseidon remained the most popular choice. These findings were supported by the preferences mentioned in the visitors' book, with the addition of the Hellenistic bronze, the so-called Jockey of Artemision (Figure 4.2b) as the next most popular choice. We finally chose[17] to focus on four[18] museum objects: the statue of Zeus/Poseidon, the Jockey, the 'Mask of Agamemnon' and the Mechanism of Antikythera dated to the first century BC, a unique piece of ancient technology (Figure 4.2d).[19] Our selection was based on a variety of reasons,

Figure 4.2 Iconic objects, clockwise from top left: (a) the Classical bronze statue of Zeus/Poseidon, dated to 460 BC, Sculpture Gallery No. 15; (b) the Hellenistic bronze known as the Jockey, dated to 140 BC, Gallery No. 21; (c) the Mycenaean gold 'Mask of Agamemnon', Prehistoric Gallery No. 4; (d) the Mechanism of Antikythera, dated to the first century BC, Bronze Gallery No. 38, National Archaeological Museum, Athens. (Source: personal archive M. Mouliou).

partly resulting from the findings of our surveys but more generally determined by the generic characteristics of these emblematic objects (e.g. age, aesthetic excellence, fame, uniqueness, mystery, distinctiveness, unusual nature, symbolism). Indeed, one of our interviewees, a young American art historian, when asked which objects he intended to see that day, mentioned all our choices except for the Mechanism, for 'they are the most prominent examples that the Museum has, maybe not necessarily the best examples of Greek art, but the ones that will stick in someone's mind when they think back on their trip to Greece'.

We then carried out the main part of this research which consisted of structured interviews[20] conducted with visitors inside the galleries, always in front of one of the emblematic objects on the shortlist. The interview consisted of open-ended questions arranged in three parts, followed by standard questions on demographic details (see Appendix):

1   An introductory part designed to encourage the visitor to reflect more intensively on the object on view, while it would help us to explore if and how the epistemological and the intervening discourses had influenced the formation of the visitor's own discourse on the object. It might also give us some clues regarding the cognitive and emotional associations this visitor–object encounter had produced, whether spontaneously or prompted by a question, exploring associations with Greek culture or their own cultural and personal identity.
2   A supplementary part through which we sought to explore the interest of the visitors in other museum objects and the specifics of these preferences.
3   A final creative and imaginative part where visitors were asked to sketch out their personal dialogue with the object in the form of a mind map.

Acknowledging the potential pitfalls a qualitative research of this kind might entail, we opted to explore fully the potential of the mind map, not only as a means of recording thoughts, but also as a way of organising and assessing data in viable and meaningful categories. At the beginning we analysed the epistemological discourse based on the predetermined generic features the conceptual mapping of the term emblematic had produced. All museum texts related to our emblematic objects (wall panels, object labels, official museum guide books and any current museum website) were recorded word for word, correlated with and mapped against these categorical features (Figure 4.3). We then completed the recordings of the epistemological perspective by incorporating into the map the curators' comments, gathered during our interviews. The analysis of the public discourse was performed in a similar way. First we charted the visitors' words corresponding to their immediate thoughts and feelings when looking at the object in question. Then we added all their views expressed in the object mind maps they had drawn themselves (Figure 4.4). Finally, the records of the epistemological and public perspectives were combined in a single mind map. We hoped that comparative analysis, based on the aforementioned discourses, would lead us to conclusions on the agency of the selected objects.

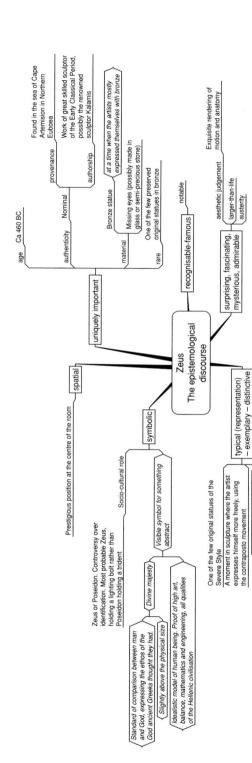

Figure 4.3 A mind map summarising the epistemological discourse on the statue of Zeus/Poseidon. The curators' views on the object are indicated in italics in hexagonal cartouches; the rest is information gathered from the corresponding written sources (e.g. exhibition labels, archaeological books).

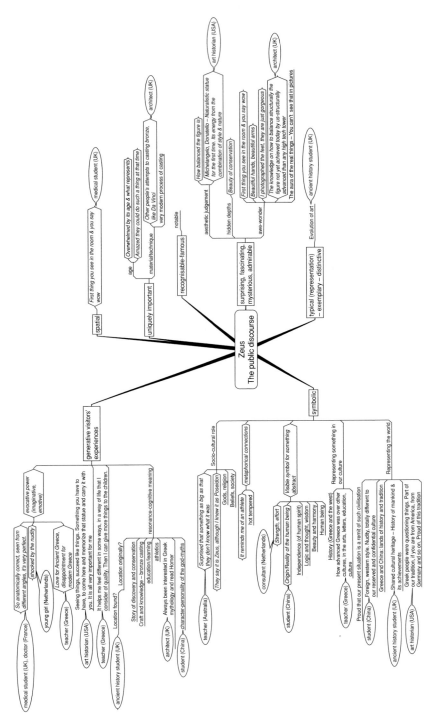

Figure 4.4 A mind map summarising the public discourse on the statue of Zeus/Poseidon. Visitors' first views on the object are given in italics in hexagonal cartouches; the rest is a summary of their comments, gathered from the mind maps the visitors were asked to draw during the interview.

Four emblematic objects in the National Archaeological Museum of Athens: brief commentary on the research findings

The Zeus/Poseidon is probably the most iconic object in the Museum. It is considered[21] one of the finest, but also one of the very few original bronze sculptures dated to 460 BC (i.e. the Classical Period). Apart from the symbolic character of the object as a Zeus or a Poseidon, the identification still being controversial, the label and the text panel offer information on the age, provenance and rarity of the object, particularly accentuating its aesthetic values and its central place among examples of the Severe Style in Greek art. Its importance in this respect is also stressed by the fact that the statue is placed on the axis of the entrance, right in the centre of the room dedicated to the Classical Period, enjoying an unhindered view from all angles (Figure 4.2a). The curators reinforce this narration by adding more information on the symbolic value of the statue, emphasising the ethos that ancient Greeks attributed to the gods and the anthropocentrism of the Greek civilisation (Figure 4.3). The statue of Zeus/Poseidon stands as a standard of comparison between man and god, as the idealised model of the human being, slightly larger than life size.

Visitors seem to follow the discourse of the museum in many aspects. They comment on the age, the rarity and the identification of the statue, and they are impressed by its aesthetic qualities; they not only express their awe and wonder, but also articulate interesting comments about the naturalism of the figure, its fine balance, and distinguish its style and place in the progression of Greek art. However, in more detailed dialogue with the visitors, other aspects arise (Figures 4.4 and 4.5a). The statue is also seen as a symbol of strength, beauty and harmony, logical thought and independence of the human spirit. These qualities are sometimes connected with the ancient Greek civilisation,[22] but they are most commonly associated with a shared cultural heritage that characterises the Western world or humanity in general, a view expressed by most of our interviewees. The visitors' personal generative readings reveal a need for more contextual information about (a) the condition in which the statue was found, and the way it was conserved, (b) what else was found with it at the same time and where it originally stood in antiquity, (c) the skill and knowledge involved in the production of the artefact, (d) ideology and religion in ancient Greek society and (e) personality traits and myths related to the god depicted. This last point was made by an Asian visitor, perhaps due to cultural differences with Western visitors who are more familiar with Greek mythology and traditions.

The Jockey[23] was discovered in the same submarine area as the Zeus/Poseidon, off Cape Artemision in Euboea (Figure 4.2b). Because of its size, it is situated at the centre of the museum in a distinctively designed room, the only room with walls painted bright red, facing a broad gallery which leads to the first floor. The statue, dated to 140 BC, is surrounded by marble Roman copies of Greek bronze originals of the fourth century BC, actually breaking the chronological order that the Sculpture Collection follows as its main interpretative device. Thus, it is

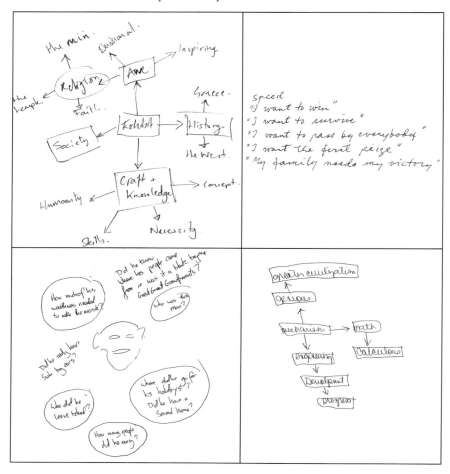

Figure 4.5 Visitors' mind maps, clockwise from top left. (a) Mind map drawn in front of the statue of Zeus/Poseidon, by a male British visitor, aged 18–24, a graduate in architecture interested in the arts (Source: survey conducted by the authors). (b) Mind map drawn in front of the Jockey, by a female Finnish retired history teacher visitor (Source: survey conducted by the authors). (c) Mind map drawn in front of the 'Mask of Agamemnon', by a male British visitor, aged 35–44, an IT engineer interested in music (Source: survey conducted by the authors). (d) Mind map drawn in front of the Antikythera Mechanism, by a female American visitor, a project manager aged 35–44, interested in documentaries and travelling (Source: survey conducted by the authors).

deprived of all contextual information related to the Hellenistic Period where it belongs. Because its presentation has isolated it from other works of its era and because it occupies a unique place in the ancient Greek heritage as the only extant bronze horse and rider of this size, the museum label focuses on descriptive and art historical details. The story of the wreck is not mentioned; no connection is made with the other famous discovery found nearby (i.e. the Zeus/Poseidon), nor the possible reasons for finding them together; no details are given about the painstaking restoration of the horse.

Visitors respond to this work of art very willingly, focusing with ease on its aesthetic qualities, but most of them find it hard[24] to integrate it in the evolution of Greek art, as it is more realistic than anything they have encountered up to that point. This reveals that the disruption already spotted in the official discourse of the Museum is often noted by the visitors. Its size and central position are the main factors giving this exhibit emblematic status, though naturally its remarkable craftsmanship and its highly evocative power are closely connected with this (Figure 4.5b). The horse is considered a universal symbol of strength, labour and freedom. Its autonomous, uncontextualised display also enables visitors to make more personal readings, such as that of a French woman, who associated the empty eyes of the horse and its frenzied gallop with fear and hell. The quest for more resonance is also present. Visitors want to know the story behind the object and details about its reconstruction.

The 'Mask of Agamemnon',[25] although 400 years earlier than the legendary king, is the best known of Schliemann's finds from the royal tombs at Mycenae (Figure 4.2c). The death mask, exclusively the funerary apparel of Mycenaean males, illustrates the dignified image, with realistic characteristics, of a Mycenaean ruler. It covered the face of one of the first Mycenaean leaders, representing an emblematic personality of the first Hellenic civilisation. It is surrounded by myth as it is connected with Homeric poems that profoundly influenced Greek thought and tradition. As the epitome of Mycenaean civilisation, the Mask dominates the entrance to the Mycenaean exhibition, being situated at the centre and visible from a distance. Visitors respond to it in a very emotional way (Figure 4.5c). Some of them comment on the exciting experience of seeing the real thing, and how it differs from what they had imagined it would be like. They mention the elegance of its realistic features and its awe-inspiring simplicity which gives it a modern look. The imposing male face evokes connotations of the male supremacy and warrior culture of the time. It also reflects the spirituality of the man depicted, that is his religious and ethical values, connotations that can be projected in surprising ways into the present day, as a belligerent, male-dominated culture still prevails. Being part of a death ritual, the Mask raises many questions about the practice of honouring the dead (something which continues to this day but is demonstrated in different ways), namely various metaphorical connections with death as well as the importance of keeping the memory alive as an expression of a people who loved their leader. Among the symbolic implications of the Mask are those that connect it with Greek mythology and the Homeric poems. What mostly engages visitors' imaginations and their sense of wonder is not an understanding of the Mask's position in our ancient Greek legacy, but details related to social history.[26] A significant proportion of the questions posed by visitors deal with the craftsmanship involved, the provenance of the gold and what this reveals, the history of the maker, or the life of the object soon after its production.

Possibly inspired by the realistic rendering of the Mask, people ask biographical questions about the person behind the object and the experience of living at that time. Visitors also require more contextual information about the archaeological evidence, namely more detailed and lively representations of the way these grave goods were found, their exact find spot(s) and the links between the objects on display.

The Antikythera Mechanism is one of the most fascinating ancient technological instruments[27] (Figure 4.2d). The Mechanism was found in the Antikythera shipwreck of about 80 BC, along with many important works of art, probably loot on a Roman ship. It is now understood to be involved with astronomical phenomena and operates as a complex mechanical computer which tracks the cycles of the solar system. The object has had an interesting career since its discovery in 1902, giving it a 'zero-to-hero' life story. The Mechanism is one of the few extant high-tech instruments from the ancient world and the only one exhibited at the Museum among what are mainly works of art and functional objects. This fact is itself a signified, for visitors are attracted to it, trying to figure out the hidden messages embedded in this uniqueness. People want to understand the reasons for its rarity, find out whether there were many things like that in ancient Greece, and know more about its function and its contemporary life story. In their personal readings visitors are attracted by the mystery still surrounding the Mechanism (Figure 4.5d). They are fascinated by its mechanical precision, the unbelievable genius of its construction and the progress of engineering in such ancient times. Its age is surely a factor in their excitement, as many responses refer to the sharp contrast between the age and the modern look of the instrument and its familiarity to our present culture. Its apparent modernity was once the reason for its not being connected with ancient Greek civilisation, but more often nowadays it leads to comments about its significance, even compared to the highly technological culture of the present day.[28] People who have studied engineering and science find a complementary, more personal reason to connect with it. Finally, comparing the epistemological with the public discourse reveals that people are interested in the information available, although they are not always able to absorb and comprehend all of it using the available media. They are intrigued by the unanswered questions that still exist and pose more questions relating to its function and researchers' attempts to decipher it. Thus, the Antikythera Mechanism offers not only a unique window on history, allowing us to view the collected astronomical knowledge of that time, but also a window on the scientific knowledge of our time, summoned up to create the most faithful interpretation. A sociocultural approach to science seems to be the most appropriate way to combine the official and the visitors' discourse successfully.

Concluding notes

Our research involved museum objects which meant that their values derived from their enduring materiality, which is an important function. Yet, it is often secondary to their role as signs and symbols, as meaning bearers and dynamic energy transformers. When dealing with sanctified museum art works, the heart of mystery lies in the uniqueness, authenticity and visual power of the master-pieces, ideally displayed in ways that heighten their charisma, compel and reward the intensity of the viewer's gaze, manifest their artistic genius. In other words, we have to take into account the objects' ability to elicit wonder. But wonder may derive not only from the beauty of the object but also its rarity, its preciousness, its technical virtuosity, its excessive, surprising nature, its poetic, marvellous quality. We know also from other very interesting studies[29] that a museum object can be caught in the conundrum of a partly false dilemma between the power of visual wonder that it can evoke in a receptive viewer and the power of cultural reso-nance. This dilemma might be artificial, for as Stephen Greenblatt reminds us:

> [T]he impact of most exhibitions is likely to be enhanced if there is a strong initial appeal to wonder, a wonder that then leads to the desire for resonance [. . .] the goal – difficult but not utopian – should be to press beyond the limits of the models, cross boundaries, create strong hybrids.
>
> (Greenblatt 1991: 54)

This hybrid is rarely fulfilled in a large traditional museum institution but can be created in many ways in the imaginative and curious minds of its visiting viewers.

This study has attempted to offer a method for analysing the epistemological and public discourse, while also to some extent exploring the intervening one, in order to arrive at a better understanding of what makes an object *emblematic* and to present in a coherent yet open-ended way the multiple dimensions of iconic objects and their agency upon visitors and the hosting museum. Although the questions used gave visitors considerable freedom to express personal views and to construct their own 'hybrid', it should be borne in mind that comments were categorised according to a preconceived coding system for the emblematic status of the objects, and this method entails subjectivity in the researchers' readings. On the other hand, these well-documented categories allowed the juxtaposition or the combination of idiosyncratic comments with formal texts, presenting rich strata of data that delineate both in breadth and depth the cultural biography of the objects.

A comparative examination of all the diagrams that map the epistemological and the public discourse of the four objects clearly showed that the Museum's stance is to present the unique characteristics of its emblematic objects, through providing details about their age and authenticity, rarity, materiality and informa-tion on technical matters. With the exception of the Antikythera Mechanism, they tend also to provide comments relating to aesthetic judgements, thus remain-ing faithful to the art historical tradition. Visitors absorb this information but they tend to expand their interest to the symbolic connotations of the objects, generating a whole set of responses that are purely evocative or ask for more resonance. When interviewed, the curators of the Museum also emphasised the symbolic associations of the objects, apparently revealing the human need to create possible meanings and personal readings that help them appropriate the material world, as previous research has already suggested (Csikszentmihalyi and Robinson 1990, Falk and Dierking 2000, Hooper-Greenhill 2000, 2007). However, these views are not incorporated in the textual information provided by the Museum.

As regards connotations of national significance, visitors rarely referred to this aspect in their initial thoughts, but most of them were able to trace some sort of association either to Greek culture or to aspects of humanity in response to the question that focused on this.

Although very demanding in terms of time, reflection and the openness required on the part of visitors in overcrowded galleries, the mind map proved to be an effective means of capturing their basic thoughts. The eagerness to talk and sketch that we encountered in almost all our interviewees may be an indication of the efficacy of our research aims and method(s); but mostly it seems likely to point to the powerful interactions that occur, whether spontaneously or prompted, between humans and objects within the space of museum galleries and the satisfaction museum visitors can feel when given the opportunity to talk about these personal encounters and reflections that they relate to their lives in a meaningful way.

Hence, our analysis clearly indicated that museums need to deploy more imaginative approaches in order to facilitate a dialogue between the visitors and the objects on display. Whether through an audio guide, a museum interactive display, a contemporary art installation, alternative textual information or an internet blog, it is crucial for museums to find new ways and interpretative means to present the context of emblematic or less famous objects and then pose open-ended questions that empower individuals to share the thoughts they evoke. In a museum environment, people – whether curators, wardens, guides, journalists, educators or visitors – offer a wealth of accumulated experiences which can enliven the objects and create a culturally enriched seam of knowledge.

Our observations essentially correspond to Nick Merriman's remarks on public archaeology and the impact of the so-called 'informed imagination' approach to museum interpretation, which respects the individual 'aura' of each object but can also be more affective, non-linear, anti-rational, self-directed and poetic. This approach seeks the knowledge of the archaeological and historical context of the material provided by the experts, but also accepts the plurality of views and the conditional nature of archaeological interpretations as well as welcoming plurality, imagination and creativity in the visitors' own constructions of the past (2004c: 101–2).

Indeed, museums are and should be three-dimensional immersive spaces of encounter, where visitors can explore things actively with all their senses and intellectual faculties. Objects and exhibitions, even the most unchanging ones, have agency that captures and potentially 'enchants' their audiences. 'Socially objectified things are imbued with meaning', as Hilde Hein says, 'layer upon layer, within sanctioned structures of reference. Museums have the option of attending to only the most prominent meaning strata of objects or of exploring the deeper layers of complexity' (Hein 2000: 64). If they go for the first option, they may become rigid and inward-looking; if they go for the latter, they may benefit in various ways from being sensitive to the non-normatively meaningful.

Appendix

Interview questionnaire with visitors in the National Archaeological Museum of Athens.

General questions

1   You are standing in front of. . . . [name of the emblematic object]. Did you make a point of seeing this museum object during your visit today? Yes..☐....No..☐ If yes, why?
2   As you see this object, what associations come to mind? (e.g. images, thoughts, feelings, sensations, memories, etc.)/Which elements make it exceptional for you?
3   In your view, what does this display project/articulate? (a) in relation to Greek culture? (b) in relation to your culture? (c) in relation to your own personality?
4   Have you read or heard anything about this display before today's's visit? Yes..☐.... No..☐ If yes, where from?
5   Did you get to know something new about this display during your visit in the Museum today? Yes..☐....No..☐ If yes, in which way (e.g. display labels, neighbouring displays, the gallery itself, your personal guide, a guide book)?
6   What else you would have liked to know about this display and the Museum did not provide the necessary information?
7   What you like it to be displayed in a different manner? Yes..☐....No..☐ If yes, how and why?

Supplementary questions

8   Which other objects of the museum collection you intend to see today and why?
9   Which museum object would you choose to have as a replica and souvenir in your own house, in whatever form (e.g. original replica, image in a postcard)?

Mind map

Looking back at the key words and concepts that you mentioned earlier on (questions 2–4), can you spot any links between them and if yes draw them on paper?

Visitor's profile

Gender: male, female
Age: 8–12, 13–17, 18–24, 25–34, 35–44, 45–54, 55–64, 65+
Nationality
Place of residence
Occupation
Favourite leisure activity
Number of museum visits per year

Notes

1 Agentive trends in social theory have led theorists to talk about the agency of objects in new ways. Appadurai's renowned anthropological theories introduced in his book *The Social Life of Things* (1986) inspired a whole new series of studies by showing for the first time how passive objects, assuming a wide range of different identities and value systems, could be successively moved about, transformed and recontextualised. Alfred Gell's descriptions of the 'instrumentality'/'agency' of objects proposed in his equally seminal book *Art and Agency: a new anthropological theory* (1998) also focused attention on the malleability of objects that, when recontextualised, could stimulate diverse emotional responses in their users or viewers. Gell's work suggested a more active model of an object's biography, in which the object could not only assume a number of different identities such as imported wealth, ancestral heirloom or commodity, but could also 'interact' with the people who looked at it. Gell spoke of 'the technology of enchantment' and 'the enchantment of technology of objects' and their magical effect on people's minds and urged us to look at how people act through objects by investing parts of their personhood into things. From the extensive bibliography on the intimate and active partnerships of people with objects, see, for example, Kopytoff (1986), Hoskins (1998, 2006), Hecht (2001), Alberti (2005), Tilley (2006), Albano (2007), Turkle (2007), Arigho (2008), Rowlands (2008).

2 On the link between antiquity, antiquities and the national imagination in Greece, there is now an extensive and insightful bibliography. Two recent seminal readings are: the collective volume *A Singular Antiquity: archaeology and Hellenic identity in twentieth century Greece*, edited by Damaskos and Plantzos (2008) and Hamilakis' (2007) book, *The Nation and its Ruins*, which deals with the use of the ancient Greek heritage and its material manifestations as symbolic capital.

3 For the history of the National Archaeological Museum, see Karouzou (1967, 1982), Kokkou (1977), Voudouri (2003: 361–72), Kaltsas (2007a: 15–22); Gazi (2008). See also the museum's website available at http://www.namuseum.gr (Accessed 12 July 2010).

4 See newspaper sources such as: *Naftemporiki* (25 June 2004), *Apogevmatini* (25 June 2004), *Adesmeftos Typos tou Mitsi* (25 June 2004), *Free Time* (25 June 2004), *Kathimerini* (21 March 2004), *Eleftheros Typos* (17 March 2004). [Clippings sourced from museum archives.]

5 There are numerous studies on the issue of national identity and museums. See, for instance, Kaplan (1994), Boswell and Evans (1999), MacDonald (2003) and McLean (2005) where further relevant references are available.

6 On recent audience research relevant to this study, see Leinhardt and Knutson (2004) and Hooper-Greenhill (2007).

7 For an account of the social lives, roles and meanings of Greek antiquities in the social context of modern Greece, see Hamilakis (2007).

8 For a general introduction to theories of discourse, see White (1978), MacDonnell (1986) and Hall (1997: 6). On discourse theories in archaeology, see Shanks and Hodder (1995: 24). See also the collective volume *Public Archaeology* edited by Merriman (2004a) and the more recent work by Hamilakis and Anagnostopoulos (2009) who, as editors of another collective volume on the subject, attempt to chart and survey an emerging transdisciplinary trend under the rubric 'archaeological ethnography' (2009: 65–6). For a discursive understanding of the museum, from an extensive bibliography, see Karp and Lavine (1991), Hooper-Greenhill (1992), Pearce (1995), Bal (1996), Hein (2000) and Lord (2005).

9 Copeland, in his essay published in the collective volume *Public Archaeology* (2004: 135), calls the epistemological discourse the 'expert construction' and contrasts it with the 'public construction'.

10 In Merriman's words, this is the 'multiple perspective' in public archaeology, for as he emphatically acknowledges 'no matter how hard archaeologists try, non-archaeologists

will re-appropriate, re-interpret and re-negotiate meanings of archaeological resources to their own personal agendas' (2004b: 6–7). Hamilakis and Anagnostopoulos also use the term 'alternative archaeologies' to describe popular, unofficial, vernacular discourses, collective practices and engagements with the material past that co-exist alongside official modernist archaeological epistemologies (2009).

11 For literature on the use of mind maps, see Novak and Caňas (2008).

12 *Webster's Revised Unabridged Dictionary*, online. Available at http://dictionary.reference.com/browse/emblematic (Accessed 12 July 2010).

13 For more information on this project see http://www.icons.org.uk (Accessed 12 July 2010).

14 For the purpose of this research, we gathered some material related to the intervening discourse, from various sources: guide books, internet sites and Greek school textbooks. This was in order to consolidate our selection of the iconic objects of the Museum and study the way these sources present them to the public. We also explored the views of some museum wardens and a tourist guide with many years' experience of working in this Museum. The study of the intervening discourse is by no means exhaustive, merely tentative. Systematic content analysis of selected sources and the tracing of their impact on visitors could be the object of a separate study, due to the amount of research time required and the need for differentiation in methodology.

15 We analysed about 1000 visitors' comments dated between 1 February and 17 August 2008. We aimed to include comments recorded during a six-month period and chose for this purpose the most recent visitors' books available in the Museum's archive. Only comments written in Greek, English, French, Spanish, Italian, Portuguese and German were analysed, as other languages were not comprehensible to the researchers. The methodology used was based on MacDonald's (2005) observations. Comments were categorised under inductively derived headings: overall impression of the museum, reference to specific exhibits, comments relating the museum with personal identity, comments referring to Greece and the Greeks. In addition, comments of a symbolic nature were categorised under several emerging themes, with the following being the most popular: History and culture, Aesthetics, Return of the Parthenon Marbles, Time dimension, Greek art and archaeology, and Heritage safeguarding. This categorisation helped us better understand at an early phase of the research the symbolic connotations that the Museum creates after being experienced in relation to its iconic dimension. It was also used as a basis for defining the scope and refining the articulation of question 3(a–c) of the structured interviews that followed (see endnote 20 and Appendix).

16 These surveys did not aim to be thorough and extensive quantitative studies, but just to test grounds of our own choices regarding the emblematic objects we had already decided to focus on. Out of the 94 answers we gathered in total, 37 were entry samples (62.16 per cent female, 43.24 per cent aged 25–44, 75.68 per cent first-time visitors, 67.57 per cent Europeans) and 57 exit samples (58 per cent female, 51 per cent aged 45+, 79 per cent first time visitors, 57 per cent Europeans). The visitors sampled in the entry survey differ from those in the exit sample. Their threshold reasons for choosing emblematic objects before their entry to the museum were evenly distributed across all the generic elements of the term *emblematic*, as follows: (a) *uniquely important* [because they are (i) connected to Mycenae, Troy, Iliad, Greece, (ii) most important pieces, (iii) acme of heroic era, (iv) extremely old]; (b) *recognisable – famous* [because they are (i) information provided by guide books, (ii) mentioned often in books, (iii) advertised often]; (c) *typical – exemplary – distinctive* [because they are (i) most representative of Greek art and of the Museum, (ii) a panorama of Greek art, (iii) forms that signal important changes in ancient art]; (d) *surprising, fascinating, mysterious, admirable* [because they exemplify (i) artistic excellence, (ii) fantastic artistic achievement, (iii) high degree of craftsmanship, (iv) high degree of animation, (v) the ability to impress the visitor];

(e) *symbolic* [because they are (i) great objects of Greek history, (ii) nineteenth-century finds, part of the early history of the Museum, (iii) the heart of Greece, (iv) a reflection of the intellectual excellence of the Greeks, (v) a legacy left to the world, (vi) of national significance, (vii) representation of human figure, (viii) representation of historical personalities]; and (f) *generative experiences – public discourse* [because the visitor (i) studied archaeology at the university, (ii) can relate them to their own artistic activities in leisure time, (iii) felt the ancient spirit, (iv) has a liking for bronze as a material, and (v) likes horses].

During the sampling process of both surveys, we had the assistance of two young researchers, Nikoletta Palaiologou (archaeologist-museologist) and Leda Papamathaiaki (social anthropologist). We thank them both for their help.

17 During a pilot phase of the project, we carried out three interviews in front of the famous marble Kouros of Aristodikos. However, we quickly understood that neither this kouros, nor any other, attracted the visitors' attention as an individual masterpiece. It was rather appreciated as part of a typological group, namely the renowned archaic kouroi. Similarly, other star objects, chosen by the visitors, could have been part of this research, such as the impressive bronze statue called The Lady of Kalymnos, found underwater near the homonymous island. However, during our research, the statue was moved to the local Archaeological Museum of Kalymnos, after a long-awaited decision of the Central Council of Museums regarding an appeal for its internal 'repatriation'.

18 For archaeological documentation on the four exhibits, see the following references, each of them containing a comprehensive bibliography: for the Mask, Demakopoulou (1990: 139–40); for the Zeus/Poseidon statue, Kaltsas (2002: 93); for the Jockey, Kaltsas (2002: 286); for the Antikythera Mechanism, online (http://www.antikythera-mechanism.gr/bibliography) as well as Freeth *et al.* (2006, 2008).

19 Although the Mechanism is scarcely mentioned in the entry and exit interviews or in the visitors' books, we chose to include it. Results from a multidisciplinary project still in progress dealing with its reconstruction and hidden meanings are constantly being announced in conferences, special exhibitions, articles in the scientific journal *Nature* (Freeth *et al.* 2006, 2008) and documentaries on the Discovery Channel, making it world famous and gradually transforming it into an icon of ancient Greek civilisation (displayed even in the pages of the new Greek passports).

20 In the space of a few weeks (October–November 2008), we conducted 33 structured interviews in front of the four chosen emblematic objects. We had 15 male and 18 female interviewees. Most of them were Europeans (19) and of those five were Greeks. We also had nine North Americans, two Asians, one Australian, one New Zealander and one South American. Their ages ranged from 18 to 55+ years old (five were aged 18–24, another five aged 25–34, nine aged 35–44, two aged 45–54; eleven aged 55+).

21 Indicatively, tourists can read in the *Blue Guide* that this statue is 'the principal masterpiece, a powerful original classical bronze of heroic proportions standing in the centre of the room' (Barber 1992: 136).

22 Our interviewees offered some relevant and fairly interesting views on the matter, when asked 'What does the statue articulate in relation to Greek culture?' We quote a selection of these comments: 'Incredibly advanced in relation to other cultures' (female, aged 18–24, medical student from UK); 'Athens, place of great civilisation' (male, aged 25–34, graduate of ancient history from UK); 'Greek people started questioning things' (male, aged 65+, art teacher from USA); 'History, strength of Greece' (male, aged 55–64, retired science teacher from Australia); 'Superiority of the ancients in the arts and letters, civilisation and education' (female, aged 35–44, primary school teacher from Greece).

23 The *Rough Guide* describes the horse with the little Jockey as 'virtuoso', 'lively masterpiece in bronze of the second century BC' (Ellingham *et al.* 1995: 97).

24 A couple of indicative comments in this respect are: 'I don't know much about Greek culture. I am not sure. It seems different from all the other things I've seen. It seems not like Greek culture' (male, aged 25–34 years old, attorney from USA); 'Usual Greek sculptures are idealistic. Beautiful young people, wonderful bodies, but this is realistic. I think this statue is global. Same feelings all over the world [. . .] Effort, I want to win, I want to survive' (female, aged 65+ years old, retired history teacher from Finland).

25 In the *Eyewitness* and *Rough Guide* it is the 'legendary and justly famous king's death mask', and 'the biggest crowd puller' [as good as Mona Lisa in Louvre] for its association with the Homeric myth (see Dubin 2009: 71; Ellingham *et al.* 1995: 95).

26 We quote at length two indicative comments from our interviewees: 'I don't know Greek culture very well. It's a beautiful gesture to cover a dead man with a golden mask. It seems that Greeks honoured their ancestry. Honouring the dead in our culture exists, but not with a funerary mask. We've seen in the museum big headstones. They reminded me of American funeral monuments in big cemeteries. It is a shared trait. I hope death is that peaceful' (female, aged 35–44, editor from USA); 'I did not connect it. I am more on [*sic*] aesthetics. I didn't search [for] historical meanings. I've seen a play in New York on how Agamemnon's children revenged his death and it was interesting to see the connections. It doesn't really connect to my culture. This is the birth of civilisation. You have to come to Greece to see the place where democracy was born, what amazing historical monuments were made. Where was the mask discovered? When? It was not exhibited before? Why is it now special? We are ignorant' (female, aged 55–64, architect from Romania).

27 For information on the history of the object and the Antikythera Mechanism Research Project, see http://www.antikythera-mechanism.gr/.

28 Some visitors expressed the following views: 'I feel it's completely connected with Greek history' (female, aged 25–34, journalist from Brazil); 'It has universal values' (female, aged 35–44, project manager from USA); 'Rare exhibit. It offers another dimension of what Greeks can achieve' (female, aged 18–24, linguist from Greece).

29 Greenblatt (1991); from the extensive literature on object studies, see also Jordanova (1989), Saumarez Smith (1989), Vergo (1989), Vogel (1991), Pearce (1992, 1994), Hein (2000: 51–68) and Tilley (2006).

Bibliography

Albano, C. (2007) 'Displaying lives: the narrative of objects in biographical exhibitions', *Museum and Society*, 5: 15–28.

Alberti, S. (2005) 'Objects and the Museum', *Isis*, 96: 559–71.

Appadurai, A. (1986) *The Social Life of Things: commodities in cultural perspective*, Cambridge: Cambridge University Press.

Arigho, B. (2008) 'Getting a handle on the past: the use of objects in reminiscence work', in H.J. Chatterjee (ed.) *Touch in Museums: policy and practice in object handling*, Oxford: Berg, pp. 205–12.

Bal, M. (1996) 'The discourse of the museum', in R. Greenberg *et al.* (eds) *Thinking about Exhibitions*, London: Routledge, pp. 201–20.

Barber, R. (1992) *Blue Guide: Athens and environs*, London: A & C Black.

Boswell, D. and J. Evans (eds) (1999) *Representing the Nation: a reader, histories, heritage and museums*, London: Routledge.

Copeland, T. (2004) 'Presenting archaeology to the public: constructing insights on-site', in N. Merriman (ed.) *Public Archaeology*, London: Routledge, pp. 132–44.

Csikszentmihalyi, M. and R. Robinson (1990) *The Art of Seeing: an interpretation of the aesthetic encounter*, Los Angeles: J. Paul Getty Museum.

DamasKos, D. and Plantzoz, D. (2008) *A Singular Antiquity: archaeology and Hellenic identity in twentieth century Greece*, Athens: Benaki Museum, pp. 67–82.

Demakopoulou, K. (ed.) (1990) *Troy, Mycenae, Tiryns, Orchomenos. Heinrich Schliemann: the 100th anniversary of his death*, Athens: Hellenic Ministry of Culture and Hellenic National Committee of ICOM.

Dubin, M. (2009) *DK Eyewitness Guide: Greece, Athens and the Mainland*, London: Dorling Kindersley.

Ellingham, M., M. Dubin, N. Jansz and J. Fisher (1995) *Greece: The Rough Guide*, London: Rough Guides.

Falk, J. and Dierking, L. (2000) *Learning from Museums: visitor experiences and the making of meaning*, Walnut Creek, CA: Altamira Press.

Freeth, T., A.R. Jones, J.M. Steele and Y. Bitsakis (2008) 'Calendars with Olympiad display and eclipse prediction on the Antikythera Mechanism', *Nature*, 454: 614–17.

Freeth, T., Y. Bitsakis, X. Moussas, J. Seiradakis, A. Tselikas, H. Mangou *et al.* (2006) 'Decoding the ancient Greek astronomical calculator known as the Antikythera Mechanism', *Nature*, 444: 587–91.

Gazi, A. (2008) '"Artfully classified" and "appropriately placed": notes on the display of antiquities in early twentieth century Greece' in D. Damaskos and D. Plantzos (eds) *A Singular Antiquity: archaeology and Hellenic identity in twentieth century Greece*, Athens: Benaki Museum, pp. 67–82.

Gell, A. (1998) *Art and Agency: a new anthropological theory*, Oxford: Oxford University Press.

Greenblatt, S. (1991) 'Resonance and wonder' in I. Karp and S. Lavine (eds) *Exhibiting Cultures: the poetics and politics of museum display*, Washington, DC and London: Smithsonian Institution Press, pp. 42–56.

Hall, S. (ed.) (1997) *Representation: cultural representation and signifying practices*, London: Sage.

Hamilakis, Y. (2007) *The Nation and its Ruins: antiquity, archaeology, and national imagination in Greece*, Oxford: Oxford University Press.

Hamilakis Y. and A. Anagnostopoulos (2009) 'What is archaeological ethnography?', *Public Archaeology*, 8: 65–87.

Harbison, R. (2000) *Eccentric Spaces*, Cambridge, MA: MIT Press.

Hecht, A. (2001) 'Home sweet home: tangible memories of an uprooted childhood', in D. Miller (ed.) *Home Possessions: material culture behind closed doors*, Oxford and New York: Berg, pp. 123–45.

Hein, H. (2000) *The Museum in Transition: a philosophical perspective*, Washington, DC: Smithsonian Institution Press.

Hooper-Greenhill, E. (1992) *Museums and the Shaping of Knowledge*, London: Routledge.

Hooper-Greenhill, E. (2000) *Museums and the Interpretation of Visual Culture*, London: Routledge.

Hooper-Greenhill, E. (2007) *Museums and Education: purpose, pedagogy, performance*, London: Routledge.

Hoskins, J. (1998) *Biographical Objects: how things tell the stories of people's lives*, London: Routledge.

Hoskins, J. (2006) 'Agency, biography and objects', in C. Tilley, W. Keane, S. Kuechler, M. Rowlands and P. Spyer (eds) *Handbook of Material Culture*, London: Sage, pp. 74–84.

Jordanova, L. (1989) 'Objects of knowledge: a historical perspective on museums', in P. Vergo (ed.) *The New Museology*, London: Reaktion Press, pp. 22–40.

Kaltsas, N. (2002) *Sculpture in the National Archaeological Museum, Athens*. Los Angeles: Getty Publications.

Kaltsas, N. (2007a) *The National Archaeological Museum*, Athens: Olkos. Online. Available at: http://www.latsis-foundation.org/gr/elibrary/1/31/book.html (Accessed 12 July 2010).

Kaltsas, N. (2007b) 'Ethniko Arxaiologiko Mouseio' [National Archaeological Museum] *Tetradia Mouseiologias*, 4: 46–7.

Kaplan, F.E.S. (ed.) (1994) *Museums and the Making of 'Ourselves': the role of objects in national identity*, London and New York: Leicester University Press.

Karouzos, C. (1981) *Arxaia Texni* [Ancient Art], Athens: Ermis.

Karouzou, S. (1967) *Ethnikon Arxaiologikon Mouseio. Syllogi Glypton* [National Archaeological Museum. Sculpture Collection], No. 13, Athens: General Direction of Antiquities.

Karouzou, S. (1982) *Ethniko Mouseio. Genikos Odigos* [National Museum. General Guide], Athens: Ekdotiki Athinon.

Karp, I. and S. Lavine (eds) (1991) *Exhibiting Cultures: the poetics and politics of museum display*, Washington, DC and London: Smithsonian Institution Press.

Kokkou, A. (1977) *I Merimna Gia tis Archaiotites stin Ellada kai ta Prota Mouseia* [Care of Antiquities in Greece and the First Museums], Athens: Ermis.

Kontrarou-Rassia, N. (2004) 'Ena neo archaeo mouseio' [A new ancient museum], *Eleftherotypia*, 20 June 2004: 14–15.

Kopytoff, I. (1986) 'The cultural biography of things: commodification as process', in A. Appadurai (ed.) *The Social Life of Things: commodities in cultural perspective*, Cambridge: Cambridge University Press, pp. 64–91.

Leinhardt, G. and K. Knutson (2004) *Listening in on Museum Conversations*, Walnut Creek, CA: Altamira Press.

Lord, B. (2005) 'Representing enlightenment space', in S. MacLeod (ed.) *Reshaping Museum Space*, London: Routledge, pp. 146–57.

MacDonald, S. (2003) 'Museums, national, postnational and transcultural identities', *Museum and Society*, 1: 1–16.

MacDonald, S. (2005) 'Accessing audiences: visiting visitor books', *Museum and Society*, 3: 119–36.

MacDonnell, D. (1986) *Theories of Discourse: an introduction*, Oxford: Blackwell.

McLean, F. (2005) 'Museums and national identity', *Museum and Society*, 3: 1–4.

Merriman, N. (ed.) (2004a) *Public Archaeology*, London: Routledge.

Merriman, N. (2004b) 'Introduction: diversity and dissonance in public archaeology', in N. Merriman (ed.) *Public Archaeology*, London: Routledge, pp. 1–17.

Merriman, N. (2004c) 'Involving the public in museum archaeology', in N. Merriman (ed.) *Public Archaeology*, London: Routledge, pp. 85–108.

Mouliou, M. (2008) 'Museum representations of the classical past in post-war Greece: a critical analysis', in D. Damaskos and D. Plantzos (eds) *A Singular Antiquity: archaeology and Hellenic identity in twentieth century Greece*, Athens: Benaki Museum, pp. 83–109.

Novak, J.D. and A.J. Cañas (2008) 'The theory underlying concept maps and how to construct and use them', Technical Report IHMC Cmap Tools 2006-01 Rev 01-2008, Florida: Institute for Human and Machine Cognition Online. Available at: http://cmap.ihmc.us/Publications/ResearchPapers/TheoryUnderlyingConceptMaps.pdf (Accessed 12 July 2010).

Pearce, S. (1992) *Museums, Objects and Collections: a cultural study*, London: Leicester University Press.

Pearce, S. (ed.) (1994) *Interpreting Objects and Collections*, Leicester Readers in Museum Studies, London: Routledge.

Pearce, S. (1995) *On Collecting: an investigation into collecting in the European tradition*, London: Routledge.

Petrakos, V. (1995) *I Peripeteia tis Ellinikis Archaiologias ston Vio tou Christou Karouzou* [Adventures in Greek archaeology as seen through the life of Christou Karouzos], No. 150, Athens: Archaeological Society.

Rowlands, M. (2008) 'Aesthetics of touch among the elderly', in H.J. Chatterjee (ed.) *Touch in Museums: policy and practice in object handling*, Oxford: Berg, pp. 187–98.

Saumarez Smith, C. (1989) 'Museums, artefacts and meanings', in P. Vergo (ed.) *The New Museology*, London: Reaktion Press, pp. 6–21.

Shanks, M. and I. Hodder (1995) 'Processual, postprocessual and interpretive archaeologies', in I. Hodder, M. Shanks, A. Alexandri, V. Buchli, J. Carman, J. Last *et al.* (eds) *Interpreting Archaeology: finding meaning in the past*, London: Routledge, pp. 3–29.

Tilley, C. (2006) 'Objectification', in C. Tilley, W. Keane, S. Kuechler, M. Rowlands and P. Spyer (eds) *Handbook of Material Culture*, London: Sage, pp. 60–73.

Tilley, C., W. Keane, S. Kuechler, M. Rowlands and P. Spyer (eds) (2006) *Handbook of Material Culture*, London: Sage.

Turkle, S. (ed.) (2007) *Evocative Objects: things we think with*, Cambridge, MA: MIT Press.

Vergo, P. (ed.) (1989) 'The reticent object', in P. Vergo (ed.) *The New Museology*, London: Reaktion Press, pp. 41–59.

Vogel, S. (1991) 'Always true to the object, in our fashion', in I. Karp and S. Lavine (eds) *Exhibiting Cultures: the poetics and politics of museum display*, Washington, DC and London: Smithsonian Institution Press, pp. 191–204.

Voudouri, D. (2003) *Kratos kai Mouseia: To Thesmiko Plaisio ton Archaiologikon Mouseion* [State and Museums: the institutional framework of the archaeological museums], Athens: Sakkoulas.

White, H. (1978) *Tropics of Discourse: essays in cultural criticism*, Baltimore: Johns Hopkins University Press.

5 Musealisation processes in the realm of art

Maria Lucia de Niemeyer Matheus Loureiro

Introduction

Musealisation is not a homogeneous process. Rather, depending on the nature of an object and the realm to which it belongs, this process can have different nuances and effects on the object itself. This chapter discusses the processes of musealisation, focusing on works of art. Intending to raise questions about musealisation of art objects, the concepts of 'museum object' and 'work of art' are approached from different perspectives. The notions of preservation *in situ* and *ex situ* are used as starting points to analyse false oppositions like objects *versus* ideas, collections *versus* territories, or classic museums versus ecomuseums. Aiming to shed light on *in situ/ex situ* as complementary approaches, a parallel is drawn with a strategy for plant conservation.

The art museum is a particularly appropriate environment to examine this issue. Works of art have been created throughout history and thus precede the recognition of art. Before society imposed certain formal values as the primary criteria for artistic and aesthetic appreciation, other values had been involved in the creation of 'works of art', most of which served specific functions (e.g. religious, political, practical). 'Work of art' is a term that is used to designate different products of human activity: painting, sculpture, song, poetry, as well as utilitarian pottery, furniture, ceremonial masks and many other kinds of objects created for a broad array of purposes. Many of these objects are preserved and exhibited in museums, whose collections include all kinds of artefacts.

Currently, collections are no longer being seen as the only way of safeguarding objects. In the 1980s, many new issues were raised in the field of museology, ranging from 'broadening the concept of museums to include new sectors of cultural and natural heritage' (Maroevic, cited in Mensch 1992), to 'abandoning the museum as a frame of reference'. The term 'museological object' has been coined in response to these discussions, a definition of which could be 'any element belonging to the realm of nature and material culture that is considered worth being preserved, either *in situ* or *ex situ*, or by documentation'. Mensch points out that a collection is an *ex situ* conservation strategy that exists alongside the countless methods of *in situ* conservation that can be pursued outside the museum environment. 'Collecting is but one of the possibilities to safeguard objects' (Mensch 1992).

Much more than simply the moment that an object enters a museum collection, musealisation is a concept that transcends and extrapolates the museological institution and has a dynamic which, according to Mensch, can be summed up in three basic forms and their variations: *ex situ* preservation, *in situ* preservation and preservation by documentation. The discussion of such issues, however, has given rise to misconceptions. One that should be raised here is the false opposition between *ex situ* and *in situ* preservation strategies, almost always to the detriment of the former. *Ex situ* preservation depends on the transfer of specimens from their original habitat to a new site and is the most commonly adopted model for safeguarding artefacts, not just in classic museums – especially art museums – but also in zoos and botanic gardens.

Far from opposing one another, *in situ* and *ex situ* strategies are complementary, often going hand in hand with what Mensch calls 'preservation by documentation'. This point is exemplified in the text of the *Global Strategy for Plant Conservation* (Secretariat of the Convention on Biological Diversity, Botanic Gardens Conservations International 2002). This strategy was adopted in 2002 after it was approved by the signatories of the Convention on Biological Diversity. It aims, among other things, 'to halt the current and continuing loss of plant diversity' and to 'be a tool to enhance the ecosystem approach to the conservation and sustainable use of biodiversity'. In order to meet its global objective, the document contains some specific goals, which include 'understanding and documenting plant diversity'. In order to do so, it recommends, among other things, 'document[ing] the plant diversity of the world, including its use and its distribution in the wild, in protected areas and in *ex situ* collections'. In recognition of the 'interaction of plants and plant communities with other components of ecosystems', the *Global Strategy for Plant Conservation* proposes '*in situ* conservation measures as the primary approach for conservation', while recommending that these be supported by *ex situ* measures. The short-term biological diversity conservation targets for 2010 include the *in situ* conservation of 60 per cent of threatened species, and the conservation of the same percentage in accessible *ex situ* collections.

While noting that 'objects embody unique information about the nature of man in society', Susan Pearce (1999: 125) asserts that what distinguishes museums from other institutions is that they have collections, which are 'at the heart of a museum'. Without neglecting the other musealisation methods and strategies – *in situ* and by documentation, which will still be addressed for the purposes of reflection – this study focuses on *ex situ* conservation, especially the concept of collections, which are the classic strategy employed by museums of art, the core topic of this work.

The 'classic' museum and *ex situ* preservation: the work of art in question

Many scholars who examine the notion of the 'museum object' see the main analytical problem as this removal of the object from its original context to an artificial context, the museum, where it becomes a document that represents its original reality. However, when we apply this thinking to the art museum, the absence of an original context points in two opposite directions, which go back as far as the genesis of the concept of art in Western Modernity. Based on this distinction, two kinds of 'artwork' are proposed:

- Objects created outside the modern Western context for different purposes, but which are recognised as 'works of art' and appreciated for their formal and aesthetic qualities.
- Objects created by professionals recognised as artists with the intention of having the function of 'works of art' and being appreciated for their aesthetic qualities.

In the former case, there is a direct correlation between the musealisation of the object and its promotion to the category of 'work of art'. A good example of this group of artworks is the marble statue of Aphrodite – better known as Venus de Milo – which was not created to be exhibited in a public space, but to represent the Greek goddess of love and beauty. It was produced around 100 BC and only in the nineteenth century was discovered and displayed in the Louvre's galleries. Works created intentionally to be publicly displayed and perceived as art, however, challenge the classic concept of musealisation, as there is no removal from an original context. The notion concerns to the act by which an object is stripped of its original functions. Mensch (1992) emphasises the act of removing an object from its original (primary) context and transferring it to a museum as a passage to 'a new reality', where the object will have the function of 'document-ing the reality from which it was separated'.

Krzystof Pomian discusses museums as a specific kind of collection, also high-lighting the removal of objects from their context of use. In his view, a collection is 'a set of natural or artificial objects, kept temporarily or permanently out of the economic circuit, afforded special protection in enclosed spaces adapted specifi-cally for that purpose and put on display' (Pomian 1999: 162). Museums can be distinguished from private collections by their permanence – they outlive their founders – and their public nature. Museum objects should be preserved and accessible to everyone. When objects are put in museums, they are exposed to the gaze not just of the present but also of future generations, as others were once exposed to the gaze of the gods (Pomian 1984: 84). Stripped of their utility, objects in collections become semiotic bearers of meanings and start to mediate between the visible and invisible, 'reveal[ing] their meaning when exposed to the gaze'. Utility and meaning are opposed and mutually exclusive: 'the more meaning is attributed to an object, the less interest there is in its utility' (Pomian 1984: 72–3).

Turning to collections of artworks, as of the fifteenth century, these attained a 'new dignity' thanks to their ability to make the invisible visible and 'make the transient last'. In a world where the invisible is presented less from the perspective of eternity than from that of the future, protecting the arts is the duty of those who aspire to glory. That is why princes become patrons and, thus, collectors (Pomian 1984: 78).

In his classic *The Origin of the Work of Art*, Heidegger (1992: 34) emphasises that transferring a work of art to a collection means removing it from its essential space. Avoiding this movement, however, does nothing to stop the inexorable and irreversible ruin and disappearance of the work. As the philosopher sees it, a work of art demands recognition (i.e. to be installed in a collection or exhibition). It should be noted here that unlike other authors, the philosopher refers only to what he calls 'great art'. For Heidegger, a work of art has an essence that distinguishes it from 'mere things'. It has a *'something else'* that added to the *'thingly character'* turns it into a symbol. In order to support his argument about the essence of art, Heidegger uses the painting *A Pair of Shoes* by Van Gogh. Unlike the painting, which allows us to uncover the truth about the thing, the fundamental nature of a shoe lies in the usefulness (i.e. its very essence).[1]

Meanwhile, art historian Ernst Gombrich stresses the non-existence of what we call 'Art', especially 'Art with a capital A'. He does, however, acknowledge the existence of artists, as, in his perspective 'there really is no such thing as Art' but only artists, who 'did and do many things'. According to the author, to call all their activities 'art' it is necessary keep in mind that 'such a word may mean very different things in different times and places' (Gombrich 1995: 15).

Philosopher Mikel Dufrenne's views on the topic also run counter to Heidegger's. He sees the work of art as 'an object to be perceived', which attains 'the very essence of its value in the fulfilment of the senses'. As such, there is no need to remove the work from its cultural context. It is enough for it to 'be properly regarded as art, i.e. as an aesthetic object and not as a utilitarian object' (Dufrenne 1981: 49–51). According to the author, this implies that the role of the spectator must be stressed, as this is the person 'who will separate the aesthetic from the religious, the magic and the utilitarian, who will perceive the essence of its value and who, in the imaginary museum, will complete the ever unfinished cosmos'. And this should occur in an inverse proportion to the role of the museum. The author would rather 'see a statue in the park than see it in a museum', since it is 'when a work can take its place in the world that it best attests to the work that engendered it and also is a potential meaning for this world' (Dufrenne 1981: 59, 245).

It is the aesthetic perception that turns an object into a work of art, which is to say that everything can be seen as a work of art, not only Van Gogh's paintings, but also the statue of Aphrodite and even landscapes and everyday objects turned into 'readymades' by Marcel Duchamp. The French artist also emphasises the role of the spectator (and therefore the spaces of aesthetic appreciation) in the creative act. According to Duchamp, 'the creative act is not performed by the artist alone'; the spectator 'brings the work in contact with the external world by deciphering and interpreting its inner qualification and thus adds his contribution to the creative act' (Duchamp 1957).

Duchamp's readymades are very interesting starting points to discuss the re-signification process that occurs when a thing crosses the threshold of a museum. In 1917, the artist submitted his readymade *Fountain* to an exhibition organised by the Society of Independent Artists, in New York. The work – a urinal signed by R. Mutt – was refused, and the case was explained in an anonymous article published in the magazine *The Blind Man*. In the article, probably written by the artist himself, the case is made clear: 'Whether Mr. Mutt with his own hands made the fountain or not has no importance. He CHOSE it. He took an ordinary article of life, placed it in a way that its useful significance disappeared under a new title and point of view – he created a new thought for that object'.[2]

Any discussion of the museum as a space for aesthetic appreciation cannot fail to take its institutional nature into account, an aspect investigated by Pierre Bourdieu (1996: 328), who defines the museum as a place that grants recognition and legitimacy to the artistic field. He writes that institutions like museums have the aim of 'offering works for contemplation that are often produced with very different destinations in mind'. By isolating and separating objects from their original context, the museum 'strips them of their different religious or political functions' and reduces them 'to their essentially artistic function'.

Exhibition in museums is, then, one of the means by which artefacts are given social recognition as works of art. As he highlights the arbitrary nature of the actions that legitimate the inclusion of the material output of human activity in the category of 'work of art', Bourdieu notes that the values produced within the 'artistic field' must be shared by all its members. The statue of Aphrodite was turned into a work of art because it became part of Louvre Museum's collection and was displayed in its galleries. The same can be said about Van Gogh's paintings and Duchamp's readymades.

The problem of *in situ* preservation: where is the place of the artwork?

Musealisation involves an almost unlimited set of processes and strategies devised to safeguard cultural material goods. It is a process that may be applied to objects (*latu sensu*) and/or sets of objects, and begins with selection strategies which (re)signify and add value. The idea of selection brings us back to the 'collection' category, but it does not stop there, since selection can also apply to pieces of land, which impinges on what is called *in situ* preservation, a strategy that is currently gaining ground. Territorial museums have a long history, which culminated in the twentieth century proposition for the ecomuseum, whose proponents argue, among other things, that removing an object from its natural environment is tantamount to killing it.

Jean Baudrillard disagrees. He compares the musealisation strategy employed at the Creusot ecomuseum to an episode that took place in 1971 involving the few remaining people of the Tasday ethnic group and the Philippines government, who returned them to their 'primitive' state. Like 'open air mummies', the indigenous people lost their identity as they came into contact with settlers, tourists and ethnologists. 'For ethnology to be alive [. . .] its object must die, taking its revenge by dying upon its "discovery" and, with this death, defying the science that wishes to understand it' (Baudrillard 1991: 14–15). No more than posthumous 'savages' who become 'representative likenesses' for a science that has become 'pure simulation'.

At the Creusot ecomuseum, entire workers' districts and living metallurgy zones were musealised as testaments of their time. 'A complete culture, men, women and children included – gestures, languages, customs included, fossilised alive as if in an instant. Rather than having boundaries like a geometric site, the museum is everywhere now, like a dimension of life' (Baudrillard 1991: 15–16).

However, this model cannot be applied to every kind of object, especially not to 'works of art'. How can works be kept in their original context? Or, in other words, what is a work's original context? If we are to reflect on *in situ* preservation in the ambit of art, we must turn once again to the distinction previously described between objects created outside the modern Western context to perform extra-artistic functions and objects created for aesthetic appreciation. Preservation *in situ* is an option for those objects that have extra-artistic functions, like the image of Our Lady of Aparecida conserved in a sanctuary in the state of São Paulo, Brazil, or for collections belonging to stately homes. It is also necessary for works that cannot be transported and were created for a particular place. Examples of these include the statue of Christ the Redeemer in Rio de Janeiro, the murals by Diego Rivera, the frescos in the Sistine Chapel, the mosaics in Westminster Cathedral, the stained-glass windows in Notre Dame Cathedral or the reliefs in the Parthenon (although many have literally been ripped out of their original context and transported to large museums, especially in the nineteenth century).

Musealisation by documentation: recording to forget

The emergence of the modern museum is repeatedly associated with the utopia of universality and the yearning for completeness.[3] Based on the assumption that citizens should have the right of access to cultural goods, which necessarily implies ongoing preservation and archival work, the museological institution has emerged in a context where information is held in high esteem.

Fausto Colombo (1991) projects this issue onto contemporary times, referring to the twentieth century's 'mania for filing' and 'obsession with memory', which, in his view, has taken many shapes: (a) recording: 'memorization of a fact in a medium through means of an image'; (b) filing: 'translation of an event into encrypted information that can be located within a system'; (c) filing the recording: 'translation of a memory-image, a mnemonic icon, into a filing sign that can be located within a system'; and (d) recording the filing: 'production of copies of signs already filed to guard against any potential forgetfulness'. The author argues that these practices serve to 'describe a cataloguing universe from the present', which is paradoxical, since they turn 'today's objects into yesterday' (Colombo 1991: 18).

He also notes the close relationship between filing and forgetting, observing that the operations listed above are present in the different kinds of 'file-form' that are created 'to guard against the potential loss of memory'. He sees the 'effort to organise and rationalise this' as emerging in 'response to the requirement of one's preventing the loss of that which has been stored'. This would suggest that things are documented and filed not to be remembered, but to be forgotten. The 'pre-emptive activation of forgetting' therefore begins in the selection of the material to be recorded. This consists of 'deciding which events or information from a set of data should be given precedence and which may be abandoned to potential obscurity' (Colombo 1991: 87–9).

Andréas Huyssen (2000: 15, 33) suggests that we live at a paradoxical time when the seduction of memory and the anguish of forgetting co-exist. This 'culture of memory' is manifested in the quest to 'record everything', the obsessive musealisation of the world, the idea that a file can be 'a counterbalance for the accelerating pace of change, a place for preservation in time and space', and where forgetting is 'the ultimate transgression'.

The concept of '*lieux de mémoire*', coined by Pierre Nora (1989: 7–8) can be useful to deepen and shed light over this question. These places, 'where memory crystallises and secretes itself' are not realms of memory, but of history. Because we are not able to live within memory, we need to 'consecrate *lieux de mémoire* in its name'. According to the author, the true memory disappeared because of its increasing objectification, and history took its place. Memory and history are in a 'fundamental opposition'. The first 'remains in permanent evolution', while the second 'is the reconstruction, always problematic and incomplete, of what is no longer'. If we take into account Nora's ideas about memory and history, this 'culture of memory' (mentioned by Huyssen) becomes 'culture of history'. We are no longer in the realm of memory, which is a 'perpetually actual phenomenon', but in the realm of history, which is 'a representation of the past'.

The documentation of performance arts, like drama, singing, dance and even visual art, like installations (documented and dismantled after the exhibition), is the only possible way of preserving them. The same could be said for works like graffiti art, since by their very nature they are short-lived. While the idea of musealising transient artefacts may seem contradictory, this is exactly what the Museum of Ephemeral Cultural Artifacts proposes, introducing itself as 'a cybergallery of transient art and artifacts'.[4] The introductory text to one of its exhibitions, called Wall Art, stresses the ephemeral nature of the works:

> This exhibit features Wall Art – art that is transient. The duration of a piece's existence is indeterminate. The artist is often unknown. The exhibit space is out in the open air, subject to the elements. The medium, instead of being canvas, is architectural – brick, stucco, etc. We have captured some of these pieces during their, possibly, short lives and present them for your viewing pleasure.[5]

A city mural is a prime example of the meeting of *in situ* and documental preservation strategies. Alongside the indispensable function of recording contemporary art production, the work of documenting artworks that, by their very nature, are doomed to extinction is comparable to the work of botanists, who collect plants from their natural habitat not just to preserve them, but also to describe and name them and thus make them known to science. Their immobility, which derives from their fragility and transience, means that *in situ* preservation must be used (when possible) and, above all, documentation.

In contemporary art, the use of transient materials is often intentional. Such is the case of Hélio Oiticica's 'parangolés', which lose their meaning when they are exhibited in glass cases. Oiticica devised his 'parangolés' (capes made of layers of coloured cloth) in the 1960s, when he was living in Morro da Mangueira (Rio de Janeiro, Brazil). Inspired by Brazilian rhythm of samba, the artist rejected traditional formats and created objects to be worn and which people should dance and play with. Despite the efforts of experts to preserve the works physically, documentation (along with the production of replicas to be worn) is the ideal strategy for preserving such works, though this in no way precludes having them restored and exhibited in glass cases, even if this runs counter to the very essence of the work and the artist's intention.[6]

And finally, some questions (or unconclusions)

In his celebrated essay, *The Work of Art in the Age of Mechanical Reproduction*, Walter Benjamin notes that originally the contextual integration of art in tradition found its expression in the cult, and that the earliest artworks originated in the service of a ritual. Although 'in principle a work of art has always been reproducible', the process of technical reproduction heralded by photography means that 'for the first time in the process of pictorial reproduction, photography freed the hand of the most important artistic functions which henceforth devolved only upon the eye looking into a lens' and the work lost its 'aura', which the philosopher defines as 'the unique phenomenon of a distance, however close it may be' (Benjamin 1994: 167–71).

According to Walter Benjamin, the whole history of art can be reconstructed from the perspective of a confrontation between two polar types of artworks: 'cult value' and 'exhibition value'. As one declines the other increases, since 'with the emancipation of the various art practices from ritual go increasing the opportunities for the exhibition of their products'. Therefore, the 'cult value' of the mosaic, fresco and the statue of a divinity ('that has its fixed place in the interior of a temple') is higher than that of a painting or portrait bust ('that can be sent here and there') (Benjamin 1969: 225).

In the view of Brian O'Doherty (1999: 14), the history of modern art is intimately related to the space in which works are exhibited. 'A gallery is constructed along laws as rigorous as those for building a medieval church. The outside world must not come in. . . .' The perception of this space that cannot be invaded by the outside world surpasses that of the artwork itself. The 'ideal gallery subtracts from the artwork all cues that interfere with the fact that it is "art"'. The work 'is isolated from everything that would detract from its own evaluation of itself'. The archetype of contemporary art is, then, the 'ideal white space', rather than any painting or artwork.

At this point, it may be interesting to review the classic idea of musealisation as removing an object from its original context (of use or life) to an artificial context. Up to what point is it reasonable to talk about an original context for modern works of art? Let us take a painting as an example. How and why would one preserve it *in situ*? Or, to put the question differently, what is a painting's original context? Paintings are objects that are created with the intention of being moved, which is what makes them easier to exhibit than frescos or graffiti, whose spaces of fruition and reception are predetermined and fixed. Unlike paintings, frescos and graffiti cannot move; the viewer must move to them. What is the place of contemporary artworks if they are almost always intentionally created with exhibition spaces like galleries and museums in mind?

'As modernism gets older, context becomes content', says O'Doherty (1999). What is the place of Duchamp's *Fountain*? How can we speak of a primary context or original function? Should we be thinking of the function for which the object was manufactured or the function devised by the artist, who made it an artwork by putting it in an art context? A readymade is only created as an artwork when it is moved into an art space (a museum or gallery). Its creation is, then, directly related to its musealisation. The work is born as it is installed in an art context and loses its meaning when it is returned to its supposed context of use. In a bathroom, the object ceases to be *The Fountain* and goes back to being a simple bathroom fixture.

Finally, it is worth returning to Heidegger's and Bourdieu's ideas about the relationship between museums and artworks. If we take the propositions put forward by the former to their ultimate consequences, some works of art would apparently have an intrinsic value that ensures their recognition as 'great art', while the rest would be relegated to the category of craftwork, as they do not have that artistic 'essence'. We should note here that the concept of art is given a transcendental, atemporal value and the prime indicator of an object's value is whether it fits these parameters. Meanwhile, Bourdieu's ideas would suggest that the artwork and the museum have a relationship of interdependence. One cannot exist without the other, and the introduction of an object into this space is precisely what gives it its status as a work of art. It should be added that a diametrically opposing proposal could also be argued: museums and artworks are correlated in the sense that one does not precede the other and the exclusion of one of the terms empties the other of all meaning; just like 'mother' and 'son', which primarily denote a relationship between terms of positional and not intrinsic or essential value. In agreement with Bourdieu and Duchamp, we would tend to support the second option, in face of the following question: is a work of art in a museum because it is art, or is it art because it is in a museum?

Notes

1 Heidegger's ideas about the relationship between the museum and what he calls 'great art' raise very interesting questions when they are taken beyond the domain of art. For a long time, the prevailing view was that some objects were predestined for museums, which were the primary spaces for harbouring exceptional, singular or notable objects (like military decorations and commemorative medals, as well as many others) to the detriment of things from daily life.

2 Anonymous. (1917) 'The Richard Mutt Case', *The Blind Man* (New York), no. 2, May 1917: 5.
3 Authors like Walter Grasskamp (1994) and Françoise Melonio (1998) discuss this utopia of universality by comparing museums to encyclopedias. Melonio defines the nineteenth century museum as an encyclopedia exposed to people's eyes, like the bazaars or department stores. Museums and encyclopedias give materiality to the desire of saving the memory of the world and confining the universe into a book or an enclosed space.
4 Available at: http://www.edgechaos.com/MECA/MECA.html (Accessed 11 March 2008).
5 Available at: http://www.edgechaos.com/MECA/WALLART/wallart.html (Accessed 11 March 2008).
6 In 2006, a gallery in São Paulo exhibited ten original 'parangolés' and also provided replicas that the visiting public could handle.

Bibliography

Baudrillard, J. (1991) *Simulacros e Simulação*, Lisboa: Relógio D'água.
Benjamin, W. (1969) *Illuminations: essays and reflections*, New York: Schocken Books.
Benjamin, W. (1994) *Obras Escolhidas: magia e técnica, arte e política*, São Paulo: Brasiliense.
Bourdieu, P. (1996) *The Rules of Art: genesis and structure of the literary field*, Stanford: Stanford University Press.
Colombo, F. (1991) *Os Arquivos Imperfeitos*, São Paulo: Perspectiva.
Duchamp, M. (1957) *The Creative Act*, Convention of the American Federation of Arts. Houston, Texas.
Dufrenne, M. (1981) *Estética e Filosofia*, São Paulo: Perspectiva.
Gombrich, E.H. (1995) *The Story of Art*, London and New York: Phaidon Press.
Grasskamp, W. (1994) 'Reviewing the museum or: The complexity of things', *Nordik Museologi*, 1: 65–74.
Heidegger, M. (1992) *A Origem da Obra de Arte*, Lisboa: Edições 70.
Huyssen, A. (2000) *Seduzidos Pela Memória: arquitetura, monumentos, mídia*, Rio de Janeiro: Aeroplano.
Melonio, F. (1998) 'La culture comme héritage', in A. Baecque and F. Melonio (eds) *Histoire Culturelle de la France – Lumière et Liberte: Le dix-huitième et dix-neuvième siècle*, Paris: Éditions du Seuil.
Mensch, P.V. (1992) 'Towards a methodology of museology', thesis, University of Zagreb.
Nora, P. (1989) 'Between memory and history: les lieux de mémoire', *Representations*, 26 (Spring): 7–25.
O'Doherty, B. (1999) *Inside the White Cube: the ideology of the gallery space*, Berkeley: University of California Press.
Pearce, S. (1999) 'Thinking about things', in S. Pearce (ed.) *Interpreting Objects and Collections*, London: Routledge.
Pomian, K. (1984) 'Coleção', in *Enciclopédia Einaudi*, Lisboa: Imprensa Nacional.
Pomian, K. (1999) 'The collection: between the visible and the invisible', in S. Pearce (ed.) *Interpreting Objects and Collections*, London: Routledge.
Secretariat of the Convention on Biological Diversity, Botanic Gardens Conservations International (2002) *Global Strategy for Plant Conservation*, Montreal, Quebec (Canada); Surrey, UK.

6   Photography – museum

On posing, imageness and the *punctum*

Klaus Wehner

Museum photography

The appointment of Roger Fenton in 1854 to be Photographer to the British Museum – the first ever official photographer to any museum – marked the official beginning of the ongoing interrelationship between photography and the museum. Ever since, museums have come to employ photography in two main ways: to record the objects of their own collections for archives and dissemination (i.e. catalogues) and to supply photographs of contextual locations and objects/ subjects not physically present in the museum. Elizabeth Edwards' *Raw Histories* (2001) provides an enlightening in-depth critical analysis of the field, which includes a wealth of references to previous studies. Based on the notion of the polysemic nature of both photographs and objects, Edwards applies the idea of a social biography to both. Further, she also refers to a certain 'merging' (Edwards 2001: 63) of displays of objects and photographs.

This chapter aims to reinforce an analogy between photography and exhibited objects, initially via a detour that examines the effect of turning the camera around: instead of supplying photographic image material into the museum, treating the museum itself as the subject of photographs. An examination of the resulting effect will supply enlightening reflections on both media. The analogy is cemented by way of the concept of the 'posed object' and the assertion that both media, by default, present constructed meaning as 'imageness'. In conclusion, a theoretical concept usually applied to photography, Roland Barthes' *punctum*, is applied to the posed object.

For several years, my own activity as practising visual artist has largely been subject to a passionate attraction to museums of all kinds and as a result I have visited and photographed many dozens of museum exhibitions across Europe.[1] What the resulting images always share with the long-standing tradition of photographic projects devoted to museums is the fact that the viewer of the photographs, by virtue of being positioned as 'external', looks at the depicted museum space *as an image*, as opposed to the actual museum visitor who focuses on individual exhibits and for whom the museum itself retains a certain degree of transparency. This applies to museum photographs that would be considered to be 'art', such as those of Louise Lawler or Hiroshi Sugimoto, as well as to images considered to be 'documentary', such as the collection of historical museum photographs collated into a series of exhibitions entitled *Camera Obscured*.[2] Georgina Born has commented on this effect in her essay: 'Public museums, museum photography, and the limits of reflexivity' (1998), in response to one of the first exhibitions of *Camera Obscured*, many images of which feature museum workers in the process of setting up dioramas and other displays, painting backgrounds, transporting objects, and so on. Born states how the 'museum photographer cannot help but produce critique' (Born 1998: 244) and further, that this produces a 'reflexivity . . . which the museums seem officially to resist' (Born 1998: 233).

However, this default critique or reflexivity is not restricted to such 'behind the scenes' images. It occurs all the same when photographing 'complete' gallery spaces. In all cases, the photographic mediation causes the viewer of the photograph to 'take a step back', and as a result, brings the museum itself into prominence. This subsequently immediately emphasises what can be seen as the main predicament that is at the base of all collecting and curatorial practice: the contrived artifice of display through the conscious staging and juxtaposing of objects produces a *composition* whose contemporaneous whole is in tension with the individual objects' historic ontology as these are incorporated. In other words, looking at photographs of exhibition spaces causes an increased awareness of the artifice that is the *curatorial composition* by presenting an image that visually emphasises that all efforts of staging and juxtaposing objects produce a sum that is by definition greater than its parts.

In cases where early photographers of museum objects, using photographic processes that required high levels of light, moved artefacts outdoors into the sunlight (Figures 6.1 and 6.2), the work of curating on the part of the photographer becomes specifically obvious as the photographers created contexts through temporary arrangements for the photographs. However, even when the photographer of a museum does not physically re-arrange objects in order to photograph them, the mere act of finding a viewpoint that *positions* certain exhibits within the image and excludes others, the act of focusing on and enlarging

Figures 6.1 and 6.2 Images from the *Album Du Musée Du Boulaq* credited to Hippolyte Délié and Henri Bechard, published in 1872, courtesy of the Wilson Centre for Photography.

Figure 6.3 The British Museum, March 2008. Photographs © Klaus Wehner, image reproduction for non-commercial purposes, courtesy of the Trustees of the British Museum.

details, in short framing, is a process that is analogous in its nature to curating (Figure 6.3).

Additionally, because a photograph always shows a frozen moment of immobility that has irreversibly passed, in photographs of exhibition spaces this inevitable pastness of the photographically recorded and preserved moment also pushes the temporality of the photographed curatorial composition into prominence. To emphasise this temporality is another reflexivity that the institutional dynamic of the museum resists, as it propagates a certain mythical timelessness over its temporality. Avoiding this reflexivity on composition and temporality may well be the reason that museum and exhibition catalogues traditionally exclude photographs of exhibition spaces in favour of photographs of individual objects in a studio set-up in front of backgrounds, perceived as neutral.

This type of image excludes anything that would overtly indicate the frozen moment of the image's coming into being (Figure 6.4). As a result, the image largely denies the artificiality as well as the temporality of the photographed set-up. The photographic moment, and even the photograph itself, recedes into invisibility in favour of a mythical a-temporality of the pseudo-neutral re-production. Thus, this type of image, as a medium, is subject to the same type of transparency as the museum: it re-presents the object but hides itself. Consequently, exhibition and museum catalogues traditionally feature series of these neutral still life photographs as a record of the collection, whereas images of exhibition spaces, which are temporary curatorial compositions, are mostly (in)conspicuously absent.[3]

Figure 6.4 Child Hiding behind Mask, also described as *False Love*. Sculpture attributed to Bartolomeo Cavaceppi, 1799, Collection T. Longstaffe-Gowan and T. Knox. Photograph © Klaus Wehner.

Returning to the perceived dichotomy of 'documentary' versus 'art' raised above, a much-discussed issue in the history of the critical reception of photography always has, and still continues to be centred on the question of whether the photograph is an objective, unmediated document, a pure and truthful reproduction of reality, described by Roland Barthes (in *Camera Lucida*) to be 'pure contingency' (Barthes 1984: 28) which 'does not invent; it is authentication itself' (Barthes 1984: 87) or if the photograph is by default subjective, artificially composed, and as much an artificial interpretation of reality as for example a painting. In short, if photography is 'document' or 'artifice', 'technique' or 'art', 'nature' or 'culture'.[4]

It appears undeniable that both arguments have validity but at the same time are also equally unable to negate the respective opposing view. Above, I compared the labour of framing on behalf of the photographer to curating and this exemplifies my position and this is also the reason for raising the issue here. It is not useful to debate whether a photograph *is* pure contingency or *is* always coded. The photograph is always both at once. The subjective, coded, artificiality is the default result of the chosen moment of the taking of the image and the camera viewpoint, which includes, excludes and arranges image components which nevertheless will be realistic imprints of objects that 'have-been-there', to use one of

Barthes' expressions. To quote Hans Belting as he discusses one of Thomas Struth's *Museum Photographs*: 'The *composition* is here the result of one possible selection out of the contingency, which the real space in fast pacing change presents to the camera' (Belting 1998: 19, my translation, emphasis added). Once again, the parallel to a curatorial composition becomes apparent as it shares with the photograph the quality of being a composition that, nevertheless, is made up from truthfully re-presented elements. In both cases the viewer is confronted with the result of an act of selecting and excluding, juxtaposing and framing. Consequently, when a photographic image re-presents an exhibition space, we are inevitably led into a hall of mirrors, as the two media reflect on each other.

Figure 6.5 The British Museum, March 2008. Photograph © Klaus Wehner, image reproduction for non-commercial purposes, courtesy of the Trustees of the British Museum.

[W]hat founds the nature of Photography is the pose.

(Barthes 1984: 78)

Photography transformed subject into object, and even, one might say, into a museum object: in order to take the first portraits (around 1840) the subject had to assume long poses under a glass roof in bright sunlight.

(Barthes 1984: 13)

Posed objects

Following the observation of the analogue between the curatorial and the photographic composition, I will extend this argument by introducing the concept of the *posed object*, which will remain the central theme of this investigation. I suggest that the museum or collector's act of exhibiting objects for visual contemplation, which allows for looking but not touching, stages the objects on display themselves as an *image* and that an examination of the ontology of the object-staged-as-image uncovers a strong analogy to the ontology of the photographic image. The viewer temporarily beholds the staged object and takes away a visual impression, or if photography is possible and allowed and the object deemed of sufficient interest, a photograph of the staged object.

Marcel Duchamp's readymade has attracted similar thoughts,[5] which to my knowledge have never been expanded in-depth nor applied beyond the readymade in 'art'. Regarding Duchamp's readymade, Rosalind Krauss points out:

> The readymade's parallel with the photograph is established by its process of production. It is about the physical transposition of an object from the continuum of reality into the fixed condition of the art-image by a moment of isolation, or selection.
>
> (Krauss 1977: 78)

In *Camera Lucida*, Roland Barthes reflects on the *pose*, describing his feeling in a moment when he himself is about to be photographed:

> Now, once I feel myself observed by the lens, everything changes: I constitute myself in the process of 'posing,' I instantaneously make another body for myself, I transform myself in advance into an image.
>
> (Barthes 1984: 10)

Hence, for Barthes, the *pose* – a moment of apprehension ready for the inscription of an image – *is* image. The moment Barthes transforms himself into an image is a momentary temporal arrest, a conscious pause/pose in the person's usual non-self-conscious positioning within the everyday flow of time and space. Through *posing*, Barthes extracts himself 'from the continuum of reality into the fixed condition of the (art-) image'. Thus, analogous to the pose of the person is any object that is exhibited, be it an object that constitutes a piece of art or craftsmanship, or an everyday object that receives special attention due to its link to a certain history or be it a piece of 'nature' or indeed any 'lump of the physical world to which cultural value is ascribed' as Susan Pearce has referred to it (Pearce 1993: 5). In all cases, the object in question will be subject to a similar temporal arrest due to its removal from its customary environment and use. The object is thus placed into a particular stasis that is distinct from the everyday flow of utility and mobility in time and space, and so the object is *posed as image* for the viewer's gaze and visual memory. This means that the act of posing an object transforms it into part of a coded, visual sign, which implies issues of absence and presence, or as Edwards has worded it: 'It is . . . pertinent . . . that both photographic and display forms work to transform objects and construct meanings through their presentation as *visual spectacles*' (Edwards 2001: 63, emphasis added).

Collection

This view can be seen as homologous to Susan Pearce's insightful analysis of collecting and collections, and the following quote further cements the equation of the readymade in 'art' and other posed objects such as a collection of natural specimens:

> The crucial semiotic notion is that of metaphor and metonymy . . . [what the collector chooses for his collection] . . . bears an intrinsic, direct and organic relationship, that is a metonymic relationship, to the body of material from which it was selected because it is an integral part of it. But the very act of selection adds to its nature. By being chosen away and lifted out of the embedding metonymic matrix, the selected collection now bears a representative or metaphorical relationship to its whole. *It becomes an image* of what the whole is believed to be, and although it remains an intrinsic part of the whole, it is no longer merely a detached fragment because it has become imbued with meaning of its own. . . . [The collection] . . . retains its intrinsic or metonymic character, but the process of selection has given it also a metaphorical relationship to the material from which it came.
>
> (Pearce 1993: 38, emphasis added)

To use one of Pearce's examples (1993: 38), the fish collected by a biologist from the Indian Ocean, genuinely is a metonymical part of the natural world and of the Indian Ocean and at the same time the collection of fish becomes a metaphorical image for 'Indian Ocean'. Regarding the collection of fish as a posed object, this shows that despite the fact that actual objects are real and present, the posed composition refers to something additional, beyond the actual objects. Thus, the viewer is faced with the same issues of presence and absence that characterise the image. Furthermore, it can be concluded that observations regarding 'collecting' can be applied to any one posed object in general, even if it is not part of a 'collection' proper. The posed object is always 'chosen away and lifted out of the embedding metonymic matrix', thus the posed object is by default 'collected' if not to say it is always part of the grand collection of posed objects.[6]

Imageness

In summary, what has been observed so far is that both photography and the posed object produce a curatorial composite resulting from the inevitable dynamic of de- and re-contextualising through choosing and excluding, juxtaposing and framing. Both media re-present real fragmented elements or (part-)objects, yet both media are simply unable to do so outside of a syntagmatic framework of constructed meaning – a framed display – which, 'adds to its nature' (Pearce 1993: 38); or in Edwards' words: 'works to transform objects and constructs meanings through their presentation as visual spectacles' (Edwards 2001: 63). Born, too, uses the word spectacle when speaking about museum photographs that show the in-progress setting up of dioramic sets: 'This is the construction of mere display as spectacle' (Born 1998: 228). Further, she describes the building of sets as 'iconic technique' (Born 1998: 230).

In other words, in the cases in question – photography and the posed object – the 'visual spectacle' is what hides the contingency, materiality and its polysemic arbitrariness underneath the appearance of the syntagmatic set-up of constructed meaning, the iconic wholeness, if not to say the simulacral, of the represented, its appearance and its meaning as spectacle – or image. As a native German speaker, I miss in the English language the ease with which one can use words like *Bildhaftigkeit* and *Bildmäßigkeit* which literally would translate as something close to 'image-like' or 'image-likeness' and which the dictionary translates as 'pictorial', yet I prefer to translate this as 'imageness', and I will use this expression when referring to the above described iconic wholeness within the syntagmatic visual spectacle/appearance that is separated from the materiality of the objects.[7]

Concluding the look at photography of the museum, and returning to the photographs of *Camera Obscured*: in these images the photographed 'incomplete' museum displays are denied their iconic wholeness or their complete imageness. In other words, the photographs present a different imageness from the one that the museum would present. Whilst in this case this happens more or less by default, this can be identified as the deliberate strategy of a project such as Louise Lawler's museum photographs as she often photographs artefacts that are in storage, resting on the floor, in the process of being installed or if she photographs 'complete' exhibition spaces her strategy consists of crops and a focus on arbitrary details of the set-up. In all cases her photographs emphasise the materiality and objecthood of the artefacts and thereby deny the iconic wholeness/imageness that the photographed objects would present to a gallery visitor if they were viewed 'properly' posed. A diametrically opposite strategy is to be found in Hiroshi Sugimoto's photographs of museum dioramas and also his series of portraits of Madame Tussaud's wax figures. In these photographs the photographed objects look more realist than the actual objects do when encountered in the gallery. His images re-present *the pose* of the photographed set-ups with such perfection that the resulting *mise en abyme*, instead of denying the objects' imageness through fragmentation, multiplies it to such an extent that all the same it uncovers its simulacral artificiality.

Figure 6.6 Museum für Angewandte Kunst Frankfurt, August 2006. Photograph © Klaus
    Wehner.

We pose things in order to drive them out of our minds.[8]

During a visit of the exhibition The Souvenir – Memory in Objects from the
Relic to the Keepsake (my translation) in the Museum for Applied Arts in Frankfurt
in 2006, I was particularly fascinated by the posed tin dish (mess tin) as seen in
Figure 6.6.[9] The label informed me that the object was an important 'tool of
survival' for Aenne Saekow, a Ravensbrück concentration camp inmate in 1945.
I was disturbed by the thought that this very dish, which shows 'traces of use'
that came into being through the handling of, thus direct contact with, the body
of this tortured concentration camp inmate, who must have been at any moment
an inch away from sudden violent death; that it was held, by her hands and
touched her lips as she consumed life-preserving drink and food out of it, fighting to survive, surrounded by grime, blood and utterly depersonalising violence.
Although no biological traces of food or lip imprints have survived on the dish
itself, I know that such *traces-have-been-there.*

Indexicality is the principal representational/ideological technique of the museum: the bringing of 'original', 'natural' or exemplary (part-)objects within the museum's space, and their framing and setting such that they speak, metonymically, of the wider practice/environment/species/oeuvre of which they form part.

(Born 1998: 229)

Index

Because indexicality is used widely in theorising photography as well as museums and the idea of the real physical trace is central for the continuation of the argument, an important distinction in the use of the word needs to be made clear. Across much semiotic theory a sign pointing to an emergency exit as well as a footprint in the sand will be described as an 'indexical sign' yet there is a crucial difference between the two. The emergency exit sign is a sign that points *at* its object by deliberately employing the *concept* of indexicality. Of the same type is the pointing finger and also the linguistic index, a 'shifter' like 'this' or 'I', which is an 'empty' signifier that receives meaning through purposeful use within specific contexts. This index is always intentionally deployed, thus posed. It is based on concept and cultural consensus and it includes arbitrary, *symbolic* elements such as the running green man and arrow indicating an emergency exit. This has been observed by Roman Jakobson in his 1957 paper, 'Shifters, verbal categories, the Russian verb',[10] in which he came to use the word *indexical symbols*.

In contrast, a footprint or a bullet hole is a residue or a trace and it is a natural sign that carries a *proof* that the object that it refers to *was* there and is now absent. Therefore, this index has one very crucial attribute and that is the element of time. A trace or an imprint always also refers to a *specific singular moment of coming into being*, which must by default be in the past, and therefore it is always 'historic'.[11]

This difference corresponds to the fact that the English language does not make a distinction between the *indice* and the *index* as is found in Romance languages. In *Philosophy of Photography*[12] Henri Van Lier refers to this issue also stating that Peirce himself covers both divergent concepts with the word *index* but in his later writings only means the *indice*.[13] Considering the issue of whether the photograph is pure authentication or artificial interpretation, the following quote by Van Lier is pertinent:

[P]hotographs can . . . be defined quite rigorously as *possibly indexed indices*. *Indicial* then refers to the natural and technical aspects of photonic imprints, while *indexical* refers to the side of the subject (the photographer) who chooses his frame, film, lens, developers and prints.

(Van Lier 2007: 118)

This means that the *index* is of the realm of syntagmatic, symbolic imageness whereas the *indice* is of the realm of real materiality and contingency. Applied to the analogy between the photographic and the curatorial composition, the posed dish from Ravensbrück too is an *indexed indice*, as the object functions as real material *trace*, thus *indice of* the murderous horrors of the Holocaust. This *indice* (of the past) is posed and made to point (in the present) *at* a whole, which in this case will be: Ravensbrück = Nazi Concentration Camps = Holocaust, rather than 'tin dishes', which is dependent on interpretative information to be either supplied at the same time as viewers encounter an exhibit or presupposed to exist in viewers.[14] Thus, the posed object in general, like the photograph, is always an *indexed indice*.[15]

For some clarity of language use I will refer to the *indice* as 'real index' and to the *index* as 'symbolic index'. As we observed, both photography and the posed object always present an amalgam of the two. Both media insert selected fragments of contingency into symbolisation.

By taking a thousand differential precautions, one must be able to speak of a *punctum* in all signs.

(Derrida 1997: 289)

Punctum

In proceeding, it is the real index of the body that touched me when encountering the dish from the concentration camp – the idea and (supplied) knowledge of touch, and the fascination this holds over many museum visitors, which will be of specific interest. I propose to adapt and apply to this real index of the body in the posed object, Barthes' notion of the *punctum*, which he developed in *Camera Lucida* as part of a quest to search for 'the essence of photography'.[16] A vast amount of literature exists on the *punctum*[17] and this complex and self-consciously paradox concept can only be crudely summed up here as a detail in the photographic image, which 'pierces' the viewer by causing a strong individual and emotional reaction that could be described as being incongruent to the viewer's perception of the *studium* of the image. The *studium* is the wider cultural context of what is seen in an image, for example the *studium* of the photographs in this essay would be: museums, exhibitions, culture, valued objects, museum-visiting, etc.

Regarding the *punctum* that would be the real index of the body, I cannot count the occasions when individuals I asked for their impression of certain exhibitions or museums have spoken immediately about the exhibits that, I would say, constituted their personal *punctum* – which most frequently related to violence to the (absent) body or, more immediate, human remains. To me the dish from Ravensbrück (in the context I saw it) is such an object. To name just a few more examples, I recall several people I asked about a major exhibition of Aztec artefacts at the Royal Academy in London in 2002, immediately mentioned the 'cruelty', referring to the carved stone vessels that – labels informed us – were used to hold blood and other body parts of human sacrifices (blood-has-been-there).

On a recent visit to Pompeii, I witnessed visitors' reactions to encountering the famous casts of the cavities left by the ancient victim's bodies (Figure 6.7):

Figure 6.7 Pompeii, August 2008. Photograph © Klaus Wehner.

'There are real bones in there!' I overheard an excited conversation next to me. Asking a 16-year-old acquaintance of mine recently if she had ever been to Pompeii, the first and only thing she mentioned were the 'dead people in the glass cases'. When I take school groups to the British Museum and later ask about their impressions, the mummies are almost always mentioned first.

I remember myself at a very young age staring at and studying intently a shrunken head and an unwrapped Egyptian mummy in the Senkenberg Museum in Frankfurt, a memory that has never left me since – and which I credit with being the trigger for my ongoing fascination with museums. A London listings magazine featuring Apsley House, a house collection brimming with a vast number of historical paintings, sculpture and furniture, lists as 'Best Exhibit: Wellington's death mask' (*Time Out* 2006) – the most paradigmatic example of a real index of the body of a historical legend.

A display at the National Maritime Museum in Greenwich shows the coat worn by Nelson during the Battle of Trafalgar on 21 October 1805, during which he received a fatal shot wound (Figures 6.8 and 6.9). The hole left by the bullet is clearly visible on the left shoulder. The coat and also the stockings on display in the case show bloodstains which are Nelson's and also 'probably of Nelson's secretary John Scott who was killed earlier in action' (text from label). Also inside the case is Nelson's hair in a pigtail as cut from his head after his death. Here the real index of the dying body of a historical legend is specifically strong. If you linger nearby this display case, you will inevitably hear numerous strong responses from visitors of all ages.

> The Photograph always leads the corpus I need back to the body I see.
>
> (Barthes 1984: 4)

By way of outlining the implications of transposing Barthes' *punctum* to the posed object, I should point out that I follow those interpretations, too numerous to list here, that have linked the *punctum* to the Lacanian real and this is the base of my transposition of the concept. Regarding the idea of imageness presented by both the photograph and the posed object, I suggest that the *punctum*

Figures 6.8 and 6.9 The display of Admiral Nelson's coat. Courtesy of the National Maritime Museum, Greenwich, London. Photographer anonymous.

is an element or detail that pierces (the generality of the) perceived imageness by way of pointing to pure materiality, contingency and singularity. Or in Lacanian terms, the *punctum* is what points to the real as it is hidden under the matrix of signification of the symbolic.

Often, but not always directly, this pointer relates to the body. Edwards begins *Raw Histories* with the description of a *punctum* she experiences in a photograph of 1873 as 'the carefully tied knots in the lashings of a bamboo palisade', which for her evoke 'a sense of presence – of fingers that had tied those knots in other times' (Edwards 2001: 1). Here the imageness of 'bamboo palisade' is pierced by the singularity of the real index of '*fingers* that had tied *those* knots'. One of Barthes' own examples is an image by Andy Warhol hiding his face behind his hands, and for Barthes the *punctum* is 'the slightly repellent substance of those spatulate nails, at once soft and hard-edged' (Barthes 1984: 45). Again the generality of the imageness: 'portrait of Andy Warhol' is pierced by pointing to the singularity of the (imperfect) materiality of the body – the corpus Barthes needed turned out to be the body he saw.

In her reflections on *Camera Obscured*, Born actually refers to Barthes' earlier notion of the 'third' or 'obtuse meaning', which is widely seen as a precursor of the *punctum* within Barthes' oeuvre (Barthes 1977). As discussed, these photographs disturb the imageness of the museum set-up. As a whole image or image collection (rather than a detail within an image) they could thus be described as a *punctum* to the museum's imageness.

Returning to posed objects, human remains and objects that are a real index of the (absent) (dead) body, by way of their absolute singularity, constitute a piercing of imageness because of the special status that the human body – alive or dead – holds within our matrix of signification and perception of ourselves and the objects around us. To paraphrase Barthes, the real index of the (dead) (absent) body within the posed object is an 'imperious sign of my future death that . . . challenges each of us, one by one, outside of any generality' (Barthes 1984: 97).

The posing of 'lumps of the material world that share this nature with ourselves' is thus a labour to insert matter – hence ourselves – into meaning, or in other words to cover the real with a matrix of signification. The pose always hovers between real materiality and our perception in mental representation. Piercing the imageness of the pose is ultimately akin to piercing the imageness of 'having a body' (symbolic), by pointing to 'being a body' (real) and thus it points to the relationship between the materiality of the biological body and the mental image in representation of the social body – the corpus I need.

Photography and the posed object are twins because the nature of both media is the *pose*, which inserts (fragments of real) contingency into symbolic imageness. The pose as such mirrors the human subject's riddle of *having* or *being* a body – or an object.

Acknowledgements

Apart from two anonymous peer reviewers, I would like to thank Dr Anna Lovatt and Dr Jerzy Kierkuć-Bieliński for valuable comments on a draft of this text. Many thanks also to the Wilson Centre for Photography and the National Maritime Museum for supplying images.

Notes

1 Samples of these images can be seen on www.museumclausum.org in the section: *Wundercamera*.

2 *Camera Obscured* is curated by artist and photographer Vid Ingelevics. On his website a selection of the photographs can be viewed at: http://www.web.net/artinfact/CameraObsc.A.htm (Accessed June 2011).

3 Regarding temporary exhibitions, it needs to be acknowledged that a practical reason for this is that catalogues are usually produced in advance, before the exhibition is set up. It is also worth noting that when it comes to the exhibition of new, contemporary art the photograph of the artwork *in situ* in a museum or gallery is often prominently included in catalogues, presenting photographic proof of the insertion of the artwork as accepted into the public and institutionalised = canonised discourse of art.

4 See: Geoffrey Batchen (1997) *Burning with Desire: the conception of photography*, especially chapters 1 and 5 in which Batchen discusses the exclusive focus on 'culture' at the base of postmodern photography theory versus the exclusive focus on 'nature' at the base of modernist, formalist photography theory. For a different clear and brief summary of the nature–culture subject see also Steve Edwards (2004) *Photography: a very short introduction*. As example of the continuous currency of these themes as hinged on the idea of 'the index', which is discussed below, see James Elkins (ed.) (2007) *Photography Theory*.

5 For another discussion of the readymade as 'photograph' see also Dubois (1989: 92–3).

6 Whilst any further discussion would exceed the scope of this essay, this also means that the concept of the posed object is by no means restricted to the museum. This will be discussed in depth in my PhD thesis *On Posing*, currently in preparation.

7 The English translations of Jaques Rancière's writings have established the use of the word 'imageness' into our vocabulary, which he uses to refer to 'a regime of relations between elements and between functions' (Rancière 2007: 4) or to a 'regime of articulation between the visible and the sayable' (Rancière 2007:11).

8 My paraphrase of Franz Kafka's quote: 'We photograph things in order to drive them out of our minds. My stories are a way of shutting my eyes' (quoted in Barthes 1984: 53).

9 The photograph I took (Figure 6.6) emphasises the fact that this battered tin dish is exhibited, in an otherwise empty, spacious display cabinet. A sense of the forlorn is increased through the fact that the blurred shape in the background suggests a visitor to the gallery whose attention is elsewhere as his or her back is turned toward the exhibit. However, it is not this photograph that is the focus here but the exhibited object itself – employing the photo as documentation.

10 Roman Jakobson (1957). See also the entry: 'Shifter' in Dylan (1996: 182).

11 This temporal distance is a temporary co-existence of cause and effect in the case of symptoms such as fever indicating disease or heat indicating a fire. These effects only exist during their moment of coming into being and are therefore different to the trace as they eventually disappear with the ceasing of the cause.

12 See 'Peirce and photography' in *Philosophy of Photography* (Van Lier 2007: 117–22).

13 To this should be added that it would have been a major intervention for translations of Peirce's texts from English into Romance languages to have altered this conflation and thus the term index is used in the same conflated manner in all Romance language translations I know of. I am aware of two other recent texts that point out corresponding different types of indexicality in somewhat different parameters also arriving at different interpretations of Peirce. Martin Lefebvre (2007) proposes a distinction between 'direct and indirect indexical relations'. David Green and Joanna Lowry also distinguish between two forms of indexicality: 'the one existing as a physical trace of an event, the other as performative gesture that points towards it' (2002: 48). Further, they argue that Peirce 'demonstrated that the indexical sign was less to do with its causal origins and more to do with the way in which it pointed to the event of its own inscription' (2002: 48).

14 This reliance on supplied information naturally implies that such information can be distorted, ideologised or altogether false and invented such as in the case of faked or misattributed artefacts.

15 The fact that the photograph is this *indexed indice* also means that writings that rely heavily on the concept of indexicality might in places be confusing but are not to be discredited. However, the distinction and acceptance that both are always present in the photograph could solve criticism of 'the index' in photography such as Joel Snyder's, who vigorously disputes the usefulness of the concept during the round table discussion recorded in *Photography Theory*: 'What I fear about the causal stuff is that it stops you from seeing the photograph as pictures' (Elkins 2007: 155); or 'The problem with attempting to discuss photographs in terms of *the* index is that the notion is so thoroughly unspecified' (Elkins 2007: 369).

16 Strictly speaking, 'Barthes' notion of the *punctum*' is problematic to define and any attempt will constitute an unjust simplification. Therefore, my premise is that what I propose here is an adaption and alteration of the concept but it is based on what I believe to be at the core of Barthes' uses of the term as is explained below.

17 For a recent publication of collected old and new essays on the *punctum* see Batchen (2009). The *punctum* is also debated in Elkins (2007).

Bibliography

Barthes, R. (1977) 'The third meaning', in *Image Music Text*, London: Fontana Press, pp. 52–68.

Barthes, R. (1984) *Camera Lucida*, reprinted (2000), London: Vintage.

Batchen, G. (1997) *Burning with Desire: the conception of photography*, Cambridge, MA and London: MIT Press.

Batchen, G. (ed.) (2009) *Photography Degree Zero: reflections on Roland Barthes's Camera Lucida*, Cambridge, MA and London: MIT Press.

Belting H. (1998) 'Photography und Malerei, *Museum Photographs*, Der Photographische Zyklus der "Museumsbilder" von Thomas Struth', in *Thomas Struth: Museum Photographs*, München: Schirmer/Mosel Verlag, pp. 5–27.

Born, G. (1998) 'Public museums, museum photography, and the limits of reflexivity: an essay on the exhibition *Camera Obscured: Photographic Documentation and the Public Museum*', *Journal of Material Culture*, 3: 223–54.

Derrida, J. (1997) 'The deaths of Roland Barthes', in H.J. Silverman (ed.) *Philosophy and Non-Philosophy since Merleau Ponty*, Evanston, IL: Northwestern University Press, pp. 259–96.

Dubois, P. (1989) *Der Fotografische Akt, Versuch über ein theoretisches Dispositiv*, with a foreword by Herta Wolf, Amsterdam and Dresden: Verlag der Kunst.

Dylan, E. (1996) *An Introductory Dictionary of Lacanian Psychoanalysis*, London and New York: Routledge.

Edwards, E. (2001) *Raw Histories: photography, anthropology and museums*, London: Berg.

Edwards, S. (2004) *Photography: a very short introduction*, Oxford and New York: Oxford University Press.

Elkins, J. (ed.) (2007) *Photography Theory*, London and New York: Routledge.

Green, D. and J. Lowry (2002) 'From presence to the performative: rethinking photographic indexicality', in D. Green (ed.) *Where is the Photograph*, Brighton: Photoforum/Photoworks, pp. 47–60.

Jakobson, R. (1957) 'Shifters, verbal categories, and the Russian verb', reprinted in *Selected Writings*, Vol. II, *Word and Language* (1971), The Hague: Mouton, pp. 130–47.

Krauss, R. (1977) 'Notes on the index: seventies art in America', *October*, 3 (Spring): 68–81.

Lefebvre, M. (2007) 'The art of pointing: on Peirce, indexicality, and photographic images', in J. Elkins (ed.) *Photography Theory*, London and New York; Routledge, 220–44.

Museum für Angewandte Kunst Frankfurt (2006) Exhibition Catalogue: *Der Souvenir – Erinnerung in Dingen von der Reliquie zum Andenken*, Frankfurt: Wienand Verlag.

Pearce, S. (1993) *Museums Objects and Collections*, Washington, DC: Smithsonian Institution Press.

Rancière, J. (2007) *The Future of the Image*, London: Verso.

Time Out (2006) 'London's best unsung museums', in *Time Out* (London), 7 July 2006.

Van Lier, H. (2007) *Philosophy of Photography*, Leuven: Leuven University Press.

Part II

Visitors' engagements with museum objects

Introduction

Jennifer Binnie

After exploring the processes that create and musealise objects, the book now moves on to look at the variety of ways which exhibitionary contexts contribute to the experience of and engagement with objects. The range of disciplinary backgrounds of the authors of these chapters reflects the breadth of influences that can impact the visitor and shape their experience. The chapters that follow discuss the implications of these influences, explore examples of interactive experiences and creative possibilities with objects and their display contexts, and examine the multiple meanings and understandings that can result.

Chapters move from the power and presence of the object as well as the qualities of its context (Dorsett, Van Eeckhaut, Katzberg, Young), through bodily experience (Saunderson, Ting), to the creative and participatory possibilities of engaging with objects and display (Clayton/Goodwin, Chubb). These authors cover such topics as the significance of an object's material stability; the value of personal responses to artworks and the apparently generalisable greater attractiveness of some objects compared with others; the impact of lighting and theatricality within exhibitions; the power of heroes' house museums; the experiential disadvantages of limited sensory access to museum objects and conversely the possibilities offered by a phenomenological approach; the use of artefacts in creating poetry; and the potential of artistic intervention for enhancing visitors' participatory interpretation of objects.

Dorsett's chapter leads on from Part I's focus on the creation of objects through a personal anecdote illustrating the similarity between the transition of objects from artistic development to finalised idea, with emphasis on the relationship between the materiality of objects and their interpretations within display context. By focusing on semiotic theory, the instability of object presence and the power of objects to divert attention from the expected presentation of interpretation are explored. Dorsett argues for the importance of noticing alterations in the material presence of an object: the experience of viewing exhibitions depends on material entities to be actually present and as steadfast as possible, but a materially unstable object introduces the possibility that an exhibited 'something' can be briefly nothing, an empty disorienting moment in which our sensory experiences resist assimilation into an existing scheme of interpretation.

Following on from this, Van Eeckhaut considers the power of contemporary art to engage an audience of more general, rather than experienced, viewers of art through the process of exhibition-making. This chapter compares the experience and output of two exhibitions created by inexperienced spectators in the Museum of Contemporary Art, Antwerp, Belgium. The two groups, one of teenagers and the other of 'New Belgians' with North African heritage, created exhibitions of artwork chosen from the museum collections to fit with their individual themes and communicate ideas and personal experiences. Through this opportunity to participate and be inspired by art objects, the two projects suggest the possibility of a general power of attraction for some of the artworks – a possibility that, it is argued, has implications for the design of exhibitions.

The design of exhibitions is also a primary focus for Katzberg, in his case with a specific emphasis on lighting and its influence on visitor interpretation and experience. The exhibition Dangerous Liaisons: Fashion and Furniture in the Eighteenth Century combined costume with decorative arts displayed within period rooms to depict various social practices of the eighteenth century. Focusing on the lighting used to surround these objects with a particular atmosphere or mood, the author explores the provenonce of lighting use within theatrical productions and its use to establish a narrative within *tableaux vivants*. By altering this feature of the display environment, it is argued that the visitor's appreciation of the exhibition is also altered and moulded to that intended within the story being told, thus enhancing their experience of the objects on display.

The experience of objects, and a sense of their power, is a theme developed in the next chapter by Linda Young, with a focus on the house museums of heroic figures. Looking at the power of visitor expectations and notions of authenticity to foster a 'magical' experience, Young examines how objects perceived to be closely connected to these heroic figures are imbued with a charisma and made numinous by the spirit of the hero believed to have been a prior resident. The chapter draws on Gell's concept of the technology of enchantment to uncover how numinous collections and sites are created and maintained, exploring how the experience of everyday material spaces can become a vehicle to experiencing the magical character of heroic achievement.

Saunderson's chapter follows this by addressing the boundaries of interaction between visitor and museum object. Today there is most often a predominance of visual experience due to the separation of display objects from the audience: the social default of not touching and the presence of accompanying text. By interweaving a reflexive experiential account and the insights of cognitive psychology, the impact of sensory information and the interaction across modalities upon attention, memory and emotion are explored in the museum context. The implications of such sensorially limited experiences and the benefits that can be gained from multi-sensorial encounters are considered.

Continuing this notion of the importance of multi-sensory experience, Ting's chapter also explores the tactile experience of objects and the possibilities of a dynamic museological approach to objecthood. Drawing on Merleau-Ponty, Ting discusses how through the incorporation of the mind and bodily experience the understanding of the embodied humanity within objects can be enhanced. This chapter considers the sensual and social aspects of interactions with objects, as well as their formal qualities, in order to illustrate the importance of the materiality of objects in how people identify with them.

The last two chapters in this part of the book explore creative forms of engagement with objects. Clayton and Goodwin, as a community museums officer and community poet, have repeatedly witnessed the potential for creativity stimulated by tactile interaction with museum objects. Their chapter discusses the linguistic responses in the form of poetry written by participants engaging in interactive workshops. Demonstrating the variety and originality of meanings created by different individuals, this chapter argues for creativity in response to objects as an important conduit for individual interpretation and expression.

Chubb's chapter concludes this part of the book neatly, by again addressing the connections between display context, object and audience. She explores two of her own exhibitions which were intended to challenge curatorial norms of display. In creating these visual art exhibitions Chubb, an artist-curator, invited the visitor to participate in a more active mode of interpretation. Using Saussure's synchronic and diachronic systems of language analysis, the chapter reflects upon the relationships created between physically distant cultures and time frames. It highlights the significance and contribution to curatorial practice within museums, of the museum's location and of artistic intervention. It also nicely signposts towards the next part of the book, and its focus upon museum representations.

Collectively, the chapters within this section each touch on the visitor engagement with and understanding of museum objects, be they contemporary art, period costume, a house or a section of mango tree with a brass plaque. The chapters bring together research from a variety of disciplines into the quality of experience and encounters within museum, galleries and other heritage institutions, and the creation and use of objects within these spaces. Taken as a whole, these chapters stress the importance of the mutual interaction between things and people, and present examples of the potential for creative exploitations of such encounters.

7 Things and theories

The unstable presence of exhibited objects

Chris Dorsett

Introduction

The *British Art Show* offers a snapshot of contemporary art in Britain in the shape of a large-scale travelling exhibition that, every five years or so, tours major museums and galleries throughout the country. Back in 1984 the show was considered to be a landmark event. The exhibition I visited that year was as busy as the streets I had walked along from the local railway station. In the most densely packed parts of the gallery, when a particular artwork held you in place for long enough to impede the perambulatory viewing of others, the conflict between your own rapt attention and the flowing crowd was palpable. Upstairs, I entered a space in which the passage of exhibition visitors across a rather shaky wooden floor was heavy enough to endanger the delicate balance of a small abstract sculpture. This diminutive two-part object, so poetically vulnerable in its construction, was suddenly lying in separate pieces in front of me. Indeed, it may have been my approach that made the sculpture finally succumb to its potential vulnerability. At this point, a state of interpretive blankness took over. This experience was like being given a cup of coffee when you expect tea. For a moment the taste is not one thing or the other, neither coffee nor tea. When an expectation is unfulfilled in this way we often cannot interpret the experience at all. Poised before the collapsed sculpture my ability to adjust my interpretive faculties from the whole object to its constituent parts was frustrated. Suddenly, and rather disconcertingly, I did not know what I was looking at.[1]

It seems that the fluctuations in perception and attention that normally accompany the viewing of objects are grounded in the stability of material presence. If that stability is destroyed, then the ebb and flow of interpretive possibilities completely disappears. However, when interpretation stops, we do not cease to form theories, and this chapter will show that, following my encounter at the *British Art Show*, I found no shortage of theoretical writing with which to frame my interest in the fragile presence of exhibited things.

In the same way that perceptual processes can be studied in illusions or hallucinations, this chapter examines interpretation within the failure to interpret. Semiotic theories will play a key role in my discussion, which ranges, appropriately for an artist-curator like myself, across artistic and museological practices. In museums, the display of historical objects tells us a great deal about the outer limits of interpretability but so does the exhibiting of artworks in doctoral examinations where a creative practice has to demonstrate new knowledge in a manner comparable to that of a written thesis. In both cases everything hangs on the viewer's engagement with material presence. Thus, my contribution to the celebration of the career of Susan Pearce brings together two contrasting 'material worlds' – that of the museum curator and that of the artist – and explores the meaningful exhibiting of what Pearce has called, in the title of her 1990 publication, 'objects of knowledge'. The failure to interpret such objects will be my unifying concept.

When things go wrong

After the moment of confusion at the *British Art Show* I was able to theorise my coffee-for-tea experience (I do not know what else to call it) as a regression to the working conditions of the studio.[2] The separate parts were no longer on display; they had lost their adaptation to the environment of the spectator. Like any serendipitous arrangement of materials on a studio floor, the horizontal disposition made it much harder to understand how, of all the sculptures these bits might become, a small rounded piece of wood and a little dish of hammered metal could come together quite as exquisitely as they had. The collapsed exhibit had restored the improvisatory moment in which a sculptor does not know what it will take for the parts to become a whole. When an attendant reassembled the piece – a task she performed easily – the sculptor's final arrangement dismissed all thoughts of improvisation. By the time this attendant had returned to her chair, the uncertainty of the studio had been banished by an act of restitution that conjured, as if from nowhere, the finished version of the artwork – now the sculpture was an entirely stable entity that merely needed routine maintenance.

The collapsed sculpture raises issues about the relationship between the material presence of objects on display and interpretive consumption. I am, as I stated above, an artist-curator and my coffee-for-tea moment – an experience in which presence overrode interpretation – seems to have implications for all kinds of exhibition practices. To notice alterations in presence is clearly not the same as registering changes in meaning, as when our interpretations of exhibited material differ or conflict. This distinction is important. When it comes to describing the experience of viewing exhibitions the distinguishing feature is surely that our interpretive engagements, in all their shifting aspects, never quite eclipse our need for material entities to be actually present and as steadfast as possible. We go to galleries and museums because we attach a value to the unmediated presence of exhibited things. Thus, the coffee-for-tea experience introduces the possibility that an exhibited 'something' can be briefly nothing, an empty disorienting moment in which our sensory experiences resist assimilation into an existing scheme of interpretation.

Non-compliant things

A core idea about presence in Western philosophy contrasts the primacy of the semiotic referent over its sign. In Plato's *Phaedrus*, the act of writing is condemned because it can function in the absence of its referents (Hackforth 1972). To write is to dislodge communication into a state of translation or codification that will always have less presence than an originating speech act. For Plato, a speaker speaking is the optimum communicative experience, writing can only refer to it, not actually be it. Needless to say, centuries of philosophical debate have interrogated this idea.[3] From the 1960s, a powerful counter-position was created by a widespread 'linguistic turn' throughout the humanities and the arts. In particular, Roland Barthes (1915–80) insisted that our world is an entirely semiotic environment; everything is encoded and mediated by endless acts of translation – we are all inhabitants of an empire of signs. As a result, artists and curators found it increasingly difficult to associate a sense of optimum presence with exhibited objects. Everyone began to 'read' exhibitions in the same way they read a text.

However, not everything about Barthes' thinking conforms to the model of linguistic expediency. The influential concept of *punctum* was developed in Barthes' *Camera Lucida* (2000) to describe the capacity of a photograph to 'puncture' our relationship with representation, to confront us with the actual presence of the past without the mediating action of signs (Barthes 2000: 63–109). The artist-photographer Klaus Wehner (Chapter 6) equates this semiotic instability with the experience of viewing Vice-Admiral Horatio Nelson's undress coat at the National Maritime Museum, Greenwich. The coat manifests *punctum* because the museumgoer is presented with the hole made by the sniper's musket ball that fatally wounded Nelson as he stood on the gun deck of HMS *Victory* whilst it engaged the French battleship *Redoubtable* during the Battle of Trafalgar. The lethal puncture, no more than a small gash beneath the left epaulette, is present enough to subvert the flow of interpretive interest that draws us to the exhibit. As with the photograph of Barthes' mother as a five-year-old which defines the *punctum* experience, the coat presents us with evidence of both a person's existence and their death (Barthes 2000: 70). The effect devastates our habits of interpretation and changes the presence of the object on display.

Wehner's research prompted a reconsideration of my coffee-for-tea experience. As a result, I turned to another essay by Barthes which touches on the matter of material presence and semiotic breakdown. In 'The plates of the *Encyclopedia*' (1989), Barthes proposes a formula for the oppositional nature of things and theories. Many of the illustrations in Denis Diderot's (1713–84) *Encyclopédie* are divided into a lower section featuring equipment or raw material laid out in inventorial rows, and an upper 'vignette' in which the same items are shown in use within lively scenes of human productivity or consumption (Figure 7.1). Barthes does not reproduce examples of these beautiful engravings but the compositional style developed for Diderot by artists such as Louis-Jacques Goussier (1722–99) is familiar from countless instruction manuals and technical drawings. In the lower section, it is as if a universe of disconnected mechanical parts exists

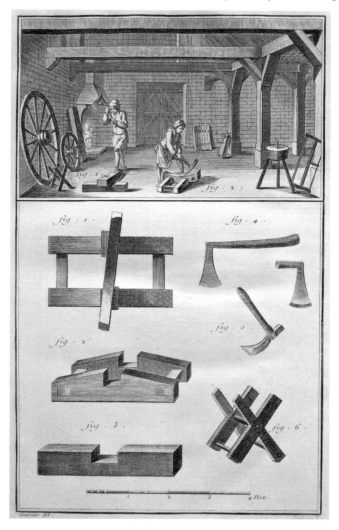

Figure 7.1 The Wheelwright, Plate 1, Vol. 3, *Encyclopedia, or a Systematic Dictionary of the Sciences, Arts, and Crafts,* edited by Denis Diderot and Jean le Rond d'Alembert, 1751–72. Photograph by Chris Dorsett, courtesy of Taylor Institution Library, University of Oxford.

independently of any obligation to a mechanistic whole. We are shown nothing but fascinating details – component after component, cog by cog. However, in the section above, we view the everyday utilisations of parts, we see what happens when all manner of 'thing' is gainfully employed in busy rooms or cavernous workshops. Diderot's plates insist on the separation of these two domains. Employing the paradigm–syntagm binary of structuralist semiotics, Barthes claims that the lower zones of these plates are like paradigmatic units awaiting configuration in a linguistic statement and the vignettes are the resulting syntagmatic combinations that bring about meaning. If you 'read' each illustration from bottom to top you follow a trajectory in which the material world is transformed into social and cultural significance. But if your eyes scan from top to bottom you descend through the realm of instrumental value into a zone of disconnected, non-compliant *thinglyness*. From this lower zone, the vignette above appears to be too full of meanings for its own good. My coffee-for-tea moment, in its *punctum*-like rupturing of semiotic coherence, is in accord with the lower non-compliance of things. In Barthes' formulation, this disruptive presence can subvert the ascending journey towards the world of lively vignettes and interpretive fulfilment.

Exhibition as vignette

Barthes describes the expansion of technological and scientific knowledge in Diderot's Europe as a process of 'fenestration' that forced the world to be docilely framed and then dominated.[4] In this sense the illustrations in Diderot's *Encyclopedia* anticipated the 'Great Expositions' of the Victorian period described in Isobel Armstrong's *Victorian Glassworlds: glass culture and the imagination* (2007). The mid-nineteenth century is the first era of public glass in which large shop windows both made visible, and physically withheld, large quantities of consumer items. This newly glazed environment would also have reflected the passing world to an unprecedented degree and Armstrong argues that the Victorian public would have associated this communal self-mirroring with a related invention: the photographic glass negative with its image-capturing emulsion. As a result, plate glass would have been a powerful stimulant to the public imagination and the metropolitan environment would have been transformed; high street consumers could now 'reflect' imaginatively upon everything and anything that was 'fenestrated' by the new technology.

Some sense of the impact of 'public glass' in the nineteenth century can be re-explored today when you visit the Pitt Rivers Museum in Oxford where ranks of Victorian vitrines display a celebrated collection of pre-industrial material culture. Today, historical significance has eclipsed technological novelty and the impressive 'fenestrating' furniture is now as curious as the objects it 'fenestrates'. The glazing can be, for eyes used to flawless contemporary glass, as materially conspicuous as the material culture it was put there to protect. Standing on the upper floors of the Museum, the visitor's eyes descend from the lofty roof to the dense arrangement of cases in the court below. The collection that lies stretched out before you is the handiwork of the Museum's many curators, whose expanding inventories have, over the years, encompassed the creative efforts of countless 'makers' from distant places and times. The sweep of one's eyes from the roof to the ground floor follows a descent from a lively 'vignette' of Victorian aspiration to a place where the overwhelming presence of objects, through the sheer volume of accumulated material, makes the desire to interpret hesitate, if not falter.

The Museum's founding collector, Augustus Henry Lane Fox Pitt-Rivers (1827–1900), clearly saw the value of immersing himself in the presence of large

Figure 7.2 An Antiquary's Billiard Table (accession number: 2002.73.14), courtesy of Pitt
Rivers Museum, University of Oxford.

quantities of objects. There is a photograph, known as *An Antiquary's Billiard Table*
(Figure 7.2), which seems to document the sorting and grouping of future exhibits.[5]
This informal assemblage of archeological specimens was gathered together for
a second museum (opened in Farnham, Dorset during the 1880s) and the horizontal arrangement of objects may show Pitt-Rivers' interpretive thinking in
progress. We see the 'inventorying effort' that Barthes associates with the lower
sections of Diderot's plates in progress. One can imagine Pitt-Rivers' eyes sweeping across individual items, noting similarities, improvising possible combinations,
speculating on how emerging typologies demonstrate theories. In doing this, the
collector would be following Barthes' bottom-to-top trajectory, selecting from an
inventory of paradigmatic units to construct a syntagmatic sequence of ideas. In
this trajectory the world of mute objects is transformed into social and cultural
meaning. A cluster of glass vessels at the back of the table and a pile of stone
tools at the front, like the ethnological objects that crowd the cases in Oxford,
become examples of a preponderance of similar forms of production and use –
perhaps evidence of the survival of the fittest technologies, the Darwinian
paradigm which is said to have influenced Pitt-Rivers' approach to material
culture. Here a bottom-to-top theoretical speculation wants to ascend vertiginously
above the non-compliance of recumbent things.

The power of the 'real' thing

Armstrong pictures the emancipated Victorian imagination soaring freely above
a newly fenestrated world. In contrast, the eminent museologist Susan Pearce, in
publication after publication, has sought to ground the fenestrated pleasures of

places like the Pitt Rivers Museum in the non-compliance of objects, in the experience we are accustomed to call the power of the 'real' thing. In 'Objects as meaning: or narrating the past' (1990) Pearce explores the transformational value of material presence and brings into view the subject–object encounter that distinguishes the lower sections of Diderot's illustrations from the interpretive vignettes on the public side of Armstrong's glass screens. We are referred to a powerfully present object displayed at the National Army Museum in London, a military jacket worn by Lieutenant Henry Anderson at the Battle of Waterloo. The jacket, known as a coatee, was damaged when Anderson was shot as his regiment stood their ground against the French Imperial Guard:

> At this moment, in the crisis of battle, Anderson fell, wounded severely 'by a musket ball which broke his left shoulder, passed through his lungs, and made an exit at the back, breaking the scapula' (Army List, 1860). The coatee shows the tears and stains which would have resulted from such a wound.
>
> (Pearce 1990: 126)

This violent moment transformed Anderson's coatee into a 'message-bearing entity' that is 'capable of a very large range of interpretations' (Pearce 1990: 127). In the immediate aftermath of the battle the jacket began to increase in interpretive significance, a process that has continued throughout the two centuries that now separate us from the Napoleonic Wars. It follows that the custodial function of the Museum has played a considerable part in maintaining this message-bearing potential in relation to our ongoing, changing collective consciousness. The Museum's particular method of combining the embodied meaning of the coatee with the ongoing process of interpretation is for Pearce a rich and complex form of knowledge construction that represents 'the greatest strength which a collection-holding institution commands' (Pearce 1990: 127).

At the time 'Objects as meaning; or narrating the past' was written, the museum world was still negotiating Barthes' semiotic legacy and Pearce considers the possibility that Anderson's coatee has no necessary connection with the signified meaning it carries (Pearce 1990: 128). This would make the capacity of the material environment to bear messages entirely a matter of the shifting efficiencies of communal agreement, of the conventionalised semiotic systems studied by Ferdinand de Saussure (1857–1913), the linguist whose theories had a formative influence on Barthes. Pearce is rightly cautious here and modifies the hard line Saussurian position to take into account the hands-on experiences of curators working with museum objects. 'The crucial aspect of the jacket', Pearce tells us, 'is that while it survives physically it retains its metonymic relationship to the battle itself' (Pearce 1990: 134). A metonym is a figure of speech built on the close, usually physical, association of a referent to its signifying substitute. If I can refer to my credit card as 'plastic', then I can certainly represent a battle with a battle-scarred jacket. Unless we have been seriously misled, Anderson's coatee was an intrinsic part of the occurrences south of Waterloo on the afternoon and evening of 18 June 1815. However, the contiguity of a particular object with a past event, whilst conforming to the synedochical conflation of the whole to a part, has other semiotic dimensions that need to be taken into account. When engaging with the power of 'real' things I do not want to feel ensnared by the linguistic absolutism of Barthes and Saussure, I want my semiotic analysis to recognise material presence in its own right.

As Sandra Dudley reports in her introductory chapter to *Museum Materialities: objects, engagements, interpretations* (2010), a 'material turn' is sweeping away older linguistic alliances. As a result, those of us still interested in semiotics seek to 'rematerialise' the sign within a broader theory of signification developed by the philosopher Charles Sanders Peirce (1839–1914).[6] With Peirce's concept of the indexical sign we can evoke a semiotic category that occurs extralinguistically, which comes about when the constituent parts of our physical environment leave recognisable traces on each other (Peirce 1931–58, Vol. 3: 359–62). It is surely the indexical dimension of the coatee that supports the ongoing diversification of cultural and social narrative which Pearce describes when she writes: 'the jacket which was once part of Lieutenant Anderson's past and present now becomes part of our own, carrying the objective reality of its red cloth and its bullet hole along the chain of meanings' (Pearce 1990: 138). Here material presence is the bedrock of interpretive possibility, the source of vignette after vignette as generations of museumgoer take ownership of the indexical signs that travel through history with the objects collected and exhibited in museums.

When words are not enough

I now want to explore this same interaction of things and theories in the context of doctoral research undertaken in art schools. The relevance to the above discussion is that, when a postgraduate student submits for examination an original piece of research in the field of fine art practice, an exhibition of artworks is given an equal role to that of theoretical writing. Given that we are talking about a doctoral examination rather than an art exhibition, this means that a collection of displayed objects is expected to carry meaning in a comparable manner to a piece of academic writing. Here the art school community wants the material presence of exhibited objects to be not only the bedrock of interpretation, but also the interpretation itself.

The doctoral group I lead at Northumbria University has researchers using fine art techniques that range from drawing, painting, printmaking, photography and sculpture to video projections, sound recordings, installation pieces and interventionist actions in public spaces. In keeping with the rest of the Art and Design sector, we call what these researchers do 'practice-led' enquiry.[7] In supporting a research process that is embodied in the creative activities of artists, a practice-led programme cannot help but commit itself to the idea that a PhD dissertation can be made like a sculpture as well as written like a book. But is this saying that the material on display, if it is not to be merely an illustrative adjunct of the dissertation, must be read like an encoded text? The artist-researchers

I supervise would certainly respond negatively to this suggestion but neither would they have a unified view on what actually happens: the sector is riven by disputes and inconclusive debates.[8] The conundrum of my student's approach to undertaking research is that their exhibits, when it comes to the doctoral examination, are neither subservient like an illustration nor communicative like a discursive language. As a result, it is difficult to know what makes these art objects comparable to a piece of theoretical writing.

Perhaps art schools have something to learn here from collection-holding institutions. Within the practice-led conflict of things with theories we have a duality that accords with the two-way principle offered in 'The plates of the *Encyclopedia*': if there is a bottom-to-top interpretive trajectory that allows historians and critics to situate artworks in lively vignettes of cultural consumption, then there is also an inverse journey in which the expansiveness of the theoretical mind is brought to a point of focus by the hard fact of objective presence. Like the studio meditation prompted by my coffee-for-tea experience, the descent from vignette to objecthood is an investigatory process driven by an object's de-adaptation within the spectatorial environment. The key idea here is that presence can meaningfully override interpretation.

I have in mind something like Martin Heidegger's (1889–1976) famous broken hammer (Krell 1993: 19–20). The philosopher says that we use this familiar kind of tool without ever needing to consider the intricate relationship of our subjectivity to objective existence. Hammering is embedded in the texture of everyday life. However, when something goes wrong – say the hammer shaft breaks – an extensive network of connected meanings suddenly comes into view, becomes present. Without the breakage, and the resulting disruption of our habitual non-attentiveness, there would be a continuous withdrawing into obscurity, a continuous veiling of presence. This is why two tiny indexical traces of bygone violence can stop us in our tracks and make us reconsider Nelson's undress coat and Anderson's coatee.[9] From a Heideggerian perspective, the *punctum* generated by a musket ball hole transforms each exhibit into an object of theoretical cognition and impels further observation and study (Inwood 1995: 346). Furthermore, from the Barthesian point of view, the *punctum* moment that initiates this theoretical cognition can only take place outside the domain of language. With this combination of ideas in place, we are in a position to appreciate the investigatory status of the practical work undertaken within practice-led research.

Disturbing things

Of all the members of the doctoral group at Northumbria University, it is John Lavell who has placed the ambiguous presence of artworks at the centre of his PhD project. This artist-researcher likes to place on exhibition large sheets of unframed 130 gram paper that have been embossed with grid-like patterns of high regularity. The quiet and undemonstrative nature of these objects appeals to our lingering love of minimalist aesthetics but the surfaces of the paper, transformed by row after row of precisely executed hammer blows or stiletto stabs, give the *sotto voce* effect an undercurrent of implied violence which is reinforced by exhibition titles derived from forensic science. One of Lavell's pieces is called *Exit Wound*. What is the viewer to think? It is as if these artworks have been lovingly crafted in order to sublimate a criminal compulsion – a rather post-modern twist on the notion of creative practice. Once again we are considering the *punctum* effect. In the context of contemporary art criticism, this term evokes rich fields of theoretical speculation. For example, Hal Foster has explored Barthes' concept in relation to the obsessive routines of artists. In *The Return of the Real: the avant-garde at the end of the century* (1996) Foster sees compulsive and repetitive creativity as a form of traumatic behaviour in which an artist's work is placed, like the unstoppable re-enactment of a tragic event, beyond the 'insistence of signs' (Foster 1996: 132). It is a feature of a Lavell exhibition that the poetic presence of his art absorbs and neutralises the evidence of its production. *Exit Wound* is displayed on its own exquisite terms – uncomfortably so because it is difficult not to be inquisitive about the insistent indexical presence of 'pattern injuries' or 'blunt force trauma'. In this way, the power of *punctum* is set against the aspirations of the forensic imagination.

For a forensic scientist, a tear or a stain is primarily a mechanism of trans-temporal meaning. In this account, the musket ball holes are evidence of the historic co-presence of the clothing and the projectiles that together generated the indexical sign. Without *punctum*-like effects, the interpretive process in museums is confined to this kind of causal connection of the past to the present. Following the top-to-bottom trajectory it has to be true that, during the Napoleonic Wars, two French combatants were in a position to inflict damage on the clothing of two British opponents to such devastating effect that we are still thinking about the outcome today. In the art school version of this experience, Lavell's sheets of punctured paper indicate that, somewhere in the recent past, an artist-researcher at Northumbria University was able to dent and pierce the surfaces of the exhibits we are now viewing. The indexical trace of this process demonstrates Lavell's authorial priority in relation to his doctoral exhibition. However, having read the candidate's dissertation on the questionable interpretive techniques of forensic science, Lavell's examiners will also have to negotiate a sense of *punctum* that is beyond the 'insistence of signs'. As a result no persuasive act of interpretation can be built on this artist's studio thought-processes without cancelling out the 'stand alone' power of his artworks.

If Lavell's doctoral exhibition is comparable to a piece of theoretical writing, then this conflict between objects and titles represents his contribution to knowledge. In this sense, what the dissertation says about the fallibility of forensic science and the creativity of the criminal mind is better seen as an elaboration of the exhibition labels rather than the artworks. For the practice-led researcher, the examination is, like all future moments of audience reception, a productively unstable event with uncertain contributing factors. In the studio, different routes of thinking will have been pursued that seemed important at the time but, in the end, counted for very little in the objects on display. Similarly, a theoretical imperative that drives forward a new piece of work may not survive the full improvisatory

Figure 7.3 John Lavell's studio, work in progress. Photograph by Christina Kolaiti.

journey of creative production in which, it often seems, anything can be made to mean anything.

This point strikes at the heart of being an artist-researcher. Whilst Lavell's sheets of paper lie horizontally on his studio workbench, they are the equivalent of the objects on Pitt-River's billiard table (Figure 7.3). Whilst surveying his work in progress, a range of associations may occur to the artist that could shape the examiner's response during the examination. On the other hand, it might be better that these associations remain outside the process of interpretive judgement. The fact that an artist has interests that are not symmetrical with those of their audience suggests, despite the presence of indexical signs, that the past should not necessarily be seen as the preparation of the present. If Pitt-Rivers had bottom-to-top ideas about the material on his billiard table, then Lavell thinks the opposite about the objects in his studio: top-to-bottom ideas insist that possibility is studied as possibility. This kind of doctoral project is situated on the shadowy side of a *punctum*-like rupture – Lavell's artworks do not support his dissertation topic once they are on display. This is, for better or for worse, definitively 'practice-led' research.

Therapeutic things

The disjunction of production and consumption is also a feature of the curatorial research undertaken by Northumbria's practice-led group. The artist-curator Poyan Yee is exploring how the Northumbria Healthcare NHS Foundation Trust can utilise the knowledge built up in art schools with the development of artist-led curatorial projects. This kind of research fits squarely in the 'knowledge transfer' category confirming a growing perception that the central value of practice-led enquiry by artists is the methodological ideas it offers for tackling research problems outside its home discipline (AHRC 2009: 6). Yee's enquiry group of patients and hospital staff plan exhibition projects with local artists for the Trust's hospitals and clinics. The group selects artworks without the interpretive pressures of display: that is, through procedures that are reminiscent of studio debate.

Let us consider how this enquiry group operates. When the artist Tuesday Nesbitt was invited to present her recent paintings to the group in November 2007,

Figure 7.4 Tuesday Nesbitt's workshop at Hexham General Hospital, Northumberland. Photograph by Poyan Yee.

she laid out her artworks on a table in Hexham General Hospital and described how these objects came to be in the world (Figure 7.4). At this point, the group was not viewing exhibits, and no one was thinking about how the artworks would be arranged in the hospital corridor that had been designated for the exhibition. Yee's documentation of the event notes that there was a vertical dimension to the workshop activities, in which Nesbitt stood narrating her studio practices, and a horizontal part, in which the group sat at the table passing around the abstract paintings. These objects did not fulfil the group's expectations of hospital art but the multi-sensory presence of Nesbitt's beautifully painted panels stimulated levels of interest that would not have been acknowledged in the works on display. As a result, it was the group's engagement with the artworks, rather than their interest in authorial narratives or exhibition themes, that prepared the staff and patients for the curatorial responsibilities involved in displaying the work of this artist in the Trust's facilities. This workshop, so reminiscent of Barthes' discussion in 'The plates of the *Encyclopedia*', was the moment that Yee established her research methodology.

The work of the enquiry group at Hexham Hospital may not seem like a pioneering contribution to knowledge. After all, its procedures are not so different from a standard gallery outreach programme, in which the insights of an exhibiting artist are made available to the exhibition's viewers in order to shape a public response to the works on display. But Yee's group works in the opposite direction; the participants dislocate themselves from the artist's intentions in order to take ownership of the artworks as a 'lay' audience with their own ideas about how the exhibits might enhance a general sense of well-being in the healthcare environment. For Yee, well-being is generated by the hand rather than the eye, an idea supported by recent research on the therapeutic value of 'touch-based practices' which suggests that giving permission to handle museum objects stimulates a sense of possession which, in turn, improves self-confidence and raises aspirations (Chatterjee, Vreeland and Noble 2009: 167). Temporarily possessing Nesbitt's paintings renders her artistic authority precarious enough to puncture a 'lay' audience's dependence on correct interpretations. Once the group has understood the contingency of Nesbitt's relationship to the paintings on the table, they can begin to understand their own potential as curators. The degree to which this process echoes the constant handling of artworks during studio tutorials suggests the far-reaching benefit of inviting artist-researchers to transfer art school practices to NHS environments.

Sign makers and sign readers

It is too soon to know if Lavell and Yee are experimenting with a form of research that could actually expand our understanding of what happens when objects are placed on display. If we can speak of an emergent field of enquiry at all it is because the parameters are entirely different from those addressed by the methods of exhibition interpretation. In my experience, artists make insightful and skillful members of museum and gallery audiences, they articulate extremely apposite critiques of most things exhibited before them, but, in the end, the bottom-to-top journey into the fullness of interpretation may not be their primary mode of doctoral investigation. One might usefully consider the nature of an indexical sign, the semiotic category most at issue throughout this chapter, and understand that the physical traces of past occurrences present themselves differently to the sign maker and the sign reader. A footprint in the sand is an interpretive challenge for Robinson Crusoe, but not for Man Friday. Artist-researchers have a similarly anterior relationship with their own indexical presence. The distinctiveness of this position is that it extends the significance of any artwork put on display during a doctoral examination. Suddenly there are two fields of enquiry symmetrically placed either side of the rupturing impact of material presence. On one side there are researchers who establish the *thinglyness* of an exhibit and, on the other, examiners who cover it over with interpretations. The two sides share, but are also held apart by, the implacable power of the 'real' thing, an existential state which can effortlessly generate the experiential blankness of a coffee-for-tea moment.

The literature on practice-led research is driven by the difficulty of matching things to theories and theories to things across this divide. Nearly a decade ago Chris Rust and Adrian Wilson complained about design students who allowed the writing of a doctoral thesis to dominate their research; so much so that the artefacts they created were reduced to illustrations of theoretical texts (Rust and Wilson 2001: 24). Not much has changed and in *Things and Theories: the unstable presence of exhibited objects* I have continued to rake over the same ground: the problem of how creative works achieve equality with theoretical writing. The clarification proposed here is that when inert things illustrate lively theories we have a bottom-to-top interpretation that does not capture what artist-researchers like Lavell and Yee actually do. It seems to me that practice-led research, if this term has any credibility at all, moves in the reverse direction: hence my interest in Barthes' alternative, top-to-bottom scan of the plates in Diderot's *Encyclopedia*.

My coffee-for-tea experience suggested that the unstable ebb and flow of theories is built on the inert stability of the exhibit. As a result, the bottom-to-top approach is unlikely to do justice to research grounded in the improvisatory uncertainty of unfinished work. Indeed, I introduced this chapter with a description of a collapsing sculpture at the *British Art Show* because the interpretive blankness this incident caused could be theorised as a regression to the working conditions of a studio. I take this to be a paradigmatic top-to-bottom journey. The artist-theoretician Brian O'Doherty contrasts the world of the artist's studio with that of the 'white cube' gallery (the coinage for which he is famous). The key distinction is that the former situates an artist in a 'nervous present' in which – here O'Doherty quotes James Joyce – 'future plunges into past, a future exerting on the present the pressure of unborn ideas' (O'Doherty 2007: 18). When we view an exhibit as a studio practitioner rather than as an exhibition interpreter, the intellectual disposition that sustains an artwork in the 'nervous present' also strives to stop artefacts becoming stabilised as illustrations of texts. In a practice-led doctoral examination, a display of artworks will achieve equality with a piece of academic writing when, as I said above, our interest in the fragility of the exhibition process stimulates its own theoretical frame. The difference is that these theories terminate in the powerful presence of an object on display and leave its interpretive afterlife to the discernment (and creativity) of the exhibition viewer.

In this chapter my theoretical frame has been museological and much of my discussion treats museum display as an exemplary opportunity for top-to-bottom viewing. Susan Pearce's theoretical writing upholds this position when she explores the museumgoer's need for material entities to be actually present. Whilst 'Objects as meaning; or narrating the past' concerns the expanding cultural and social significance of Lieutenant Anderson's coatee, Pearce's essay also reminds us that the tears and stains that resulted from Anderson's wound are directly linked to an event that seemed 'confused, spasmodic and incoherent to most of the individuals who took part in it' (Pearce 1990: 127). Here the metonymic-indexical incoherence of a 'real' thing subverts and challenges the stable object of our interpretations. This top-to-bottom subversion chimes with Klaus Wehner's description of the *punctum* of Nelson's undress coat at the National Maritime Museum; it also corroborates the efforts John Lavell and Poyan Yee have made to let their practice actually *lead* their research. The point about using exhibitions to construct and convey knowledge is that, in both museums and fine art doctoral examinations, an exhibited 'something' can suddenly become 'nothing' and return us to the confusion and incoherence that marked the moment before meaning-making was possible. In making this instability the topic of this chapter I have sought to explain why curators and artists, however theoretically minded, must continue to explore the unmediated presence of exhibited things.

Acknowledgements

I would like to thank my doctoral students John Lavell and Poyan Yee for the inspiration and support they gave to the development of the ideas explored in this chapter. I am also grateful to Tuesday Nesbitt for permission to cite her work at Hexham Hospital. In addition, I want to express my appreciation of the research undertaken by two other members of my practice-led doctoral group, Jolande Bosch and Hiroko Oshima, whose engagement with studio practices has enriched my understanding of the practice-led approach. In relation to the theme of the artist's studio I also thank an anonymous peer reviewer for recommending Brian O'Doherty's *Studio and Cube*. I am indebted to the Pitt Rivers Museum and Taylor Institution Library for allowing me reproduce images from their collections as well as Paul Sims at Techunique for his expert work on the illustrations. Finally, I gratefully acknowledge the support of Northumbria University in granting me sabbatical leave whilst I was writing the final draft of *Things and Theories: the unstable presence of exhibited objects*.

Notes

1 This is my second attempt at making sense of the experience of a sculpture collapsing at the *British Art Show*. In my chapter 'Exhibitions and their prerequisites' (Rugg and Sedgwick 2007) I discuss this incident in relation to my 'curated' walk for *Trees Walking* (2003), an exhibition at the Royal Botanic Gardens, Kew (Dorsett 2007: 77–87).

2 The coffee-for-tea idea has evolved, over many years, in seminars on studio practices held in the Department of Arts at Northumbria University. In these sessions I explore the intricate relationship between studio production and exhibition reception using Alexander Liberman's atmospheric photographs of the studio of the celebrated Modernist sculptor Constantin Brancusi. An important source of ideas on this topic is Sidney Geist's book *Brancusi: a study of the sculpture* (1968). Geist offers many insights into how Brancusi's practices 'created the idea of the artist's studio in our time' (Geist 1968: 167). Liberman's images show, in Geist's words, 'precious objects gleaming among rough blocks of wood and stone' (Geist 1968: 167). The beautifully top-lit studio, now reconstructed at the Pompidou Centre in Paris, appears as a 'temple and laboratory of art, the site of a confrontation of man-made order and natural chaos' (Geist 1968: 168). In the photographs this confrontation can be seen in the carefully arranged encounter between the 'precious objects' on upright pedestals and the 'rough blocks' strewn across the studio floor. My discussion of the serendipitous arrangements of sculptural materials on a horizontal plane owes a great deal to the impact of these images in a contemporary art school.

3 There is a concise and informative discussion about presence in Amanda Bell's entry on the *Theories of Media* pages of the University of Chicago website (Bell 2004).

4 In 'The plates of the *Encyclopedia*' Barthes introduces the concept of 'fenestration' within a highly emblematic passage that pictures Noah's Ark as a huge floating 'goods locker' containing thousands of animals docilely sticking their heads through windows in order to be divided, named and domesticated (Barthes 1989: 222). This is a symbolic reference to the role of encyclopedism in the expanding sphere of European influence during the eighteenth and nineteenth centuries.

5 *An Antiquary's Billiard Table* comes from a photograph album held at the Pitt Rivers Museum entitled 'Rushmore and Environs' (Rushmore House was Pitt-Rivers' home on the Wiltshire–Dorset border). The Museum's website gives an account of a visit by Hilda Petrie (wife of the Egyptologist William Flinders Petrie) to Rushmore in 1898:

> The hall consisted of two immense rooms, crammed with every imaginable object, and a corridor, stacked with curios all over its floor, led to a billiard room whose table was piled with Romano-British bronzes, and dozens of early Syrian glass vases.
>
> (Pitt Rivers Museum 2009)

Perhaps the horizontally arrayed objects described here (not just on the billiard table but also 'all over' the corridor floor) deserve more consideration than I have room for in this chapter. For example, Douglas Hofstadter's (1997) experiments with what he calls 'tabletop' analogies may be a way of understanding cognitive processes that do not contribute to viewing vertically displayed exhibits but do come into creative play when comparing material on a flat plane (Hofstadter 1997: 323–58).

6 For more on the explanatory force of Peircian semiotics, particularly in relation to the curatorial uses of 'iconic', 'indexical' and 'symbolic' signs, see my chapter 'Making meaning beyond display' in Sandra Dudley's *Museum Materialities: objects, engagements, interpretations* (2010).

7 The 2007 AHRC *Review of Practice-led Research* describes the creative activities of artists, designers and architects as 'instrumental' in the process of practice-led enquiry (Mottram, Rust and Till 2007: 11). However, the discipline of fine art is wary of this definition. Whilst artists know that new ideas have to be absorbed in order to create new artworks, and that art students need to develop a wide range of skills for acquiring and utilising new knowledge, they also know that making artworks answer questions destroys the autonomy of art objects. In this sense, practice-led research in fine art has a very different potential from that of design or architecture.

8 For examples of these debates see James Elkins' *Artists with PhDs: on the new doctoral degree in studio art* (2009). In an online review of Elkins' book, Hugo Ortega calls the practice-led doctoral degree the 'hot topic in art instruction in the US' (Ortega 2009). This review is written from the perspective of American art schools, which have been slower to embrace postgraduate research than their counterparts in Great Britain and Australia. However, as Ortega points out, assimilation has not protected the practice-led PhD from controversy. The art and design sector in the UK continues to worry about appropriateness (why would an creative practitioner want to undertake doctoral research?) even though British institutions now expect junior art school staff to have a research degree. In *Things and Theories: the unstable presence of exhibited objects* I side-step these discussions in order to focus on the issue of compatibility (can artworks demonstrate and disseminate 'findings' in a comparable fashion to established forms of doctoral research?). Those of us who are in their second decade of supervising practice-led PhDs know that this is a core problem. As the ceramic artist Maarit Mäkelä writes in her interesting article 'Knowing through making: the role of the artefact in practice-led research', 'artefacts seem to be unable to pass on their knowledge' (Mäkelä 2007: 157).

9 There is good reason to link Nelson's undress coat and Anderson's coatee with the philosophical motif of the broken hammer. Heidegger analogises the unveiling of presence, so strongly brought to mind by the sudden interruption of habitual manual work, with 'the "setting up" of something on display', a process in which 'a normally inconspicuous object is brought into salience by being put on exhibition' (Young 2001: 38). Similarly, in 'The origin of the work of art', Heidegger (1971) uses Vincent Van Gogh's painting of a pair of peasant's shoes to describe the ontological power of 'unconcealment', a state of displacement that lifts our experience of things into the present by disrupting the flow of everyday existence. As Heidegger writes: 'In the nearness of [Van Gogh's] work we were suddenly somewhere else than we tend to be' (Krell 1993: 161).

Bibliography

Armstrong, I. (2007) *Victorian Glassworlds: glass culture and the imagination 1830–1880*, Oxford: Oxford University Press.

AHRC (2009) *Future Directions for Arts and Humanities Research: a consultation*, Bristol: Arts and Humanities Research Council.

Barthes, R. (1989 [1980]) 'The plates of the *Encyclopedia*', in S. Sontag (ed.) *Barthes: selected writings*, London: Fontana, pp. 218–35.

Barthes, R. (2000 [1980]) *Camera Lucida: reflections on photography*, tr. Richard Howard, London: Vintage.

Bell, A. (2004) 'Absence/Presence', *The University of Chicago: theories of media: keywords glossary*, online. Available at: http://csmt.uchicago.edu/glossary2004/absencepresence.htm (Accessed 27 July 2009).

Chatterjee, H., S. Vreeland and G. Noble (2009) 'Museopathy: exploring the healing potential of handling museum objects', *Museum and Society*, 7: 164–77.

Dorsett, C. (2007) 'Exhibitions and their prerequisites', in J. Rugg and M. Sedgwick (eds) *Issues in Curating, Contemporary Art and Performance*, Bristol and Chicago: Intellect, pp. 77–87.

Dorsett, C. (2010) 'Making meaning beyond display' in S.H. Dudley (ed.) *Museum Materialities: objects, engagements, interpretations*, London and New York: Routledge, pp. 241–59.

Dudley, S.H. (2010) 'Museum materialities: objects, sense, feelings', in S.H. Dudley (ed.) *Museum Materialities: objects, engagements, interpretations*, London and New York: Routledge, pp. 1–17.

Elkins, J. (ed.) (2009) *Artists with PhDs: on the new doctoral degree in studio art*, Washington, DC: New Academia Publishing.

Foster, H. (1996) *The Return of the Real: the avant-garde at the end of the century*, Cambridge, MA: MIT Press.

Geist, S. (1968) *Brancusi: a study of the sculpture*, London: Studio Vista.

Hackforth, R. (tr. and ed.) (1972) *Plato's Phaedrus*, Cambridge: Cambridge University Press.

Heidegger, M. (1971) 'The origin of the work of art', in D.F. Krell (ed.) (1993) *Martin Heidegger: basic writings from Being and Time (1927) to The Task of Thinking (1964)*, London and New York: Routledge, pp. 139–212.

Hofstadter, D. and the Fluid Analogies Research Group (1997) *Fluid Concepts and Creative Analogies: computer models of the fundamental mechanisms of thought*, London: Penguin.

Inwood, M.J. (1995) 'Martin Heidegger', in T. Honderich (ed.) *The Oxford Companion to Philosophy*, Oxford: Oxford University Press, pp. 345–9.

Krell, D.F. (1993) 'General introduction: the question of being', in D.F. Krell (ed.) *Martin Heidegger: basic writings from Being and Time (1927) to The Task of Thinking (1964)*, London and New York: Routledge, pp. 1–35.

Mäkelä, M. (2007) 'Knowing through making: the role of the artefact in practice-led research', *Knowledge, Technology and Policy*, 20 (October): 157–63.

Mottram, J., C. Rust and J. Till (2007) *AHRC Research Review: practice-led research in art, design and architecture*, Bristol: Arts and Humanities Research Council.

O'Doherty, B. (2007) *Studio and Cube: on the relationship between where art is made and where art is displayed*, New York: Buell Center/FORuM Project Publication.

Ortega, H. (2009) *Artists with PhDs: new book by James Elkins*, online. Available at: http://artpracticeasresearch.com/topic/blog/page/3 (Accessed 29 July 2010).

Pearce, S. (1990) 'Objects as meaning; or narrating the past', in S. Pearce (ed.) *Objects of Knowledge*, London and Atlantic Highlands: Athlone Press, pp. 125–40.

Peirce, C.S. (1931–58) *Collected Papers*, Vols 1–6 C. Hartshorne and P. Weiss (eds), Vols 7–8 A.W. Burks (ed.), Cambridge, MA: Harvard University Press.

Pitt Rivers Museum (2009) *Rethinking Pitt-Rivers, Eyewitness at Farnham*, online. Available at: http://web.prm.ox.ac.uk/rpr/index.php/article-index/12-articles/177-eyewitness-at-farnham (Accessed 13 July 2010).

Rust, C. and A. Wilson (2001) 'A visual thesis? techniques for reporting practice-led research', *Designjournalen*, 8: 23–9.

Young, J. (2001) *Heidegger's Philosophy of Art*, Cambridge: Cambridge University Press.

8 Inexperienced museum visitors and how they negotiate contemporary art

A comparative study of two visitor-driven visual art presentations

Marijke Van Eeckhaut

Questions and focus

Contemporary artworks are curious items in our material world. Being contemporary, it is sometimes supposed that they are more subject to interpretation than older art; however, they frequently remain a closed book under our enquiring gaze. Even when created out of the most familiar of materials, using everyday images and referring to our own surroundings, contemporary artworks can still evade clear interpretation. The more experienced know how to deal with an artwork's open-ended questions and provocations, how to come to an interpretation and how to form an opinion. However, museum visitors with less experience vis-à-vis contemporary art can find themselves faced with an impenetrable blur of images without any means of making the subject 'speak' to them.

In this chapter, I explore the relationship between contemporary art and museum visitors with little or no experience of it, consequently lacking the specific knowledge and skills that more adept visitors have developed over the years (usually as a result of their upbringing and/or education), thus enabling them to interpret contemporary art and negotiate the often predominantly self-referential exhibitions in art museums. In what ways do visitors with less experience try to make sense of contemporary art? What are they looking for in artworks? Are there certain features of artworks that appeal in particular to a less experienced audience? And is this true of various groups of less experienced visitors: are there features in artworks that possess a more generalised power of attraction going beyond traditionally defined museum-audience target groups?

My focus is on two exhibitions at the Museum of Contemporary Art in Antwerp, Belgium (M HKA) and created by two such sets of inexperienced members of the public. These experimental projects are suitable for exploring the above questions because the participants had varied backgrounds but little or no experience of contemporary visual art and had been asked to pick through the museum's collection in order to develop an exhibition. Not all of the participants were already visitors in the strict sense – some of them had never visited a museum of contemporary art before – nevertheless, they fitted the profile of an audience with little or no pertinent experience and were invited to form their opinions and define their preferences with regard to particular contemporary works of art. My account draws on observation of the participants' processes, interviews and conversations with the people involved (participants and staff – educational, artistic as well as on the museum floor), documentary sources (such as reports from meetings and working documents prepared by the participants, e.g. a mind map and associations with the artworks), texts by the participants (such as catalogue and wall texts) and on-site observation (content, design and organisation of the exhibition; working of the mediation tools through the entirety of the exhibition), complemented with messages left by visitors (who were invited to write down their comments during the second exhibition). I was employed at the M HKA at the time of the first exhibition. This allowed me to witness the creation of the exhibition from a front-row seat. By the time of the second exhibition I was working on my doctoral dissertation at Ghent University, researching the M HKA as a prominent case. Consequently, I had not only full access to the museum but also to the people employed there and their internal documents.

My objective in this case is to examine the relationship between the artworks and the participants through all the aspects of the exhibition-making process up to and including the final presentations. I also explore any patterns found in these relationships and discuss the validity of the traditional view concerning the correlation between the engaging power of works of art and the specificity of the target group to which the visitor (i.e. the participant) belongs.

Introduction

In the past, several attempts were made to support the visitor's interpretation – some attempts more successful than others. On the whole, however, museums of modern and contemporary art concentrated chiefly on creating aesthetically sound white cubes cleared of interpretative clutter for the purpose of highly focused viewing and private contemplation (Duncan 1995, McClellan 2008). Nowadays, even more curatorial emphasis is placed on the independent contemplation of artworks, given that the display of art's evolution through different movements has ceased to be the dominant model (one which, at least, offered a narrative, albeit somewhat inefficient). The many solo exhibitions or isolated displays of (groups of) work by single artists concentrate the focus, '[obliging] us to develop our own reading of the work rather than relying on a curatorial interpretation of history' (Serota 2000: 10). As Serota rightly points out, the fact that artists often create their work with museum environments and specific viewing conditions in mind has a decisive impact on display policies.

Thus, it is little wonder that research shows that the art museum audience consists of a predominantly adept public of culturally cultivated visitors. Over the years, attendance has indeed increased. However, more recent visitor surveys at museums of modern and contemporary art generally show no significant changes to the public's profile; as the educated population grows, so does the art museum audience (Bourdieu and Darbel 1969, Bennett 1995, McClellan 2008). Those who visit art museums are usually predisposed to learning and, therefore, are more often than not well educated; they consider their visits to be a worthwhile investment in their lifelong learning process (Falk and Dierking 2000).

In recent decades, external pressures, such as the funding conditions arising from the political demand for the further democratisation of museums, combined with rising operational costs, have rendered visitors equal or even greater in priority to the collection, study and conservation of objects (McClellan 2008). Museums of every type and size are making efforts to increase attendance through a variety of educational and outreach initiatives. They are embracing the idea that it is not only the experienced who can enjoy and interpret objects, thus building on the concept that a lack of expert knowledge and well-trained interpretative skills on the part of the visitor can be overcome through well thought-out arrangements on the part of the museum. As Hein (1998), Falk and Dierking (2000), Hooper-Greenhill (2000) and others have argued, interpretation is a dynamic relationship in which it is important for visitors to be able to connect what they know and feel with the objects on show. Visitors create meaning and make objects meaningful according to their own experience of life, cognitive frameworks, interpretive communities, meaning-making strategies and, not least, their own personal agendas. Museums that take current educational and communication theory into account have succeeded in creating the circumstances in which encounters between diverse visitors and various types of objects can be both meaningful and enjoyable.

This new educational turnabout aimed at helping visitors with heterogeneous backgrounds and varying levels of experience to interpret museum objects occurs in all kinds of museums. In general, however, museums and other organisations involved with contemporary art are lagging behind, more often than not failing to assist the inexperienced with making sense of what they see. Recent research in Belgium, for example, has shown that such developments in the contemporary art world are in many instances still taking their time (Van Reeth 2009). Curatorial habits, opinions and attitudes regarding the public are slow to change, and the deep divide between curators and educators still persists in too many cases. The primacy of artworks and artists in contemporary art museums stands in the way of an understanding that consideration of the visitor will not mean art being left out of the equation as a result. In a manner of speaking, there is often no equation to speak of as things stand today. The artistic and educational departments each focus on their own area of interest; curators build up their collections and create their exhibitions regardless of future visitors, while educators try to open things up, frequently creating a completely different package of the art on show for different target audiences. Unfortunately, keeping art and visitor conceptually apart in this way is neither elegant nor truly efficient. Nevertheless, art museum practice shows that it does not need to be like this. I discuss two cases below in which it has been inexperienced members of the public rather than expert curators who have produced a contemporary art exhibition. The process involved, as well as the results from these experiments, point to some interesting aspects of the relationship between contemporary art and museum visitors with little or no experience of it.

Two experimental museum projects

Ever since the M HKA's opening in 1987, the largely constructivist-inspired aspirations of its educational department have conflicted with the predominantly art-focused approach of its artistic department. Over time, the museum began to move on occasion away from this classic juxtaposition in search of a balance between these art-focused and visitor-focused approaches. Instead, it tried to focus more on the encounter between artwork and visitor. One of the more interesting lines of investigation at the M HKA concerns experimenting with visitor involvement in the domain, hitherto traditionally exclusive to the artistic sphere, of working with art objects and creating exhibitions. In the two projects of interest here, members of different target audiences were invited to enter into a profound relationship with the artworks in the museum's collection by having an entire exhibition-making process placed in their hands. Both projects were aimed at finding a new, more balanced approach towards the encounter between artwork and visitor through the means of a visitor-driven process. On the one hand, the projects were expected to shed new light on the possible appeal, interpretation and value of the museum's collection regarding different target audiences and, on the other, to create greater intellectual accessibility to the public at large. The educational department took the initiative for the first project. The second one was proposed by the artistic director and then handled by the educational department which may indicate a shift in the museum's vision.

The first project dates from 2000, when teenagers were invited to participate; the initiative fitted in with the museum's educational programme for this target audience. The idea was that younger spectators would be able to relate more easily to a presentation created by their peers, thus drawing them more to contemporary art and museums. A notice was published in the press and, as a result, five participants were grouped together to create a collection presentation. The youngest was 16 years old, the oldest turning 18 on the last day of the show. They all lived and/or went to school in or near Antwerp and were general or art secondary school students. Four were girls; one was a boy. All were native Belgians interested in art, although not with any profound experience of contemporary visual art. Together, they went through a process lasting several months. They were the ones who were really in control; the M HKA's involvement was limited to that of moderator: initiating, sustaining and stimulating the process when necessary. The exhibition ran from 21 May to 31 August 2000 and was situated in three small rooms (approximately $200\,\text{m}^2$) that accommodated fourteen relatively small works of art.

'New Belgians' with North African roots recreated the experiment in 2007. The museum wanted to address visitors less familiar with art and museums due to their different cultural background; the underlying idea was again that a presentation by the visitors' peers would be more familiar to the target audience.

This was organised in collaboration with Moussem, a volunteer organisation established by people of Moroccan descent wanting to present their new homeland with more Arab and Islamic culture, primarily performing arts. A group of eight Moussem volunteers – all being unfamiliar with contemporary visual art – committed themselves to the project. They lived and/or worked in Antwerp and had foreign roots, mainly Moroccan in origin. The volunteers represented a mixture of first and second generation immigrants; there were seven women and one man, all being between 24 and 35 years of age, and they had a variety of professions ranging from labourer to surgeon. Their collection presentation was the result of a year of collaboration and, once again, it was they who were the ones in charge with the museum acting as their coach. The exhibition ran from 15 March to 13 May 2007. The scheme was much more elaborate on this second occasion, resulting in a larger exhibition which occupied the entire second floor (approximately $1,800\,\text{m}^2$) with twenty-six works, including several series, large sculptures and installations.

Influence of level of experience on interpretation and preference

Both projects provide much food for thought. My focus is on what they reveal about the relationships between inexperienced museum visitors (i.e. the participants) and contemporary artworks – especially when compared with one another. More specifically, it is by comparing the actions, interpretations and choices of inexperienced visitors from very different backgrounds being confronted with contemporary visual art that we seem to gain an impression – despite some telling differences – of certain patterns in these relationships, suggesting the existence of more general preferences both in terms of art and in their approach towards interpretation. These preferences appear to differ in some important respects from what one finds more traditionally in contemporary art exhibitions. Consequently, they seem to indicate divergent views on (what is interesting and worthwhile in) contemporary art as held between inexperienced visitors and adept visitors who, as explained above, constitute art museums' typical visitors. Admittedly, the participants could hardly have been called inexperienced by the end of their M HKA adventure. All the same, the scope of their experience was still too narrow to raise them to the level of the typical adept public of culturally cultivated visitors with a profusion of knowledge and skills in the domain of interpreting contemporary art. As indicated previously, the process was directed by the participants themselves with neither group choosing to immerse itself in extensive study or intense interpretive training, instead preferring to discuss the given works together, aided only by the basic information provided by the museum for its audience.

Pursuit of pleasure and emotional experience

Both exhibitions were the result of a long and intensive process during which the participants acquainted themselves with the M HKA collection (and in most cases with contemporary art), next interpreting favourite artworks in order to develop an exhibition concept to guide their final selection and following this up by designing the presentation and interpretive devices for their future public. While not unexpected, it was striking how the participants' intellectual activity concerning learning about contemporary art and creating an exhibition was closely intertwined with the pursuit of pleasure and emotional experiences. As Falk and Dierking (2000: 73) found, 'for the overwhelming majority of museum visitors, education and entertainment are not mutually exclusive motivations for coming to the museum but are complementary aspects of a single, complex leisure experience'. Learning and fun are both elements that visitors seek in their interactions with museum objects, which of course fits in with the idea of an intellectually demanding activity during one's leisure time: it should be pleasurable as well. When asked about their reasons for visiting museums, visitors also occasionally cite 'a desire for an emotional/aesthetic experience' (Falk and Dierking 2000: 72). Especially in art museums, visitors seem to be looking for such experiences in order to connect emotionally, to be carried away, to be able to make free associations and to let their imagination take wing. Just as efficient learning goes hand in hand with fun, so, argues James Young (2001), emotions have an important role to play in the knowledge we can derive from art.

In this respect, the inexperienced visitor appears not to differ from the majority of museum visitors and thus from the adept visitor. In both groups, learning, entertainment and emotional experiences were encountered in nearly all aspects of the process. For instance, the teenagers took pleasure in writing the texts for the catalogue and exhibition labels (each taking on their favourite works), especially enjoying coming up with their own interpretations, subsequently hunting down anything the artists had said concerning the works themselves and then confronting both versions. To take an example, the Moussem group undertook some significant outings together during their interpretive process, such as attending a performance by poet Ramsey Nasr, visiting the Antwerp museum of ethnography and going to the 0110 concerts for tolerance.

Preferences for certain features in art

The first part of the project consisted of exploration, interpretation and selection, and the process was similar in both cases. The participants started out – one more hesitantly than the other – by exploring the collection and thereby different expressions of contemporary art. It was not long before some definite, generally shared preferences began to take shape. Both groups were fairly quick to begin looking for a theme that might dictate their final selection of works, because – within their broad preferences – each of them had developed some very personal relationships with favourite artworks which were too different in respect of content to fit all together and which, in any case, were too numerous to be contained within the space available. The themes were inspired by their own interests and their own interpretation of the artworks, which were allowed free rein separate from orthodox explanations. The 2000 group decided on the theme 'weaknesses', while the 2007 group chose 'identity in relation to society'. Each theme allowed all the participants to include one or more of their favourites. In both cases this resulted in works being selected that were predominantly recognisable, connected to reality and pleasant to look at.

Both selections obviously favoured distinct evocative possibilities: it was clear that the inexperienced participants valued the possibility of 'reading' stories and shared emotions in the artworks over and above more abstract concepts. In addition, the selections also betrayed a sensibility for beautiful images and what one might call the seductiveness of material qualities. As might be expected, this is consistent with Parsons' earlier stages of aesthetic development (Parsons 1987). Works that offered fewer leads, works that referred mainly to art and art theory, and works that offered a visual provocation were conspicuously passed over. Satisfactory interpretation of such works demands a command of the more mature stages of aesthetic development, only to be mastered through extensive experience and learning in art. Where an adept visitor can interpret and appreciate very different art, a less experienced visitor, as can also be discerned in the cases in question, will narrow the choice according to preferences described above: an evocative power with respect to content and/or emotion and a pleasing quality with respect to the image and/or materials.

Two works were selected by both groups, thus emphasising these generally shared preferences: *Spreken* (to speak) by Berlinde De Bruyckere and *Divisione e moltiplicazione dello specchio* (division and multiplication of the mirror) by Michelangelo Pistoletto (Figures 8.1 and 8.2). These works are indeed quite representative of the aforementioned preferences. De Bruyckere's figures are beautiful to look at with a certain translucent quality to the wax and with blankets that appeal to our sense of touch. They evoke strong emotional responses, associations of cuddling

Figure 8.1 Berlinde De Bruyckere, *Spreken*, 1999, M HKA collection.

Figure 8.2 Michelangelo Pistoletto, *Divisione e moltiplicazione dello specchio*, 1978, M HKA collection. Photograph: A4A vzw.

juxtaposed against hiding, of covering juxtaposed against suffocation and of childhood camping juxtaposed against makeshift refugee shelters familiar from the news. As such, the artwork links in with stories ranging from sharing secrets, hiding from the pressures of the world, to fugitives with only a blanket to their names. Pistoletto's work is a large mirror divided into two equal parts mounted in an impressive gilt frame. Visitors are reflected (possibly multiple times and from different angles, depending on how the mirror is set up) and become part of the artwork, asking themselves what reality is, where life stops and art begins, and, more mundanely, whether or not they cut a good figure. They are inspired to contemplate (their own) lives for a moment. Other examples that perfectly illustrate these features so particularly valued in artworks are *Conversation Piece with a Stick* by Juan Muñoz and *Betonmolen* (concrete mixer) by Wim Delvoye (Figures 8.3 and 8.4). Muñoz's bronze sculpture, for instance, has a powerful narrative quality, evoking emotionally rich stories that touch on personal reflections of loneliness and relationships, as well as on broader topics such as social isolation. It is a figurative work that is easy to recognise and to connect with one's own experience, as is the case with Delvoye's concrete mixer. Additionally, both works are interesting to look at, even pleasing to the eye, being clever descendants of a long tradition of classic bronze figures and of ornate craftsmanship, respectively. Evocative power and pleasing visual qualities are not exclusive to figurative work, as illustrated by the inclusion of a work such as *Untitled* by Anish Kapoor (Figure 8.5). This cubic stone with its enigmatic blue hole does not in fact refer to particular events, objects or feelings in everyday life, yet it intrigues and incites poetic reflections on infinity and eternity as well as more mundane speculations concerning how it was made.

Figure 8.3 Juan Muñoz, *Conversation Piece with a Stick*, 1994, M HKA collection. Photograph: Syb'l S. – Pictures.

Figure 8.4 Wim Delvoye, *Betonmolen*, 1993, M HKA collection.

The evidence from these two selections suggests that artworks selected by inexperienced visitors (i.e. the participants) are more intellectually accessible than those in an average art exhibition because they are more connected to familiar experiences, knowledge, thoughts and feelings; they are more evocative and visually attractive, allowing a range of visitors to relate to them. As one visitor to the 2007 exhibition put it: 'your artworks show keen social commitment. Moreover, the meaning is clearer than in many examples of western contemporary art, and the aesthetic style invites to look closely!' On the other hand, this type of selection

Figure 8.5 Anish Kapoor, *Untitled*, 1991, M HKA collection. Photograph: Syb'l S. – Pictures.

also represents just as much of a personal vision as when made by a professional curator – although it is more accessible, one visitor will always be more drawn to it than another. This could be corroborated by the notable difference in the selection of works showing nudity or referring to an erotic theme. The group of teenagers did include such works in their selection (following on their theme of weaknesses) while the Moussem volunteers did not (even though it would have been in line with their theme, but it is not self-evident in their culture). Nevertheless, as one might expect, it is clear that artwork that is less evocative or attractive is less popular with an inexperienced public and therefore needs more attention given to it when exhibited.

Choices regarding interpretation and mediation

During the second part of the project, the participants were asked to develop some mediation tools to help their future visitor's interpretation. Both groups wanted to communicate their chosen theme in the presentation, but their approaches were very different. The 2000 group opted for an itinerary along the course of which their story of weaknesses could clearly unfold, ending in a self-confrontational climax. The 2007 group built its presentation around several smaller clusters connected in some way to identity and society; this was to be experienced independently without a fixed beginning or end. Their titles suited the theme. Concerning 'Watch me (this is my truth)', the 2000 group's intention was to refer to the weaknesses of vanity and arrogance, and to show that, while this was their interpretation, other people might have different ideas (it was by this means that they opened up the storyline). In 'Encounter', the 2007 group wanted to communicate their view of the presentation as a meeting point, where art and visitor would be able to enter into a dialogue and through which works of art would be able to start a discourse between widely divergent people. In addition to the title, both groups created various mediation tools in which their personal experiences were also strongly represented. As a result, the visitor was addressed as an equal by equals; in presenting the interpretations, thoughts and emotions of the teenagers and the Moussem volunteers as valid opinions about art in their respective exhibitions, visitors were encouraged to form their own ideas.

It is clear that the participants took their own experiences as a model for their future public's interaction with the artworks, because they valued these more than the classic approach such as is typically seen in labels and texts in art exhibitions. Therefore, both cases presented a mixture of opening up and directing visitors' interpretations, although each had a different balance. These different approaches seem characteristic in this respect: the teenagers emphasised their vision, while the non-native Belgians were loath to impose this upon the visitor. However, both groups understood the vulnerability of both artwork and visitor in such an open encounter and tried to empower their public by providing their own example while at the same time offering different visions and sufficient openness to safeguard the artworks against any interpretation that was too 'one-dimensional'. Striking was their emphasis on the pleasure of immersing oneself in a work of art once a person has dared to take the first leap.

The participants' views on interpretation and their choices concerning mediation were characterised by strong connections with the interpreter's own experiences, ideas and feelings, an interest in different voices and empowering visitors to do this for themselves and enjoy the experience. As was the case with their selection, their handling of interpretation and mediation departed somewhat from what is customary in a typical contemporary art exhibition. Set against the criteria of constructivism (Hein 1998), their approach was more tailored to the requirements of a wider audience than on average, although the very personal nature of the projects did impose some limitations since the groups always took themselves as points of departure. Nevertheless, comments left by the public at the Encounter exhibition supported the idea that their outlook had been especially visitor-friendly: for example, 'stories . . . everybody's after them. I like yours so far'; 'draws people out' and 'inspiring, carrying, jointly more supportive! Nice to look at, lovely to hear the stories . . .'. However, this appreciation was not the general view given as the museum staff reported some comments about the presentation and mediation's subjectivity; it was made clear that a museum's classic neutral tone of voice was preferred. The museum assessed that these comments had come from adept visitors, and that does seem probable. The adept category of visitor is often critical of comprehensive measures to improve intellectual accessibility (Bourdieu and Darbel 1969), although that is not to say that this group does not appreciate any mediation at all. As pointed out above, the adept visitor and the traditional contemporary art exhibition seem to be more or less balanced in terms of supply and demand: adept visitors usually know their way around art without the need for more extensive and empowering mediation, being able to find any background information they might want via the labels and texts typically provided.

Transcending traditionally defined target group boundaries

Issues relating to participation and intellectual accessibility are often approached on the basis of a target audience concept, as was the case in these two M HKA experiments. Museums habitually divide their audience into target groups based on parameters such as the visitor's education, age and cultural background, and they prepare specific packages for each of these groups. By engaging target group members to create an exhibition, the museum was hoping for a result that would offer greater access to art to that specific target group. The observed differences between the two exhibitions do suggest a certain target group effect. Naturally enough, differences such as the choice of themes, the issue of including or excluding nudity and the matter of confidence in and expression of one's own vision have everything to do with the group that created the exhibition. In this sense, it can be concluded that each project did indeed bear the mark of the group that worked on it and, therefore, was specifically recognisable to that group.

At the same time, however, the M HKA opposes the target group concept in its policy documents, wishing to be accessible to all. In order to increase and broaden its accessibility, it entered into a dialogue with certain inexperienced visitors, hoping to develop strategies that, ideally, would be successful in addressing everyone. It was certainly demonstrated that inexperienced visitors make remarkably similar choices in art and the handling of interpretation and mediation: choices that broaden and increase intellectual accessibility effectively compared with traditional exhibitions. Clearly, this accessibility is neither generally felt nor universal, but the responses that the museum received from the public confirmed that intellectual accessibility increased regardless of traditional target groups.

Therefore, analysis and comparison of these two projects suggest that we need to refine the traditional view concerning the correlation between the engaging power of a contemporary artwork and the specificity of the target group to which the visitor belongs. Consistent with target audience thinking, it was anticipated that two different exhibitions would emerge, each with a distinctive choice of artworks and a characteristic way of approaching the public. However, the actual differences seem minor when compared with their striking similarities. Regardless of the visitor's background as traditionally discerned within target groups (in this case, particularly those differences concerning age, religion and culture), the findings suggest that certain qualities in works of art are more generally preferred, such as a strong evocative power with respect to content and/or emotion and the appeal of the image and/or materials. Clear value was in both cases placed on points of contact with everyday life and with one's own experiences, ideas, feelings and interests. This was not only reflected in the selection of artworks, but also in the handling of interpretation and mediation. These results fit in with current educational and communication theory (Hein 1998; Hooper-Greenhill 2000). Moreover, once initial hesitation and feelings of vulnerability have been overcome, interaction with artworks appears to be generally characterised by the pleasure of interpreting them independently of a prescribed canon and sharing these interpretations with others, ever conscious that the artworks are not pinned down to one interpretation and inviting others to add their own. This sharing of interpretations is indicative of the importance of the social component of learning, as identified, for example, by Falk and Dierking (2000).

Of course, the intention is not to gloss over all individual, cultural, educational and other differences that naturally affect the public's encounters with any part of the material world. Nor is it the intention to give an impression that contemporary art is easy for inexperienced visitors to interpret or natural for them to enjoy. However, both of the projects under discussion here suggest that certain features of contemporary artworks have a marked appeal for inexperienced visitors, notwithstanding their diverse backgrounds. This indicates that certain works of art possess a more general power of attraction for heterogeneous visitors due to the presence of such valued features. Naturally, there could never be any question of confining collections and exhibitions to similar works of art. Nevertheless, these findings might function as an aid to museum staff to assess potentially more difficult artworks and to design appropriate mediation. As for the approach taken with regard to interpretation and mediation, we need to consider the apparent differences between inexperienced and adept visitors: adepts, who appreciate the selected artworks as well as other, for example more art theoretical ones, can be less enthusiastic about far-reaching measures to improve intellectual accessibility. Therefore, concerning target group thinking, it seems that a more relevant distinction should be made between adept and inexperienced visitors, but on the whole we should conclude that the appeal of contemporary art is often underestimated.

Bibliography

Bennett, T. (1995) *The Birth of the Museum: history, theory, politics*, London and New York: Routledge.

Bourdieu, P. and A. Darbel (with D. Schnapper) (1969) *L'Amour de l'Art: les musées d'art européens et leur public* [*The Love of Art: European art museums and their public*] trans. C. Beattie and N. Merriman (1991), Cambridge: Polity Press.

Duncan, C. (1995) *Civilizing Rituals inside Public Art Museums*, London and New York: Routledge.

Falk, J.H. and L.D. Dierking (2000) *Learning from Museums: visitor experiences and the making of meaning*, Walnut Creek, CA: AltaMira Press.

Hein, G.E. (1998) *Learning in the Museum*, London and New York: Routledge.

Hooper-Greenhill, E. (2000) *Museums and the Interpretation of Visual Culture*, London and New York: Routledge.

McClellan, A. (2008) *The Art Museum from Boullée to Bilbao*, Berkeley, Los Angeles and London: University of California Press.

Parsons, M.J. (1987) *How we Understand Art: a cognitive developmental account of aesthetic experience*, Cambridge: Cambridge University Press.

Serota, N. (2000; 1st edn 1996) *Experience or Interpretation: the dilemma of museums of modern art* (Walter Neurath Memorial Lectures, 1996), New York: Thames & Hudson.

Van Reeth, I. (2009) *Bemiddeling tussen kunst en publiek in hedendaagse beeldende kunst*, Research report by order of BAM (Flemish centre for visual, audiovisual and media arts), Ghent.

Young, J.O. (2001) *Art and Knowledge*, London and New York: Routledge.

9 Illuminating narratives

Period rooms and *tableaux vivants*

Michael Katzberg

[T]he manner in which light illuminates an object shapes our impressions and understanding of what we're seeing.

(Gillette 2008: 2)

In 2004, the Metropolitan Museum of Art in New York organised an exhibition entitled *Dangerous Liaisons: Fashion and Furniture in the Eighteenth Century*, curated by Harold Koda and Andrew Bolton. The exhibition took place in the Museum's Fifth Avenue building from 29 April to 6 September 2004, within a suite of period rooms. It was not only a presentation of decorated spaces but was, moreover, a spectacular display of costumes in dynamic interaction with their furnished surroundings. The exhibition showcased costumed mannequins posed in accordance with the norms of eighteenth century demeanour. Because of its presentation techniques and its ability to instruct viewers about eighteenth century social practices, the exhibition occupies a significant position at the intersection of theatricality and didactic display.

In addition to setting the costumes in period rooms rather than in conventional exhibition spaces, the unique aspect of the show was that a *story* was told, aided by the effects of light. Eleven scenes presented in the style of *tableaux vivants* comprised the show, which was based on Choderlos de Laclos' epistolary work *Les Liaisons Dangereuses* (1782) and Jean-François Bastide's libertine novella *La Petite Maison* (1758) (Koda and Bolton 2006: 11). More specifically, the notion of rivalry between the sexes securely links the novels with the exhibition, in which the curators exposed how the elegant artifice of French design became a tool for seduction. The illumination techniques deployed in this exhibition are unusual. They are theatrical and generally uncharacteristic of ethnographic and art historical exhibitions. Philippe de Montebello writes that 'the narratives that linked the rooms [. . .] were a kind of theatre, and unusual for an art museum' (Koda and Bolton 2006: 9).

In this chapter, I first consider the museum's period rooms as theatrical stages where the action of the story takes place. Here, I argue that decorated galleries within the Metropolitan Museum of Art have been transformed into expository dramaturgical spaces where mannequins enact ritualistic scenarios of seduction. As I demonstrate, the curators and creative director have imported theatrical techniques such as staging, lighting and the use of props to intensify the visual presentation of each exhibit. Secondly, I consider the presentation style and techniques deployed to bring this exhibition to fruition. There, I suggest that the presentation style draws influence from painting, literature and the theatre of the period. Specifically, I propose that this exhibition is a narrative story partly told with special illumination effects; one in which chastity is metaphorically hunted. I demonstrate that the exhibitionary story is, in fact, a pictorial text comprised of multiple chapters and I suggest that the inclusion of specialised lighting instruments and effects advance and even propel the narrative of each scene. Finally, I turn my attention to a close analysis and discussion of several key tableaux. Here, I demonstrate the different ways in which light influences viewers' interpretations and contributes to the narrative of *Dangerous Liaisons*. The narrativity of these tableaux will be examined through the framework of Mieke Bal's theory of narratology. In discussing aspects of the illumination deployed throughout *Dangerous Liaisons*, I argue that light does indeed affect the viewer's interpretation of contemporary museum exhibitions by conveying a mood, or a prevailing state of mind through the agency of light as a narrative and rhetorical device.

Period rooms as theatrical stages

Period room displays are a type of exhibitionary technique where museum artefacts are drawn together across typological lines to recreate a decorated space for display purposes. Furniture, decorative arts, inlaid parquet floors, carved ceilings and wall coverings are introduced into a gallery where they are arranged to recreate a generic interior environment characteristic of a historical period. In the case of *Dangerous Liaisons*, an existing suite of period rooms was used for this temporary 'costume' exhibition. These rooms, with names derived from defining characteristics of their furniture, architectural elements and origin, house the museum's renowned collection of European furniture.

What makes this exhibition noteworthy and different from most contemporary period room displays is the inclusion of articulated mannequin figures attired in period costumes. 'While clearly dummies, the figures were posed in naturalistic postures derived from period paintings and prints', write Koda and Bolton (2006: 12). Within these vignettes, figures with names such as 'The Admirer', 'The Voyeur' and 'The Connoisseur' allude to the visuality and the spectacle of the act of looking. 'The Voluptuary', 'The Reckless Suitor' and 'The Girl in Flight' collude to generate an interpretation of libidinous hunting and seduction. The exhibits show how people moved and acted within the confines of (social and physical) spaces and establish a discourse between objects and viewers.

Different sources of light combine in such a manner to create theatrically inspired period rooms. Luminous atmospheres envelop individual exhibits and concurrently, viewers are immersed in these effulgent spaces. The effects of light actively interact with viewers' interpretations of the exhibited artefacts, similar in function to theatrical productions. The curators have also chosen to include 'occupants' within the rooms, which shift the focus from the display of art and architectural elements to that of the interaction of decorative arts with costumed mannequins. The 'population' of these enlivened spaces become actors in the story. In so doing, the curators transformed a display object 'into [a] dramatic subject, a character in interaction with other characters' (Sandberg 2003: 70). Through this rhetorical act, the period rooms are equally transformed into theatrical stages where their costumed occupants become a spectacle for viewers. As Mimi Hellman argues, 'They seem to take on a knowing, conspirational air – poised for our admiration, *inviting us to join the game,* daring us to take a seat' (Hellman 2006: 23; emphasis added). This suggestion facilitates the perspective that the mannequins can and should be interpreted as metaphorical stand-ins for the viewers themselves, which in turn augments their engagement with the objects on display.

Rhetorically speaking, the period rooms become a series of *mise-en-scènes,* the environments in which the exhibition takes place. These period rooms 'shelter' and 'foster' the performance of the story by creating a visually enriching theatrically illuminated environment. In her essay 'Limited visibility', Maaike Bleeker makes a distinction between 'theatrical' and 'theatricality', writing that '[r]ather than define theatre as an unchanging identifiable object in the real, we might rethink it as a culturally conditioned mode of staging the construction of the real' (Bleeker 2007: 150). Bleeker argues that '[t]he theatrical apparatus as "vision machine" stages ways of looking that respond to a particular culturally and historically specific spectator consciousness' and that 'theatre and reality appear as parallel constructions appealing to similar ways of looking' (2007: 326–7). There is an uncertain pressure between similarity and difference which brings Freedman to define theatricality as:

> [T]hat fractured reciprocity whereby beholder and beheld reverse positions in a way that renders a steady position of spectatorship impossible. Theatricality evokes an uncanny sense that the given to be seen has the power both to position us and displace us.
>
> (Freedman 1991: 1)

In these theatricalised spaces viewers are separated by not only a physical barrier, but also by an illumination device. 'To further emphasize the artifice and theatrical nature of the scenarios, [creative director Patrick] Kinmonth introduced footlights to the existing diffuse daylight and candlelight effects of the rooms resulting in an "up-lit" effect of a Watteau painting' (Koda and Bolton 2006: 11), such as in his *Comédie Italienne* (1720). Footlights, or strips of lights arraigned in a linear form, demarcate one zone for spectators and another for the mannequin actors. That is, they create a physical barrier for the spectators and a psychological barrier that contains the dramaturgical players. On the one hand, *Dangerous Liaisons* responds to the eighteenth century spectator consciousness by the way it groups mannequin occupants in a configuration that is historically specific. On the other, the exhibition employs modern delineation devices (footlights acting as barriers) that the modern viewer experiences as a cultural and historical statement.

Tableaux vivants

Dangerous Liaisons consists of exhibit groups presented as *tableaux vivants*. The *Oxford English Dictionary* defines the term as 'a representation of a personage, character, scene, incident, etc., or of a well-known painting or statue, by one person or a group of persons in suitable costumes and attitudes, silent and motionless' ('tableau vivant, n.' *OED Online*). Simply stated, the actors strike a pose. The term describes a visually striking group of figures carefully posed, arranged and, I want to stress, theatrically lit. The parlour game of staging *tableaux vivants* in imitation of well-known paintings was a favourite pastime during the late eighteenth century, 'conceived as a form of edifying sociable re-creation among French aristocracy' (Grey 1997: 39). As Holmström explains, '[t]he purpose of these tableaux was to visualize an historical or literary episode; imitation of the figure composition in some well-known painting was only a means to this end, not an end in itself' (Holmström 1967: 223). Far from an isolated phenomenon, the *tableau vivant* is an act of prolonged or sustained stage direction that has clear links to the theatre, painting and Neapolitan nativity cribs.

These contemporary *tableaux vivants* were created to re-enact scenes of everyday life of the French aristocracy during the eighteenth century. However, strictly speaking they are not actually a 'living' tableau, as the mannequins are not sentient. Rather, they are presented in the tableau style. The authors have invoked the 'slice-of-life model' to borrow a phrase from Mark Sandberg in his *Living Pictures, Missing Persons* (2003: 85). The exhibition's tableaux teach modern viewers not only about how people dressed, but also how they acted in relation to their possessions and surroundings during the eighteenth century because their behaviours are at once similar to, and yet different from our own. They are familiar and relatable and thus enhance the mutual interaction of modern viewers and objects. I would suggest that *Dangerous Liaisons* exploits these interactions successfully and creatively. This approach marries the art forms of the stage with painting and exhibition design.

In the exhibition spaces of *Dangerous Liaisons* the *tableau vivant* was adapted as a vehicle to display period costumes in dramatic and reciprocal interaction with furnishings of the period. From the *tableau vivant* as a parlour game it took the domestic setting and its inspiration for posing mannequins in 'real-life' situations that demonstrate social mannerisms, etiquette and seductive rituals of the period. It should be highlighted here that previously mentioned texts of the period played an important part in the inspiration and didactic content of this exhibition. These texts are interpreted by the curators by visual means: using presentation techniques that allow the texts and viewers to interact and engage with one another. As in all these historical forms of the *tableau vivant*, light is central to the contemporary exhibition.

A difference between the exhibition *tableaux vivants* and the historical forms concerns the fact that the exhibition's figures do not re-enact an actual historic, pictorial or literary episode; they depict a generalised social discourse through the reciprocal interaction of mannequins. The figures in fact acquire, in Sandberg's words, 'an impression of life through the display's relational structures (dead/ alive, sleeping/walking, unconscious/conscious)' (2003: 91). Thus, in the exhibition, mannequins imitate eighteenth century personages attired and posed in compositions similar to painted depictions and literary descriptions of the period, while at the same time drawing influence from the theatre of the same era. Various media are at work in the exhibition which fuses theatre with 'tableau' in the sense of painting. The raising of the curtain at the Comédie Italienne's Paris performance of *Les Noces d'Arlequin* (1761) is significant in this regard because in *Dangerous Liaisons* the figure in the opening tableau or prologue ('The Connoisseur') ushers in the visitors and admits their entrance to the exhibition by raising his curtain. In a way, this also makes the viewers part of the theatrical spectacle. They need to enact this ritual of passing through in order to enter the exhibition.

All of the figures are engaged with one another, appearing as if they were 'at home' in these spaces where acts of seduction take place, viewed through a voyeuristic mode of looking. 'Every amorous episode can be [. . . .] endowed with a meaning: it is generated, develops, and dies [. . . .] this is the *love story*' writes Roland Barthes in *A Lover's Discourse* (1979: 7). With each successive scene the viewer is seduced into making meaning aided by illumination.

In addition, the figures are depicted as being 'absorbed', in Michael Fried's sense of the term. He defines this frame of mind as 'the state or condition of rapt attention, of being completely occupied or engrossed or [. . . .] absorbed in what he or she is doing, hearing, thinking, feeling' (Fried 1980: 10). In his book *Absorption and Theatricality*, Fried argues that:

> The depiction of figures involved in 'absorptive' tasks or situations requiring concentration turns them inward on the depicted world; their apparent obliviousness of the painting's beholder in turn frees up that observing position for a voyeuristic appreciation of the scene.
>
> (Fried 1980: 87)

Their absorption means that viewers are at once physically present but not acknowledged or involved in the action and hence adopt a voyeuristic mode of interaction. *Dangerous Liaisons*' tableaux are carefully staged exhibits which, I propose, include absorbed figures within extended theatrical scenes which facilitate a voyeuristic mode of looking (Fried 1980, Bal 1991).

Narrative exhibition

Dangerous Liaisons actualises the dramatically forceful tableau exhibition technique, which is clearly narrative on several rhetorical levels. Bal, in *Narratology*, argues that '[a] *narrative text* is a text in which an agent relates ("tells") a story in a particular medium, such as language, imagery, sound, buildings, or a combination thereof' (Bal 1996: 5). I consider the exhibition as a narrative text that utilises the medium of imagery. Each vignette is a chapter in this visual exhibitionary narrative. The story is not only comprised of the exhibits themselves, but also

Figure 9.1 (a) 'Déclaration de la Grossesse'; (b) 'Le Souper fin', Jean-Michel Moreau le Jeune. *Monument du costume physique et moral de la fin du dix-huitième siècle ou tableaux de la vie, ornés de figures dessinées et gravées/par Moreau le jeune et par d'autres célèbres Artistes.* 1789. Neuwied sur le Rhin. Courtesy of the Universiteit Leiden.

of the illumination used. The story layering is further complicated by the use of visual 'texts' such as Jean-Michel Moreau le Jeune's *Monument du Costume* (1789) on which the composition of several tableaux is based. This is particularly evident in the composition of 'The Levée' corresponding to an engraving entitled the 'Déclaration de la Grossesse' (Figure 9.1a) and 'The Card Game' which is similar to 'Le Souper fin' (Figure 9.1b).

Specifically, the tableaux of *Dangerous Liaisons* can be compared to the events in a libertine novel, a popular literary genre during the period under discussion here. Libertine writers like the Marquis de Sade, Denis Diderot and John Wilmot espoused ideals that in modern times are associated with sadomasochism, nihilism and free love. In libertine novels, themes included anti-clericalism, anti-establishmentarianism, eroticism, deception, seduction and the corruption of innocence. In *Dangerous Liaisons*, each tableau expresses some aspect of libidinal life that could have easily found its way into libertine novels such as *La Petite Maison* in which similar episodes appear.

The staging and illumination of the tableaux make statements about the way courtship may have been conducted. For instance, in 'The Music Lesson', the authors have placed a figure entitled 'The Chaperone' peering from behind a screen to oversee the progress of the lesson. By placing 'The Chaperone' in such a position, she leads the viewer to believe there is something going on that may be improper and requires surveillance. By deploying a light to increase the localised brightness on this figure, the curators make a statement that she is important to the narrative. The tableaux are staged in such a way as to present to viewers not a mere display of clothes, but a drama set in motion by mannequin actors. This drama is a rich concoction of historically based fiction supported by genuine costumes, props and set decorations. Furthermore, this vision is 'focused by a subjective point of view, an agent of vision whose view of the events will influence our interpretation of them' (Bal 1996: 270). I consider the mannequins to be agents of vision acting as rhetorical figures: the seducer and the seduced. This demonstrates how the technical aspects of the exhibition enact intellectual discourse, which is indeed at the core of this chapter.

Viewers of this exhibition can switch viewing positions between their own and that of the seducer and seduced, or, in narratological terms, the focalisors. In *Narratology*, Bal defines focalisation as 'the relationship between the "vision," the agent that sees, and that which is seen' (1996: 146). In this case, viewers can 'read' the exhibition from another subjective viewing position, as if from the position of the focalising figures. The mannequins focus the viewer's vision, so to speak. The focalisors 'show' viewers a subjectivised array wherein they are the focus of the story, and, simultaneously, focus our eyes through their vision of the action. Significantly, in a visual display, lighting takes on part of the task of organising and assigning focalisation. Although there are many differences between painting, theatre and museums, the impact of light on the way we as viewers perceive the represented story is one thread that runs through them all.

Thus, in *Dangerous Liaisons*, the illumination is deployed in service of the narrative. That is, the illumination helps tell the story and focalise it through its effects. Through the effects of a theatricalised light, the deployment of strategically focused devices, the tableaux become alive with activity. The addition of visible theatrical instruments into the galleries enhances the effectiveness of the exhibition technique and propels the agency of the exhibitionary story. For example, in 'The Withdrawing Room', a woman has fainted, and is lying facedown on the floor with two other women about to attend to her. This dramatic action is highlighted by conical shafts of light and a localised light pool that falls on 'The Fainter'.

In order to argue this point, I distinguish three (rhetorical) levels regarding light and compare them with Bal's narratological levels, which become the basis for my discussions of several key tableaux below. I will call the first rhetorical level the *technique level* which is compared with the narratological text level. On this level I place the luminaires and their physical position within the rooms in relation to the beholding viewer: for instance, the distribution, intensity or colour of the light used to illuminate aspects of the tableaux.[1]

Light as a tool is located on the second *agency level* which is compared with the narratological level of focalisation. On this level, light acts as a kind of agent, which determines how and what is rendered visible or, conversely, what remains unlit and obscured. As such, it not only influences the narrative through suggestion, emphasis or the degree to which the beam of light is narrowly or broadly focused, but it supports, and propels the narrative.

On the third rhetorical *elemental level*, light functions as a device on the narratological fabula level, which Bal defines as 'a series of logically and chronologically related events' (1996: 5). Various times of day are depicted in the fabula: from morning through to late night and on to the early morning hours. Light is deployed to develop the temporal perspective of the exhibition. Narrative chronology is created by the ways in which light is distributed within each tableau. Streaming sunlight through a window or the warm glow of candlelight orients viewers' interpretation of a particular tableau. Visual chronology was also created by using colour media.[2]

It is almost impossible to discuss one rhetorical level without touching upon another. These levels are not distinct; they accrete and coalesce. For example, the technique level combines with the elemental level when artificial sunlight, projected through a false window, orients viewers' perceptions of chronology, such as in 'The Levée' and 'The Music Lesson'. And the agency level interacts with technique level when a candelabrum is 'lit' and deployed to illuminate wooden inlays of a side table, such as in 'The Card Game'.

Light in painting and the theatre arts

Creators of eighteenth century *tableaux vivants* drew inspiration from paintings with depictions of historical events and used the lighting conditions as a basis for the illumination of their 'living pictures'. In *Lighting in the Theatre*, Gösta Bergman identifies 'two early declarations of principle about differentiated stage lighting with reference to painting' (Bergman 1977: 178). One was made by Count Francesco Algarotti in his *Essai sur l'opéra* (1755). 'Algarotti dreamt of an art form, where all the elements: text, music, singers, scenery, [and] light co-operate to form a whole [. . . .]. Algarotti sees Rembrandt's *clair-obscure* transported for the stage, the light and shade [. . . .] that calls forth a sense of atmosphere' (Bergman 1977: 178). A 'sense of atmosphere' created by lighting effects can be observed in many eighteenth century paintings, especially works by Joseph Wright of Derby, Jean-Honoré Fragonard and Jean Antoine Watteau, which are intentionally similar to lighting effects observable in the exhibition.

Segueing from a historical to a contemporary application, what we see in 'The Connoisseur' is a modelling of light that gives volume to the scene or, as Gillette proposes: '[l]ight can be thought of as a plastic sculptural medium that is used to reveal form through the creation of a pattern of highlight and shadow' (Gillette 2008: 8). The relief forms of the embroidery and, moreover, the cut and proportions of the suit are revealed by the creation of shadows, highlights and brightness gradients. Thus, the appearance of the tableaux is altered to a great extent by this modelling effect. Gillette argues that 'dramatic changes in meaning can be affected by simply changing or reversing the normal patterns of highlight and shade' (2008: 10). Supplementing this idea, I would like to suggest that the meaning of the tableaux is not merely affected but even created through a variation in lighting patterns. To some extent this technique is deployed in all of the tableaux. The use of footlights adds a theatrical dimension, while still retaining a sense of realism requisite for this type of exhibition. As a result of the illumination, a message is conveyed that implies something, creates a mood and encourages viewers to engage with the narrative of the tableaux. Light adds to the illusion of the visual text by enhancing the exhibition's narrative and visual attributes. It presents the curator with a tool that can be focused to highlight different aspects of the exhibitionary story. For example, in 'The Withdrawing Room' pools of light illuminate both single figures and groups. They have a distributive rhythm and are therefore on the technique level of the narrative rhetoric.

Light in this tableau not only illuminates the scene in a theatrical manner, but also acts as what Bergman calls a 'binding agent' (1977: 11). It facilitates cohesiveness between the various scenic elements. On the level of technique, a semi-focused light illuminates the figure and makes shadows possible in 'The Connoisseur'. The figure is illuminated by lights that create sharp-edged shadows on the curtain and the wooden crate-cum-plinth. Based on a consideration of the shadow patterns, it can be deduced that the primary light source enters this tableau from stage left at a low angle and travels upward, giving the scene an uplit effect similar to Watteau's paintings. Rhetorically speaking, light on the agency level makes connections between the scenic elements and the elevated figure, while creating a visual wholeness from disparate elements.

Light as agent further 'conveys a lulling suggestion of illusory reality, the atmospheric light that helps the spectator to identify himself with the parts and settings of the stage' (Bergman 1977: 13). Light acting in such a manner facilitates the figuration of the viewer. One way in which light propels the exhibitionary narrative is by facilitating a change of viewing positions. Viewers can enter into the narrative 'through' 'The Connoisseur'. The viewer can, by proxy, see him or herself through his eyes. Viewers' interpretations of the tableau are influenced by the luminous atmosphere created by the active agency of light which binds the seen, seer and scene. We now see what he sees, focalised from his point of view. What we now also see is the subjectivity of his sight.

Every light has been placed intentionally to contribute to the performance of the story in one way or another. Viewers progress through several stages of daylight illumination. On the elemental and agency levels of 'The Levée', light acts to produce a bright sunny morning. Light on the agency level is vibrant and cheery; on the elemental level it signifies the early time of day. A mental image of an unseen morning sun is conveyed by the light entering through the blind-window apertures, and also by the highly contrasting and defined shadow patterns that appear on the figures. The light reflected from the floor is diffused and appears as if it is emanating from window openings.

In this tableau, light not only transmits messages about chronology and time of day, but it also transmits interpretable messages about feelings, moods and social relations. The illuminations of *Dangerous Liaisons* echo a reaction to an even, unaccentuated style of lighting. This is dramatically evident in 'The Card Game' where the luminous landscape is populated by pools of light amongst the shadows. Unevenly distributed light punctuates and illuminates some areas more brightly than others. A diminutive table-top lamp, gilded girandoles and a central chandelier distribute light disproportionately across the visual array.

The addition of footlights has skewed the scene visually by adding a light from an improbable position. This augmentation adds to the theatricality – breaching the illusion of seeing figures in their 'homes' – and transmits a message that this scene is not to be interpreted as being realistically depicted; it is a re-enactment; a theatrical contrivance and the illumination tells us so. On the agency level, the variations in intensity instruct us where to look. The skewing of the scene and the highlighting of figures enriches the visual spectacle by reversing or altering the viewer's perception of 'normal' shadow and highlight patterns. Placing a light below or spotlighting a figure changes the viewer's psychological interpretation of the scene and is a further example of light acting as narrator and agent. The deployment of simulated moonlight seen through the windows lies rhetorically on both the agency and elemental levels. The moonbeam-effect beyond the window demonstrates that the scene is set at night. I propose that the moonlight rhetorically frames the tableau in this way. Moonlight acts in more ways than modelling; it tells time and is consequently located on the elemental level, where time and chronology reside. However, if the moonlight is understood as a mood-inducing effect, it is therefore located on the agency level. The moonlight is theatrical in the sense that evokes action; the viewer must suspend their disbelief because, as we well know, moonlight cannot stream into the exhibition space.

Directing the viewer's attention with light to a specific area of an exhibit entices our eyes to look selectively at different elements such as the costumed figures, furniture and architectural embellishments. In so doing, other areas of the tableau become less brightly lit and of secondary importance. This creates what Christopher Cuttle calls in *Lighting by Design* an 'illumination hierarchy' whereby the perception and subsequent interpretation of object attributes, is significantly affected (Cuttle 2003: 66). A visual hierarchy was created in 'The Withdrawing Room' which facilitates viewers' interpretative abilities by punctuating the narrative with light. Variable intensities of luminance within each tableau guide interpretations of the narrative in continuous dialogue with its viewers by challenging our eyes to move about and search out the brighter highlighted areas. But we are also intrigued by darkness, drawn to try and make out what remains hidden, in for example, 'The Shop: The Obstruction'. By selectively illuminating different aspects of a display, the authors describe with light and darkness, while writing the so-called sentences of the exhibitionary narrative.

In this epilogue, light works differently from the previous scenes in order to create a silhouette. On the level of technique, the silhouette-effect produces a view, usually in black, consisting of a profile outline and a featureless interior. In this tableau, the figures are seen in semi-silhouette against a backdrop. Differences in light and darkness, including shadows, also advance the narrative effects by creating an appropriate mood. Victor Stoichita writes in *A Short History of the Shadow* that the 'shadow had been integrated into the area of a complex representation to suggest the third dimension – volume, relief, the body' (Stoichita 1997: 7). By rendering shadow, Kinmonth not only integrated the bodily figures into the staged narrative, but he did so with the effects of the absence of light. Thus, 'darkness and light can be introduced as important elements to create the right atmosphere' (Bergman 1977: 181). This creates an illusory, poetic style of lighting within the tableaux with a direct link to painting of the period. On the rhetorical level of agency this effect obscures our vision of the events. This in itself is unusual for museums, as they do not normally obscure viewers' vision but generally try to increase visual acuity and develop the way objects and people interact. It is not what museum visitors are accustomed to seeing. This is significant precisely because it flouts convention and supports the narratological theatricality of the exhibition. However, judging by the semi-concealed poses of the figures, it is indeed clear that 'The Girl in Flight' is attempting to extricate herself from the clutches of 'The Reckless Suitor'. Not only does the silhouette-effect add depth to the scene, but it visually separates the figures from the background.

On the basis of these analyses, it is clear that illuminations of the tableaux are not uniform. The lighting is differentiated and unevenly distributed across the visual scene, and many parts of the fabula (a figure, an object or grouping) are highlighted – or actually spotlighted – through the use of lighting effects similar to those employed in painting and theatre. Furthermore, lighter and darker areas have been created within the tableaux in order to motivate the attention of the viewing public and to convey a feeling or accentuate an action. The luminous atmospheres of *Dangerous Liaisons* are the result of an artistic process wherein messages are communicated to viewers. Light is used to convey meaning through the use of *distribution, intensity* and *colour*; it therefore has an effect on objects and the way viewers perceive them. Lighting theories and techniques first developed during the eighteenth century have been thus transferred to a twenty-first century museum setting. One of a museum's primary functions is to exhibit, and the way in which objects and artefacts are lit contributes to way they are perceived by the viewer. The choices about the lighting are neither purely utilitarian nor arbitrary; instead, they expose the judgement or opinion of the curators about an object. By providing light that is not just utilitarian in nature agents expose objects, physically and rhetorically, including surface attributes and internal qualities. At the same time, they make a pedagogical argument with the effects of light through the discourse of the museum and interpretation by the viewer. In line with Bal's work, I suggest that this specific way of exposing objects in a museum constitutes a dialogic relationship between viewers and objects. Light is one of the tools, or mediums, that establish such relationships.

Acknowledgements

Dr Hanneke Grootenboer (St Peter's College, University of Oxford) deserves much appreciation for first drawing my attention to this exhibition. Images of the exhibition can be found at: http://www.metmuseum.org/special/Dangerous_Liaisons/fashion_images.htm

I would also like to express my sincerest gratitude to Academy Professor Mieke Bal (ASCA, Universiteit van Amsterdam) for her critical remarks on earlier drafts of this chapter and especially for her personal tutelage.

Notes

1 For more on these controllable qualities of light see Gillette (2008) especially chapter 1, 'Controllable qualities of light'; Keller (2006) especially the chapter entitled 'Choosing lighting angles'; and Cuttle (2003, 2007), especially 'Visible characteristics of lighting' (2003, chapter 2).
2 For a full description of the physical and psychological associations of coloured light see Keller (2006).

Bibliography

Bal, M.G. (1991) *Reading Rembrandt: beyond the word-image opposition*, Cambridge: Cambridge University Press.

Bal, M.G. (1996) *Narratology: introduction to the theory of narrative*, Toronto: University of Toronto Press.

Barthes, R. (1979) *A Lover's Discourse* (trans. R. Howard), London: Jonathan Cape.

Bastide (de), J-F. (1758) *La Petite Maison*; reprinted in R. El-Khoury (trans.) *The Little House: an architectural seduction* (1996), New York: Princeton Architectural Press.

Bergman, G.M. (1977) *Lighting in the Theatre*, Stockholm: Almqvist and Wiksell.

Bleeker, M. (2007) 'Limited visibility', in M.G. Bal and M-Á. Hernández-Navarro (eds) *Migratory Politics: technology, time, performativity*, Amsterdam: ASCA Press, pp. 317–40.

Cuttle, C. (2003) *Lighting by Design*, Oxford and Burlington, MA: Architectural Press.

Cuttle, C. (2007) *Light for Art's Sake: lighting for artworks and museum displays*, Amsterdam: Elsevier.

Freedman, B. (1991) *Staging the Gaze: postmodernism, psychoanalysis, and Shakespearean comedy*, Ithaca and London: Cornell University Press.

Fried, M. (1980) *Absorption and Theatricality: painting and beholder in the age of Diderot*, Berkeley: University of California Press.

Gillette, J.M. (2008) *Designing with Light: an introduction to stage lighting*, 5th edn, Boston: McGraw-Hill.

Grey, T.S. (1997) 'Tableaux vivants: landscape, history painting, and the visual imagination in Mendelssohn's orchestral music', *19th Century Music*, 21.1: 38–76.

Hellman, M. (2006) 'Interior motives: seduction by decoration in eighteenth-century France', in H. Koda and A. Bolton (eds) *Dangerous Liaisons: fashion and furniture in the eighteenth century*, New York and New Haven: Yale University Press, pp. 15–23.

Holmström, K.G. (1967) *Monodrama Attitudes Tableaux Vivants: studies on some trends of theatrical fashion 1770–1815*, Stockholm and Uppsala: Almqvist & Wiksell.

Keller, M. (2006) *Light Fantastic: the art and design of stage lighting*, 2nd edn, Munich: Prestel.

Koda, H. and A. Bolton (2006) *Dangerous Liaisons: fashion and furniture in the eighteenth century*, New York and New Haven: Yale University Press.

Oxford English Dictionary (2004) '*tableau vivant*, n.' *OED Online*. Draft revision. Oxford University Press, online. Available at: http://oed.com/ (Accessed 6 May 2007).

Sandberg, M.B. (2003) *Living Pictures, Missing Persons: mannequins, museums and modernity*, Princeton and Oxford: Princeton University Press.

Stoichita, V. (1997) *A Short History of the Shadow*, London: Reaktion Books.

10 Magic objects/modern objects

Heroes' house museums

Linda Young

Introduction

Museums are often compared with temples as the religious sites of the modern age, and museum visiting is correspondingly regarded as a ritual enactment of communion with the sacred values of modern society. The church built on faith and the museum grounded in science constitute an institutional binary that bookends the great shift of modern society that Weber called the disenchantment of the world. Yet more and more cases are being presented to suggest that magical modes of understanding not only persist but thrive in the shadow of the dominant ideology of authoritative, scientific knowledge (Hughey 1979, Saler 2006). Cases of persistent magical thinking are partly fed by resistance and may be dedicated to undermining the scientific paradigm, such as alternative medicine; and are partly condoned by the majority view, permitted in some circumstances, even enjoyed in a playful suspension of disbelief, as with astrology. Further, some magical survivals translate fluently into the modern era under the rubric of civil religion, the mightily effective mobilisation of the forms of ecclesiastical religion to the service of the state, epitomised by rituals of patriotism.

Despite the reputation of the museum as a peak location of scientific knowledge, the institution can also be seen to contain, express and even exploit many tenacious habits of magical thought. One technique is the reverent stress on collections as 'the real thing', projecting the rhetoric of authenticity in support of the special value of the museum, yet simultaneously deploying the physical form of the sacred shrine. Another is the trend to affective, experiential modes of interpretation which focus on visitors' emotional responses to collections and exhibitions.

This chapter explores how these and other magic-based expressions are brought to bear in what would seem to be the disenchantment of the shrine when transformed into a museum. The relics of culture heroes are often collected individually, and are sometimes preserved in the entirety of the hero's dwelling, in which case the house as well as its contents function as a shrine under the name of house museum. The cottage, house or mansion is decked with historical apparatus that guarantee the meaning of the museum visit, whether it is intact and *in situ*, partial or even retro-created. The house museum is managed according to professional standards of access, conservation and security. At the same time, an unspoken agenda permits and encourages visitor communion with the hero in frankly worshipful terms – often inarticulate, for how can a thoroughly modern institution explicitly condone forms of magic-based apprehension?

To make sense of a visit, the ritual of communion requires that visitors arrive with at least some knowledge of the hero, enough to inform the value of a visit. To a degree, it can be taken for granted with a Shakespeare or a Washington. But in the case of heroes of another age who are known only vaguely by today's audiences, the sense of communion may be fed by the post-modern discourse of celebrity, in a curated vision of the private life of someone 'well known for being well known'. The highly personalised presentation of the hero's domestic circumstances can be traced to social history interpretive approaches, but it also happens to correspond neatly with the contemporary style of personal revelation that encourages onlookers to consider themselves intimate participants in another's life. Theorists of celebrity concur that the interaction generated between celebrity and beholder is a site of interrogation and elaboration of cultural identity which contributes to the integration and normalising of identity construction, a view not distant from sociological approaches to the functions of religion, and with refractions on the social role of museums (Turner 2006: 23–6). The conundrums of these entangled modes of apprehension and presentation indicate that heroes' houses and their contents present museological dilemmas beyond the usual challenges that museums engage every day.

This chapter focuses on a sub-species of culture heroes' houses – those that have been entirely relocated from their original sites. They are not as rare as one might think, and their translation from site to site stresses the relic-nature of the building itself in its new career as a museum. Starting with the precursor of a house-relic with enduring magico-religious significance, the Santa Casa of Loreto, the continuity of the practice into the modern era of the house museum is demonstrated by Abraham Lincoln's birthplace home in Kentucky, via a parallel problematisation of authenticity, relics and faith. A case study of Captain Cook's cottage in Melbourne suggests that what motivates the continuing public interest in heroes' houses is the survival of the pre-modern mentality of magical thinking that continues to penetrate a generally secular, rational, managerial world, now enhanced by the concept of celebrity.

Two houses translated

It is said that in 1291, a stone cottage was carried by angels from Nazareth in Palestine to Tersato in Illyria (Croatia) and, in 1294, was again transported by angels across the Adriatic to a village near Ancona, where, after another small hop, it settled in a laurel grove. The trees gave the name Loreto to the structure, which was acclaimed as the very house where the Virgin Mary had received the Annunciation and where the Holy Family subsequently brought up the Christ Child. In Loreto, the cottage (roofless, but containing a door and a window) was enclosed in a basilica built about 1470, and encased in a magnificent carved

Figure 10.1 The marble screen designed by Bramante in 1517–33, set with sculpture and reliefs by several Renaissance sculptors, to enclose the three brick and stone walls of the Santa Casa. Photograph by courtesy of Carlo Bononi, 2008.

marble screen (Figure 10.1). Known as the Santa Casa or Holy House, it became a popular shrine, attested by papal blessings and continuing pilgrim devotion, specially by women (Meistermann 1911, Thurston 1912).

In 1911, another cottage was relocated to a temple-shrine in Hodgenville, Kentucky, on the site of the farm where Abraham Lincoln was born and lived his first two years. A single room built of notched logs, it exemplified the American pioneer cabin tradition, demonstrating the humble origins of the sixteenth President of the United States. After the Lincoln family moved on, the cabin logs were said to have been reused on an adjacent farm; they and the Lincoln site were purchased by an entrepreneur in 1894, and the cabin re-erected on site in

Figure 10.2 The Memorial Building constructed to shelter the reconstructed logs of the cabin in which Lincoln was claimed to have been born in 1809. Photograph by courtesy of the National Park Service.

1895. Thereafter the now well-travelled logs were demounted and exhibited, reconstructed, in various cities for some years. The site was sold in 1905, the logs having also passed on in ownership. The property was acquired by a benefactor who established the Lincoln Farm Association in 1906, when the cabin logs were also purchased for $1000 and returned in triumph, their authenticity was affirmed by old timers (suppressing the doubts of others). The Association commissioned an imposing neo-classical temple to house the yet-again reconstructed cabin (Figure 10.2), and when it opened in 1911, transferred the site to the state; in 1916, it shifted to US federal government ownership, and has been managed by the National Parks Service since 1933 (Peterson 1968: chapters 2 and 3).

The Santa Casa of Loreto constitutes an illustrious source of the tradition of the house of a great person being translated into a shrine to its inhabitant, and the Lincoln Birthplace Historic Site proves how the tradition endured. Both structures have been critiqued in modern times for doubtful historical provenance. Addressing this problem, the judgement of religious authority applies equally to its modern manifestation in the civil religion of heritage: both regimes have struggled with histories, proofs, revisionisms and, in the end, with the kernel of faith. In fact, management agency sources on both the Santa Casa and the Lincoln Birthplace now acknowledge that each is more an object of inspirational faith than a historical reality. At the same time, in contemporary popular belief, the rationale for preserving houses associated with heroes, sacred or secular, remains fundamentally justified by the claims of the built fabric to authenticity.

Authenticity and faith

The Santa Casa's authenticity was reviewed by the Roman Catholic Church in the early twentieth century, surveying knowledge about the house's career in Palestine and in Italy (Figure 10.3). Church historians traced pilgrim sources

Figure 10.3 The walls of the Santa Casa bear some patchy fresco survivals; the room
contains the 1921 replacement of an older statue of the Virgin, her robe
adorned with jewellery – the traditional offering at this site. © P. Ferdinando,
Santuario della Santa Casa, Loreto.

demonstrating that a basilica had been erected around the Virgin's house in
Nazareth very early in Christian history, perhaps in the fourth century. The
Muslim conquest of Palestine in 637 introduced conflict over the site for many
centuries, but the basilica was definitively destroyed by 1010, then rebuilt by
Crusaders in 1101, and destroyed again in 1263. Not until 1620 was another
church constructed on the site, by then structure-less and referred to as the Grotto
of the Annunciation. At the same time, Church scholars largely agreed that no
reliable records described the Santa Casa's presence in Italy before the fifteenth
century, but that a church dedicated to the Virgin had existed on the Loreto site
since the thirteenth century. The historicity of Mary's house in either Palestine
or Italy had to be acknowledged as dubious.[1] The *Catholic Encyclopedia* sidesteps
the obvious conclusion with the gesture that faith trumps reality: 'there is no
reason to doubt that the simple faith of those who in all confidence have sought
help at this shrine of the Mother of God may often have been rewarded, even
miraculously' (Thurston 1912).

The authenticity of Lincoln's birthplace was initially founded on affidavits by
old residents, while a handful of dissenters were not asked to make statements.
All doubt was sidelined at the time the Lincoln Farm Association began its commemorative project, and again in 1933 when the National Park Service took
control. In 1948, an amateur historian published a devastating analysis of the
presentation, arguing that the cabin was a hoax (Hays 1948). The Park Service
responded with its own research, which supported the critique, though not the
implication of intent to deceive. But recognising that the cabin had metastasised
into a key element of the legend of the martyred president, which could not be

Figure 10.4 The cabin reconstructed of logs which might have housed Abraham Lincoln's
birth in 1809 – now enclosed in a Doric temple built in 1911. Photograph by
courtesy of April Rygg, 2009.

simply abolished, staff introduced the descriptive qualification, the 'traditional'
birthplace of Lincoln – a distinction with 'authentic' that, they acknowledged,
escaped most visitors. Presentation of the cabin within the temple in the formal
landscape is today more forthright (Figure 10.4), being referred to as a 'symbolic'
birthplace, and paired with a second cabin, ten miles away at Knob Creek, where
Lincoln lived from the age of two to seven. The Knob Creek cabin is frankly a
replica, fully furnished, as is a third Lincoln childhood cabin near Lincoln City,
Indiana.[2] The abundance of houses associated with Lincoln points most obviously
to the sacral character of the hero's touch and the faith it evokes, yet all contain
an element of the real history of the man, a 'factual' basis of belief. As a former
Chief Historian of the NPS reflected on the mediating role of the authorising
agency: 'The public's perception of the Lincoln cabin is important to the nation's
image and an indispensable part of the nation's ritualistic public tribute to its
own humble origins' (Pitcaithley 2001: 252, Steers 2007: 2).

    'Authenticity is a slippery topic' writes Peter Howard with brief understatement.
In a heroic effort to address the topic in textbook dimensions, he tabulates nine
fields in which authenticity is discussed within the heritage business: authenticity
of material, creator, function, history, ensemble, style, context and experience
(Howard 2003: 227). The spectrum of applications indicates the possibilities for
multiple and interpreted authenticities, comprehensively undermining the concept
of unique truth. Indeed, the arguments against authenticity as an absolute are
blunt. Ontology posits that if something exists in certain conditions, then it is
necessarily authentic within those conditions (Muñoz-Vinas 2005: 94). Change
the conditions and authenticity persists in line with the changes. This points to the
problem of the essentialist view that the material character of things defines their
authenticity. If changes to the fabric affect the authenticity of the item, as held
by the dominant modern conservation focus on original materials and historically

correct technique, then the passage of time and its historic evidence inevitably distort the 'truth' of things – a classical dilemma of conservation (Phillips 1997: 42–3). Further in this direction, the emphasis that Western thought puts on the first, the oldest, the original, endows these conditions with an apparently natural primacy or authenticity, which devalues subsequent eras and manifestations of objects' careers. Thus, to acknowledge a range of possible authenticities demonstrates that, unless limits are specified (contingently admitting the existence of other limits), a judgement of authenticity is an argument of conviction. In other words, recognising authenticity is a choice, a taste, an act of faith, imbuing the believer with agency. The willingness of the subject to believe goes far to relieve the managing authority of charges of duplicity (especially if alternative information is available in some form), thus locating the act of faith in the field of heritage as social practice.

Faith in authenticity is easier to interrogate at the coalface of managing its manifestations than in the interface with the minds and hearts of believers (Starn 2002: 1–16). Priests and heritage stewards possess the specialist knowledge and intellectual techniques to justify their decisions, which may derive from complex, even casuistical, processes. Reflecting on shifts in understanding authenticity over thirty years of heritage conservation practice, David Lowenthal traces the history of contemporary professional judgement which now comes to the conclusion that no criterion of authenticity is valid for all times and cultures. In fact, he suggests that it can be acknowledged that 'The dynamic processes of change are now more durably authentic than their transitory products', and he uses the argument to call for a more humble and tolerant approach to the authenticities of other times and cultures (Lowenthal 2008). It is an appropriate lesson for the agents of authenticity-management and it also addresses the integrity of the faithful, who comprise the larger part of the authenticity-appreciation equation.

The pilgrims and tourists who visit the Santa Casa and the Lincoln Birthplace anticipate a spiritual satisfaction or emotional affect beyond the rational order of things. It was the normative mentality in the Middle Ages, which is assumed to have been overtaken by modern values and behaviours – yet the enchantments of magical explanation clearly infiltrate more than a few institutions of modernity. A growing number of revisionist challenges to the Weberian secularisation thesis demonstrates that residual irrationalities abound, and, combined with the willing suspension of disbelief for faith-sustaining, romantic or utilitarian purposes, enable a current of Frazerian magic to be observed, practiced and advocated within an otherwise disenchanted world (Meyer and Pels 2003, Styers 2004, Bell 2007). Museums have been eloquently analysed as one such channel (Bouquet and Porto 2005).

The relics and rituals of saints and heroes

Visiting the Santa Casa is a religious ritual conferring communion with the numinous via the building in which a holy person lived, confirming spiritual identity and achieving intercession with the godhead: in the sphere of Christian faith, the Virgin Mary is the peak agent of intervention between the human and the divine. This heroine's relics manifest an old tradition of magic – contagious magic – whereby supernaturally endowed objects can transmit the power of their owners to others across time and space (Frazer 1922). For the sake of this transcendent connection, relics of saints and martyrs were venerated from the earliest era of the Christian Church, though its later, more intellectual branches grew wary of the primitive enthusiasm. Primary charisma was located in bodies and body parts, leading to a vigorous medieval trade in, and even theft of, famous relics, which could also be channelled into objects close enough to receive the impress of the body such as clothes, possessions and, by extension, tombs and, occasionally, houses (Thurston 1911). Bodies, parts and possessions were honoured by making them accessible in finely worked reliquaries, whose precious materials and captivating design magnified and decentred the allure of the sacred object, facilitating supplicants to project their own desires onto the relic. On a larger scale than most, the relic of the Santa Casa itself is enclosed by a marble reliquary screen, designed by Bramante.

The cult of relics transfers easily into the rituals of civil religion, whereby adoption of parallel forms of religious practice legitimises state power or other ideological objectives with solemnity and ritual (Bellah 1967: 1–21, Parsons 2002: 1–5). In the absence of a god, civil religious expression often focuses around heroes political and cultural. Being products of the genteelising enlightenment mentality, civil relics tend less to bodies or corporeal parts, and more to objects associated with the hero's personal or physical environment.[3] While bloodstained pieces such as Nelson's coat or Lincoln's handkerchief are not infrequent, it is much more common to find that heroes' possessions – personalia, equipment and furnishings – are deemed to contain sufficient charismatic aura for civil relic status. In this context, museumised houses fulfil the role of both intrinsic relic and reliquary of further relics.

Lincoln's Birthplace is one of five Lincoln-associated houses museumised to enable visits by patriotic citizens, instantiating a further type of museum-as-ritual-site as theorised by Carol Duncan. Her view of art museum visits as 'civilizing rituals' in institutions that 'publicly represent beliefs about the order of the world, its past and present, and the individual's place within it', suggests also the modern purpose of conserving and museumising the relic houses of culture heroes (Duncan 1995: 2). In the sphere of US patriotic civil religion, Abraham Lincoln, the murdered redeemer, is second only to George Washington, the father of his country (Schwartz 1987: 196–7). All the more to ritualise it, features of the Beaux Arts temple containing the reconstructed cabin were ascribed with numerological significance (the origins possibly informal and maybe retrospective): sixteen rosettes in the ceiling coffers of the chamber said to represent the sixteenth President; fifty-six stairs climbing to the podium of the temple numbered equivalent to the President's age when he was assassinated.[4]

Not every hero's house museum is so explicitly divided from the world by symbolism or reliquary structure, but all exist within curtilages that serve the same function of separation. The gate or door of the house museum is the same kind of portal as the church narthex, a transition from the mundane world to the sacred. Where the power of a visit to the Santa Casa is grounded in the other-worldliness of religion buttressed by the relic house, a visit to Lincoln's Birthplace relic house is girded by history, draped in the veils of civil religion. And so is Captain Cook's Cottage.

The story of Captain Cook's house

In 1929, road-widening in the West Yorkshire village of Great Ayton required the demolition of a modest eighteenth century house, unexceptional but for its connection with the family of Captain James Cook, Royal Navy navigator and explorer of the Pacific. The house had been acknowledged for this fame since shortly after Cook's death at the hands of Hawaiians in 1778, even though the link was attenuated: it was a house built by Cook's father some years after James had left home to go to sea, and there is only circumstantial evidence that he may have ever visited it (Figure 10.5). But relics of mobile heroes such as sailors are scarce, and Cook had no others, so after half the house had been demolished, the owners announced in 1933 that they would sell the remaining portion for reconstruction elsewhere as a memorial to Cook (Dixon 1996: 4–5). Expressions of interest from an American buyer induced the caveat that it would only be sold for relocation within Britain. By this time, an Australian interest in the house had been alerted, and following some deft argument that the patriotic sphere of the British Empire fulfilled the vendor's nationalist requirement, a philanthropist purchased it for re-erection in Melbourne, to celebrate the 1934 centenary of establishment of the state, formerly colony, of Victoria.[5]

Figure 10.5 The house built by Captain Cook's father in 1755, sketched by George Cuit after the explorer's death. Watercolour in the Gott Collection (Yorkshire views). Image by courtesy of The Hepworth, Wakefield.

Cook's significance in Australia derives from his 1770 voyage, which identified the east coast of the country and claimed it for King George III. A British settlement was established at Sydney in 1788, but unfortunately for the honour of the subsequent colony of New South Wales, it was a prison establishment, manned largely by convicts and their guards. Once the colony and others had begun to thrive, the shame of a tainted genealogy led Australian colonists to prefer a history that recognised Captain Cook as discoverer, rather than Captain Phillip who commanded the First Fleet of exiles. Thus, Cook came early to wear the mantle of Australia's foundation hero.

The philanthropist who funded the translation of the Great Ayton house to Melbourne in 1933–34 seems to have been motivated by British loyalism, but his agent in the deal was more picturesquely inspired by the associative magic he inferred from the bricks and stones of what he called the Cook Cottage (Figure 10.6). Invoking the justification of reliquary honour for relocating it to Australia, he appealed to faith in the materiality of the building to enact a supposed visit to his parents by Captain Cook: 'Its doorstep rang to his heel as he entered. Its walls heard his voice . . . Within them must be stored memories' (Gill 1934: 13). Just as the 'sacred theft' of saints' bones around medieval Europe brought the blessings of their presence to their new owners, so would the patriotic delivery of material (faintly) connected to the foundation hero endow legitimacies on white Australians.

The Cottage was received in Melbourne with vast public enthusiasm. It had been quaintly rebuilt to accommodate the loss of half the original house and furnished with appropriate antique furniture acquired in York; cuttings of original ivy were planted to grow over the reconstruction. From 1934, the people of Melbourne swarmed in, and wrote ebullient thanks to the patron who had brought this slice of the Old World into the antipodes. They expressed pride in the nation's British descent; they identified with positive characteristics ascribed to manly

Figure 10.6 The truncated house with 'stable' and lean-to created to cover the entrance door, now known as Cooks' Cottage in Melbourne. Photograph by courtesy of Richard Dobson, 2010.

Yorkshire heritage; they relished the aura of antiquity in this, the oldest house in Australia (Grimwade Papers 1933–34).[6] The opening of Captain Cook's Cottage (as it was referred to) endowed the overwhelmingly Anglo population with a token of its origins which was true and resonant but also alternative to the self-made, gold-rich novelty of the colony of Victoria and the Commonwealth of Australia. The cottage enabled a ritual that asserted not a land without history, represented by peculiar mammals and back-to-front seasons, but communion with the Empire via its domestic bones, with a highly appropriate sea-going connection to the motherland.

Contemporary visitors showed practically no interest in doubts about the cottage's authenticity, though the topic gained some currency in newspaper commentary. This doubt informed reluctance among public land managers to provide a site and ongoing management for the donated cottage. Melbourne City Council eventually won the dubious prize and soon began to undermine the patron's vision by making the small building as simple to manage as possible. Measures such as cutting in a new door to improve traffic flow and closing off the upper room on account of the narrow stairs undermined the sense of sacred fabric, and the beautiful but somewhat marginal park in which it was rebuilt permitted graffiti which grew into vandalism within a few years. The Cottage was rehabilitated after the Second World War for the 1956 Olympic Games, regaining its aura of shrine to the national foundation hero. But the period was the beginning of the end for the ancestral relationship between Britain and Australia, and as that sense of blood loyalty faded, the Cottage required a new justification.

It arrived in the 1970s, a decade begun with the bicentenary of Cook's 1770 voyage of discovery, and shaped by the 1972 election, which ended a long conservative government for a social democratic one with cultural nationalist leanings. A new popular interest flourished in Australian history and heritage, and in its light, the Cook Cottage was revised for the first time. The National Trust brought together scholars and connoisseurs to apply authoritative standards of research to the building and its presentation. In this process, the peculiarities of the building were analysed, though the absence of the missing half remained unknown and the post-eighteenth-century internal stud walls which established a display of gender-divided sleeping rooms were unremarked. Colonial revivalist furbelows were extracted from the furnishings (though bed-warming pans and samplers remained) and plain finishes were introduced to windows, walls and beams. A professional librarian introduced the new Cottage booklet with an account of Cook's historical achievements for the first time in a site publication; an architectural historian discussed the Cottage in the context of Yorkshire vernacular building; a well-informed furniture collector pointed out the humble dimension of furnishings that had acquired the glamour of antiquity in the twentieth century (*Cook's Cottage* 1978). The booklet represented a challenge to hagiography by acknowledging the remote connection of the Cottage to Captain Cook himself, but nonetheless strengthened the authentic reputation of the structure by contextualising it in time, place and class. The scientific refocusing thus managed to incorporate a proof of authenticity into a bigger story of the hero, and although technically disproving both, left epistemological space in which the 1934 magical aura could be maintained in public perception.

The overwhelming power of Captain Cook's sacred presence in the material Cottage was peculiarly proved in the 1990s, when professionalised heritage management standards were introduced in the first conservation management plan prepared for the place (Sands 1993). Research was commissioned in Britain to review the documents as known and discover any more; it turned up a c.1788 drawing of the original double-cell house, demonstrating the extent of its truncation. It validated the sources that had long been understood as proving Cook-senior ownership, producing a sound property history (Cuit c.1788). But the Melbourne-era history of the translated Cottage was prepared in the intellectual atmosphere of post-colonial revisionism, positing Captain Cook as a focus of social memory in constructing the white history of Australia. This perspective was somewhat incoherently attached to the building history and, in best practice conservation terms, it determined the management plan's statement of significance. Theoretically, the basis of management decisions about the site and its fabric, the statement of significance was composed without mentioning Captain Cook at all. The statement focused instead on the symbolism of the Cottage as a statement of national origin for the white population of Australia and a statement of dispossession for Aboriginal people; in this duality, the statement also aimed to demonstrate the constructedness of histories (see Young 2008). It is a sophisticated interpretation, in tune with its time, but according to Cottage staff it was unconvincing to many visitors.

Visitors continued to visit the Cottage, now named Cooks' Cottage, minus the Naval rank and with the apostrophe in a critical position to indicate it was the house of multiple Cooks. Again, enough slippage remained in the compromise title to permit the assumption that it included the only famous Cook, the Captain. Logic demands this interpretation: 'Why would anyone want to visit the house of Captain Cook's father and mother?' as the presenter of a 2007 BBC television programme on Captain Cook asked in an astonished tone, gazing at the Cottage (Collingridge 2007). And not only logic: the presence of a shrine manifestly indicates the relics of a hero; its scientifically demonstrated authenticity guarantees the hero. It must be Captain Cook's Cottage, or else why is it there?

Does authenticity matter?

A further question arises if the answer to this question is negative: does it matter if the relic is not authentic? The Roman Catholic Church offered one answer, cited above, that faith is itself sufficient to make a fake relic meaningful. As also recorded above, the US National Parks Service concludes that the fake can take on meanings unjustified by history but no less meaningful. My 'does it matter?' question was recently answered confidently by the current manager of Cooks' Cottage: no – visitors get a thrill even when they know it is not true.

To explain this observation, a new way forward is suggested by the parallels of religion and celebrity culture, both draped in the tradition of magical thinking.

The spectrum of saint-to-hero-to-celebrity contains many a sequence of divergences, but the primary one in this argument is the shift in honour from revered distance to (pseudo-) up-close vantage. Most modern visitors to heroes' house museums arrive equipped with some or little knowledge of the aura of the hero, and a mentality predisposed to expect intimate personal communion with famous strangers. They see a house of a different era, infused with the expectations of what a house is today. The vision of nuclear family domesticity presented in the Cook cottage matches the ubiquitous magazine photo-spread of stars' homes, albeit in humble mid-eighteenth-century vernacular form. Guides point out to school students how small the rooms are, how basic the furniture, how absent the comforts of our time, but the frame of the visit is veneration of the great man. Associative magic infects it all with glamour on the same principle as the authenticity of the Cottage itself: it is here in a sacred setting; it must be real.

The (re-created) narrow stump bedstead placed in a closet downstairs is there to cradle the hero on his visit home; it is as simple (allowing for period) as John Lennon's childhood bed (also re-created) in Liverpool. No ecstatic shaking and weeping has been reported in Cooks' Cottage as it is in 'Mendips', but the tones of vulnerability and sexuality in the beds of the famous hint at the intimate contact that celebrity pretends to permit. Though even celebrity has its practical limits: Elvis Presley's bedroom is not open to the public in Gracelands for fear of fan hysteria (Marling 1996: 226). The claim 'Queen Elizabeth/George Washington slept here' refers to pure relic character, yet in its frequency it is now famous as a credulous visitor joke, a parapraxis which reveals the strength of magical thinking in the era of celebrity, tourism, heritage interpretation and other constructed forms of experience.

Should museums condone magical approaches to their collections and exhibits? Could they control them anyway? Sharon Macdonald addresses the power of 'enchanted looking' at museumised sites of disturbing history and discovers dilemma that is best addressed with a consciousness of the political agency of institutions (Macdonald 2005: 224). The canon of 'heroes' is inevitably determined by political interests too, though the effects of time reduce many heroes to anonymity and irrelevance. But where heroes maintain currency, there is no doubt their political efficacy is enhanced by magical thinking. Captain James Cook is one of numerous eighteenth and nineteenth century explorers who extended the borders of the British Empire and thereby paved the way for white colonialism in Africa, Asia and the Pacific. As a British hero he was soon remembered merely as one of many in the pantheon of Empire. In Australia, however, he was endowed from the 1870s with specific glory as national founder, a century after his voyage up the east coast. Generations of children learned about Captain Cook; he was marked in civic expressions such as commemorative plaques and the relocated cottage; and came to permeate popular consciousness in rhyming slang and schoolyard chant.[7] The survival of Captain Cookery after the history wars of the 1990s, which turned on the presentation of Indigenous rights, suggests that his heroic status persists in Australia, uneroded in the national psyche (Macintyre & Clark 2003: 119–41). The Cottage in Melbourne is still touched by popular magic.

Hero worship and celebrity adoration need an enchanted public, served by agents with some perspective on the constructedness of their role as guardians or gatekeepers. At the same time, the curatorial approach is grounded in the paradigm of scientific knowledge which demands that the hero is presented in the contexts of history and power; and the visitor perspective is coloured by anticipation of contagious magic and intimate revelation. This is not so much a case of the disenchantment of the shrine transformed into a museum, as the museum being assumed enchanted by its audiences – and hence, constructed as a shrine. It is harder for some artefacts to be modern today, than to be magical.

Notes

1 A building in Ephesus, Turkey, said to be the house of the Virgin Mary's old age and death, has been a pilgrimage site since its miraculous revelation in 1821 and restoration in the 1890s. Archaeologists date the building to the sixth to seventh century, but note older foundations which may date to the first century (http://www.sacred-destinations.com/turkey/ephesus-house-of-the-virgin.htm).
2 Lincoln's adult family house in Springfield, IL, and Ford's Theatre in Washington, DC, where he was assassinated, are also NPS sites. The village of New Salem, IN, where he lived as a young single adult but never owned a house, has a historic park of re-located cabins, known as Lincoln's New Salem. Rounding out the ancestral dimension of the family, the Lincoln Log Cabin State Historic Site near Charleston, IL, is a rep-lica of the house inhabited by Lincoln's father and step-mother well after he had left home. Knob Hill, New Salem and Charleston were all constructed by the Civilian Conservation Corps in the 1930s.
3 In this, civil relics are distinct from personal in memoriam relics, where hair is a very frequent keepsake of the departed.
4 These features are not discussed in Robert Blythe *et al.*, *Abraham Lincoln Birthplace National Historic Site Historic Resource Study*, NPS, 2001, but can be found in sites such as Abraham Lincoln Online.Org: http://showcase.netins.net/web/creative/lincoln/sites/birth.htm.
5 For a range of histories, see Jillian Robertson (1981), Maryanne McCubbin (1999) and Chris Healy (1997).
6 The house was built in 1755, thirty years before white settlement in Australia.
7 A Captain Cook = a look (search), now used with nostalgic irony; 'Captain Cook chased a chook, all around Australia/Lost his pants in the middle of France and found them in Tasmania' (and many variations) – I learned this one at school in the 1960s.

Bibliography

Abraham Lincoln Online.Org: http://showcase.netins.net/web/creative/lincoln/sites/birth.htm (Accessed 22 January 2011).

Bell, K. (2007) 'Breaking modernity's spell: magic and modern history', *Cultural and Social History*, 4: 115–22.

Bellah, R. (1967) 'Civil religion in America', *Daedalus*, 96: 1–21.

Blythe, R. *et al.* (2001) *Abraham Lincoln Birthplace National Historic Site Historic Resource Study*, NPS. Available at: http://www.nps.gov/abli/historyculture/upload/ABLI_Historic_Resource_Study.pdf (Accessed 22 January 2011).

Bouquet, M. and N. Porto (eds) (2005) *Science, Magic and Religion: the ritual processes of museum magic*, New York: Berghahn.

Collingridge, V. (2007) *Captain Cook: obsession and discovery*, ABC DVD.

Cook's Cottage (1978) Contributions by M. Lewis, M. Lewis and J. Rogan, Melbourne City Council.

Cuit, G. (c.1788) *South East View of a House at Great Ayton which was Built by Capt. Cook's Father which House He Sold previous to His Going to Live at Redcar*. no. 41, Gott Collection (Yorkshire views), Wakefield Art Gallery.

Dixon, J. (1996) *History under the Hammer: why did the Dixon family sell Captain Cook's Cottage to Australia?* York: North York Moors Historical Society.

Duncan, C. (1995) *Civilizing Rituals: inside public art museums*, London: Routledge.

Frazer, J. (1922) *The Golden Bough: a study of magic and religion*, London: Project Gutenberg eBook.

Gill, H. (1934) *Captain Cook's Cottage*, Melbourne.

Grimwade Papers (1933–34) Series 15/8, University of Melbourne Archives.

Hays, R. (1948) 'Is the Lincoln birthplace cabin authentic?' *Abraham Lincoln Quarterly*, 5: 1948.

Healy, C. (1997) *From the Ruins of Colonialism: history as social memory*, Melbourne: Cambridge University Press.

Howard, P. (2003) *Heritage: management, interpretation, identity*, London: Continuum.

Hughey, M. (1979) 'The idea of secularization in the works of Max Weber', *Qualitative Sociology*, 2: 85–111.

Lowenthal, D. (2008) 'Authenticities past and present', *CRM: The Journal of Heritage Stewardship*, 5 (1) Available at: http://crmjournal.cr.nps.gov/Print.cfm?articleIDN=4256 (Accessed 22 January 2011).

Macdonald, S. (2005) 'Enchantment and its dilemmas: the museum as a ritual site', in M. Bouquet and N. Porto (eds) *Science, Magic and Religion: the ritual processes of museum magic*, New York: Berghahn Books, pp. 209–27.

Macintyre, S. and A. Clark (2003) *The History Wars*, Carlton: Melbourne University Press.

Marling, K.A. (1996) *Graceland: going home with Elvis*, Cambridge, MA: Harvard University Press.

McCubbin, M. (1999) 'Cooked to perfection: Cooks' Cottage and the exemplary historical figure', *Journal of Popular Culture*, 1: 35–48.

Meistermann, B. (1911) 'Nazareth', in *Catholic Encyclopedia*, Vol. 10, New York: Robert Appleton Company. Available at: http://www.newadvent.org/cathen/10725a.htm (Accessed 22 January 2011).

Meyer, B. and P. Pels (eds) (2003) *Magic and Modernity: interfaces of revelation and concealment*, Stanford: Stanford University Press.

Muñoz-Vinas, S. (2005) *Contemporary Theory of Conservation*, Oxford: Elsevier.

Parsons, G. (2002) *Perspectives on Civil Religion*, Aldershot: Ashgate/Open University.

Peterson, G. (1968) *An Administrative History of Abraham Lincoln Birthplace National Historic Site Hodgenville, Kentucky*, National Park Service. Available at: http://www.nps.gov/history/history/online_books/abli/adhi/adhi.htm (Accessed 22 January 2011).

Phillips, D. (1997) *Exhibiting Authenticity*, Manchester: Manchester University Press.

Pitcaithley, D.T. (2001) 'Lincoln's birthplace cabin: the making of an American icon', in P. Shackel (ed.) *Myth, Memory and the Making of the American Landscape*, Gainsville: University of Florida Press.

Robertson, J. (1981) *The Captain Cook Myth*, Sydney: Angus & Robertson.

Saler, M. (2006) 'Modernity and enchantment: a historiographic review', *American Historical Review*, 3: 692–716.

Sands, R. (1993) *'Cooks' Cottage, Fitzroy Gardens*, Melbourne: Conservation Management Plan.

Schwartz, B. (1987) *George Washington: the making of an American symbol*, New York: Free Press.

Starn, R. (2002) 'Authenticity and historic preservation: towards an authentic history', *History of the Human Sciences*, 15: 1–16.

Steers Jr, E.J. (2007) *Lincoln Legends: myths, hoaxes and confabulations associated with our greatest president*, Lexington: University of Kentucky Press.

Styers, R. (2004) *Making Magic: religion, magic, and science in the modern world*, Oxford: Oxford University Press.

Thurston, H. (1911) 'Relics', in *Catholic Encyclopedia*, Vol. 12, New York: Robert Appleton Company. Available at: http://www.newadvent.org/cathen/12734a.htm (Accessed 21 January 2011).

Thurston, H. (1912) 'Santa Casa di Loreto', in *Catholic Encyclopedia*, Vol. 13, New York: Robert Appleton Company. Available at: http://www.newadvent.org/cathen/13454b.htm (Accessed 20 January 2011).

Turner, G. (2006) *Understanding Celebrity*, London: Sage.

Young, L. (2008) 'The contagious magic of James Cook in Captain-Cook's Cottage', *ReCollections* 3. Available at: http://recollections.nma.gov.au/issues/vol_3_no_2/papers/the_contagious_magic_of_james_cook/ (Accessed 20 January 2011).

11 'Do not touch'

A discussion on the problems of a limited sensory experience with objects in a gallery or museum context

Helen Saunderson

Whiling away time in a queue, discussing pornographic images of women that were blu-tacked to the inside of a shipping cargo container. Only then to clamber into a chest freezer, and descend a wooden ladder to a shaft. The shaft (which was scrambled through on all fours) opened out into a cavernous space containing a huge musty smelling earth 'mammoth'. That was just one element of my experience at Christoph Büchel's *Simply Botiful* exhibition (2007).[1] Sight, smell, touch, sound and taste (in the accidental consumption of earth as dust!) were all crucial elements of the experience. What would it have been like if the work was only encountered encased within protective glass? What impact would the reduction of the encounter to a purely visual one have had? Did the other sensory information influence how the work was experienced?

In this chapter, after an initial overview of the dominance of the visual in museum contexts, the implications of this convention are considered, including the possibility that it may lead to less attention upon the actual museum objects. Thereafter, the chapter discusses the idea that potentially an impoverished experience can result if only visual information is presented. By considering empirical psychological literature which investigates multi-sensory experiences, findings from selected experiments are presented that suggest that having experiences with more than one sense can influence emotions, memory, attention and the overall perceptual experience. Having presented empirical research suggesting that various aspects of human experience are influenced in multi-sensory ways (including situations where that which is perceived in one sense is actually affected by information from another), a proposal of what this might imply in a museum setting is outlined in the final part of the chapter.

In addition to the aim of answering the questions posed in the introductory paragraph, I also intend to illustrate the enormous potential to expand knowledge by cross-disciplinary pollination between museum studies and empirical psychology. It is, in my opinion, important that the two sometimes disparate extremes of methodologies and philosophical approach consider literature in one another's fields, as, by considering another discipline's body of knowledge forces researchers to consider their own discipline's methodological framework and its implicit assumptions, many of which have never been explicitly tested; the cannon of museum studies literature can be used to provide interesting and novel angles for insightful psychological research;[2] and it may lead to empirical evidence and methods from psychology being identified as potentially illuminating for theoretical debates in museum studies (as illustrated in this chapter). Specifically, I focus upon relating a small number of selected examples, based partly upon my areas of expertise (as an artist and vision psychologist) and accessibility of the written research papers to a non-psychology audience. The aim is to illustrate how the theoretical and logical extrapolation of psychological research can provide novel knowledge within which to consider current debates, in this instance the importance of multi-sensory experiences in museums. In the hope that the potential advantages of cross-disciplinary pollination is illustrated and in the future explicit (and less extrapolated) research into museum studies issues using scientific/psychological methods will be more widely undertaken; as partially started with touch and the handling of museum objects (Chatterjee 2008).

Glass cases and the dominance of vision in museum contexts

What would it have been like if the work (*Simply Botiful*) was only encountered encased within protective glass? If *Simply Botiful* had been encased, pragmatically it would have been very difficult to process through it physically, as climbing into the freezer would have been impossible. Also, the experience would have been partially disconnected rather than an interactive encounter. This particular artwork could be considered an 'anomaly' as it is specifically designed to elicit a multi-sensory experience, so it is important to consider the impact of barriers by comparing *Simply Botiful* with a more conventional example, such as the Lewis chess men. The Lewis chess men (Figure 11.1), in the National Gallery of Scotland, are now encased and can only be experienced visually. However, the convention of wrapping objects in transparent containers, only to be viewed, is a relatively modern phenomenon, as traditionally touch was regarded as an important factor in enabling the museum visitor to gain a special kind of knowledge of an object.

Indeed, as an upper class Victorian it would have been possible to handle the Lewis chess men as 'museum visitors, as polite guests, were expected to show their interest and goodwill by asking questions and by touching the proffered objects' (Classen 2005: 275). In addition, as Classen points out, touch offers, firstly, an opportunity to verify what the visual sense implied. If, for example, you picked up what seemed to be a Lewis chess figure and it had the lightness of plastic it may be easier to identify it as a replica than purely through looking. Secondly, it enables people to intimately experience the object and, lastly, have a sense of what it would have been like to be the original possessor of the object. And so:

> [T]his oft-perceived ability of touch to bridge space and time gave it special value in the museum setting, where visitors were separated by considerable spatial and/or temporal distances from the cultures of origin of many of the objects displayed.

(Classen 2005: 278)

Figure 11.1 Author's sketch of the Berserker Lewis chess piece from the National Museum of Scotland, 2009.

Therefore, handling and touching an object was (and by some still is) regarded as an essential aspect of the experience (Chatterjee, Vreeland and Noble 2009).

However, perhaps it is important to consider if there is a distinction between art galleries and museums: in a gallery context sometimes the artist intends the dominance of vision and specifically chooses to encase in glass. For example, vitrines (Rebecca Warren's *2001, 2002, 2003, 2004 or 2005 2006,* 2006[3]) and glass cases (including the studio works in *Eva Hesse: Chain Polymers* at the Fischbach Gallery, New York, 1968) may be used to confer status and attention upon art objects. Indeed, it has been argued that 'When things are put in a glass case it tends to make you look at them differently: like a frame, it forces you to look, maybe harder, according to another set of habits' (Fer 2009: 84). In addition, specifically in relation to Hesse's work, it has been stated that:

When you look at the work that fills the glass cases there is no doubt that your eyes get caught up in them as if they were a trap for looking. It is almost as if we are lured to look and to get our eyes caught in there intricacies, but then just as surely be brought up short at their almost visceral materiality.

(Fer 2009: 86)

So, galleries and modern museums often tend to give preference to vision (though in certain instances this is an intentional artistic decision) for experiencing the actual object.

What happens when the encounter with an object is predominantly a visual one? Correlation evidence from a real world, eye tracking experiment by Fukuda *et al.* (2009) provides some interesting findings. Fukuda *et al.* tracked the eye movements of a small number of people (one person in each of eight pairs) whilst they freely navigated the Nagasaki Museum of History and Culture. The following was found in relation to three displays: when the environment was a wall covered in information, inset with objects in cases, large amounts of time were spent looking at the text, and only a small amount of time on the objects themselves. Interestingly, when a screen object was displayed outside a case but had a touch screen in front of it, observers looked longer at the touch screen than the screen object right behind it. People tend to spend the most time looking at objects in traditional cases, which had little accompanying text. Perhaps this means that if a visual modality is depended upon, textual information in a real life encounter can predominate, seriously reducing attention to the object. So, potentially, the predominance of vision and the visual pull of text in a museum context may reduce attention on the actual physical object.

However, traditionally, touch was regarded as an important factor in enabling the visitor at a museum to gain a special kind of knowledge of an object. Further, it is normal that an everyday experience that involves touch and vision is coupled with congruent information from the other senses, like smell, taste and sound, and sometimes this is also true of museums. Whilst ascending the stairs to the attic of the Fisherman's Cottage at the Scottish Fisheries Museum in Anstruther, the visitor encounters the onslaught of an indeterminate smell, which may have been a mixture of jute and preservatives, and possibly the taste of the salt of the sea. Once in the attic it is possible to see the numerous ropes and fishing equipment displayed (Figure 11.2), and to then gently touch and feel the roughness of the ropes, and the structure of the braiding. The very high personal saliency this experience engendered perhaps implies that multi-sensory experiences tend to be more memorable. Empirical psychological research into the various senses (also referred to as modalities) and the interactions between them (be that two, three or more senses/modalities – all referred to here as multi-sensory) will potentially illuminate the importance, or not, of a multi-sensory encounter in a museum context, which anecdotal examples and museum studies theoretical arguments appears to imply may be important.

Figure 11.2 Part of the attic room of the Fisherman's Cottage at the Scottish Fisheries Museum, Anstruther. Photograph by the author. Reproduced with permission of Scottish Fisheries Museum.

Empirical psychological research into multi-sensory experiences and subsequent specific implications for museums

There is strong evidence, from empirical psychologists using a variety of research techniques, that the interaction between various senses does influence how things are experienced by a person, though not always in an obviously straightforward way (including those focused on below: Easton, Greene and Srinivas 1997, Herz, Beland and Hellerstein 2004, Seitz, Kim and Shams 2006, Auvray *et al.* 2008, Mozolic *et al.* 2008). Arguably, various aspects of an encounter with an artwork or museum object would be influenced by (or have an influence upon) multi-sensory experiences, including emotions, memory, attention and perception, and each of these aspects will be discussed in turn. However, it should be noted that the psychological experiments described have been selected on the basis of their relevance and interest – a comprehensive literature review revealing the complexity and subtleties of each field is beyond the scope of this chapter. In addition, the extrapolation to museum studies is my personal view and not the opinion of the researchers, but I aim to illustrate with these examples the potential for using empirical psychological findings and approaches in relation to museum studies, and thus indicate the potential for developing a future cross-disciplinary investigative framework.

Starting with emotion, and focusing upon smell: Herz *et al.*'s (2004) research involved people playing computer games (a multiple-sense activity) accompanied by a smell. The smell was not congruent with all the other sensory information involved in playing the computer game. The computer game was either frustrating (inducing negative emotions) or interesting (promoting a positive mood). The emotional state induced affected the participant's ratings of the smells. Smells were more negatively rated if experienced during negative emotions and visa versa. In that instance, the perception of the smells was influenced by an induced mood; others (Cinel and Humphreys 2005) have also identified the inverse relationship, namely where sensory information may influence mood. Together this may imply that if a person was viewing an object and there was a smell of coffee from the café at a museum it would be possible that your experience with the object you were currently encountering would be related to the emotional state that coffee induced in you. Therefore, even an 'accidental' smell in a museum context (as highlighted as occurring by Drobnick 2006) could produce interesting effects through associations.

Moving on from emotions to memory, Easton *et al.* (1997) have found that the 'test results for three-dimensional objects revealed modality specificity, indicating that the recognition system keeps track of the modality through which an object is experienced', therefore implying that although information from one modality can be transferred to representations in another modality, the brain keeps track of the modality within which the object was encountered. Presumably, if the encounter was multi-sensory this would also be represented in the memory. Easton *et al.* (1997) have shown that information from more than one sense are integrated and can enhance basic memory.

Further, in relation to memory, it has been shown that bi- and tri-modal sensory inputs improve basic types of learning (Hecht, Reiner and Karni 2008) and in addition that sound information can improve long-term learning (Seitz *et al.* 2006). Seitz *et al.* divided participants into two groups and, over a period of time, trained them on a particular task (motion detection) either in a purely visual condition or in a visual and auditory condition. Results show faster learning when congruent auditory and visual information was available during training. Indeed, the researchers concluded that:

> Under such a regime, encoding, storing, and retrieving perceptual information is intended by default to operate in a multisensory environment, and unisensory processing is suboptimal because it would correspond to an artificial mode of processing that does not utilize the perceptual machinery to its fullest potential.
>
> (Seitz *et al.* 2006: 1424)

In other words, as humans are designed to function in a multi-sensory environment, learning though multiple senses is the most efficient method or approach, while learning from information available through only one sense provides a more limited understanding and is less effective as a result.

Experiences through a single sense may also be detrimental in relation to attention. There are situations where the perception from one sense can interfere with information received from others, including in relation to touch and vision (Auvray *et al.* 2008). Auvray *et al.* showed that change blindness (an inability to detect changes between two stimuli separated by a short pause) between two tactile stimuli can be increased either when a tactile or visual stimulus is presented in the intervening time. In other words, both touch and vision interfere, to the same extent, with a person's ability to notice a change in a stimulus they are touching. Indeed, when individuals complete simple tasks 'it has been shown that attention can alter multisensory interactions' (Mozolic *et al.* 2008: 51). The individual's performance was relatively impaired if his/her attention was focused on one sense, instead of being split into the two senses, assuming the information supplied was congruent. In more complex situations, including an experience with art (or those lucky enough to handle museum objects) it would be logical to assume that some form of the same relationship would occur.

Multi-sensory experiences with art or museum objects are arguably distinct from single sensory ones, which tend to favour a particular form of attention, and hence experience. Generalising the specific findings of Mozolic *et al.* to a gallery situation could imply that an individual, whilst viewing *20:50* by Richard Wilson (1987), would experience the smell of the oil at the same time as viewing the mirrored surface created by the substance. Due to congruent sensory information, performance (otherwise defined as an enhanced experience) would be improved by splitting attention to both modalities and impaired by focusing solely on one. This may mean that, if museums and galleries are biased towards one modality (vision) the 'normal' expected behaviour would be to defer all attention to that one modality in that context; which may mean a multi-sensory experience cannot achieve its full potential. All this shows that attention, memory and emotion are influenced by multi-sensory versus single modality experiences, including in relation to touch and vision. The research suggests that normal human encounters are multi-sensory. Therefore, the brain has evolved to reflect this, and hence single sense experiences may be detrimental and often a multi-sensory experience is optimal. The following example shows just how important multi-sensory experiences may be.

Imagine that somebody in the street asked you for directions then, after your momentary distraction, were substituted with someone else. Do you think you would notice? Simons and Levin (1998) have shown that many people do not. The experiment involved an individual (collaborator) going up to someone (participant) in a university campus, and asking for directions to a building. During the conversation about directions, two other people carrying a door interrupted the conversation by walking between the participant and collaborator; and the collaborator (who originally asked for the directions) was substituted with another experimenter. Half the participants did not notice the switch. This is an example of change blindness, the powerful phenomena where dramatic visual changes are often not explicitly noticed.[4] Another type of change blindness involves showing two images where there is a significant alteration, for example an object

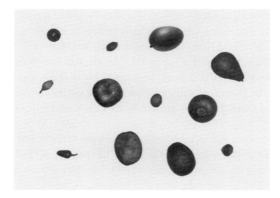

Figure 11.3 Image from Symes *et al.* (2008) showing the array of fruit and vegetables used as stimuli. Reproduced with permission of Rob Ellis.

changes, separated by a blank screen. In this situation it often takes individuals some time to identify the change, although in the static images it is reasonably easy to do so. This method is often used in experiments and provided the basis for the following pertinent investigation.

Symes *et al.* (2008) used images of fruit and vegetables in their change blindness experiment (Figure 11.3). Certain of the fruit would be grasped if picked up (for example, the apple) while others (such as the pea) would require a pinch movement to be successfully physically manipulated. A display of numerous fruit and vegetables were presented, followed by a blank screen, and then substituted by an identical image to the first, with the exception that one of the items had changed. Individuals responded when they identified any change using a device that either required them to make a pinching or a grasping motion. It was found that when the response to an image was a pinching motion, then if the change to the image was to a fruit or vegetable that could be physically manipulated by a pinch, then participants were faster at noticing the change – because there attention was biased towards objects congruent to their hand movement. So, if the person had had to respond with a grasp, and was presented with a display in which the apple changed they would be faster at identifying the change than if they had had to respond using a pinching motion. The results imply that the input to one sense can actually affect the perception of another sensory modality.

Broader implications of multi-sensory research for museums

This research has implied the great importance of the distinctive type of experience gained during a multi-sensory encounter; perhaps best illustrated by the fact that visual perception can be influenced by information received through touch. Returning to the experience with Büchel's *Simply Botiful*, the interaction of the physical experience of grasping the side of the fridge to enable oneself to clamber would have changed the experience of the visual perception of the object, from that where it was encountered without being able to touch.

So what does this imply for museums and art galleries? Generally, the current set-up in these institutions favours the predomination of vision, which provides only a certain type of experience. How the objects are perceived in this environment would be different if people were able to touch the objects. In addition, Fukuda *et al.* (2009) have presented preliminary evidence that suggests, rather ironically, that in purely visual encounters where people look is often not upon the actual object, but rather the accompanying text (partially dependent upon the display set-up). Arguably, this could be because attempts to gain information focus upon the text sources rather than the object. In contrast, if it was possible to handle the object, more information would be easily available, for example what material it is made from. A multi-sensory experience is, therefore, very different from a single modality one, including in terms of how the objects are perceived and knowledge is gained.

Therefore, it is important to consider *how* an individual is gaining their experience with the object. In my view, there are broadly two ways of gathering new knowledge from a museum object, which are here coined as infobject and objectext. Infobject is information gained by an encounter engaging with the actual object: this could be through looking and seeing the dimensions and texture of the materials, or handling and feeling the weight, balance point and temperature. In contrast, objectext is where knowledge external to the object is gained, for example from the accompanying context, including text, audio guide information and discussions with other people. The relationship between infobject and objectext knowledge, and what ratio or emphasis gives the 'best' experience as measured either by longevity of memory, fullness of encounter or desire to repeat the experience needs investigation. It may well be, as suggested by researchers such as Seitz *et al.* (2006), that a multi-modal engagement would result in the richest experience.

However, it is not entirely clear what type of multi-sensory experiences would be advantageous. An encounter with an object behind glass whilst listening to an audio guide is perhaps rather unfulfilling, though when using an audio guide at a ruin where it is possible to navigate within the architecture and experience various sense information, potentially it enhances the experience.[5] Indeed, if an immersive environment such as multi-sensory displays in digital domes – which already have as standard vision and audio, but where there is also the potential for smell and even movement – then the quality of being totally surrounded by the 'object' would perhaps be rich enough to provide an enlightening experience, and this is especially the case in relation to objects that are not easily accessible due to geographical location, or are no longer in existence. However, perhaps the most straight-forward method of generating a multi-modal experience is allowing people to handle original objects, as purported by Susan Pearce (personal communication 2010).

Unfortunately, there is a tension between the pragmatically understandable 'do not touch' policies of art galleries and the evidence supporting the importance of handling original objects. While visiting the Whitechapel Gallery (2003), exhibiting Cristina Iglesias, where one work was a structural labyrinth which you were allowed to enter and navigate, the gallery assistant watched me eagle eyed, and commented that I should be careful not to touch the work. I became so aware of the importance of not touching the work that the focus of my experience became upon avoiding contact with the labyrinth, rather than engaging 'normally' with the work. This experience made me consider the difficulty for an artist creating a work that seemingly needs audience interaction, to only then arguably have the artistically intended experience altered as people are distracted by the 'do not touch' philosophy. Preservation of objects and full experiences are often at opposite ends of the scale and careful consideration needs to be taken to consider how to balance these requirements.

What other advantages might a multi-sensory encounter confer? Personally, the anticipation of knowing that I was going to be allowed to handle a Lewis chess man piece and then doing so would have an amazing frisson, and this suggests there is the potential for engagement with an original object to increase the pleasure gained from the experience. Generalising from an experiment involving the tasting of wines (Plassmann *et al.* 2008), the researchers found that when people were given samples of an identical wine, if they were told it was more expensive it stimulated the pleasure-giving areas of the brain more than if they were told it was cheaper. So, in addition to the intuitive and technical arguments for the importance of an original object encounter, it is also possible that such an experience with the authentic original may influence how it is perceived, including in terms of pleasure. The special 'magic' of encountering an original object, especially handling it, may be a reflection of increased pleasure due to our expectations.

Conclusions

'Please do not touch. This work is extremely vulnerable. Touching even with clean hands, will damage it. Please respect the work and keep children in hand'[6] is just one variation of the 'do not touch' philosophy adopted by many museums and galleries in relation to their original objects. Indeed, so naturalised is this 'hands off' attitude that it can be hard to break even with permission. My experiences at the Franz West exhibition (Whitechapel 2003) were that although exhibits were clearly marked to be interacted with, it took some time for me to summon up the nerve to sit in one of the seats that are part of the artwork, and my observations were that other visitors would circle exhibits, repeatedly read the instructions that they were allowed to touch, and yet still seemed to have a guilty demeanour if they touched the artworks. Currently, a 'do not touch' concept is engrained in both the visitor and institution, but perhaps a shift in philosophy is needed. To achieve this, museum and gallery curators arguably need to ask themselves the following questions. What do I want my audience to gain from this experience? What level of interaction with the actual object do I want? What relationship between infobject and objectext do I desire? What trade off will be needed? Do I vary the experiences (so that sometimes it is more information focused and other times more object focused)? How does display facilitate the different types of experience? Perhaps it seems that I have raised more questions than I have answered, but arguably this chapter has shown that factors like being able to experience an object through multiple senses provides a different experience from peering through glass; neither is worse, it is just important to consider the target audience and aim and adapt the encounter to elicit the desired outcome of experience, which is what the questions raised above must answer. To answer these questions fully it would be advantageous to test them empirically in further psychological research. So, perhaps the conclusion of this chapter is 'to be continued'.

Acknowledgements

I would like to thank Sandra Dudley and Susan Pearce for giving me the opportunity to write this chapter and also for their support, Alice Cruickshank for her helpful editing and advice, the various anonymous reviewers for their insightful criticism which assisted in improving the chapter greatly, Dipak Soma for his IT assistance and Rob Ellis for providing the change blindness illustration.

This chapter is dedicated to Ambalavanar Kumaran, Betty Robson, Leicester Spokes, Sarah White, Kathryn Wilkinson and Dean Wood.

Notes

1 I visited the exhibition at the Hauser and Wirth's East London project space on multiple occasions during the period 11 October 2006–18 March 2007.
2 My doctoral research aims to question assumptions made in psychology in the light of humanities literature, and to empirically investigate issues identified and theoretically discussed in the humanities literature.
3 Displayed as part of the Turner Prize installation.
4 There are various explanations for why change blindness occurs – for a clearly written review see Bruce, Green and Georgeson (2006).
5 Especially when it is Terry Jones talking about Doune Castle which featured in the film *Monty Python and the Holy Grail*.
6 Quote from information display boards at the exhibition of Eva Hesse's work *Studiowork* at the Fruitmarket Gallery, Edinburgh, as visited by the author on 15 September 2009.

Bibliography

Auvray, M., A. Gallace, J. Hartcher-O'Brien, H.Z. Tan and C. Spence (2008) 'Tactile and visual distracters induce change blindness for tactile stimuli presented on the fingertips', *Journal of Brain Research*, 1213: 111–19.
Bruce, V., P.R. Green and M.A. Georgeson (2006) *Visual Perception, Physiology, Psychology and Ecology*, Hove, UK: Psychology Press, pp. 415–16.
Chatterjee, H. (2008) *Touch in Museums: policy and practice in object handling*, Oxford: Berg.
Chatterjee, H., S. Vreeland and G. Noble (2009) 'Museopathy: exploring the healing potential of handling museum objects', *Museum and Society*, 7: 164–77.

Cinel, C. and G. Humphreys (2005) 'Multisensory integration', in D.T. Rosen (ed.), *Trends in Experimental Psychology Research*, New York: Nova Science.

Classen, C. (2005) 'Touch in the museum', in C. Classen (ed.) *The Book of Touch*, Oxford: Berg.

Drobnick, J. (2006) 'Volatile effects: olfactory dimensions of art and architecture', in D. Howes (ed.) *Empire of the Senses: the sensual culture reader*, Oxford: Berg.

Easton, R.D., A.J. Green and K. Srinivas (1997) 'Transfer between vision and haptics: memory for 2-D and 3-D objects', *Psychonomic Bulletin and Review*, 4: 403–10.

Fer, B. (2009) *Eva Hesse: Studiowork*. Edinburgh: The Fruitmarket Gallery.

Fukuda, R., M. Morii, K. Ohata, K. Ichihara, S. Ogura, D. Igari, *et al.* (2009) 'What do we look at in a museum?' Oral presentation at the European Conference on Eye Movements, at Southampton.

Hecht, D., M. Reiner and A. Karni (2008) 'Enhancement of response times to bi- and tri-modal sensory stimuli during active movements', *Experimental Brain Research*, 185: 655–65.

Herz, R.S., S.L. Beland and M. Hellerstein (2004) 'Changing odor hedonic perception through emotional associations in humans', *International Journal of Comparative Psychology*, 17: 315–38.

Mozolic, J., C. Hugenschmidt, A. Peiffer and P. Laurienti (2008) 'Modality-specific selective attention attenuates multisensory integration', *Experimental Brain Research*, 184: 39–52.

Plassmann, H., J. O'Doherty, B. Shiv and A. Rangel (2008) 'Marketing actions can modulate neural representations of experienced pleasantness', *Proceedings of the National Academy of Sciences of the United States of America*, 105: 1050–4.

Seitz, A.R., R. Kim and L. Shams (2006) 'Report sound facilitates visual learning', *Current Biology*, 16: 1422–7.

Simons, D.J. and J.T. Levin (1998) 'Failure to detect changes to people during real-world interaction', *Psychonomic Bulletin and Review*, 5: 644–9.

Symes, E., M. Tucker, R. Ellis, L. Vainio and G. Ottoboni (2008) 'Grasp preparation improves change detection for congruent objects', *Journal of Experimental Psychology: Human Perception and Performance*, 34: 854–71.

12 Living objects

A theory of museological objecthood

Wing Yan Vivian Ting

Thinking about objects

A myriad of objects are fused with our lives to fulfil our needs and desires and to assign meanings to our world. We are so used to living in a world of things that we rarely consider their existence and the extent to which objects shape our practices and cultures – thus furthering our desire for possessions and the production of new meanings (Gell 1998, Ingold 2000, Miller 2005). Given the intimate relationships between objects and human life, how does an object extend our personhood?

In this chapter, I draw upon Merleau-Ponty's perceptual phenomenology to consider the intersubjectivity of an object in reflecting upon our relationship with objects. Turning to Chinese material culture, I examine how Merleau-Ponty's notion can be integrated into the study of objects. In essence, highlighting materiality would connect with an object's perceptual qualities through our bodily experiences which, in turn, would enhance our empathetic understanding of the humanity that is embodied by the object.

Being in the world of things

Merleau-Ponty (1962: 5) is concerned that 'We are caught up in the world and we do not succeed in extricating ourselves from it in order to achieve consciousness of the world.' His philosophical project thus focuses on giving perception primacy, and enabling it to operate within a matrix of objects, persons and situations, as an extension of our mind, metaphorically drawing the world to us (Kelly 2005: 98–9). In this respect, Merleau-Ponty's perceptual phenomenology illuminates the intriguing object–human relationship in dissolving material and culture sensuously.

To material culturalists, Merleau-Ponty's theory suggests that objects speak for themselves through our perception. He denies that we have innate knowledge that constructs our understanding of objects. For example, a 26-layer hollowed-out ivory ball of openwork demonstrates ingenious craftsmanship, which is likely to draw visitors' attention, even those having little prior knowledge or interest in Chinese decorative art. Curiously, my audience survey conducted in the Bristol City Museum revealed that visitors who had never before seen an intricate object like the ivory ball tended to express greater interest in the artefact than the 'experienced' viewers. One of the experienced viewers stated (19 November 2007), 'That's nothing spectacular. I have seen this before.' Clearly, objects cannot be understood in our minds alone, and in some cases, our ignorance creates the novelty in such object–human encounters, to heighten our sensory pleasures (Merleau-Ponty 1962: 33).

Emphasising the objectivity of the phenomenal world and its impact on our perception, Merleau-Ponty does not agree that an absolute truth is obtainable about the phenomenal world, where we learn about objects through definite atomistic sense data which eventually lead us to an objective overview. Considering our established perception and prior knowledge, we cannot communicate with an object in an initially unbiased manner. For instance, the lack of context or insufficient lighting may cause a visitor to mistakenly identify a blue and white exportware from China as a Wedgwood piece decorated in a similar style. Thus, our knowledge of the external world can be acquired through sense experiences, which are grounded by our common sense of the perceived object and the objective conditions of perception (Merleau-Ponty 1962: 7–8).

To dissolve the dichotomy between the objectivity of things and the subjectivity of our perceptions, Merleau-Ponty proposes the notion of 'lived body'. According to Merleau-Ponty (1962: 94), the body is 'a vehicle of being in the world' that mediates between subject and object, and consciousness and materiality, enabling one to be interwoven into the phenomenon world. The body is not a separate part of our being, providing us with sense data about our surroundings, but a living organism that draws us into the world and enables the world to communicate with us. As Merleau-Ponty argues, 'I am not in front of my body, I am in it, or rather I am it, we are our bodies' (1962: 173). He uses the phenomenon of a phantom limb to illustrate this.

Physiological evidence has shown that patients who have had a limb amputated may still feel sensations from the missing limb and continue to act instinctively as though it is still there in situations where use of the missing limb would be needed. Merleau-Ponty (1962: 92–3) argues that if our body could be separated from our mind, patients would live on without feeling the urge to use a phantom limb. In fact, this phenomenon demonstrates that our body and consciousness comprise an integrated operation of sense, which enables us to connect our mind with the 'external' world. Our bodies, or more precisely, our bodily perceptions, encounter an overlapping experience between the world of things and us, which enables us to be conscious of various possibilities in relation to our surroundings. Merleau-Ponty proves that our body is immanent, engaging us in the world of things as an extension of the mind; and also transcendent, shaping our sensory experiences according to the objects we encounter.

Based on the premise that our body is the centre of the world, Merleau-Ponty further suggests that our sense of being is not only an organic totality of mind and body, but also correlates within a matrix of objects, people and situations. Merleau-Ponty states:

> The system of experiences is not arrayed before me as if I were God, it is lived by me from a certain point of view; I am not the spectator, I am involved, and it is my involvement in a point of view which makes possible

both the finiteness of my perception and its opening out upon the complete world as a horizon of every perception.

(1962: 354)

We can never experience the world out of our bodies; and objects from the world only exist when they are experienced by us. We are not detached entities, but involved in the world within a body that can only see things from certain particular perspectives in a particular content. Even elements of our sensory stimulation are not atomic definites. For instance, a shade of blue does not exist in its own right; rather, it is a colour of *something* that feels different in various textures (Merleau-Ponty 1962: 365). In other words, we are enmeshed in a matrix of things with our being understood only in relation to the world. These bodily experiences are intersubjective, partial and in flux, enabling inexhaustible possibilities which can unfold to us. To Merleau-Ponty, this state of 'in-betweenness,' the interweaving of subjective self with the objective world, heightens our sense of being, in rediscovering ourselves and as we experience the multi-layered phenomenon world to its fullest extent.

In touch with objects

Merleau-Ponty contends that the in-betweenness of our bodies, on one hand, mediates our mind and body, for it operates in the world of things as an extension of the mind. On the other hand, it engages us with the world through sensory experiences. Living intimately within a matrix of objects, we could find the sensory world stimulating, but confusing and difficult as well. How do we communicate with objects in making sense of the world?

According to Merleau-Ponty (1962: 45, 275), an object can be defined as an 'organism of colours, smells, sounds and tactile appearances' and body defines as another form of object, which is also sensitive to these sensory stimulations. Highlighting the sensations our bodies experience through an object–human relationship, he justifies his claim that humans understand the 'tactile language' of an object because both parties actually share the same means of communication. In addition to this shared 'language', Merleau-Ponty (1968b: 123) argues that objects are alive in the sense that they are an extension of our being. He observes that when we look at something, our body is looked at. This reciprocality of object–human communication suggests that materiality shapes our bodily perception of the world and reveals part of ourselves, such as feelings, thoughts or desires, through this bodily experience. We may not have prior knowledge or personal experiences related to an object, but by feeling its materiality, the double sensations of our bodies are absorbed into a dialogue with the object.

To illustrate the reciprocity between objects and our sensory experiences, I refer to Chinese connoisseurs' description of glaze colour as an example. *Gangdou* red is literally translated as red, akin to the skin of beans; it is a copper-red glaze developed by the imperial kiln during the late-seventeenth century (Kerr 1998: 74–5). It is praised for its sophistication, in that moss-greens puff out from the lustrous layer of reds and suffuse like a cloud of smoke (Chen 1994 [1910] I: 4A-B, II: 15A). Connoisseurs refer to the glaze as 'drunken beauty' (*Meiren zui*), 'peachbloom' (*Taohua pian*) or 'baby cheeks' (*Wawa lian*) in highlighting the subtle transmutation of colours (Zhao 1973 [1942]: 93–4, Liu 1993 [1925]: 46–7, Xu 1993 [1925]: 60–1). What is the colour of intoxication, flourishing blossoms or a child's cheeks? These descriptions seem to be less than helpful for accurately identifying the colour of the copper-red glaze. Curiously, they attempt to relate the interfering effects of feminine grace, natural beauty or budding youth, and draw readers to imagine how the soft, ruby-red shades touch the tiny spots of forest-green. In this sense, the terms are metaphors that evoke an aesthetic imagination based on the materiality of the glaze. As the connoisseurs project their education, taste and aesthetic imaginations onto the glaze, the materiality shapes their perceptions, sensory responses and appreciation criteria of the glaze.

Highlighting sensory experiences as the primordial contact with the world, Merleau-Ponty holds that bodily perception is an embodiment of our personal history, embracing tactile expressions, passion and feelings (1962: 150). Hence, our feelings, instead of thinking, enable us to grasp tactile language in experiencing the density of the world. The fundamental phenomenon of the world is its organic totality, in which objects and people interweave within a tempo-spatial context. Hence, Merleau-Ponty (1968a: 35) suggests that reflective bodily perception 'turns back over the density of the world in order to clarify it, but . . . coming second, reflects back to it only its own light'. In other words, the tactile language of objects is understood by the heightening of our senses in choosing different ways to relate to the world.

Taking the perspective of material culturalists, Merleau-Ponty's notion suggests that studying an object can be an intersensorial experience, since what is seen is physically, cognitively and emotively related by the researcher to the sounds, touch, smell, taste and feelings that are evoked by the object in its specific cultural context. Through the sensuous stimulations that are shared by the objects and their human agents, researchers can become involved in the world as others would have experienced it in the past. Material cultural studies should, then, look into the blurred zone of in-betweenness, where the formal qualities of objects can be fully experienced, and where personal narrations, such as desire, emotions or memories can emerge from the human stories embodied within the objects.

In the following discussion, I use Chinese material culture as an example to investigate how Merleau-Ponty's notion of perceptual phenomenology can be implemented into the study of objects. This modest attempt considers the possibilities of material culture research for understanding the bodily extension of humanity that might otherwise be ignored.

Function and bodily experiences

By positioning material culture at the nexus of tactile consideration, Merleau-Ponty suggests that objects are agents, which shape human culture with their materiality. He states:

The thing is inseparable from a person perceiving it, and can never be actually *in itself* because its articulations are those of our very existence, and because it stands at the other end of our gaze or at the terminus of a sensory exploration which invests it with humanity.

(1962: 373, emphasis in original)

At a basic level, objects are created to serve a particular function and are therefore empowered to act on behalf of human beings (Gell 1998: 6). Our intention is the human agency embedded in our actions, which elicit sensuous experiences and reveal the interaction between the materiality of an object and our bodily perception. Thus, an object may be considered as a bodily auxiliary in materialising our intention (Merleau-Ponty 1962: 152, Gell 1998: 20–1).

For example, conventional forms of Chinese tableware demand certain etiquette; this suggests that eating is more an intimate sensory experience, rather than simply the ingesting of food. A rice bowl, shaped with a flared mouth and foot rim, rests comfortably in one's hand, bringing the food closer to the holder, to feel the warmth and aroma. A porcelain bowl, with a simple design, would thus be a piece of delectable tableware to flesh out the colours of the rice and the various elements of the dish (Yuan 1913 [1716–98]: 3a, Wang 1994: 334–5). A rice bowl then materialises the human intention of serving a hot meal, enabling a better appreciation of the food. This can be understood as an extension of our bodily perceptions and potential action.

To a certain extent, the use of a rice bowl encourages Chinese table manners in serving dishes with larger plates placed at the centre of a round table, so that one may have a few bites from every plate. It helps to create an enjoyable eating space, which is both individual and communal, since one feels free to taste various combinations of food according to personal preference and be able to socialise with others by sharing the dishes. Objects of daily life, like tableware, further organise our habits in a natural way that may be imperceptible; for example, holding a rice bowl while eating, or managing a pair of chopsticks to pick up food. In fact, our bodies need to develop certain kinds of manners, knowledge and skills. In this sense, objects are the extension of our bodily synthesis to bridge our needs with the social life of the world. They also extend our physical bodies, to help transform us into social beings.

At first glance, such an approach to studying material culture has much in common with research that examines function and sociocultural practices in a particular cultural context. Besides taking this line of enquiry, the approach also emphasises a return to the sensations of how an object feels when being used, rather than considering just the relevant sociocultural context. This suggests that a rice bowl is not merely a vessel that extends one's bodily function, but that it is a crucial performative agent that transforms eating into a multi-sensory experience, also embodying dining etiquette and manners that are deep-rooted within culture. Therefore, sensory stimulations would be a medium, which draws the Chinese culture of eating to our bodily experiences, and communicates subtle connotations of culture that would otherwise be neglected.

Feelings and bodily experiences

Highlighting sensory experiences as a cornerstone of understanding the phenomenon world, Merleau-Ponty's notion also prompts researchers to consider how feelings could be integrated into the study of material culture. That is, investigating how we become attached to an object to resolve conflicts within our inner psyche; for example, to gain confidence or overcome grief. The psychological concept of the 'transitional object' is helpful for explaining this. According to Winnicott, a teddy bear or a blanket creates the illusion of a motherly figure, bringing a sense of security for a baby (Winnicott 1971, Csikszentmihalyi and Rochberg-Halton 1981: 23–4). In the case of adults, emotional attachment is far more complicated and subtle than simply recovering from insecurity. In fact, the ways in which we become attached to specific objects vary and the meanings they can trigger may be reversible and somehow contradictory, depending on the demands of the particular situation, the emotional state of the person and personal history (Dant 2000). Nonetheless, the emotional comfort we yearn for is not an abstract idea. Either metaphorically or realistically, it is a form of sensuous satisfaction that can only be fulfilled by materialised being: the perceptual qualities of an object or the sensuous experiences it conveys (Dant 2005: 62–3).

In the context of Chinese material culture studies, this approach of studying how materiality embodies sensory and emotional responses brings new ideas to the examination of funeral objects. Funeral items, including paintings, manuscripts, ceremonial vessels, musical instruments, dining utensils, daily life necessities and pottery figures, are made, arranged and buried in a meticulous manner for the dead. The genre of objects is distinctive, since people believed that the deceased should be shown respect by being treated as if they were alive (Pu 1993: 219–22, Yu 2008: 121). These objects have long been categorised according to their function and/or medium and considered as leftover material that informed researchers about the decorative style and technical development of artefacts, religious beliefs, symbolism and daily life experiences of people in specific historical contexts (Xiao *et al.* 2000: 121–2). By examining the categories of artefacts systematically, a typology of objects or a chronological order of the related cultural practices can be constructed. Nevertheless, this approach ignores the bodily experiences that a set of objects would be expected to perform, or how the objects might embody a potential emotional bond with the dead (Wu 2008: 81).

To illustrate this, consider Lady Dai's tomb, from *Mawangtui*, an archaeological site dating from the Western Han Dynasty (207 BCE–25 CE). Lady Dai was the wife of the Marquis of Dai, who was Prime Minister for the state of Changsha. Lady Dai is buried in four embellished lacquered layers of coffins, surrounded by over 3,000 funeral objects distributed in four different chambers. The northern chamber is of particular interest, as the enclosed space has walls that are decorated with silk tapestries and bamboo mats which provide exquisite flooring. At the back, a comfortable settee, with embroidered pillow and lacquered armrest, is set in the middle against a colourfully painted screen. In front of the settee, a lacquered table holds a great variety of culinary dishes, lacquerwares and glittering drinking vessels. Next to the seat, personal items, such as a walking stick, cosmetic accessories and wigs, are there for the owner. Lady Dai – or more precisely, her soul – probably looks to the left where a group of pottery figurines are dancing and playing various musical instruments (Hunan Provincial Museum 1973: 3–37, 97–101).

Apparently, the set of funerary objects were meant to ensure that Lady Dai would enjoy opulent living, with an abundance of food and drink, glamorous clothes and accessories, and endless dances and musical performances. The chamber was her underground household, where her soul, an immaterial yet conscious being, was expected to experience all sorts of sensory pleasures in the fullest sense (Wu 2008: 84–5). The emphasis on sensory experiences for the deceased confirms that Han Chinese believed that death was a transformation of life cycle, and that the afterlife was an extension of the living world (He and Zhang 1982: 33–7, Yu 1987: 377–9). Still, the multiple-layered coffins and the fact that Lady Dai was wrapped in more than 20 layers of silk suggests that the deceased was completely disconnected from the living; and that the dead belonged to the realm of the underground, with its darkness, spirits and mystery (He 2004: 26–7, Yu 2008: 181–4). The funeral objects may be considered as consolations for the living, when contemplating the uncertainty of death, but still embodying complex feelings (including fear, anxiety and, perhaps, intrigue). Preparing the objects would likely have been the last and a crucial opportunity for the living to pay tribute to the dead.

Focusing on the sensory experiences that the objects would provide for the deceased, the aim is to contextualise the funeral objects in their original tomb environment. The funeral objects are considered as an integral whole that helps to unpack ancient beliefs and the people's response to the otherworld. By looking at the bodily experiences and emotional responses to an object, new research questions arise, such as why a tomb builder would design such chambers for the deceased; what is the significance of the different layers of coffins and personal possessions of Lady Dai and her family; and how does the setting reveal changing concepts about the soul in the Western Han Dynasty (Wu 2008: 84–5)? By positioning material culture research within the context of bodily experiences, researchers are able to construct various scenarios for objects, and explore the human stories embodied by the materials.

Action and process

In addition to considering how objects are experienced sensuously, Merleau-Ponty's theory focuses on interactions between body and materials. In terms of material culture studies, perceptual phenomenology reminds researchers to look into the making process of objects: how the materials would be handled by craftsmen while materialising their ideas. Thus, researchers consider how craftsmen would develop a certain skill and technique for exploring a range of aesthetic possibilities according to their role in a particular social context. Consequently, social and technical dimensions are involved in examining the formal qualities of artwork through the craftsmen's bodily actions and the process of making.

In a workshop environment, the production facilities contextualise the working space and regulate a set of routines for team members for collaborating with one another towards the common purpose – becoming part of the production process (Dant 2005: 111). This is critical for the study of decorative art or ceremonial objects, which are produced by anonymous artists according to a prescribed set of instructions, whether they be porcelains from the Jingdezhen imperial kiln or ritual portraits of emperors made by Chinese court artists. In these cases, the artists' autonomy was compromised in that they were detached from the creative process, being guided by prototypes of various forms. Nonetheless, the intentionality of artists, as social beings working collectively, is revealed by the social network that mediated interactions between artists, the media and the patron-recipient during the production of art. In other words, objects, the finished products of a technical process, acted as effective mediators for enquiring into the social characteristics and significance of art production.

In looking at a polychrome vase (Figure 12.1), we can appreciate its perceptual qualities, including the translucent and refined texture of the porcelain body, different layers of coloured glazing which confer a poetic touch, and the asymmetric composition of pomegranate trees and magpies which accentuate the globular form. We can also see how these dissolve into a vivid brush painting

Figure 12.1 Polychrome vase with pomegranate and magpie, Qing dynasty, c. eighteenth century, Bristol City Museum collection. Photograph taken by author (2006). Reproduced with permission of Bristol City Museum and Art Gallery.

that enhances the three-dimensional view of the vase as an organic whole. The exquisite qualities of the vase, and especially the imperial reign mark inscribed on its base, suggest that it was produced by an imperial workshop at Jingdezhen. Every piece of porcelain may have gone through more than twenty procedures, conducted by seventy workers (Kerr 1998: 35–7, Lan 1991 [1870]: 1.53–64, Zhu 1994 [1774]: 1.63–84). For example, the painting of the polychrome decoration was divided into smaller tasks, such as designing the prototype, outlining the decoration, mixing coloured glazes, and filling in colours and applying overglaze, where each craftsman excelled at his appointed task (Lan 1991: 3.82, Zhu 1994: 1.2–13). This meticulous division of labour enabled the team to work mechanically, with each member developing a bodily response to the materiality that led to more efficiency.

The effect of a ceramic object's formal qualities portrays a materialised, sensuous display of the artist's technique and skills in working with the materials. For example, the dramatic form of the vase (Figure 12.1) implies that in mastering their throwing skills, the potters were familiar with the low plasticity of porcelain clay. Following the motion of the rotating wheel, the potter first established a base by slightly pressing the clay to flow freely between the fingers, then held the outer wall with one hand and pushed from the inside to shape the clay body with the other. To a certain extent, porcelain clay is resistant to being shaped, yet the potter developed a bodily sense to enable the handling of the unstable clay while managing the wheel, which rotated at a high speed, so that a desirable form was created, despite its durability and shrinkage rate after being dried and fired (Huanan Gongxueyuan *et al.* 1981: 77–8). The globular form of the vase is thus a material agent, demonstrating a bodily interaction between the potter and the medium. The static, final artwork's perceptual qualities do not stand alone, as the artwork is infused with the artist's bodily action, a vigorous performance of technical process and a meticulous plan of production.

In any case, porcelain making is an art of fire, as well as clay. Clearly, the experience and skills of kiln workers were critical in controlling the kiln environment and locating various forms of porcelain to different parts inside the kiln, to prevent distortion and cracking of the finished products. In fact, in the production line for the vase shown in Figure 12.1, many workers were assigned to the different procedures, like trimming, polishing the body surface, cutting the vase from the wheel and replenishing the water, each of which contributed to the perfect form of the product. In the imperial workshop, each team member was focused on a single task, but the work was interrelated to the extent that even a tiny mistake from the biscuit-loading worker would spoil the form of the porcelain ware (Wang 2004: 108, 206–9). All of the workers were working towards a common goal – creating an anticipated effect with porcelain ware for the imperial court. The vase form, which embodies the technical virtuosity of the Qing dynasty, points to the collective actions of craftsmen in mastering the resistance of material.

This example demonstrates that enquiry into a technical process considers the social fabric of a community working with a medium. By looking into the artists' bodily experiences, such studies consider how they work collaboratively during the production process and explain why the finished work was made in a particular manner. Instead of asking how an object is made technically, such an enquiry considers how the makers created the object. Technical production is then considered as a tactile conversation between craftsmen and medium in moulding the craftsmen's bodily experiences and the medium into a desirable piece.

Sensuous beings – materiality and personhood

In positioning material culture within the context of bodily experiences, I have appealed to perceptual phenomenology to theorise how we identify with objects. Emphasising the in-betweenness of objects, Merleau-Ponty suggests that an object can be defined as the material result of human experiences that replicate and shape human cultures, bodies and persons, both symbolically and materially. In other words, the object is not a 'dead body' of materials, but a living extension of human beings from different places and times. This idea reminds researchers to broaden the studies of material culture from the formal qualities of an object to include the sensory stimulations it embodies. Encountering an object thus goes beyond an intellectual exchange; it is a sensuous experience of feeling how an object's varied perceptual qualities are coordinated in unifying materiality and humanity.

Bibliography

Chen, Liu. (1994 [1910]) *Tao ya*. [*Pottery Refinement*], Chengdu: Bashu shushe.

Csikszentmihalyi, M. and E. Rochberg-Halton (1981) *The Meaning of Things: domestic symbols and the self*, Cambridge: Cambridge University Press.

Dant, T. (2000) 'Objects in time: modernity and biography', in *Material Culture in the Social World: values, activities, lifestyles*, Buckingham: Open University Press, pp. 130–52.

Dant, T. (2005) *Materiality and Society*. Maidenhead: Open University Press.

Gell, A. (1998) *Art and Agency: an anthropological theory*, Oxford: Clarendon Press.

He, Jiejun (2004) *Mawangdui Hanmu* [*Han Tomb at Mawangdui*], Beijing: Wenwu chubanshe.

He, Jiejun and Zhang Weiming (eds) (1982) *Mawangdui Hanmu* [*Han Tomb at Mawangdui*], Beijing: Wenwu chubanshe.

Huanan Gongxueyuan *et al.* (1981) *Taoci gongyixue* [*Techniques of Pottery Making*], Beijing: Zhongguo jianzhu gongye chubanshe.

Hunan Provincial Museum (1973) *Changsha Mawangdui yihao Hanmu* [*Han Tomb No.1 at Mawongtui Changsha*], Beijing: Wewu Publication Limited.

Ingold, T. (2000) *Perception of the Environment: essays in livelihood, dwelling and skill*, London: Routledge.

Kelly, S.D. (2005) 'Seeing things in Merleau-Ponty', in T. Carman and M.B.N. Hansen (eds) *The Cambridge Companion to Merleau-Ponty*, Cambridge: Cambridge University Press, pp. 74–110.

Kerr, R. (1998) *Chinese Ceramics: porcelain of the Qing Dynasty, 1644–1911*, London: Victoria and Albert Museum.

Lan, Pu. (1991 [1870]) *Jingdezhen Tao Lu* [*An Account of Pottery at Jingdezhen*], Beijing: China Bookshop.

Liu, Zifen. (1993 [1925]) *Zhuyuan taoshuo* [*Remarks on Pottery from the Bamboo Garden*], Shanghai: Shanghai keji jiaoyu chubanshe.

Merleau-Ponty, M. (1962) *Phenomenology of Perception*, London: Routledge.

Merleau-Ponty, M. (1968a) 'Reflection and interrogation', in *The Visible and Invisible*, Evanston: Northwestern University Press, pp. 3–50.

Merleau-Ponty, M. (1968b) 'Interrogation and intuition', in *The Visible and Invisible*, Evanston: Northwestern University Press, pp. 105–29.

Miller, D. (2005) 'Materiality: an introduction', in D. Miller (ed.) *Materiality*, Durham, NC: Duke University Press, pp. 1–51.

Pu, Muzhou. (1993) *Muzang yu Xhengsi: Zonggou Gudai Zongjian zhi Xingsi* [*On Burial, Life and Death: Reflection on Chinese Ancient Religion*], Taipei: Lianjing Chubanshiye Gongsi.

Wang, Renxiang. (1994) *Yinshi yu Zhongguo Wenhua* [*Dinning and Chinese Culture*], Beijing: Zhonghua Xuadian.

Wang, Guangyao. (2004) *Zhongguo gudai guanyao zhidu* [*The Ancient System of Imperial Kiln in China*], Beijing: Zijincheng chubanshe.

Winnicott, D.W. (1971) 'Transitional objects and transitional phenomenona', in *Playing and Reality*, London: Tavistock Publications, pp. 1–34.

Wu, Hung. (2008) *Meishu shi shiyi* [*Ten Discussions on Art History*], Beijing: Sanlian Shudian.

Xiao, Kezhi *et al.* (2000) *Handai taoqi yu gudai wenming* [*Han Pottery and Ancient Civilization*], Beijing: Zhongguo nongye chubanshe.

Xu, Zhiheng. (1993 [1925]) *Yinliuzhai shuoci* [*Remarks on Porcelain from the Studio of Wine Lover*], Shanghai: Shanghai keji jiaoyu chubanshe.

Yu, Ying-Shih. (1987) ' "O Soul, Come Back!" A Study in the Changing Conceptions of the Soul and Afterlife in Pre-Buddhist China', *Harvard Journal of Asiatic Studies*, 47: 363–95.

Yu, Ying-Shih. (2008) *Donghan Shengsiguan* [*Views of Life and Death in later Han China*], Taipei: Lianjing Chubanshiye Gongsi.

Yuan, Mei. (1913 [1716–98]) *Suiyuan shidan* [*The Recipes from Sui Garden*], Shanghai: Zhonghua Tushuguan.

Zhao, Ruzhen. (1973 [1942]) *Guwan zhinan* [*Guidebook for Collecting Antiques*], Taipei: Wenhai chubanshe.

Zhu, Yan. (1994 [1774]) *Tao shuo* [*On Pottery*], Taipei: Yiwen yinshuguan.

13 The poetic triangle of objects, people and writing creatively

Using museum collections to inspire linguistic creativity and poetic understanding

Nikki Clayton and Mark Goodwin

Introduction

This chapter stems from an interactive workshop that was given at the Material Worlds conference. The wordshop focused on the potential of museum objects to release participants' linguistic creativity, and so engender deeper and more various understandings of the material world. (In this context 'understandings' are more often emotional and poetic, although conceptual and reasoned understanding can also be enhanced.) Wordshop participants were invited to experience this potential directly by engaging in a series of creative writing games (or exercises) stimulated and inspired by museum objects from one of the Open Museum's loan collections.

As an officer with Leicestershire's Open Museum and as a community poet, we have been working together on numerous community museum projects for over eight years. During this work we have witnessed the truly amazing[1] potential of museum objects to release linguistic creativity and, through this release, unlock people's latent and intuitive grasp of the phenomenology[2] and multiple meanings of objects. This can be described as a poetic triangle of objects, people and writing creatively. It is important to be aware that 'poetic' is not being used here to denote 'poetry' or 'of poetry'. 'Poetic' refers to a state of imaginative conscious-ness where awareness of the world is heightened through creative possibility and transformation, or, as Bachelard would have it: 'ecstasy of the novelty of the image' (1998: 97). It is also important that 'image' is not confused with 'visual image'; a poetic image, which can encompass all the senses and emotions, is characterised by being both startling and impossible to fix. 'Poetic' is forever open and forever in a state of becoming.

Often the daunting canon of literature and the perceived authority of museums inhibits people from relating significantly with creative writing and museum objects. Through our community work we have discovered that people can feel 'overwhelmed', 'intimidated' or 'stuck' when faced with the prospect of writing a poem or interacting with a museum object; there is a feeling in both situations that they will somehow 'get it wrong'. However, through combining museum objects free of glass cases with a sensitively facilitated creative environment, it is possible to give back to people recognition of their natural abilities to create with verbal language and read the world of objects around them. Sadly, it must be noted that people (adults and children alike) can often demonstrate astounding poetic and interpretive abilities but cannot be convinced to recognise them as valuable (we will briefly explore this point later).

The imagination, particularly when it is channelled through creative speaking and writing, can be a powerful hermeneutical tool. Certain poetic writing (and speaking) games and procedures can be utilised to explore juxtapositions and dialectics, and to also excavate emotional depths from surface appearances. (To obtain depth from mere surface is, through logical discourse, an impossibility; however, poetic thinking is not bound by logic.) 'Dialectics' in this context is not to do with the logical critical investigation of truth or opinions (as utilised by Marx, for example), but refers rather to metaphysical contradictions and the processes of the unification of opposites. Poetic images (and poetry itself) are often characterised by the yoking of opposites. Metaphor is an example of a yoking of disparate elements. Poetics can be used to pursue 'truths', or to get to the 'essences' of things, or even a single thing. We cannot stress enough the importance of the plural 'essences' in relation to one thing. The plural term 'essences' in relation to a single object is paradoxical if considered logically and in terms of the definition of 'essence': 'The intrinsic nature or character of something; that which makes it what it is; the attributes, constituents, etc., that something must have for it not to be something else and that serve to characterise it' (*Shorter Oxford English Dictionary* 2007). However, if considered poetically, the word 'essences' honours the forever transformational, multiple and yet unified nature of poetic consciousness. Such poetic thinking can be used to identify, with reasoned certainty, what a particular object is not. Poetics always presents or creates a field of possibilities, and if embraced can dispel the pressure of 'getting it wrong' to reveal a phenomenological hermeneutics that is not fixed, but rather multiple and transforming. However, for the purposes of this chapter we will not dwell on this kind of philosophical discourse but focus on the relatively simple notion that *interacting actively and imaginatively with objects through verbal language can allow people to become confident in making their own unique interpretations of the material world.*

So, within this chapter, we draw more on our own experiential sources than from philosophical explorations offered by theorists such as Bachelard (see for example, 1994 and 1998) or Merleau-Ponty (see 1962). We share ideas that have been formed through our experiences of delivering museum-object-inspired creative writing workshops and projects for learning providers; community groups; people of differing ages and from a broad range of backgrounds. These experiences are underpinned by a wealth of documented evaluation undertaken for such community work. The poetry examples we use to illustrate the chapter have been taken from the Write:Muse initiative[3] and from the Behind the Scenes series of poetry workshops (BSPW),[4] both run by the Open Museum. The chapter also presents a poem collaged by Mark from fragments of creative writing that were generated by the participants of the conference workshop, and demonstrates how people can speak through 'things'.

Why creative writing and things?

Leicestershire's Open Museum comprises three loans collections of over 5,000 artefacts, models, replicas, artworks and touring displays of museum objects.[5] The wealth of resources it holds (as diverse as an eighteenth century bronze cockerel-shaped Chinese incense burner to stuffed owls in simulated flight) can fascinate, surprise and even amaze. There are also over fifty museums and heritage sites in Leicester and Leicestershire, ranging from an eighteenth century windmill to a major museum store located in a twentieth century industrial unit, all of which house a huge diversity of objects.

For community artists and outreach workers, these collections and sites are a never-ending source of inspiration and wonderment; something which as museum staff we can all too easily take for granted. Through evaluation and feedback, the Open Museum has discovered how the general public are not always comfortable engaging with museum objects; whether that be a primary school teacher using objects as part of a lesson or a young person encountering them during a fun day at their local community centre (see for example Boyd 2003, 2005, Dacombe and Daniels 2006, Mair 2009). A writer who facilitated a creative writing workshop with learning providers, commented: 'I was surprised that people did not seem to engage with the objects . . . there was not much voluntary picking up and handling of objects . . . not sure whether this was fear of handling them . . . ?' (Dacombe and Daniels 2006: 36).

As a museum service we work hard to help people get the most from our resources. We particularly strive to enable people to engage with objects in a way that is significant and consequential. We also try to encourage people to explore the multiplicity of meanings that 'things' provoke. A number of the Moving Objects touring displays, for example, are themed: the Beauty Myth display explores the cost of beauty in relation to health concerns, animal rights, human rights, monetary costs, etc. – the thirty or so historical and modern objects in the display do not physically change, but the stories and meanings you can draw from them certainly do.[6]

Barriers still exist that inhibit people from getting the most from the collections. However, one of the most successful ways we have discovered to challenge and break down these barriers is through employing experienced writers and poets to facilitate wordshops using museum collections as inspiration for creative writing, particularly poetry. However, creative writing is not without its own barriers; the canon of poetry, for example, can be intimidating for many and the mere mention of the 'P' word can send people hurrying away. When we use the word 'experienced' relating to writers and poets, our emphasis is on their ability to encourage others to write. Poetry workshops have to be undertaken in a sensitive manner, and we often use the term 'creative word-play' as a more appealing description of what participants become engaged in.

The benefits and value of 'creative word-play' are significant. As poets Deborah Tyler-Bennett and Mark Goodwin state in *Words and Things: writing creatively from objects and art*:

[P]laying with words and imagination can empower adults and children alike to become confident about expressing their distinct world-views and emotional selves. However, as well as language skills, this is also relevant to personal development. Engaging in imaginative writing and speaking will always teach us about language and how it works, but above all how to be better and more assured at making use of words. People need to use words, and are often far more talented and skilled at doing so than they realize. Writing creatively can reveal these unacknowledged talents. Playing with words in a small social group, i.e. in a workshop setting, can be a fulfilling and even profound sharing experience.

(Clayton and Featherstone 2008: 4)

Combine poetry/creative word-play and museum objects in a sensitive workshop, and people can unlock their ability to manipulate words, and reach a deeper understanding of objects and the world around (and within) them. As Write:Muse workshop participants have commented: 'It brought stuff out of me I didn't realise was there'; 'Using objects to fire imagination and turn it into something else . . . [I was] surprised how well this worked . . . a story behind each object' (Dacombe and Daniels 2006: 19).

Merely handling museum objects can engender this, as the quote below from a learning disabilities development worker reveals:

I think I couldn't believe sometimes the interest that people had of handling the objects. And how the objects could get people to reflect on things that people had dreamt of . . . a whole bit of their life that we [staff] had never heard about before. These objects would trigger off these memories which enable people [staff] to have a different perspective of people [they are caring for].

(Atkin-Barrett 2008)

However, using those objects for creative writing encourages this process even further:

You know things like the Poetry Engine [see below], stuff like that . . . these were all working great, and I'd just invent my own sort of binary system if you like. . . . going for a walk in the town I was so aware of what was underneath the surface . . . I can still remember that night even though I was tired, about midnight that night insisting on trying to get this particular poem together.

(Dacombe and Daniels 2006: 26)

I found working with museum objects really useful. They provided a good starting point for images, and I found myself trying to find human characteristics in the artefacts. The whole process was good for my self-esteem and I really enjoyed working with the poet.

(Leicestershire's Open Museum 2010: 14)

Creativity could be described as a process of unlocking. And when it comes to creative writing, for those not accustomed to writing creatively, to gain confidence it is often about being given 'permission' to speak outside conventions and received language registers. Permission can be given through validating ways of using verbal language that are unique to an individual. Using museum objects to inspire writing and speaking creatively in this way can encourage people, enable them to see their world differently and, as the above quote declares, raise their self-esteem.

For those our society marginalise, such as people who use mental health services or who have learning disabilities, the value of this process of unlocking to gain a voice can be profound and life-changing. Some of the positive effects of writing and speaking creatively for people who use mental health services have been identified by mental health professionals who have participated in Write:Muse wordshops:

> 'My hope is that we will inspire people to write/create in order to gain confidence in their abilities'; 'To encourage [them] to use community facilities, to gain interests in arts and be able to feel confident to access services available to them'; 'Patients suffer with huge low self-esteem. Hope it can get them out into the 'real world'; 'Social interactions with others increases confidence to share thoughts and feelings. Learn to listen to others.'
>
> (Leicestershire's Open Museum 2008)

So, writing creatively from objects can contribute towards increased confidence, self-esteem, self-efficacy and motivation. In turn, recovery from ill mental health is promoted, and ultimately people can begin to develop social networks and become socially included (see further evidence in Leicestershire's Open Museum 2010).

Writing creatively from museum objects is not only of value to those marginalised by our society. As Write:Muse workshops have shown, learning providers such as teachers and community tutors can also benefit hugely, and not only in terms of raising confidence, but also in bringing out previously undiscovered creative talents and skills (which they can pass on to their learners). As the following selection of feedback quotes from Write:Muse workshops declare:

> 'Very inspiring, I feel more energised about writing and much more confident on a personal level and teaching level'; 'Inspiring – I didn't know I could write stories! Amazed I'd written poems!'; 'I never thought I could be this creative!'; 'The teachers themselves insisted that the work they had written in these workshops were typed up and displayed in the area ... they're so proud of it.'
>
> (Dacombe and Daniels 2006: 91)

Seeing things differently

Bachelard has commented: 'This grip that poetry acquires on our very being bears a phenomenological mark that is unmistakable ... It is as though the poem, through its exuberance, awakened new depths in us' (1994: xxiii). Although here he is referring to the act of reading a poem, it is also true for the act of creating poetry. Playing poetic word-games can enable people to transform the ways in which they see the world (or rather, worlds). We have both witnessed a wordshop participant's profound amazement on discovering that they have created a poetic transformation. We have not only seen this in people's facial expressions and body language, we have also heard people declare their amazement and we have listened to them explain what their discovery means to them.

The poem that finishes this chapter is a case in point – it is full of transformational images rich with possibilities of multiple meaning. The following line from that poem was written by someone with very little creative writing experience, and yet it is a profound and beautiful discovery:

> A man in a desert seems
> a container of history.

If the person who wrote this line is enabled to value it, and so is allowed to see in it the possibilities it 'contains' for understanding fresh ways we can view 'history', 'men', 'containers' and 'deserts', then inevitably their view of those things and how they relate will change. Sometimes such transformation of view is small, but it can be considerable. Of most value perhaps, is the realisation in that person of their being able to use their imagination to transform the ways they view objects, concepts, emotions and people. Such a realisation is hugely empowering. It can allow us to shake off old ways of thinking and behaving that hinder us, be they imposed on us by others or by ourselves.

As workshop facilitators, we have discovered that it is really quite easy to get people to produce startling fragments or even substantial passages of poetry, and especially easy when utilising objects. However, when it comes to getting them to realise just how valuable their discovery and creation is, we very often fail. It is difficult to understand fully why this should be so. Often participants will reject the work they produce; they will either dismiss it or feel embarrassed about it. It is too easy for an eager poet to feel that everyone should have the opportunity to 'play' with poetics and phenomenology. However, such transformational and emotive creativity can be threatening. And as facilitators we have learned that for some there are very good reasons for not exploring the poetic imagination – for some, such exploration can even be dangerous.

On a basic level, writing creatively can encourage people to look closer at the material world around them. Simple creative writing exercises, for example, can encourage people to describe objects through simile and metaphor as the following poems illustrate:

Buttered Hands

> In pride of place at the front of the shop
> Warm honey, flecked with brown

Smooth, hard edges with corrugated sides
A flattened door wedge
A slice of supporters' rattle
Buttered hands for shaping butter into blocks

(Boyd 2008)

Haiku:

Crumpled Filing Card:
Starched collar worn by lawyer
Thrown down defeated.

(Atkin 2008)

Bottle

distortion bubble
ghost bulb
winter foetus
window bladder
eye sculpture
monopod chesspiece

(Johnson 2008: 69)

Museum objects also provide means to access meanings and memories constructed through the realms of society and the personal. Museum objects have traditionally been used for reminiscence work, with people with Alzheimer's or dementia, or with the elderly for example (see Kavanagh 2000, Arigho 2008, Jacques 2008, Phillips 2008). A focus of this work is to encourage individuals, through objects, to make connections to their past life and self/identity they now have trouble accessing. Using objects for poetry can also encourage this, as the following excerpt illustrates:

It would be like old times.
When an Alsatian guarded
scrap merchants you'd take me
to hunt for Ford Zephyr shock absorbers.
And I'd steal cigarette lighters
from the wrecks,
while you set to work
with a socket set.

(Stewart 2004: 39)

Objects 'turbo-charged', as it were, with creative writing can become powerful vehicles to transport us elsewhere. However, within poetic realms those *other* places, times (and the characters inhabiting them) are not limited to one's own memory and personal experience (as tends to happen in reminiscence).

The object can become a conduit for collective memory and time travel. Through poetic imagination incited by objects participants can even become objects:

> Sold from the workshop with the misshapen others
> Into Wylf the Pedlar's stock,
> For two years I travelled the donkey roads
> Jiggling in his greasy sack.
> Hawked at markets hereabouts
> Through fingerfulls of crowds
> I was that damnthing he could not sell.

(Twell 2007: 32)

When writing creatively, however, an individual can never escape their own life experiences. The same objects will always inspire diverse poetic responses drawn inevitably from the personal. The same collection of 1950s women's headscarves, for example, inspired BSPW participants to imagine the following very different fictional characters:

> The scarf she left
> Still hanging on the palm-hammered nail in the back of the door.
> He takes it down, faded now
> Yet, still half-silky, through his rough long-nailed fingers.

(Maslowski 2006: 64)

> My atomic cocktail-bubble-gum lipstick, scarves patterned
> Madrid, Paris, Rome, worn at *Butlins*,
> (a favourite, the Bridge of Sighs).
> Stilettos, candy-flossed underskirts flash.

(Tyler-Bennett 2006: 62)

Whilst experienced writers can create imaginary characters without the aid of museum objects, it is our experience that museum objects can actually make character-creation easier, and have certainly generated surprising characters that could not have been conjured without having been 'born' from a particular object (as the above examples demonstrate beautifully). Poetic contemplation of an object can open up channels of imagination through the very tangibility of the object's material.

Using the 'museumyness' of things

Through years of facilitating workshops and projects, we have witnessed how the experience of writing creatively from objects outside a museum setting and not contained behind glass, leads people to engage all the senses when considering an object. Through handling things the dominance of the visual is challenged as participants also engage their senses of touch, smell and hearing. The physicality, the materiality, of objects stimulates the imagination. (See Dudley 2010 for a wider exploration of museum materialities.)

However, when the public experiences museum objects from a loans collection or directly out of a museum store, the museum objects are often housed in boxes of varying sizes and materials to protect them. These containers can also act as focal points of inspiration, as the following poem, inspired by a Resource Box loans box, illustrates:

This box is empty

except for its noise
a tiny noise
a tinkling

the chest is a box for the heart
and the heart like the noise
is happy in its box

neither wants to be let out
both are happy to be locked.

(Gardner 2006: 25)

Indeed, the mere opening of a box resonates a certain expectancy and theatricalness which can inspire participants to look more closely. As Mark wrote in *Words and Things*:

A box of objects slowly opened, the tissue-paper-wrapped contents slowly unveiled by group members – this casts a spell! No one can fail to be fascinated. In being fascinated self-consciousness dissolves – suddenly some very surprising creativity is unleashed.

(Clayton and Featherstone 2008: 9)

The compelling, theatrical experience of unwrapping artefacts is not limited to objects associated with the great, good and famous (as is the case in Hancock 2009, for example). Indeed, the historical or personal provenance of an object need not be known at all for that object to resonate and capture the imagination. The phenomena of all objects, be they considered unique, common, exotic, cheap, mundane or precious have the potential to activate the imagination in profound ways: paperclip, a pharaoh's mummy, laptop computer, Indonesian Shamanic tunic, huge ruby gem stone, pedal bin.

The 'museumyness' of objects can also be explored (and revealed) in other ways through the creative act. The material culture contained within museums is not neutral. The very act of 'taking-in' objects by museums means that those objects become subject to processes of authority and control (Karp and Levine 1991, Bennett 1995, Macdonald 1997, Hooper-Greenhill 2000, Kavanagh 2000).

These relationships of power and control can be revealed through creative writing. A BSPW which used the Natural Life collections in storage, inspired the following:

> so it's good to find you skewered under glass,
> tiny thorns on your front-legs feeling for air;
> hinges on your back-legs no longer oiled.
>
> How I hope the death chemical was slow;
> that you fought with the pin through your wings,
> through your shell

(Thompson 2008: 74)

Through poetic imagination, the author of the poem above has revealed that the human desire to collect and classify has a brutality. The material world contained (and constrained) by the institution of 'Museum' is revealed as not being neutral nor passive. The poet 'hopes' that the victim 'fought'. The poem inevitably becomes a critique of the whole process of museumification.

Techniques for freeing the mind – getting to the essence of things (and oneself)

Imagination, particularly channelled through creative speaking and writing, can be a powerful hermeneutical tool. It can provide the means to enable a lay person to access and experience depths of otherwise hidden meanings of objects.

The following poem, written by a teacher in a Write:Muse workshop, was inspired by a Tibetan bell from the Open Museum's loans collection:

And the objects on the table spoke

> The Indian bell rang itself to death
> But just then
> Before passing over to the place that bells go
> Heard the others
> Resuscitating its colour,
> Blowing deep into its brass lung,
> Palming its figured handle.
> 'If I stay completely still
> And mould myself into this lie
> Perhaps no one will sound me out'.

(Richmond 2008)

Through the activity of focusing on an object to engage the poetic imagination, here the author has accessed a field of possibilities concerning interpretations of one culture by another. As it is a poetic text it cannot be fixed, and so presents a constellation of shifting 'truths', which in turn are open to further interpretations by different readers or listeners.

However, the shiftiness and multiplicity of interpretations are rooted in the almost tangible quality of the re-imagined object. If we are open to the poetics and alert to the rootedness of the senses evoked in this poem then we can experience interpretations of an object, and the kind of material culture it 'belongs' to or 'relates' to, that we could not have otherwise accessed. An observant curator would notice that the poet has mis-identified and 'mis-labelled' what is 'in fact' a Tibetan bell rather than an Indian one. However, it is not the job of a poetic hermeneutics to establish facts, but rather express possibilities of innate understandings.

Techniques can be as simple as just speaking freely in the moment, rather than writing words down (if necessary others can scribe). As teacher Rob Cooper observed about his students:

> The students loved the objects and were inspired by the atmosphere they helped to create. Scribing for them allowed their imaginations to run wild, free from the limitations of their literacy skills. The ideas that came out could not have happened without the objects.
>
> (Clayton and Featherstone 2008: 18)

Certain poetic games can be played which facilitate this further. One warm-up exercise that Mark uses in his workshops is the 'Outpour'. Participants write for three minutes about an object, and in that time they must not stop writing; the pen must keep moving; they must not stop to 'think' (nor worry about the conventions of spelling, grammar, etc.).[7] It can take some practice to move away from having the conscious and rational parts of our minds try to vet the output from our unconscious. However, if set up in the right kind of way, in a conducive environment and atmosphere (often enhanced by museum objects), an outpour can quickly generate some surprising and strong creative writing from complete novices. Through this exercise, participants are not only helped to overcome the horror of the blank page, but are also often surprised by the inevitable expression of ideas about an object that they could never have accessed if they had thought rationally about the object before writing. This exercise demonstrates how writing creatively is in itself a way of thinking – the writing process is the thinking.

Another exercise, what Mark has called the 'Poetry Engine', provides a particularly effective means to explore the hermeneutical possibilities of objects. Participants fold a piece of A4 paper in half length-ways, creating two thin columns to write in. This exercise was undertaken with the Material Worlds conference delegates, and in this instance, they inserted the word 'house' at the top of one column. They then had to write down that column about 'house', 'home', 'shelter', 'hearth' and so on, while looking at small models of houses from the Open Museum's loans collections (Figure 13.1). Then, at the top of the second column they put the word 'desert', and were asked to write about this subject/object from their imaginations. Once both columns were full of text it was then possible to splice lines from the two columns by effectively ignoring the columns and reading across the entire width of the page, thus creating new sentences by editing at will.[8]

Figure 13.1 Teeth and houses from the Leicestershire Open Museum Resource Box collection. Photograph by Nikki Clayton.

The 'Poetry Engine' can be used to get to the 'truths' or 'essence(s)' of things, and is particularly effective relating to opposites or dialectics. In the conference workshop the dialectics of sheltered and unsheltered, wild and domestic, inside and outside, civilised and uncivilised, hidden and exposed, and even private and public were 'processed' by the poetry engine through using the words 'desert' and 'house'. The exercise led some of the conference delegates to reveal fears associated with home, and the anxiety of losing the security 'home' offers in the face of 'wilderness' (or even the face of the 'wilderness' of society):

> Somewhere there are houses, homes where the
> heart is, little yellow home
> But here it is cold, uninhabited, trackless,
> No people, no dogs but wild wolves
>
> (Susan Pearce)

> County homes are dry and exposed
> market towns are empty and alone
> Home has been carried away on the breeze.
> Need to go away from the city.
>
> (Amy)

When choosing the words for each half of a poetry engine care has to be taken. It tends to be ineffective to simply use adjectives, and more often fails completely if abstracts are used. So, rather than 'wet' and 'dry' it is better to have 'water' and 'dust', and rather than 'love' and 'hate' it is essential to have somethings[9] like 'ring' and 'knife'. 'Thingness' is the important quality here. Poetry only happens in relation to 'things', and in turn only happens in relation to emotions. The humanness of poetics reveals objects through emotions and reveals emotions through objects. Museums, the custodians of objects, could much enhance their roles by considering further the triangle (or equation) of object–emotion–poem, and so could perhaps also become repositories of emotional potential.

Conclusions

We have presented some evidence to show how encouraging people to be creative and imaginative is intrinsically valuable. The social and emotional benefits people can gain from writing creatively about museum objects include: an expanded world-view and consciousness; a facility to look outwards and beyond oneself; an opportunity to consider the world and one's position in it anew; raised confidence and self-esteem; permission to speak with a unique voice; enhanced well-being and health.

We hope that through this chapter we have begun to reveal how the imagination, particularly channelled through creative speaking and writing, has the potential to be utilised as a powerful hermeneutical tool. The imagination can act as fascinating and exciting transport through the shimmering of poetic meanings within the material world. We have explored how the poetic triangle of objects, people and writing creatively can provide the means to enable lay people to access and experience the depths of hidden meanings in the relationships between people and objects; how the creative act, facilitated in a sensitive and supportive manner, can be one of unlocking, and of being given permission to speak poignantly and uniquely.

To finish, we offer a poem which Mark has collaged from the poetic fragments produced from the imaginations of the Material Worlds conference delegates in our interactive workshop.[10] Though on first reading it might appear non-sensical, and indeed will defy being pinned to any certainty, we are certain it reveals beautifully how humans, through their words, cannot help but react and relate to objects, and to each other.

A Museum of Desert-as-House

How to start? A man in a desert seems
a container of history. How powerful!

Frost roses on the window stare
at this endless home
of quiet snow. I have a roof
over this white, white
head of mine and colour I can dream

I can flower . . .

. . . five houses, all different, lie in the hot sun.
Sand, wind, chimneys, windows, doors,

yellow and red bricks in solitude's silence.
Village, city, region, difference
home this ground. Here,

little yellow home. Home
where a heart is. I am running

on top of void images.
Standing upright is a mark of existence.
I have to find out how to balance.
My eyes merge with horizon.
Feeling so small and immense I
could fly away from this house.
Where would I land?

Perhaps we have already gone
through the wardrobe to a place
of tiny houses. See

my concealed shoes:
do not stop them
on a cold night,

for my soul's body
has glass windows
through which stars twinkle.

Darkness and absence surge
around my shelter, fighting
to unmake it –

a shelter
of becoming a house.

I look for the purple house to put
in this beauty of nature.
What I need for myself is this
wilderness of freedom:

like the snake, me, swimming through
grains of sand. The smells.
The sands stalking their prey.

House/home –
what's the meaning
of that when you have
a beautiful desert in your heart?

Home has been carried
away on the breeze.

Everything is under
this heavy load
of snow waiting

like a flower in a pot . . .

Notes

1 This is not mere rhetoric – we do mean the truth of actual amazement.
2 This paper draws mostly from Bachelardian phenomenology.
3 Write:Muse is an ongoing initiative which enables learning providers such as teachers, adult learning tutors, youth workers, museum and library staff to experience creative writing workshops facilitated by practicing writers. The workshops make use of the Open Museum's loans collections as inspiration, and the emphasis is on engaging participants in creative word-play through which, ultimately, they explore their own creativity and increase their confidence with poetry and prose.
4 The Behind the Scenes series of poetry workshops makes use of museum spaces, sites and collections that are not normally accessible to the public. These workshops are open to adults, and include anyone interested in poetry, from novices through to experienced poets.
5 For further information about Leicestershire's Open Museum and the Resource Box, Artworks and Moving Objects loans collections, visit http://www.leics.gov.uk/open_museum.html
6 For more information about the Beauty Myth Moving Objects display, visit http://www.leics.gov.uk/open_museum/movingobjects/moving_objects_collections/beauty_myth.html
7 For a more detailed explanation of this exercise, see Clayton and Featherstone (2008: 73).
8 For a more detailed explanation of this exercise, see Clayton and Featherstone (2008: 127).
9 'Somethings' should not be confused with 'some things'. 'Somethings' refers to the multiple possibilities ('somethingness') of what we often, in passing, consider to be fixed 'things'. For example, 'knife' holds possibilities relating to surgeons, murderers or cooks; and the possibilities of meanings for each of us is unique, depending on our personal memories.
10 There have been hardly any changes made to fragments of text lifted out of participants' work. The fragments have been collaged with the full permission of the participants: Alice Semedo, Amy, Despina Kalessopoulou, Giota Kasimi, Magnus Gestsson, Mark Hall, Marlen Mouliou, Sue Pearce, Poyan Yee. This poem is thus an example of a collaboration between ten creative minds.

Bibliography

Arigho, B. (2008) 'Getting a handle on the past: the use of objects in reminiscence work', in H. Chatterjee (ed.) *Touch in Museums: policy and practice in object handling*, Oxford: Berg.

Atkin, L. (2008) 'Haiku', in N. Clayton and K. Featherstone (eds) *Words and Things: writing creatively from objects and art*, Leicestershire: Leicestershire County Council.

Atkin-Barrett, J. (2008) 'Valuing people evaluation', unpublished report, Leicestershire County Council.

Bachelard, G. (1994) *The Poetics of Space* [trans. M. Jolas], Boston: Beacon Press.

Bachelard, G. (1998) *Poetics of Imagining: modern to post-modern* [trans. R. Kearney], Edinburgh: Edinburgh University Press.

Bennett, T. (1995) *The Birth of the Museum: history, theory, politics*, London and New York: Routledge.

Boyd, M. (2008) 'Buttered Hands', in N. Clayton and K. Featherstone (eds) *Words and Things: writing creatively from objects and art*, Leicestershire: Leicestershire County Council.

Boyd, N. (2003) 'Audit of the Leicestershire Heritage Services' Resource Box loan service', unpublished report, Leicestershire County Council.

Boyd, N. (2005) 'An audit of the Moving Object touring displays', unpublished report, Leicestershire County Council.

Clayton, N. and K. Featherstone (eds) (2008) *Words and Things: writing creatively from objects and art*, Leicestershire: Leicestershire County Council.

Dacombe, J. and K. Daniels (2006) 'Write:Muse evaluation report', unpublished report, Leicestershire County Council.

Dudley, S. (ed) (2010) *Museum Materialities: objects, engagements, interpretations*, London and New York: Routledge.

Gardner, A. (2006) 'This box is empty', in N. Clayton and K. Featherstone (eds) 'The trick of watching', unpublished poetry anthology, Leicestershire County Council.

Hancock, N. (2009) 'Virginia Woolf's glasses: material encounters in the literary/artistic house museum', in S. Dudley (ed.) *Museum Materialities: objects, engagements, interpretations*, London and New York: Routledge.

Hooper-Greenhill, E. (2000) *Museums and the Interpretation of Visual Culture*, London and New York: Routledge.

Jacques, C. (2008) 'Easing the transition: using museum objects with elderly people', in E. Pye (ed.) *The Power of Touch: handling objects in museum and heritage context*, Walnut Creek, CA: Left Coast Press.

Johnson, H. (2008) 'Bottle', in N. Clayton and K. Featherstone (eds) 'The skin between two worlds', unpublished poetry anthology, Leicestershire County Council.

Karp, I. and S. Levine (eds) (1991) *Exhibiting Cultures: the poetics and politics of museum display*, Washington, DC: Smithsonian Institution Press.

Kavanagh, G. (2000) *Dream Spaces: memory and the museum*, London and New York: Leicester University Press.

Leicestershire's Open Museum (2008) 'Creative experience: exploring the potential of museum objects and creative writing in a mental health context', unpublished event evaluation, Leicestershire County Council.

Leicestershire's Open Museum (2010) 'Opening minds: mental health, creativity and the Open Museum', unpublished advocacy report, Leicestershire County Council.

Macdonald, S. (1997) *The Politics of Display: museums, science and culture*, London and New York: Routledge.

Mair, S. (2009) 'Evaluating the Moving Objects scheme', unpublished report, Leicestershire County Council.

Maslowski, P. (2006) 'Memory', in N. Clayton and K. Featherstone (eds) 'The trick of watching', unpublished poetry anthology, Leicestershire County Council.

Merleau-Ponty, M. (1962) *Phenomenology of Perception* [trans. C. Smith], New York: Humanities Press.

Shorter Oxford English Dictionary (2007) *Shorter Oxford English Dictionary*, Oxford: Oxford University Press.

Phillips, L. (2008) 'Reminiscence: recent work at the British Museum', in H. Chatterjee (ed.) *Touch in Museums: policy and practice in object handling*, Oxford: Berg.

Richmond, M. (2008) 'And the objects on the table spoke', in N. Clayton and K. Featherstone (eds) *Words and Things: writing creatively from objects and art*, Leicestershire: Leicestershire County Council.

Stewart, C. (2004) 'The value of memory', in N. Clayton and K. Featherstone (eds) 'Some intrinsic value', unpublished poetry anthology, Leicestershire County Council.

Thompson, P. (2008) 'Stag-beetle', in N. Clayton and K. Featherstone (eds) 'The skin between two worlds', unpublished poetry anthology, Leicestershire County Council.

Twell, T. (2007) 'Kitchen bowl – Donington-le-Heath', in N. Clayton and K. Featherstone (eds) 'You hear us on wires', unpublished poetry anthology, Leicestershire County Council.

Tyler-Bennett, D. (2006) '3 character poems', in N. Clayton and K. Featherstone (eds) 'The trick of watching', unpublished poetry anthology, Leicestershire County Council.

14 Location and intervention

Visual practice enabling a synchronic view of artefacts and sites

Shirley Chubb

The museum site can be perceived as a permeable membrane where specific ethnographic or anthropological meanings communicated through display are exchanged with the personal experience and knowledge of the viewer. In addition, the significance of displayed objects shifts as their meaning interacts with contemporary events. This flow of meaning creates an interstitial territory between museum, artefact and audience, a connective space where new understandings may be fleeting or considered, but are often unrecorded. The two visual art exhibitions considered here, *Hold* (1995) and *Thinking Path* (2003), manifested this interstitial space through artworks that intervened in the curatorial norms of display and suggested a synchronic view of artefacts and site.[1] The work responds to the museum as a catalyst and used visual methodologies to question the relationship between the museum site and the external world of the viewer.[2]

The aim of this chapter is to provide a reflexive analysis of this process by considering the relationship between the physical and conceptual elements that form the work and the theoretical considerations that underpin it. From the perspective of the artist the concepts implicitly embedded in the work are communicated visually through the use of materials and modes of presentation. However, the work also allows for a textual analysis that considers how this visual practice fused the relative cultural positions of artefact, location and audience by investigating potential meanings as a hybrid visual whole. Drawing from existing curatorial structures and the inherent cultural position of each museum, the process of intervention invites the viewer to challenge accepted norms of looking in response to a hybrid visual outcome that articulates potential relationships between the past and the post-colonial present.

Susan Pearce's incisive analysis of the intimacy between the engaged viewer and the displayed object, and her description of artefacts as 'material equivalents to the grammar of language', is of particular relevance here (Pearce 2006: 21). In considering Saussure's principles of *la langue* as the 'underlying system which makes possible various types of behaviour', and *la parole* as 'the actual instances of such behaviour' (Culler in Saussure 1978: xvii), Pearce recognises the museum as a physical redefinition of *la langue*, or an indicator of what, paraphrasing Saussure, she describes as the 'structured whole' of society (Pearce 2006: 21). Within the museum itself, artefacts can be understood as expressions of *la parole*,

with individual items combining into 'sets' where meaning 'depends upon relationships, and categories are created by the distinction which divides one set from
another' (Pearce 2006: 21).

The work cited here continues from this point to build a visual interpretation
of Saussure's further definition of diachronic and synchronic systems of language
analysis, where the *diachronic* acknowledges the chronological development of a
language whilst the *synchronic* attempts to construct an understanding of a given
language as a whole in any given period (Culler in Saussure 1978: xx). An
example of Saussure's theoretical tools is the linguist who, in a *diachronic* study,
would follow the evolution of a language within a given timeframe, such as French
from the thirteenth to the twentieth century, where similar facts are analysed in
order to establish general truths (Saussure 1978: 99). A *synchronic* study, however,
would forgo tracing the history of a language such as Old French between two
historic points, in favour of analysing the similarity of facts and principles revealed
in other languages, such as Bantu or Greek (Saussure 1978: 99). This approach
considers the relationships encountered between languages when 'passing from
one to another' (Saussure 1978: 99).

Hold and *Thinking Path* developed individual and cumulative works that utilised,
questioned and interpreted the diachronic reflection of history often expressed
in museum displays. Simultaneously, each exhibition developed to combine artefacts, timeframes, site and location to create visual interpretations that reflect
Saussure's relational synchronic system. By identifying key issues between 'interrelated items', the combined nuance of artefact, artwork and site was defined by
the individual history of each element as well as by their cumulative relationship
within broader cultural systems (Culler in Saussure 1978: xxi).

The history of artistic interventions within museums, archives and heritage
sites has covered increasingly broad frames of reference, from the anthropological or ethnographic to the economic or social, the scientific or the mythical. Of
particular relevance here is the work of Joseph Kosuth who, amongst others,
used intervention to critique the foundations of power and control that underpin
museums and the consequent influence upon public perception. Kosuth questions
what constitutes artistic practice by presenting existing works from various sources
alongside extracts of pertinent critical theories. Within *The Play of the Unmentionable*
(1990) he comments that:

> If art is to be more than expensive decoration, you have to see it as expressing
> other kinds of philosophical and political meaning. And that varies accord-
> ing to the context in which you experience it. This particular exhibition tries
> to show that artworks, in that sense, are like words: while each individual
> word has its own integrity, you can put them together to create very different
> paragraphs. And it's that paragraph that I claim authorship of.
>
> (Kosuth in Freedberg 1992: 27)

An additional work of intrinsic relevance here is Fred Wilson's exhibition
Mining the Museum (1992). Wilson's work has been widely acknowledged for its

forceful engagement with America's racist past and the representations of slavery that exist in particular museums. Wilson's racial identity is at the core of his practice and the strength of his work lies in his ability to engage with selected artefacts objectively, suppressing the imposition of a personal moral stance by employing a 'questioning process' as the underpinning basis for his work (Corrin 1994: 13). As with Kosuth, the viewer is implicated in the work and it is they who are asked to question 'Where am *I* in all this?' in response to the deeply uncomfortable and penetrating scenarios that Wilson presents to them (Corrin 1994: 13).

Both *Hold* and *Thinking Path* grew from a focused interest in the high Victorian era of African colonialism and considered the seminal relationship between this relatively recent past and the present, giving visual form to Edward Said's observation that:

> Appeals to the past are among the commonest of strategies in interpretations of the present. What animates such appeals is not only disagreement about what happened in the past and what the past was, but uncertainty about whether the past really is past, over and concluded, or whether it continues, albeit in different forms, perhaps.
>
> (Said 1993: 1)

Hold

First exhibited in 1995, *Hold* resulted from an invitation by Anthony Shelton, then Keeper of Non-Western Art and Anthropology, to explore Brighton Museum and Art Gallery's Non-Western Art collections. At the core of the exhibition was a consideration of the symbiotic relationship between the original use of artefacts and their contemporary location. Reflecting what Pearce has described as the power of 'the actual object' (Pearce 2006: 25), six works built upon African artefacts and used visual practice as a communicative tool for the content or meaning extrapolated from each artefact (Biggs 2006: 191). Embedding the artefacts within the contemporary artwork directly represented the force of encounter experienced as each item, previously held in storage, was reaffirmed through public display. The resulting combination manifested the diachronic trajectory between the original provenance of the artefacts and their current status within the holdings of a regional British museum, a journey that Michael Ames describes as the 'career' of an object (Ames 2000: 141). The juxtapositional form of presenting hybrid work which 'both physically and conceptually "holds" the objects' was a critical element in the equation of new synchronic meanings (Shelton, Hilty and Reason 1995: 23). The original act of handling the artefacts is further reflected in the exhibition title *Hold*, which conveys the empathic response set in motion by the physical act of holding and examining artefacts. It also communicates the notion of a museum's collection or holdings and reflects how these two realities, the personal and the institutional, become reliant and accentuated by the other, held together.

Initial explorations within the museum stores yielded an item of particular relevance, namely a section slice of a mango tree bearing a brass plaque upon which was inscribed the legend:

> Piece of the mango tree
> cut down in October 1930
> under which
> Henry M. Stanley
> met
> David Livingstone
> at Ujiji
> Lake Tanganyika
> Central Africa
> November 10th 1871

The plaque, which in isolation identifies a diachronic point in the development of colonial Africa, became the literal and metaphorical centre of the exhibition. Taking the origin of the artefact as a title, *Tanzania* uses the meaning indicated by the significant historic provenance of the plaque to dictate both the materials and size of the respondent artwork. An indicator of an iconic historic encounter, accounts of Stanley's preparations for the journey to meet Livingstone were translated into material form in the work. In preparing for his journey in January 1871, Stanley describes sourcing a substantial store of items for barter, tribute or bribes and the need for cloth, beads and brass wire to negotiate progression through the interior (Newson-Smith 1978: 67). Having identified the contemporary equivalent to the gauge of wire used by Stanley, it was cut to 1.5-cm lengths. Laid end to end each segment signified individuals involved in the intervening period between past and present and formed a spiralling ribbon linking the original plaque to an identically shaped version bearing the names of contemporary African states (Figures 14.1 and 14.2). The connective line of brass wire initially forms a diachronic visual representation of the relationship between colonised and contemporary Africa, where form manifests 'temporal antecedents' linked 'in a causal chain' (Culler 1985: 74). When seen within the expanding environments of *Hold*, the museum and the external social context, the visual language of *Tanzania* recognises the plaque as a catalyst of interrelated systems creating a 'move from the diachronic to the synchronic perspective' (Culler 1985: 74).

The diachronic 'projection back and forth of historical readings' was explored further through artefacts such as a small woven food basket catalogued as originating from Angola (Hilty in Shelton *et al.* 1995: 29). Here the initial acceptance of the basket as familiar craft object was challenged by its placement alongside identical cases bearing short phrases taken from *The Times* newspaper. Each phrase was extracted from anniversary accounts of Angola's ongoing civil war, moving the viewer from independence in 1975 to the point of exhibition.[3] The linguistic element further references Saussure, as selected phrases create an individual language in the form of a bleak cumulative poetry that is worryingly familiar.[4]

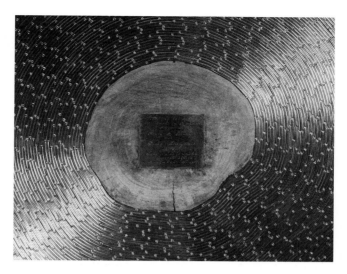

Figure 14.1 Tanzania (detail), 1995. Commemorative plaque mounted on section of mango tree, cut brass wire. Photograph © Fred Woodley with permission of Royal Pavilion and Museums, Brighton and Hove.

Figure 14.2 Tanzania & Ghana I, 1995. Mixed media, Brighton Museum and Art Gallery. Photograph © Nicholas Sinclair with permission of Royal Pavilion and Museums, Brighton and Hove.

Language becomes physical, positioned at the interface of text, image and object within each case. Although the placement of text is sequential, its presentation as a physical visual phenomenon within *Angola* invites the viewer to create individual patterns of viewing and reading with consequent connections.

The immediacy of Asante brass weights as signifiers of cultural values prompted *Ghana I*, a physically and conceptually synchronic work that revealed a matrix of associations. The work replicated the lost wax process used to make the original weights by using unrefined beeswax sourced directly from Africa. Here, however, the fabrication technique stopped at the point of the wax positive, momentarily inverting familiar systems of colonial trade, as the wax itself became the product. No longer seen in isolation, the visual language of each small artefact appears literally and metaphorically caught between two stages of development, generated by one culture they are consumed within another, and point to the problematic evolution of post-colonial cultures and economies.

Within *Hold*, casing systems also became an active participant in the accumulation of meaning. Replicated within the artworks, and obscured by specific materials, cases were effectively transformed into surrogate artefacts. This was most apparent in *Provenance Unknown*, a work that responded to the forceful signification of a powdered milk tin that had been transformed into a drum by the addition of animal hide. The resulting item becomes an arresting example of the coalescence of cultures, reaching us in a state of, in Annie Coombes' terms, original hybridity (Coombes 1994: 218). A synchronic understanding of the artefact is indicated by the addition of eight cases coated with milk powder referencing the gestation of a child. These cases invited the viewer to consider contemporary debates surrounding the marketing tactics of multi-national companies within non-European countries, broadening and re-aligning our understanding of the divergent uses fused within the artefact. As a drum it can be seen as an archetypal symbol of non-Western culture; however, when fabricated as a by-product of European commerce, Western systems of taxonomy become confused. The accepted ethnographic title becomes a synchronic pointer to both the idiosyncratic nature of the artefact and the social dilemmas that it manifests.

The range of synchronic associations explored within *Hold* were further expanded as the exhibition toured to new venues. The location of the exhibition at the University of Essex Gallery (1996) reflected what Coombes has observed as the 'weight of meanings' attributed to objects (Coombes 1992: 41). At this venue, the nuance of the work engaged with an institution whose purpose is to explore, debate and define understanding and knowledge in a variety of educational spheres. At Ferens Art Gallery, Hull (1997), *Hold* was exhibited alongside a newly commissioned work, *Sampler acc.806* (1997), based on a rare sampler held by the Wilberforce House Museum. Dating from around 1807 and promoting the anti-slavery campaign, the original sampler was reconstituted within a new work featuring additional imagery linking its original production to the present. The significance of the newly reconstituted work within *Hold* and its location within the city known as the home of the abolitionist William Wilberforce added further to the synchronic breadth of the exhibition.

Thinking Path

Thinking Path, first exhibited in 2004, was a visual response to the life and influence of Charles Darwin. Commissioned by Shrewsbury Museum and Art Gallery, initial research was undertaken with the support of English Heritage at Down House, Darwin's family home in Kent.[5] Down House was bought by Darwin in 1842 (English Heritage 2007). He and his family grew to love the house and associated lifestyle and in 1846 Darwin commented 'My life goes on like clockwork and I am fixed on the spot where I shall end it' (Wilson 2000: 31). The grounds to the house show Darwin's fascination with every aspect of his natural environment and include the Sand-walk, a small tract of land that Darwin leased and eventually bought from local landowner Sir John Lubbock (Keynes, Coulter-Smith and Forgan 2004: 15). Habitually walked by Darwin on a daily basis, the Sand-walk became a haven from external pressures and a vehicle for the meticulous long-term observations that fuelled his emerging theories (Figure 14.3). Predominantly a solitary exercise, Darwin also enjoyed company whilst walking, with his friend the botanist Sir Joseph Hooker recounting how they often visited the Sand-walk 'round which a fixed number of turns were taken, during which our conversation usually ran on foreign lands and seas, old friends, old books, and things far off both to mind and eye' (Keynes *et al.* 2004: 16). Later anecdotes describe the Sand-walk as Darwin's 'thinking path', a phrase which, when adopted as the exhibition title, acknowledged the actuality of Darwin's physical and mental presence, whilst also enabling the path to signify the broader impact of his theories.

In considering the relationship between the study of linguistics and biology in the early nineteenth century, Culler identifies potential links between Saussure and Darwin. He states that both theorists recognised the need to break with history by treating 'individual languages or species as autonomous entities which could be described and compared with one another as wholes' (Culler 1985: 63).

Figure 14.3 The *Sand-walk* (2003). Down House, Kent. Photograph © Shirley Chubb by kind permission of English Heritage.

Diachronic forms of study provided the sequential basis to new forms of thinking that re-aligned historic relationships in order to provide new synchronic overviews.[6] Within *Thinking Path* the diachronic progression of Darwin's life and theories, and their relationship to the present, are reconstituted through a process of recording the Sand-walk. Here the experiential element of encounter explored in *Hold* played an increasingly formative part, as the house, grounds and more specifically the Sand-walk itself, become the pivotal core of the exhibition.

By accentuating a sense of contemporary physical presence in an external space, documentary video footage of re-walking the path reflected Rebecca Solnit's observation that 'Walking shares with making and working that crucial element of engagement of the body and the mind with the world' (Solnit 2002: 29). This documentation also became an essential means to curate ideas by using visual form as an openly associative alternative to the myriad texts analysing Darwin, his theories and legacy. During the exhibition tour the video footage was shown on small LCD screens within museum cases, effectively transforming experience into artefact. The performative element of retracing Darwin's footsteps re-animated the micro-environment of the path as the judder of each pace created a sense of faltering movement through the landscape and a collective movement through time. The 1,600 paces of the walk became a way to structure these thoughts as each step was imbued with an individual figurative or representational identity. Layers of diachronic reference were further defined by documenting the path on the anniversaries of four significant dates in Darwin's life: his birthday; the return of the *HMS Beagle* from its five-year voyage; the publication of *The Origin of Species* (1859); and the day he died. This enabled a numerical subdivision of the 1,600 paces into four day-groups of 400 images each. A further subdivision orders the days into sequential panels of 20 images that ascend in number from 1 to 20. The resultant image panels were used as an episodic means to curate meaning.

Stills from the video documentation captured blurring, sunbursts and shadow, enhancing the sense of a fleeting experience as split seconds of time were frozen and extracted from the sequential whole. Each still alternates with found imagery detailing aspects of Darwin's life and contemporary manifestations of his theories, creating a framework of synchronic references that cross timeframes and physical spaces. Specific to particular historic, cultural and environmental references, the accumulation of imagery considered aspects of the anniversarial qualities of each day, from the fragility of birth and death, to the empowerment of travel, and the inexorable accumulation of global knowledge. Images of the path therefore provide a literal continuum for the narrative imagery, the combination of which suggests further interwoven synchronic interpretations and anticipates Tim Ingold's consideration of the multiple linearities that shape our engagement with the world and his suggestion that 'Retracing the lines of past lives is the way we proceed along our own' (Ingold 2007: 119).

Individual glass lenses were used to animate each image as the viewer scanned or analysed the accumulated array presented to them (Figure 14.4). The lenses reference Darwin's use of the microscope to reveal, literally and conceptually,

Figure 14.4 Beagle Journey 02.10.1836/2003 #7 (2003). Glass lenses, polypropylene and digital print, 255 × 260 mm. Photograph © Shropshire Museum Service with kind permission.

what cannot be seen with the naked eye. Simultaneously, they reference how contemporary technology enables a vicarious experience of reality and how science has expanded our vision of the world. Tracey Bowen has observed how we increasingly understand the 'materiality, physicality, corporeality' of the world through electronic technologies, and how haptic space is 'disrupted by the mediation of technology . . . disappearing behind the screen or monitor' (Bowen 2008: 3–4). The static images of *Thinking Path* traverse this issue, digitally sourced and indicative of multimedia displays, they are reconstituted through the physicality of the lens. The slight shift prompted by the curvature of each lens suggests movement as the simultaneous imagery accumulates a filmic fluidity. However, the choice of reading sequence is relinquished to the viewer who can alter the pace of connection between images which 'like evolution, . . . does not have a beginning or an end, just a constantly changing middle' (Coulter-Smith in Keynes *et al.* 2004: 31).

Darwin drew upon and compiled an eclectic mix of knowledge in the construction of his theories, a process that maps on to *Thinking Path* and is particularly pertinent within the development of each set of anniversary panels, where groups of imagery were generated, selected and juxtaposed to create narrative subdivisions. The diachronically structured system of presentation adds order to the accumulation of images whilst simultaneously animating various synchronic frames of reference and interpretation. Of particular note was Darwin's heightened awareness of the relationship between distant and domestic environments. Whilst articulating with acute insight how apparently mundane encounters could reverberate with meaning and association, Darwin was also able to cross-reference between disparate experiences in order to formulate generic theories (Darwin 1985: 459). His account of experiencing a Brazilian forest for the first time is a prime example of his contagious enthusiasm as he describes how:

> [I]f the eye attempts to follow the flight of a gaudy butter-fly, it is arrested by some strange tree or fruit; if watching an insect one forgets it in the stranger flower it is crawling over, – if turning to admire the splendour of the scenery, the individual character of the foreground fixes the attention.
>
> (Darwin quoted in Browne 2003a: 211–12)

Such observations show how Darwin explored processes of association that directly influenced the accumulation of imagery within *Thinking Path*, where the eye is invited to flicker and roam through images encouraging a consequent mental journey of association for each viewer.

Also of crucial significance is Darwin's ability to frame what were essentially abstract ideas, a process that is directly referenced in the use of the grid format to enable sequential cross-referencing between images.[7] Janet Browne's articulation of Darwin's methods can be applied to the aims of *Thinking Path*, which acknowledge the breadth of Darwin's influence through accumulation rather than the identification of a single definitive image. As Browne states:

> Darwin had no crucial experiment that conclusively demonstrated evolution in action. He had no equations to establish his case. Everything in his book was to be words – persuasion, revisualization, the balance of probabilities, the interactions between large numbers of organisms, the subtle consequences of minute chances and changes. Like Charles Lyell in his *Principles of Geology*, he had to rely on drawing an analogy between what was known and what was not known.
>
> (Browne 2003b: 55)

Building on processes of collaboration initiated in *Hold*, *Thinking Path* toured to a series of venues specifically relevant to Darwin, and involved a heightened curatorial role in negotiation with host venues. The synchronic nature of the panels was enhanced at each museum by the addition of core artefacts chosen for their ability to resonate with the themes explored in each anniversary. These included items that variously acted as metaphors for Darwinian theories on natural selection or adaptability, whilst other items referenced the constant human pursuit of knowledge. Of particular note was the incorporation of the *Grinshill Sandstone* showing fossilised ripple marks from the Triassic Period, an item that exquisitely signifies the interconnectedness of vast expanses of time and simultaneously displays the fleeting nature of all organic life. The additional use of a satirical *Darwinian Ape* (c.1890) showed how acutely Darwin upset the hierarchies of existence that dominated his contemporary Victorian society.[8]

In addition to the core artefacts, display systems at Shrewsbury Museum and Art Gallery and subsequent venues were redefined in response to the site as chosen artefacts were relocated from permanent collections to be seen alongside *Thinking Path*. At Down House the house and gardens themselves became the wider installation site as, exhibited in a small domestic room, the dense grid of wall panels immersed the viewer within the 1,600 images, suggesting new associations that re-animated both the internal site and the external grounds that inspired the work as a whole. At Plymouth City Museum and Art Gallery a series of ceramic figures depicting the elements, seasons, continents and senses accompanied the work. Representing ancient order systems seen as the bedrock of understanding, the figurines were shown in a pyramidal form contemplated by the Darwinian Ape which, placed at the apex of the display, was seen to condense contemporary knowledge and question former hierarchies. The intervention of *Thinking Path* at Russell-Cotes Art Gallery and Museum in Bournemouth involved the relocation of statues and busts alongside specific panels, where they re-animated issues such as the Victorian predilection for sentimentality as a vehicle for expression and the role of museums in the definition of cultural identity (Figure 14.5).[9] The

Figure 14.5 Thinking Path. Mixed media. Russell-Cotes Art Gallery and Museum (2004). Photograph © Mandy Schaller by kind permission of Russell-Cotes Art Gallery and Museum.

Origin of Species panels were implacably observed by a series of sculptures of British political, social and military figures, whilst at the centre of the group were two works by Pietro Calvi, entitled *An Arab Chief* (c.1860) and *A Black Queen* (c.1881). Sculpted in marble and bronze, this couple are very much 'the other' amongst the iconic figures that surround them and epitomise nineteenth century attitudes to non-Western races, where difference was eroticised in order to make it palatable to Victorian sensibilities.

As *Thinking Path* redefined itself at each venue the exhibition moved beyond the format of a biographical survey and reflects what Albano, paraphrasing Lyotard, has described as a 'self-contained narrative' that enabled the visitor to move 'into an artificial, hence, illusionary, temporal and spatial dimension as the exhibition subject unfolds' (Albano 2007: 24). The internalised world of accumulated imagery induces a sense of location in relation to Darwinian thought within the audience, whilst the context of the museum suggested new connective taxonomies and a heightened awareness of cultural positioning as each viewer negotiated a personal path through the display.

Conclusions

This chapter has described how two exhibitions, *Hold* and *Thinking Path*, considered the problematic relationship between colonial pasts and contemporary realities and sought to identify modes of presentation applicable to, and reflective of, the heightened awareness of contemporary society. Investigated within regional museums, both exhibitions reflected the uniquely evolved nature and cultural position of host collections and developed visual expressions that explored artefacts in relation to their particular origin and current location.

Of particular relevance to this practice has been Susan Pearce's effective articulation of the relevance of linguistic theory within the museum context. Her insight has shown that Saussure's principles can provide a logical framework for understanding the interrelation and evolution of material cultures, and the practical work described here has sought to further define this relationship in visual form. Reflecting and building upon Pearce's application of Saussure, the text has described how *Hold* and *Thinking Path* developed specific and focused visual responses to diachronic and consequently synchronic understandings of artefacts and sites.

Within *Hold*, connective processes created physically and conceptually dependent works that manifested tangible links between the current site of the collection and the geographically distant realities underpinning the artefacts within it. The hybrid approach of curatorial practice became actual rather than implied, shaping the artworks and re-aligning the reception of the artefacts themselves. In *Thinking Path*, the role of artist curator evolved further to include specifically targeted collections forming the exhibition tour. The communicative aspects of the work were further expanded through the heightened curatorial role adopted at each venue, where the repositioning of artefacts and artworks in particular relation to each other created synchronic meanings that remained negotiable for the viewer on an individual basis.

Both *Hold* and *Thinking Path* used artefacts 'actively as evidence rather than passively as illustrations' (Prown 1982: 1). Material processes were used to manifest empathic links between the represented world of the artefact and the actual world of the viewer (Prown 1982: 8), mirroring Prown's observation that 'encounter between an object with its history and an individual with his history shapes the deductions. Neither is what they were nor what they may become' (Prown 1982: 9). The description of key stages of production within each exhibition and the significance of encounter as a fundamental spur to research and production 'in pursuit of the direct rendition of experience' defined the diachronic and synchronic in visual form (Macleod and Holdridge 2006: 11). The identification of a numerical basis linked to the provenance of an object, or the scale of a site, was used to form a diachronic understanding of the ensuing artwork, manifesting factual links between the past and the present. The consequent inclusion of additional historic and contemporary references related to the trajectory of the artefact, or the resonance of the venues, created further connective synchronic links. In this way each exhibition became a flexible catalyst of meanings that enabled a permeable interface of understanding between artefact, artwork, site and audience.

Notes

1 Aspects of this text first appeared within Shirley Chubb's PhD thesis 'Intervention, location and cultural positioning: working as a contemporary artist curator in British museums', undertaken within the School of Arts and Communication, University of Brighton (Chubb 2007).
2 The exhibitions were exhibited as follows:
   Hold: Brighton Museum and Art Gallery, 11 March–2 April 1995
   University of Essex Gallery, 16 January–9 February 1996
   Ferens Art Gallery, Hull, 5 April–3 May 1997
   Thinking Path: Shrewsbury Museum and Art Gallery, 7 February–17 April 2004
   Plymouth City Museum and Art Gallery, 1 May–30 August 2004
   Russell-Cotes Art Gallery and Museum, Bournemouth, 29 September 2004–23 January 2005
   Down House, Kent, 2 February–29 May 2005.
3 Angola became independent on 10 November 1975, itself an anniversary of the meeting of Stanley and Livingstone 104 years earlier.
4 The sequential journalistic extracts read as follows: the flag / clash / shot dead / third anniversary / 'victories' / aid and comfort / dogfight / national day / contradictory claims / quest / plea / one white and one black / dispute battle credit / mediated talks / legacy / cycle / family / stands on the brink / each day / called off.
5 Darwin was born in Shrewsbury and *Thinking Path* was commissioned by Shrewsbury Museum and Art Gallery to launch the 2004 Darwin Festival.
6 Culler goes further to state that 'Any purposiveness in biological evolution, Darwin saw, does not lie in changes themselves but wholly in the process of natural selection, which is, in a sense, a synchronic process' (Culler 1985: 64).
7 Rosalind Krauss' essay 'Grids' in *The Originality of the Avant-Garde and Other Modernist Myths* is pertinent here (Krauss 1993: 9–22).
8 Core artefacts exhibited at each tour venue alongside *Thinking Path* included:
   From the collections of Shrewsbury Museum and Art Gallery:
   Darwinian Ape c.1890, ceramic with bronze finish, probably Austrian
   Fragment of Log-boat Date unknown, possibly prehistoric Chelmarsh, south-east Shropshire

Grinshill Sandstone with Fossil Ripple Marks Triassic period, Grinshill, north Shropshire. From the collections of Plymouth City Museum and Art Gallery:
Pregnancy Garment, early twentieth century, East South Africa
20 Quartz Specimens from the J.F. Manteau Collection, the René Gallant Collection, the R. Barstow Collection, the Sir John St. Aubyn Collection and the Babbington Collection.
9 The Darwin family used to holiday near Bournemouth and the Russell-Cotes Art Gallery and Museum collection is renowned for its expression of high Victorian sensibilities.

Bibliography

Albano, C. (2007) 'Displaying lives: the narrative of objects in biographical exhibitions', *Museum and Society*, 5(1), University of Leicester. Online. Available at: http://www.le.ac.uk/ms/museumsociety.html (Accessed 21 June 2007).

Ames, M. (2000) *Cannibal Tours and Glass Boxes: the anthropology of museums*, Vancouver: University of British Columbia Press.

Biggs, M. (2006) 'Modelling experiential knowledge for research', in M. Mäkelä and S. Routarinne (eds) *The Art of Research: research practices in art and design*, Helsinki: University of Art and Design.

Bowen, T. (2008) 'Disrupting the lines between materiality and virtuality: exploring "aura" as a pedagogical site for personal projections of aesthetic sensibilities', paper presented at Mobility of the Line symposium, University of Brighton, January 2008.

Browne, J. (2003a) *Charles Darwin: voyaging*, London: Pimlico.

Browne, J. (2003b) *Charles Darwin: the power of place*, London: Pimlico.

Chubb, S. (2007) 'Intervention, location and cultural positioning: working as a contemporary artist curator in British museums', unpublished thesis, University of Brighton.

Coombes, A.E. (1992) 'Inventing the "postcolonial", hybridity and constituency in contemporary curating', *New Formations*, 18: 39–52.

Coombes, A.E. (1994) *Reinventing Africa: museums, material culture and popular imagination*, New Haven and London: Yale University Press.

Corrin, L. (ed.) (1994) *Mining the Museum: an installation by Fred Wilson*, New York: The New Press.

Culler, J. (1985) *Saussure*, London: Fontana Press.

Darwin, C. (1859, reprinted 1985) *The Origin of Species by Means of Natural Selection*, London: Penguin.

English Heritage (2007) Online. Available at: http://www.english-heritage.org.uk/server/show/ConProperty.102 (Accessed 22 February 2007).

Freedberg, D. (1992) *The Play of the Unmentionable: an installation by Joseph Kosuth at the Brooklyn Museum*, New York: The New Press.

Ingold, T. (2007) *Lines: a brief history*, London: Routledge.

Keynes, R., G. Coulter-Smith and S. Forgan (2004) *Thinking Path*, Shrewsbury Museums Service.

Krauss, R.E. (1993) *The Originality of the Avant-Garde and Other Modernist Myths*, Cambridge, MA and London: MIT Press.

Macleod, K. and L. Holdridge (2006) *Thinking Through Art: reflections on art as research*, London: Routledge.

Newson-Smith, S. (ed.) (1978) *Quest: the story of Stanley and Livingstone*, London: Arlington Books.

Pearce, S.M. (ed.) (2006) *Interpreting Objects and Collections*, Abingdon, Oxon: Routledge.

Prown, J. (1982) 'An introduction to material culture theory and method', *Winterthur Portfolio*, 17: 1–19.

Said, E. (1993) *Culture and Imperialism*, London: Chatto and Windus.

Saussure, F. de. (1978) *Course in General Linguistics*, Glasgow: Fontana Collins.

Shelton, A., G. Hilty and D. Reason (1995) *Hold: Acquisition, Representation, Perception: work by Shirley Chubb*, Brighton: The Royal Pavilion, Art Gallery and Museums.

Solnit, R. (2002) *Wanderlust: a history of walking*, London: Verso.

Wilson, L. (ed.) (2000) *Down House: the home of Charles Darwin*, London: English Heritage.

Part III

The uses of objects in museum representations

Introduction

Amy Jane Barnes

In this part of the book, we turn to the different strategies and forms through which museums might utilise objects to make representations and to tell stories. It follows on logically from the second part: for although it continues to explore and problematise the role of objects within exhibitionary settings, the previous emphasis on how *visitors* experience and respond to objects as material things is now complemented with a focus on the different strategies and forms through which *museums* do, or could, use objects to make representations and tell stories. The diversity of subjects represented in the following chapters – contemporary art museums, historical costume, collector-donors, missing and absent objects, and 'relics' of Arctic expeditions – reflect not only a range of museum representations generally, but also the breadth of Susan Pearce's interests and some of the spheres in which her writing and teaching has been influential.

The section begins with Roger Sansi's examination of exhibition strategies in two Spanish art museums: the Museum of Contemporary Art in Barcelona, and the Guggenheim Bilbao. He argues that these two institutions demonstrate the diversity of contemporary art museums, by utilising contrasting, but relatively successful, interpretive strategies to conceptual art. However, Sansi puts forward a third, more participatory possibility – a relational museum which engages the audience in the production of artwork, forging a middle ground between the museum as spectacle and the museum as archive. In this respect, his chapter provides a neat bridge between this section and Chubb's exploration of interstitial space at the close of Part II. But it also serves to set up the overarching narrative of the remainder of this part of the book, by thinking about objects in relation to people – those being represented, and those being represented to.

Subsequent chapters engage with different incidences of liminality in the museum context – things, feelings, people and legacies of past interpretation which are at the very edges of perceptual awareness, difficult to pin down, but which may, nevertheless, contribute enormously to audience experience. Chapters 15 and 16 are linked by the paradoxical relationship between museums and the intangible. In his chapter, Sansi considers the tension between the art museum and the dematerialising goal of conceptual art. Julia Petrov then begins her exploration of costume collections and imagined space, with the assertion that as visitors we experience museums immaterially. She argues that historic clothing embodies a palpable, sensory association with a body absent, and may offer powerful opportunities to transmit cultural knowledge to museum audiences. On display, Petrov suggests, objects of dress operate as triggers for the recollection of lived experience. Through facilitating acts of imagined embodiment – feeling through seeing – fashion offers museums a unique interpretive shortcut to comprehension and participation.

The interpretive role of the individual behind the object – the wearer, the owner – is a theme furthered in the next chapter. In charting the lingering, frequently problematic vestiges of donors' past collecting discourse perceptible in works and collections of art, Caroline Bergeron (Chapter 17), employs the Maussian principle of the gift and its resultant obligations – giving, receiving and reciprocating – to analyse the complex, and occasionally uncomfortable materialised relationships that develop between collector-donor and museum-recipient. She presents the exhibition *All for Art! Our Great Private Collectors Share Their Works* (Montréal Museum of Fine Arts, 2007–08) as an example of how the potential for tension between the needs and expectations of the collector-donor and those of the institution may be assuaged, while providing visitors with an insightful experience of the personal motivations and collecting discourses of those individuals who choose to donate objects to museums.

Helen Rees-Leahy's chapter continues the theme of absence foregrounded in the preceding chapters through their discussions of the body and the collector-donor. But instead of seeking to interpretively resolve 'lack' in display contexts, she explores absence, in both theory and practice, in all its novelty and unsettling potency. Drawing on the observations of Hazlitt, Malraux and Latour, and providing examples as diverse as Libeskind's Jewish Museum in Berlin, the disappearance of the Mona Lisa, the explicit absence of the Parthenon Marbles at the new Acropolis Museum in Greece, the Sigmund Freud Museum in Vienna and Veronese's looted *Marriage at Cana*, she analyses such concepts as the empty plinth which symbolises absence, loss and longing, the *musée imaginaire*, which conceptualises forgotten or elusive objects in the museum space, and the vacuum left by missing works of art, in order to address the reflexive potential and rhetorical effects of curating absence rather than presence.

Finally, in a chapter that provides a neat link with the last part of this volume and its focus upon the material culture of difficult histories, Claire Warrior considers the ways in which museums have constructed and displayed the relationships between objects and people, through an analysis of material held in the National Maritime Museum's Polar collections. She looks at the legacy of nineteenth century constructions of artefacts – connected with Arctic exploration – as 'relics' of particular expeditions or explorers, and the political ramifications of the continued presentation of such narratives in the museum context.

As with the rest of this volume, the chapters in this part of the book represent a series of interdisciplinary encounters: art history meets art practice; fashion history connects with sensory studies; anthropology informs the accession and display of art objects; memory and museums collide; and the politics of representation challenges museum interpretation. Together they are connected, not least by their focus on objects, or the absence thereof, but also by their passionate avowal of novel approaches to museal representation.

15 Spectacle and archive in two contemporary art museums in Spain

Roger Sansi

As many chapters in this book point out, there is a curious paradox in museum studies. On the one hand, many writings on museums in the last decades have an explicitly critical approach, describing museums as institutions that reproduced the structures of social power. But at the same time that this institutional critique emerged, the museum has become the star of cultural policy: museums have blossomed, expanded and multiplied, becoming symbols of absolute modernity – the places one has to see, now. In this chapter, I look at how this paradox has been addressed in two new contemporary art museums in Spain, which were created after, and partially in response to, institutional critique.

The criticism directed to museums stems from the age-old suspicion of Western scholars towards objects and images, as appearances that hide the truth, and are used to impose ideologies. This suspicion is still present in much contemporary writing, which identifies the new success of museums with fetishism. But a few scholars have gone beyond this criticism, giving a fairer reading of the power of objects and images, and the value of museums. Susan Pearce has been one of them, when she has affirmed, for example, that objects constitute social life and bring it into being (Pearce 1992: 262). Along with anthropologists like Miller or Latour, Pearce insists upon the fact that ultimately our ideas, and our social life, can only be realised through objects in the real world. But we are suspicious of them because at the same time that they are the means through which we construct our understanding of the world, they are also real things out there, autonomous from our understanding (Pearce 1992: 257). And sometimes, these two sides of objects collide, or go in different directions.

Nowhere is this more evident than in the realm of contemporary art. Contemporary art faithfully follows the Western tradition of suspicion of objects. In the last decades, many artists have tried to control any possible form of objectification, fetishisation or idolatry of their work. 'Conceptual' art is not only one more tendency, but *the* contemporary art of today. Most of this art is not made to be seen in a museum, but on the contrary, it has been explicitly made to resist any museification and spectacularisation. More than objects or images, conceptual artworks are performances, installations, actions, processes, events. They are ephemeral and they are in process; they are practices, more than things. But, as Lucy Lippard (1973) pointed out long ago, these conceptual artistic practices inevitably end up being identified as discrete things, artworks, which can be commodified and museified. Thus, the dematerialisation of art is never complete. However, this has not stopped conceptual art from thriving; on the contrary, many conceptual artworks play with this ambiguity (Buskirk 2003). Maybe they cannot fully achieve dematerialisation, but by playing with it, they can open up a lot of questions about the relationship of people with things.

And still, this dematerialisation opens up a lot of questions for museums. Museums of modern art like MOMA, Tate or Beaubourg have their collections firmly grounded in modern, objectual art from the first half of the twentieth century. But how to start a museum of the age of conceptual art? In Spain, several museums have opened their doors in the 1990s, and their answers to this issue have been radically different. There are two museums that have proposed two radically opposed models, and have been relatively successful in doing so. One is the Museum of Contemporary Art of Barcelona (MACBA). The other one is the Guggenheim Bilbao.

The MACBA has seriously attempted to be a museum of conceptual art since the 1960s, and because of that, it has had to become something more, or something else, than a museum. More than as artworks, the MACBA has started to organise and display its contents as documents with a social and political value, offered to public use, to make a statement in current political debates. The MACBA presents itself both as an institution of public service and a space of public debate, both as an Archive and as an Agora. The Guggenheim Bilbao, on the other hand, has embraced the society of spectacle, becoming the centre of spectacle in itself: it is all about the building, not its content. The contents are accessory and transient, and rarely have they been conceptual art: most have been blockbuster exhibitions, from the archaeological treasures of China to motorbikes or Armani suits. The Guggenheim is a new form of museum, the 'exciting museum' (Cuno 2001: 45) which draws the masses and stimulates tourism. Spectacle and Tourism: nothing more opposed to the Archive and the Agora.

To what extent are these two personifications compatible? In the next pages, I discuss the two models, which in their radical opposition can shed light on each other's strategies and contradictions.

The Guggenheim Bilbao: spectacle

When the Guggenheim was built in 1997, it was hailed as the first building of the twenty-first century, a world marvel, the masterpiece of Frank Gehry. It certainly did not look like anything that had been built before: the irregular, fluid, inapprehensible form of the building and the changing colours of its titanium surface against the background of the Bilbao estuary became instantaneously an icon. Shortly after it was built, one of my supervisors at the University of Chicago, a famous and respected anthropologist, told me that he was going to Bilbao to see the 'most beautiful building of the world'. He did not have any intention to visit any other place in Spain but the Guggenheim. There was a sense of emergency in this rush to see the building: it was not just a building, but an event.

Bilbao itself was almost an excuse: the building was not making reference to the city, on the contrary. Bilbao is the economic capital of the Basque country, but it has never been known for its beauty, and the economic crisis since the 1970s has resulted in the abandonment of many of its industrial areas. The Guggenheim was a 'miracle', which had transformed a shabby, post-industrial town on the Atlantic coast of Spain into the light of modernity. It was necessary to see it right now (right then).

Much has been written on the controversial 'making of' this building-event, in particular by Joseba Zulaika (1997, 2005). Zulaika described Krens, the director of the Guggenheim Foundation, as the ultimate gambler, a seducer who convinced the government of the Basque country to give him a two million dollar cheque plus another hundred to keep the Museum. Krens spent the two million at Shoteby's. In exchange, Krens was giving the franchise of having a Guggenheim building in Bilbao to the Basque government. Krens had total autonomy to plan the exhibits in the museum, and never had to pay attention to the political requirements of Basque cultural policy. What is more, he rejected incorporating Basque artists into the collections, unless they lived in New York. With time, Basque art has made its way into the collections, but the initial position of Krens could not be more meaningful: the Guggenheim was an international contemporary art museum, and as such only international artists were worth collecting. And international artists live in New York.

But that was probably a lesser issue for Krens, since his plan was not to propagate the gospel of New York art to the world. His ambition was bigger than that: to build an emblem, a focus of attraction that would make anybody in the world want to come and see it; an object of desire, a fetish of modernity. As previously mentioned, what is important is the building more than its contents (Guasch and Zulaika 2005: 17). Or better: it is the prestige of the Guggenheim building that, in return, enhances the value of the objects contained. The space does not pretend to be a neutral white box, but on the contrary, the biggest of the artworks on display, which reverberates its value on the objects contained, like the motorbikes, which by association can also be seen as artworks. Of course, we know that the 'white cube' art gallery is never the neutral space that it is supposed to be; exhibits like Susan Vogel's *Art/Artifact* (1988) had already pointed out how the value we give to objects in the 'white cube' are radically different than in other representational settings. But the Guggenheim Bilbao was re-writing this into a new level: there was no attempt to hide that it was the space that was adding a value to its contents – that is clear in the case of the Armani or motorbike exhibits.

As Fraser (2005) points out, we should not think that this is an attempt to make museums more 'popular' and less elitist. On the contrary, this is a way of multiplying the value and the commodification of its contents: there is no surprise, and no shame, in the fact that the motorbike exhibit was promoted by BMW. Why should there be? Krens, as Zulaika (2005) said, has brought the logic of modern financial capitalism and advertisement to the museum world, buying and selling fame: he sold the name of the Guggenheim to Bilbao in the same way that he rents a space to motorbike companies, which use it as a luxury publicity stunt. What the Guggenheim sells is status.

Politics, and diplomacy, also work following a similar logic. The Basque government saw in the Guggenheim the best possible way of polishing the image not only of the city of Bilbao, but also of the Basque country, associating it with modernity, luxury and fabulousness instead of terrorism. The 'franchise' model of the Guggenheim Bilbao was transposed to other locations, such as Brazil and Dubai, with uneven success. The *Brazil Body and Soul* exhibit at the Guggenheim New York in 2000, a reduced version of the extraordinary exhibit of the 500 years of Brazil in São Paulo, was part of the deal to open a Guggenheim franchise in Rio. The project, following the model of Bilbao, would cost around $250 million, three times the budget of the Brazilian Ministry of Culture. The reaction to the project was of public outcry, especially amongst the local art world in Rio, and even rallies were organised against the Guggenheim in June 2003. Finally, the project was stopped in the Brazilian courts.[1] However, the Abu Dhabi project is still going on, a project that has literally been labelled by Krens as 'pharaonic',[2] again without any shame.

To come back to the Bilbao case: despite all criticisms, it seems that in fact, the Guggenheim *did* operate a miracle. It changed the look of the city; it made it into a tourist destination. Again, we could ask if this is only because of the Guggenheim, and not also because of the political will of the Basque government, which has improved the surroundings of the museum and the infrastructures in the region. Maybe they, in fact, needed a Guggenheim to believe in their own potential. At all these levels, the Guggenheim Bilbao operates as a fetish, as an object of desire that has a radical historicity – it has to be seen *right now*; a building-event. It is still early to see if the Guggenheim will overcome the urgency effect of its first years, and people may want to see it again. If its does, it will probably change status, from fetish of its time to monument of history.

In the meanwhile, we can be sure that there is a before and after the Guggenheim Bilbao. The white box has been overcome by the fetish-building that has to be seen, the building-event that is more important than its contents. The content is contingent.

Is that the future of contemporary art museums? Are we destined to see every year more and more spectacular buildings, technically to house 'contemporary art'? There are other, very different models, like the MACBA. And that is the case I would like to consider next.

The MACBA: archive

A long-awaited project, the MACBA was originally conceived in 1986 as an autonomous institution with both public and private funding. The museum was not finally opened until 1995, in the Raval neighbourhood of Barcelona. The Raval was the poorest area of the historic centre of Barcelona back then. The MACBA was meant to be the catalyst of the gentrification of the Raval. The building was commissioned to the American architect, Richard Meyer, who claimed to make a building in response to its historical environment but in fact produced an international modernist white cube structure. For a while the building was the pride of Barcelona, until the Guggenheim made it instantly old fashioned.

This, however, was not the major problem for the MACBA. From the very beginning, the discussions on its contents and the art it had to display were quite intense; the original idea was to show the collections with a historical narrative, starting with the post-war 'rebirth' of modernity with informalism. But a younger generation was more interested in using the MACBA as an international 'Kunsthalle', a space for international contemporary art with temporary exhibits. Three directors of the museum were replaced after short tenures for political reasons. Finally, the Museum Foundation decided to take seriously the idea of the 'autonomy' of the museum, and they hired a professional curator who was allowed to develop his own project: Manuel Borja-Villell (Borja from now on).

Borja had a clear project, which was at once a national museum and an international Kunsthalle. He proposed a different historicity of Catalan art, starting in the 1970s with conceptual art, rather than in the 1940s with informalism. He discovered a 'hidden tradition', whose heroic origin was the historical Grup de Treball ('Workgroup', GT from now on), a collective of artists and filmmakers working in the last years of Franco's dictatorship. GT's work was very political and also, alas, very ephemeral: its emblematic 'piece' was a private announcement in a newspaper, with the following message: 'due to temporary absence of country, we are seeking direct information on its reality. Appointments from 5 to 7 or write to: Muntadas, Comercio street 64, Barcelona 3, T. 319-09-03'.

Other preserved 'pieces' are posters, typed texts and films. In other terms, precariously preserved documents; remains, leftovers of actions, containing information of past events. The importance of these pieces is radically historical rather than aesthetical, in the sense that they are not objects to be seen as images, as art objects, but as traces of the past.

Borja was critical of the 'rational' model of the historical museum, with a lineal narrative, and preferred to see the development of the collection as a constellation or network, acquiring materials that would fit with the existing collections, expanding in new directions. Inspired by Benjamin and Broodthaers, he understood collections as an accumulation of diverse sources that, in their juxtaposition, can generate new associations, awakening hidden memories. In this sense, 'a true collection is not just the mere accumulation of souvenirs and "dead materials", but it can constitute an immense reservoir of experiences and images, opened and polymorphous' (Borja 2003: 16). Of course, ultimately who made the connections and opening the networks was Borja and his team, building *their* narrative.

Thus, for example, Borja's focus on the GT contributed to MACBA's interest in similar 1970s artist-activists groups in Latin America, like Tucumán Arde. The MACBA bought a whole archive of materials from Tucumán Arde as an art collection. Most of what it contained were posters, leaflets, photographs and films: documents from the actions of the group. In this direction, the MACBA developed a wider interested in political art and documentation, and on the topic of the archive.

The exhibits included a profusion of documents hung on walls or on tables with journals, books, photographs, typed texts, etc. Interestingly enough, the focus on documentary materials generated some contradictions within the architecture of the Museum. Richard Meier's building was the perfect white cube of pure modernist lines, pristinely illuminated by its glass façade, ideal for exhibiting king-size paintings, but not to show films, small photographs, leaflets or typewritten pages. The museum had to become darker; shades and panels were used to obstruct the light. For the GT show (1999), the tables had a very austere look, with trestles, making reference to a working table, reproducing the aesthetics of the workshop. However, there were no chairs: the public could look at the documents, but was not allowed to touch them. This was still an art show, after all. In following shows, the tables would include glass boxes, building further and clearer barriers between spectators and 'artworks'.

The museum presented itself as an archive that was making public a hidden or alternative tradition, in theory to open certain artistic, cultural and political issues to debate. But in the forms of exhibiting, and in the value it attributed to this material, the discourse did not always correspond to the practice of an archive or a library. At the museum, as opposed to the actual archive, the documents are displayed not just to be accessible, read, give information and awaken consciousness. They are there to be *looked at*, and not necessarily touched or used. That is why they are in glass boxes. In most of the displays at the MACBA, it is materially impossible to see all the images and films, read all the texts in display, not only because it is almost impossible to sit but also because of their sheer volume. The museum is *not* a library. There is a very important *visual* component of display that overcomes its informational dimension: the display of information becomes the artwork to be seen and experienced. Thus, visitors will enter in these ambiences that reproduce the look of a workshop or a classroom as if they were walking through an installation, looking here and there at one or another image, or text. I would argue that an important part of this visual experience is also technical curiosity for images and texts made with techniques that already belong to the past, like Super8 films or cyclostyled texts. The nostalgia for these forms of material documentation and its now perceived ephemerality, in an age of uniform, apparently extemporal and immaterial digital archives, is an important component of what, after all, is an aesthetic of the archive. In this sense, the material and visual qualities of these apparently immaterial documents become the focus of attention for the public. The archive is presented in spectacular ways, with overwhelming amounts of information which are impossible to absorb, but only to admire and appreciate in fragments. In spite of the MACBA, yes, they are building an aesthetic discourse, and yes, they are valorising a collection of texts and images not just as documents, but as artworks. The spectacle of the archive.

This spectacle of the archive is, of course, deeply embedded in Dadaist and Surrealist montage, and an ambiguous approximation to archives – both critical to and fascinated by it – can be found at the roots of conceptual art (Sekula 1989). In an interesting recent work, Sven Spieker analyses this aesthetics of the archive. Archives fulfil two main functions: administrative and historical. The second function is contingent on the first, since more archives are born out of the administrative impulse to classify documents. It is only once they are archived that these documents acquire a historical value – as records, discrete traces of contingent time. For Spieker, what the Dadaist collage questions is not just the administrative order of the archive by putting together apparently incongruent bits and pieces, but it also questions the figure–ground relationship – the archival base and what the archive stores. For example in Schwitters' work, the presentation of unreadable texts underscores this disjunctive interrelation between text (figure) and image (ground). This blurring of figure and ground, container and content, is also explicit in the 'archival' exhibits that MACBA presents, as we have seen. As a corollary to this Dadaist blurring, surrealism adds an explicit reflection on the contingent nature of the archive:

> Contingency, this archive implies, is not the same as randomness. Chance is organized, yet its precise morphology can be detected only by accident (literally). The archive does not give access to history: it is, or aims to be, the condition of historicity itself.
>
> (Spieker 2008: 174)

This emphasis on 'objective chance' is also explicit in the MACBA, which underscores the non-linear, contingent nature of its collections/archives. Yet, the question remains, how to organise a collection/archive on the basis of a modernist aesthetics of chance and the debasement of the distinction between documents and works of art? These contradictions, in fact, have become clear to the direction of the museum. As the collection grew bigger, it became apparent that a certain separation between documents and artworks had to be made. In other terms, an administrative principle of *classification* was necessary. The Documentation Center of the MACBA opened last year, bringing together the library and the archive. How the archive is going to be organised, separated from the collection, and displayed, is still a contentious issue within the museum. The general idea is that collection and archive are a continuous whole. Between the library and the museum, the archive will be, in the words of the director of the Documentation Center,[3] a 'fish-bowl', a restricted access space where authorised visitors will be allowed to consult the documents. Thus, between the glass boxes of the museum, where one can read from a distance, and the library, where everyone can grab a book and read, the archive will be a bigger glass box, a fish-bowl that will allow some people in to actually sit and read the documents. I have to say that this image of the fish-bowl is deeply alluring to me, and I cannot wait for the day I can sit down inside, and maybe hold in my hands a cracking newspaper from 1973, with an announcement written by the mythical Grup de Treball. I do not know if I will learn much from it, but I will certainly enjoy the (aesthetic?) experience.

Spectacle, archive and relational aesthetics

Borja and Krens left the MACBA and Guggenheim more or less at the same time – at the end of 2007 and the first months of 2008. At that point, their trajectories and reputation in the international art world were diametrically opposed, if at a different scale. Borja's work at the MACBA has in general been well received within the international art world; in 2007 he was designated president of the International Committee for Museums and Collections of Modern Art (CIMAM) and at the end of that year he was also appointed director of the Museo Nacional de Arte Centro Reina Sofia (MNCARS) in Madrid, the most important public collection of modern and contemporary art in Spain. At the MNCARS, Borja plans to apply some of the ideas he developed at MACBA. First and foremost, the rejection of a lineal, Euro-American narrative, developing an exhibition and acquisitions policy based on 'lines of force' and 'case studies' which does not privilege a single discourse of modernity but a plurality of discourses and artistic traditions – in particular in relation to Latin America. Secondly, Borja also wants to challenge the limits between the museum and the art centre model. This challenge is explicitly related to a new acquisition policy, based on 'case studies' and lines of force, or in other terms, curated temporary exhibits, more than on 'filling the gaps' of a historical narrative (Artfacts 2009).

There are elements of Borja's discourse, however, that seem to have taken a different direction: the rejection of the society of the spectacle seems to have been replaced by a reconsideration of the Museum as a temple of consumption. In an interview to *El Pais*, the most important Spanish newspaper, Borja explained that:

> We have gone from an era of production to an era of consumption. In the era of consumption, everything that is not productive, what is merely cognitive, an exchange of experiences, is central. The foremost example is art. In fact those who think that nobody goes to museums are wrong. They are more popular than ever. (. . .) in this cognitive world, where the exchange of experiences is more important than the production of things, education is very important. There are two forms of education: one based on curricula, which is circular, repressive, that wants to make children into little adults, without elements of equality. On the other hand, there is another kind of education, art, which is more complex, ambiguous, and fragile.[4]

Education seems to be the function of museum in these cognitive times (Borja makes reference to theories of cognitive capitalism). The museum, the big museum in particular, is not only the agora envisioned at the MACBA, but also an institution of education for the masses. In this sense, the function of the Museum does not seem contradictory with the society of the spectacle; it only aspires to provide an educative show.

Borja's ideas are clearly borrowed from the situationist rejection of the society of the spectacle, but also from relational aesthetics, a more recent reformulation of situationism by the art critic, Nicolas Bourriaud. Bourriaud (2002) has explicitly defined contemporary art as a 'situation of encounter', an exchange of experiences, as Borja says. Bourriaud was making reference to art practices that include the public in the production of the artwork – practices of 'participatory art'. Bourriaud's formulations were explicitly rejected in texts produced by MACBA, which accused it of being apolitical and too narrowly focused on the sphere of institutional art and 'aesthetics'. But in the long run, Bourriaud's adaptation (or containment) of situationist discourse to the art world seems to have provided Borja with the 'discourse' in which he can bring together the apparently contradictory nature of his discourse – how to transform a museum into an actively political institution, or at least something that looks like it.

Is Borja's project finally meeting Krens'? To go back to our other case, Krens' trajectory in the last years has been exactly the opposite. The first explicit markers of the crisis in Krens' project were a result of the Rio de Janeiro fiasco, in 2003, when the Board of trustees asked him to rethink his bold strategy of world domination; but in the end, his position as director was not only maintained but he was promoted to head of the foundation, causing the withdrawal of Peter B. Lewis, its chairman and biggest benefactor. After that, Krens was unable to reproduce Bilbao's success at other venues. The projects of expansion of the Guggenheim at New York were unsuccessful due to lack of funding, and the exhibitions at the Central Park building were increasingly criticised in the art world. Krens ended up resigning from his position in February 2008, to concentrate on the Abu Dhabi 'pharaonic' project. His resignation was welcomed in the art world as a 'goodbye to wackiness' (Yablonsky 2008). And still it is obvious that Krens' approach to cultural merchandising has been extremely influential in institutions like the Louvre, or the Tate, who still feel compelled to constantly 'renew' their image.

Interestingly enough, one of the first exhibits at the post-Krens New York Guggenheim was *Theanyspacewhatever* (2008), an exhibit of 'relational art'. Recently (Winter 2010), Tino Seghal had a solo show in the New York Guggenheim that consisted essentially of people who addressed the public with different questions. The museum, literally, was only filled with people.

Is the relational museum becoming, then, the middle ground between the museum spectacle and the museum archive? It certainly could, because relational art implies at the same time a sense of spectacle, since it is based on events of encounter, and yet it is nonetheless defined as a democratic, or horizontal practice, since it is explicitly participative and engages the public in the production of the artwork.

Conclusions: ambiguous dematerialisations

Coming back to our starting point, we have seen two different strategies to deal with the dematerialisation of contemporary art. One strategy is an 'empty' museum where the building, the container, becomes the central object that gives value to its content. The second one is to shift the content of the museum from objects to documents, proposing to transform the museum into an information centre and a public agora, more than a container of art objects. In both cases, as we have seen, the museums have been relatively successful, but they have also had problems. In the first case, the emblematic spectacularity of the Guggenheim Bilbao building has not been powerful enough for Krens to build the global empire he envisioned. The power of the fetish, in this case, has not been enough. In the second case, the replacement of art objects by documents in the MACBA has had some unintended effects, like the spectacularisation of these documents, in what I have defined as a spectacle of the archive. The archive in itself becomes an object of aesthetic contemplation, an art object. As Susan Pearce implied, the material autonomy of objects from our values sometimes can lead to unpredictable effects.

Reacting to these limitations, one of the possible alternatives is to use relational art to fill the empty museum with encounters (in the Guggenheim's case) and transform the archive into a lively experience (in the MACBA's case). With all, relational art has been questioned explicitly, for being too conservative and too 'arty', or, on the other hand, for pretending to be something more than institutional art (Bishop 2004). And yet it seems an adequate solution if contemporary art museums have to be defined as a specific kind of institution substantially different from other cultural venues – such as theatres, concert halls or universities, for example. Of course, the ultimate criticism of this model is that in these terms of replacement of production by consumption, art seems to be reduced to a sort of 'cultural service' (Kwon 2004), and museums to good, cultural shopping malls articulating an 'experience economy' (Pine and Gilmore 1999) . . . but shopping malls nonetheless?

Notes

1 Americas: 'Brazil: Court Bars a Guggenheim Museum', *The New York Times*, Wednesday 3 December 2008.
2 'Krens' museum for global contemporary art Guggenheim Abu Dhabi Will be "pharaonic"', *Spiegel Online*, 27 March 2008.
3 Personal interview, 25 October 2008.
4 Hemos pasado de una época de producción a una de consumo. En la de consumo, todo lo que no es productivo, lo que es meramente cognitivo, de intercambio de experiencias, es central. El máximo ejemplo de intercambio es el arte. De hecho, todos los que creen que ya nadie va a los museos están equivocados. La gente viene más que nunca. (. . .) Que en este mundo cognitivo, donde prima el intercambio de experiencias frente a la producción de cosas, la educación es muy importante. Hay dos formas de educación: la curricular, que es represiva, en la que a los niños se les quiere hacer pequeños adultos, sin elementos de igualdad. Frente a ésta hay otra, la del arte, que es más compleja, más ambigua, más frágil. Así que me niego a que se imponga la otra (Ruiz Mantilla 2008).

Bibliography

Artfacts.net (2009) Interview with Manuel Borja-Villel, director of MNCA Reina Sofia (Madrid 12.2.2009). Available online at: http://www.artfacts.net/index.php/pageType/ newsInfo/newsID (Accessed 20 October 2010).

Bishop, C. (2004) 'Antagonism and relational aesthetics', *October*, 110: 51–79.

Borja-Villell, M. (2003) 'Museu, memòria i identitat', in *MACBA Collection*, Barcelona: MACBA.

Bourriaud, N. (2002) *Relational Esthetics*, Dijon: Les Presses Du Reel.

Buskirk, M. (2003) *The Contingent Object of Contemporary Art*, Cambridge, MA: MIT Press.

Cuno, J. (2001) 'Against the discursive museum', in P. Noever (ed.) *The Discursive Museum*, Vienna: Hatje Cantz.

Fraser, A. (2005) 'No es un lugar maravilloso? El tour de un tour por el Guggenheim Bilbao', in A.M. Guasch and J. Zulaika (eds) *Aprendiendo del Guggenheim Bilbao*, Madrid: Akal, pp. 39–62.

Guasch, A.M. and Zulaika, J. (eds) (2005) *Aprendiendo del Guggenheim Bilbao*, Madrid: Akal.

Kwon, M. (2004) *One Place after Another: site-specific art and the location of identity*, Cambridge, MA: MIT Press.

Lippard, L. (1973) *Six Years: the dematerialization of the art object from 1966 to 1972*, Berkeley: University of California Press.

Pearce, S.M. (1992) *Museums, Objects and Collections: a cultural study*, London: Leicester University Press.

Pine, J. and J. Gilmore (1999) *The Experience Economy*, Boston: Harvard Business School Press.

Ruiz Mantilla, J. (2008) 'Los museos han pasado a ser como centros comerciales', *El País Dominical*, 6 January 2008.

Sekula, A. (1989) 'The body and the archive', in R. Bolton (ed.) *The Contest of Meaning*, Minneapolis: University of Minnesota Press, pp. 342–88.

Spieker, S. (2008) *The Big Archive: Art from Bureaucracy*, Cambridge, MA: MIT Press.

Vogel, S. (1988) *Art/Artefact: African art in anthropological collections*, Exhibition Catalogue: New York, Center for African Art and Prestel Verlag.

Yablonsky, L. (2008) 'Goodbye to Guggenheim's Krens, Franchising, Wackiness', *Bloomberg News*, 28 February.

Zulaika, J. (1997) *Crónica de una seducción: El Museo Guggenheim Bilbao*, Madrid: Nerea.

Zulaika, J. (2005) 'Desiring Bilbao: the Krensification of the museum and its discontents', in A.M. Guasch and J. Zulaika (eds) *Learning from the Bilbao Guggenheim*, Reno: University of Nevada Press, pp. 149–70.

16 Playing dress-up

Inhabiting imagined spaces through museum objects

Julia Petrov

Introduction

It may initially seem paradoxical to consider that museums, with all their vast stores of objects, are actually immaterial in nature. However, the typical museum visitor is often reduced to only their visual sense to respond to their surroundings, filled with physical objects. In the literature of the 'New Museology', this has resulted in critiques of museums as didactic institutions, filled with unreflexive curator-centric discourse, where audiences are passively indoctrinated into hegemonic sociocultural world views. This literature is now nearly three decades old, and a new generation of ideas reclaiming visitor agency in museums is emerging, describing subtle and nuanced ways in which museums can facilitate, and not just impart meaning.

In collections of the decorative arts, especially, the museum visitor can be seen as an expert-connoisseur. Their experiential knowledge of physical objects in the mundane reality of their everyday lives allows them to negotiate the physical and temporal space of the gallery without having to rely on direct haptic input. Even in a museum, the object can serve the function of an *aide-memoire*, just as it would in a private collection: to remind the beholder of a past experience, and to mediate the space between memory of the past, and the imagination of the self. As Wehner (Chapter 6) suggests, museal conventions take on a type of transparency. Drawing on the works of Gathercole (1989), Moore (2000), DeBolla (2001) and Feldman (2006), this chapter explores how theories of embodiment, materiality and aesthetics can supplement traditional conceptions of the museum experience by positing the viewer as capable of bypassing curatorial conceits through acts of imagined embodiment.

Throughout the speculative discussion that follows, I will most closely focus on a class of museum objects frequently encountered in everyday life: clothing. It is my view that the body missing from vacant displays of fashion galleries can be a vehicle for fantasy and memory, straddling the difficult boundary between active and passive knowledge. My aim is to begin building a vocabulary and theory for the types of (dis)embodied interactions that occur around the material culture of musealised dress.

Materiality and museology

The term materiality is underpinned by the assumption that one sensory experience is not interchangeable with another like a metaphor, but is unique and individual, grounded in physical and psychological responses that vary (within a set of cultural conventions) from person to person, object to object. These contrasting interpretive theories clash most obviously within museums, where objects placed in glass cases are experienced mostly visually, and relinquish much of their material power. Even though curatorial practice is highly haptic and relies on connoisseurial distinctions that are multi-sensory; even though galleries are filled with artefacts that serve as witnesses to the past; and even though objects are scrutinised as closely as scientific evidence for their significance, yet still the actual experience of a museum is, for most visitors to most museums, mainly a visual one, where objects are staged in tableaux.

This staging is made possible by what Tony Bennett has described as 'the methods of exhibition, display, and spectatorship' (2004: 363) that manage meaning in viewers – the norms and systems of visual experience within the museum environment, and constructed scopic regimes for sense-making. Objects, carefully arranged according to rules of two-dimensional composition, are locked away in Plexiglas cases, lit dramatically to highlight their appearance, and made to speak with text panels. The galleries are hushed, the security is stern, and a reverent distance is maintained at all times. Museums are about ideas – the emphasis is placed on the process of intellectual discovery, and sequences of rational thought, rather than on the materiality of the places, processes, people or things under examination. The message is: 'Look, but don't touch; think, but do not experience'.

As craft historian Pamela Johnson has argued, traditional visual analysis, as practised by art historians and frequently, curators, does not examine the material function of objects, privileging as it does 'the conceptual, the idea separate from skills and materials' (Johnson 1997: 293). Her further point is that in reality, 'a literacy of touch' (1997: 293) is an important way by which meaning is attached, projected and received to objects. Similarly, Alan Wing, Christos Giachritsis and Roberta Roberts write that:

> Vision often appears to determine the way we perceive the world. However, touch is the sensory modality that verifies the reality of what we see by allowing us to confirm the physical presence of objects and the people around us. Vision may prompt us to make contact with an object or person, but by touching, we reinforce the subjective impact of that object or person.
>
> (Wing *et al.* 2007: 31)

According to these critics, then, materiality is the touchstone that defines human experience, and how objects are integrated into physical interactions with humans is therefore a useful counterpoint to visuality.

However, the conventions of visuality within the exhibition space die hard, as Fiona Candlin has argued:

> Relinquishing the notion of the museum as a purely optical space does come at some cost, particularly in relation to institutional expertise. This could be understood in relation to the challenge of accepting lay opinions and the necessity of mastering new skills. It would require a paradigm shift, in that curators would need to accept that sight is not the sole route to aesthetic experience and knowledge and that embodiment is not disassociated from thought.
>
> (Candlin 2007: 103)

Thus, while museum curators rely on the material properties of objects to make assertions about their history, paradoxically the material existence of the same objects is often neglected in favour of other priorities. As Peter Gathercole (1989: 73) has noted: 'To put the question more generally, are artefacts regarded by curators as basic to the existence of museums, or is it the knowledge concerning artefacts which is basic, the artefacts being merely illustrative of that knowledge?' Dorsett (Chapter 7) discusses this dilemma in the context of artistic practice, but on many levels, this is also an ontological debate, striking deep at the heart of Western epistemology; if objects are essentially different from words and images, then how they operate and are interpreted becomes a question of vital importance. If the nature and function of an object displayed in a museum is inadequately or incorrectly interpreted, the museum system itself may be to blame.

Staged display

Object connoisseurship is a practice deeply rooted in an intuitive understanding of materiality, and museums have traditionally assembled public collections out of the private stores of individual connoisseurs. The practices of curatorship and collections conservation and management are also all based on a profound appreciation of materiality; both as objects that have their own physical properties and how these physical properties affect or are affected by their interactions with humans. Museum interpretation within a gallery setting, however, does not often make these material qualities evident, either as a result of the conventions of museum display (in which objects are placed out of reach behind protective glass or on plinths and pedestals which more subtly discourage touching), or as a result of the narratives used by curators to define and describe objects (in which the objects themselves are often secondary to a broader cultural theme under discussion, making them virtually dispensable or interchangeable). This situation has historical precedents, and certain categories of museum object, such as fashion, are more susceptible.

It was the close association between the visual and dramatic arts in the nineteenth century that caused a connection in the public imagination to be made between historical costume and theatrical display, even in 'serious' venues like museums (Petrov 2008). The display of dress in museums harnessed familiar visual codes to construct a popular vision of a shared public past; these drew their rhetorical power from association and repetition. Audiences expected the costumes inside museums to reflect the ways they were presented outside the gallery space. While no one seriously expects the antique porcelain in a museum to be regularly hauled out for fun and fundraising tea-parties, yet, as late as 1972, museum literature was still encouraging dressing up in historical costumes to 'create a social occasion which will draw attention to your society, amuse the membership, intrigue the public, and please the press' (Briggs 1972: 1). Even where live models were not used, lifelikeness in the displays was and continues to be valued. Of the 1834 display of Cromwell's clothing, *The Times* noted, 'the figures are arranged in two rooms, and have the appearance of living beings' (Anon 1834: 3). In 1911, discussing the desirable arrangement of a set of newly acquired eighteenth century period rooms by the Metropolitan Museum of Art (the Met), the *New York Times* waxed nostalgic: 'We recall a little local museum in Butzbach, Germany, with a room delightful in its minute detail of reconstruction, a sturdy realism having furnished lay figures in the costume of the period representing the members of a numerous German family engaged in work and play' (Anon 1911: 8). Ninety-three years later, perhaps in the very same period room described in the article, the Met followed the Edwardian author's advice in its 'Dangerous Liaisons' exhibition (Petrov 2004, McNeil 2005, Koda and Bolton 2006). Even now, displays of dress feature frozen mannequin actors in tableaux, acting out in perpetuity the domesticated past, icons of a narrative first adopted as a model in the nineteenth century.

This type of staging is commonly excused as a means of 'bringing the past to life'. Mannequins, such as those in the exhibition discussed above, are dressed to be as recognisable as possible, using familiar visual conventions. In some cases, the faces of the mannequins themselves may be familiar – the Brooklyn Museum's use of mannequins featuring the faces of contemporary English actors for their display of historical male costume (*Of Men Only*, 1975–76; see Coleman 1975) is a case in point. It only takes a moment of reflection to consider the result: a false sense that the past was familiar, and that the people who populated it were not so very different (West 1999: 1–3). There is a kind of dramatic irony in the fact that these mannequins were based on actors, as many museums (the Met is but one notable example) use elements of theatrical *bricolage* to add a sense of verisimilitude to their shows, and note only the 'authentic' objects on display in labels, ignoring the reconstructed or reproduced elements completely. Often, the theatricality can overwhelm the sense of the real.

For this reason, materiality has become an important point of critique in museum studies. Museologist Kevin Moore (2000) has argued that materiality, not visuality, is key to the visitor's experience of understanding. According to him, it is materiality that lends a sense of authenticity to history. While multi-sensory engagement can heighten the reality-effect of a heritage attraction, this is only a theatrical illusion unless it is backed up by authentic physicality. He writes:

> Museums and heritage attractions which have or create this double power
> of real things and real place powerfully engage all the senses. We have a
> sense of being transported back in time, we are there, in sight, sound, smells,
> and touch, and sometimes even taste.
>
> (Moore 2000: 142)

Furthermore, he argues that:

> We can only appreciate and understand material culture when we gain some
> awareness of its meaning, whether now or in the past, for the people who
> created or used it. [. . .] in focusing on material culture we need to consider
> a third element: 'real things in their real place as experienced by real people'.
>
> (Moore 2000: 142)

Decorative arts displays, especially those set up in ways that mimic how those
objects were encountered in their commodified existence (within a market economy
of value exchange), create an effective stage for this reality-effect. Associated as they
are with everyday lived experience, having once been a part of it, the decorative arts
arouse strong feelings of empathy, and consumer desire; that may be why they
have been traditionally associated with morality, taste and control over the material
world (see Potvin and Myzelev 2009). Thus, the decorative arts lend themselves much
more effectively than the traditional fine arts to being used to create a microcosmic
world within the museum environment. The sense of verisimilitude that may result
requires a very specific set of interrelationships between the objects on display,
their now-missing original owners and the contemporary viewers who behold
them in a gallery. The act of looking can trigger sense memories, and heighten
a material understanding of objects that seem distant by their difference.

Embodied expertise

Archaeologist Carl Knappett has pointed out that, 'For humans, generally, an
understanding of what an object is seems to be fundamentally linked to how that
object is encountered in active situations' (2005: 44). This understanding is not
merely form-related, but also comes from cultural norms. Non-representational gallery
settings only succeed if they are merely surreal, and not unreal: some connection
to quotidian presentations of similar objects must be maintained. For this reason,
the relatability of scale and proportion of exhibited object to viewer is one of
the key aspects of any museum display; it can be significantly assisted by props
such as mannequins which serve as yardsticks of human measurements. As the
philosopher Maurice Merleau-Ponty wrote in *The Phenomenology of Perception*:
'In other words: to look at an object is to inhabit it, and from this habitation to
grasp all things in terms of the aspect which they present to it' (2002: 79).

In my professional practice as a curator of historical dress, I have found that,
to some extent, even the most highly decorated, exaggerated or expensive garment
will be accessible to a viewer because of this very phenomenon: even if the

museumgoer in question will never have worn such a garment themselves, and indeed may never encounter one like it again, they will instinctively know exactly how it related to a body in space because of the long cultural conditioning they have had with clothing and character play, in their roles as consumers.

Jules David Prown hit upon the truth in his essay 'The truth of material culture' when he wrote:

> The human body constantly provides a sense of scale. It all adds up to a tremendous body of experience that is common and transcultural. This experience is transformed into belief that finds material expression in arte-facts, the analysis of which – material culture – provides privileged paths of access for us to an understanding of other people and other cultures, of other times and other places.
>
> (Prown 1993: 17–18)

In his assertion that 'Artefacts constitute the only class of historical events that occurred in the past but survive into the present. They can be re-experienced' (1993: 2–3), Prown reveals the fundamental strength of materiality: its apparent transferability backwards and forwards through time due to its continuing action on the human senses. On some level, therefore, the interpretation allowed by the materiality of an object appears to be simple and easily generalised: if humans across cultures have had roughly the same physiological needs and responses, then the objects they produce to meet those will be readily identifiable to any other human. More recently, archaeologist Christopher Tilley put the same idea this way: 'Past experiences are carried forward through the activity of the incarnate subject and provide structures through which that subject is able to interpret the world or fit it into a pattern. The body carries time into the experience of place and landscape' (2004: 12).

Bodies past and present

Within the museum landscape, visitor bodies encounter past bodies: clothing on mannequins. Yet the mere fact of a dress having once been on a body is not enough; it requires a particular physicality to engage with viewers. For a displayed dress to retain sufficient talismanic power to serve as what *Harry Potter* aficionados might refer to as a 'portkey' (Rowling 2000) – an object which, through its physical and psychological associations seems to 'take one back' to a given historical period – it needs both verisimilitude and anonymity. The typical visitor response to different display modes was well-described by Alexandra Palmer:

> The use of made-up faces, wigs and complete accessories leads one to explore social history, manners and custom. Abstract faces and minimal detailing tend to represent the costume as art object, the mannequin providing the frame. Realistic faces draw our attention as we tend to 'read' them before focusing on other details. This can act as a tool to attract the public's attention

and initiate interest. Alternatively an abstract face or headless form can be used to demonstrate the costume as the prime target of interest.

(Palmer 1988: 9)

Symbolically, a dress on a mannequin is only a silhouette. It is a chalk outline of a missing person, needing a body to fill it. The moulded shape of a mannequin can do so physically, but museum visitors are only too happy to fill in the mental outline and restore the imagined spirit of the occupant inside. This can be very conducive to museum-based learning, as it is to some degree participatory. A Canadian Conservation Institute handbook for constructing mannequins confidently states that, 'Studies have shown that people visiting a museum to view costume displays are inclined to let their fantasies roam while looking at the display. They often imagine themselves wearing a period costume from the display' (Anon 1988: 13).

Imagination and memory, as argued above, can be stimulated by personal experience. In an insightful essay titled, 'Preserving human packaging', dress curator Elizabeth Ann Coleman outlined exactly what makes clothing important from a historical point of view, yet compelling from a personal one. She wrote:

> Articles of apparel allow us to approach, in a very personal form, our immediate ancestors and see what they really wore. They also allow us to contemplate what some renowned personage may have owned. Garments tell us that people, then as now, were short or fat, tall or skinny, rich or poor, disabled or robust.
>
> (Coleman 1993: 6)

The significance of dress, according to Coleman, therefore, is not so much in the object of dress itself, but in what it can tell us about the now-missing body of its original wearer, and how that body navigated the physical space around it. Just as importantly, Coleman highlights the way in which seeing the 'packaging' reveals the world of objects and human relationships, which once surrounded it.

However, this world of relationships is a highly constructed one. There is a sense of play in the way that period rooms are laid out as a proscenium stage, a life-sized doll house, frequently peopled with mannequins in period dress and stylised/stereotyped poses as the inhabitants of the doll house. Perhaps the similarity between the museum visitor and the mannequin inspires also a sense of habitation, a desire to live among the liminal objects within the gallery space: neither dead nor alive. The mannequins so often placed in historic houses, or in room settings within museums, add to their interpretation precisely because they are stand-ins for the living humans who, for reasons of conservation, can no longer interact with the spaces as they were meant to. This staging presents evidence of the performance of shared human behaviour using artefacts as props.

Sameness and otherness in context

Looking at clothes in a museum is a recognition of difference: while the physical experience of other decorative art objects, different though their individual stylistic features may be, may be quite similar to modern parallels, antique fashion styles engage the body in ways that are very different, and immediately palpable to the onlooker. Even if clothing comes from a different culture, and may not have modern parallels in the observer's everyday lived experience, the intuitive act of mentally 'trying on the garment for size', as it were, 'walking a mile in someone else's shoes', and similar idiomatic expressions, speak to the translation of the imagined physical experience through cultural and temporal bonds.

Blogger Ingrid Mida captured just such an exchange when she related her experience viewing a gown believed to have belonged to Marie Antoinette, displayed at the Royal Ontario Museum in 2008: 'While studying the dress, I heard one visitor remark that the dress was much "*smaller*" than she expected. She explained that she had envisioned "*something larger than life*" given the notoriety of Marie Antoinette' (Mida 2008). The visitor had measured herself up to Marie Antoinette, and found the historic queen lacking – partially due to her own preconceptions of what Marie Antoinette was supposed to look like: a short queen with an extravagant style far beyond her personal proportions. That idea, of course, stems from the legends surrounding the French Revolution: the portraits, written accounts and later Hollywood representations of the doomed monarchy.

Nancy Millar's book on underwear contains a similar description of on how museumgoers confront the materiality of the past through clothing.

> For if I were to look at a dress in a museum, one from Victorian times, say, I'd notice the dress and all its features, but I'd also be thinking of the body that must have worn it, how slim she must have been, how hard it must have been to drag all that fabric around. So I'm imagining that dress on a body. I'm embodying it. Body and dress as a package. Sometimes more of the body is in the equation, sometimes more of the dress.
>
> (2006: 31)

Millar's quote illustrates succinctly the symbiotic relationship between fact and fantasy, viewer and object, past and present, all mediated through clothing, supported by the physical body.

Evoking the past

Clothing's dual character, at once mundane and spectacular, makes it one of the most evocative categories of museum object. While all of us have experiential knowledge of dress – a basic competence in its feel, sound and appearance – seeing the discarded clothes of another sparks also a desire to wear them, with the implication that one could almost become them by so doing. This empathy, combined with experience, is what drives the dressing-up games that children (and adults) play. However, it is also what makes a museum display of dress so uniquely potent; capable of convincingly communicating directly not just about the generalities, but the intimate specifics of the past. In Jeffrey Feldman's terms, this might be called a 'contact point,' which he defines as 'a general category of object that results from physical contact with the body, and then the subsequent removal or destruction of the body' (2006: 245). He writes:

> When museum objects are treated as contact points, the senses become historical links between histories and representation, thereby opening onto unexpected discourses of domination, agency, and material value that might otherwise be silenced or excluded by critiques of museums as markets.
>
> (2006: 255)

Feldman's focus is on undermining colonial narratives, but imagined embodiment can just as easily disrupt the curatorial ideologies modern museology is so keen to criticise. By inserting one's body in place of the missing historical body to whom the historical objects exhibited in the museum belonged, the visitor can gain a valuable understanding of the absent person's experience.

In his book on aesthetics, Peter DeBolla has clarified how the museum object might function in arousing remembered responses:

> Immediate somatic responses may quickly give way to a variety of thoughts associated with formally similar presentations [. . .] When this happens, the frisson of the physical encounter rapidly mutates into a jumble of thoughts, as if an impulse – call it a spark of affect – sets in motion a series of reactions that leave their trace in whatever permeable surface they encounter. For some viewers that surface is identifiable as 'emotion,' for others it is more like ratiocination.' [. . .] This state of 'in-between-ness', as it were, part physical and part mental, in the orbit of the emotive yet also clearly articulated or potentially articulatable within the higher orders of mental activity, is one way of describing wonder.
>
> (DeBolla 2001: 2–3)

Although DeBolla writes about the processes of seeing artworks, even this is not a purely ocular experience within a gallery setting. If viewers could also touch the artefacts, their affective experience would be stronger, but the most interesting point that DeBolla makes is that this is not a prerequisite for stimulating memory processes. The subjectivity of touch may serve to reify the past: to make it immanent through acts of the imagination. Conversely, however, imagination can substitute for physical touch.

Because materiality has an apparent metaphorical or mnemonic link with the past, objects have traditionally been housed and interpreted within those contexts in museums, themselves institutions of cultural memory. There, artefacts serve to represent and recreate the material conditions of the past, evoking modern understandings of its reality. Even the practice of remembering is disciplined and altered within a museum, where visitors are educated to remember appropriately. Personal memory, the associations that come from a lifetime of building literacy in 'reading' objects and relating them to one's own life, is often less valued in a museum experience than cultural memory: associating oneself with a narrative greater than the individual.

Viewers looking at a dress in a museum see a body – gone. On one hand, this often elicits a naïve and crassly commercial response so often decried by museum practitioners and theories, particularly in the decorative arts. Spurred on by acquisitive instincts, visitors often are heard to make comments to the effect of 'I wish I owned that', or 'I could never wear that', or remarks similar in spirit. The micro-blogging site Tumblr allows individuals to post images with comments, and many of the responses to museum items also reflect such consumer desires; for example, an eighteenth century *robe à la française* from the collection of the Royal Ontario Museum (925.18.1) prompted user Glendora to remark: 'Can I wear this? I want to wear this. What do you mean it's a little too much!?' (Glendora 2010). Yet there is a deeper, darker, more metaphysical aspect to this. Certainly, if there is no one currently wearing the dress, it may mean that you can wear it. But more frequently, it means that someone else already has; and they are not able to wear it anymore. Suddenly, the viewer is face-to-face with the shocking proof of mortality – a human mortality that objects in museums can transcend, at least for a time.

Our culture is full of myths and images about objects coming to life, ghosts animating once again their abandoned bodies: the classical myth of Pygmalion, the 1933 horror film *The Mystery of the Wax Museum* and subsequent remakes, and the classic children's film *Bedknobs and Broomsticks* are just some examples. There are also the philosophical questions about the limits of death posed by the contemporary artist Damien Hirst in his installations of animals floating in formaldehyde limbo. What all these, and many others, suggest to me is an underlying cultural discomfort with the borderline between the lifeless and the living, which is most effectively embodied by mannequins. Freud called this 'the uncanny', but this frisson caused by the emotional engagement of living people with inanimate things is just one part of aesthetic experience. As Kate Soper writes:

> Much of our clothing and bodily adornment will outlive us, sometimes by many years, thus escaping the relatively speedy post-mortem decomposition of our fleshly selves; and it is arguably this combination of proximity with the organic body and alterity from it that is responsible for the poignancy of lost or no longer needed clothing.
>
> (Soper 2001: 22).

So displayed dress can marry the spectacular and the tangible, and there are implications of this for museums attempting to communicate through this medium, as the quote from Elizabeth Ann Coleman, above, suggested. Objects of dress, as triggers for memories of lived experience, can be powerful means for transmitting cultural knowledge.

Conclusions

It is therefore vitally important to consider the issues of a usable public past, as well as visual literacy within a wider consumerist culture of images. Museums are, after all, a convergent medium, and while text and image together offer a powerful message about social identity, when combined with objects, they are even more effective. The object can often initiate social processes – and this is why museums, at their best are relevant and exciting; my further point is that fashion is a unique medium in this exchange.

I concede that this assumes that the museumgoer in question has actually had experiences with particular types of objects, or with objects similar enough that they could mentally extrapolate that experience and imagine how an exotic object might have been used. The effectiveness of a museum display may rest upon this fact. My point, therefore, is that the focus of the formula of museum learning may need to be rewritten: it is not always that a museum merely dictates and a visitor understands. Instead, more often, a visitor brings to a museum their own bundles of cultural understandings, their personal narratives and experience-honed skills, which they can mentally lay over the objects they are presented with, performing an intangible comprehension (Haldrup and Larsen 2006: 279) – feeling through seeing. They may not gain new expertise, only merely hone that which they already have. Far from being a Lockean *tabula rasa* waiting to be filled with expert wisdom, the audience shapes their museum experience through pre-existing knowledge. For museum practitioners to understand this, therefore, is a first step towards creating exhibitions and activities that facilitate debate and reminiscence, rather than relying simply on a one-way flow of didactic pedagogy. Without necessarily changing their long-established form, the complex intertwining of the visual and the material in museum displays can be more carefully developed to ensure that their content considers their fluid, discursive function.

By engaging with an object, one can participate in the past, thereby making it present through an act of imagination. There is nothing physical in the memories or the feelings evoked by objects, but they form just as vital a link to human experience. Fashion's representation within the museum space, and outside of it, can influence how the public thinks about history. As museum practice in interrogating fashion as a simultaneously aesthetic, sensory and material artefact of material culture develops, curators need to better understand the efficacy of the fashion museum (or the fashion exhibition) as a medium of social control and communication, to allow visitors to create their own meanings.

Bibliography

Anon (1834) 'Exhibition of ancient costume', *The Times*, 9 June 1834: 3.

Anon (1911) 'Bringing the past to life', *New York Times*, 13 August 1911: 8.

Anon (1988) *Mannequins: considerations and construction techniques*, Ottawa: Canadian Conservation Institute.

Bennett, T. (2004) 'The exhibitionary complex', in D. Preziosi and C. Farago (eds) *Grasping the World: the idea of the museum*, London: Ashgate, pp. 413–41.

Briggs, R.T. (1972) 'Displaying your costumes: some effective techniques', American Association for State and Local History Technical Leaflet 33, *rev. ed.*, *History News*, 27 (11).

Candlin, F. (2007) 'Don't Touch! Hands Off! Art, blindness, and the conservation of expertise', in E. Pye (ed.) *The Power of Touch: handling objects in museum and heritage contexts*, Oxford: Berg, pp. 89–106.

Coleman, E.A. (1975) *Of Men Only: a review of men's and boy's fashions, 1750–1975*, Brooklyn: The Brooklyn Museum.

Coleman, E.A. (1993) 'Preserving human packaging', *Museum International*, 45 (3): 4–7.

DeBolla, P. (2001) *Art Matters*, Cambridge, MA: Harvard University Press.

Feldman, J. (2006) 'Contact points: museums and the lost body problem', in E. Edwards, C. Gosden and R. Phillips (eds) *Sensible Objects: colonialism, museums and material culture*, Oxford: Berg, pp. 245–68.

Gathercole, P. (1989) 'The fetishism of artefacts', in S. Pearce (ed.) *Museum Studies in Material Culture*, Leicester: Leicester University Press, pp. 73–81.

Glendora (2010) 'Woman's overdress or robe à la française of Chinese floral-painted silk, with petticoat'. Available online at: http://glendora.tumblr.com/post/903960128/marieantoinettereine-vintagevision-womans (Accessed 30 July 2010).

Haldrup, M. and J. Larsen (2006) 'Material cultures of tourism', *Leisure Studies*, 25 (3): 275–89.

Johnson, P. (1997) 'Out of touch: the meaning of making in the digital age', in T. Harrod and H. Clifford (eds) *Obscure Objects of Desire: reviewing the crafts in the twentieth century*, London: Crafts Council, pp. 292–6.

Knappett, C. (2005) *Thinking Through Material Culture: an interdisciplinary perspective*, Philadelphia: University of Pennsylvania Press.

Koda, H. and A. Bolton (2006) *Dangerous Liaisons: fashion and furniture in the eighteenth century*, New York: Metropolitan Museum of Art.

McNeil, P. (2005) 'Exhibition review: Dangerous Liaisons. Fashion and furniture in the eighteenth century', *Fashion Theory: The Journal of Dress, Body and Culture*, 9 (4): 477–85.

Merleau-Ponty, M. (2002) *Phenomenology of Perception*, Florence, KY: Routledge.

Mida, I. (2008) 'Marie Antoinette's dress at the ROM: photos'. Available online at: http://fashionismymuse.blogspot.com/2008/10/photos-of-marie-antoinettes-dress-at.html (Accessed 3 November 2008).

Millar, N. (2006) *The Unmentionable History of the West*, Calgary: Red Deer Press.

Moore, K. (2000) *Museums and Popular Culture*, London: Cassell.

Palmer, A. (1988) 'Exhibiting costume', *Museum Quarterly*, 16 (4): 9–14.

Petrov, J. (2004) 'Exhibition review: "Dangerous Liaisons; Fashion and Furniture in the 18th Century"', *Dress: The Journal of the Costume Society of America*, 31: 76–7.

Petrov, J. (2008) '"The habit of their age": English genre painters, dress collecting, and museums, 1910–1914', *Journal of the History of Collections*, 20 (2): 237–51.

Potvin, J. and A. Myzelev (eds) (2009) *Material Cultures, 1740–1920: the meanings and pleasures of collecting*, Farnham: Ashgate Publishing.

Prown, J.D. (1993) 'The truth of material culture', in S. Lubar and W.D. Kingery (eds) *History from Things: essays on material culture*, Washington, DC: Smithsonian, pp. 1–19.

Rowling, J.K. (2000) *Harry Potter and the Goblet of Fire*, London: Bloomsbury.

Soper, K. (2001) 'Dress needs: reflections on the clothed body, selfhood and consumption', in J. Entwistle and E. Wilson (eds) *Body Dressing*, Oxford: Berg.

Tilley, C. (2004) *The Materiality of Stone: explorations in landscape phenomenology*, Oxford: Berg.

West, S. (1999) 'Introduction', in S. Tarlow and S. West (eds) *The Familiar Past? Archaeologies of later historical Britain*, London: Routledge.

Wing, A., C. Giachritsis and R. Roberts (2007) 'Weighing up the value of touch', in E. Pye (ed.) *The Power of Touch: handling objects in museum and heritage contexts*, Oxford: Berg, pp. 31–44.

17 Material object and immaterial collector

Is there room for the collector-donor discourse in the museal space?

Caroline Bergeron

Museums offer their visitors the possibility of appreciating a multitude of artefacts, many of which do not necessarily come from the institution's own collecting efforts. Besides loans from other museums and acquisitions from the specialised art scene, there are also artefacts that used to adorn the interior domestic spaces of private collectors. Experienced museumgoers may be able to pick out the legacy of collector-donors among the various works on display, but what do they truly understand of these indispensable partners of the museum? Often forgotten about, the relationship between collectors and museums, and more precisely between 'collector-donors' and 'museum-recipients', is nevertheless unavoidable. This article addresses this issue by focusing on notions of collecting and giving, and by examining how the mechanisms linking these concepts are interdependent. These ideas are developed in two parts: first, how collectors create a discourse around their collections and, second, what vestiges of this discourse remain once the collection is given to a museum or collecting institution. This research question occurred to me after more than twelve years of professional activity in the philanthropic field.[1] Professional experience has allowed me to witness and participate in numerous gift transactions, some of them difficult, few of them perfectly fluid.

Collecting: in pursuit of one's self

Constant and varied interactions between people and objects lie at the centre of human life. Those relations consist in an expression of the 'material culture' which is both characteristic of and specific to humans (Schiffer 1999). Among human activities linked to the material world, collecting is a very meaningful occupation. From the field of consumer research, Russell Belk observed that personal possessions are used as an identity device as well as a tool of representation of the self. Studying the collecting phenomenon, Belk (1988) concluded that collecting is an identity-driven process occurring as a part of consumption. Often, material possessions are indeed signs of the relative wealth, power and importance – whether real or symbolic – that their owners exercise in their milieu. His research on consumer behaviour even concludes that possessions are an 'extended self', acknowledging the notion of personal and symbolic assets in a sense previously developed by the French sociologist Pierre Bourdieu (1987).

Within this approach, the collection is considered to be a pure 'extension of the self', an idea that I follow in this chapter. Indeed, if personal possessions contribute significantly to how an individual establishes his or her identity and conveys this identity to others, then the collection, as a representation vector, is among these identity-based strategies. By defining who he or she is, the collector becomes the artisan of a discourse that conveys their worldview to a chosen audience (Bal 1994). In addition to building identity through objects, the collector also searches for social connections via material culture. As Baudrillard (1968) states in *The System of Objects*, there is, indeed, a major difference between accumulating things for accumulation's sake and consciously acquiring objects to assemble a cohesive collection and cultivate an ideal. Thus, building a collection is an act inseparable from shared community culture. In fact, it could be argued that a collection directs itself towards culture, that this culture leads people towards each other via objects and that this dynamic includes social exteriority and human relations. In more recent work, Baudrillard (1994) studied the act of collecting, coming to the conclusion that collectors wall themselves in a closed and reflexive system that we can describe as a narration about their own cultural identity.

These visions of the collection suggest that both actions, collecting and giving, can share similarities as both actions rely on the importance of the self within the community in order to be completed. The self emerges from the collection as a significant component, and a *sine qua non* condition for the authorship of the gift. Both collecting and giving have cultural purpose, creating a particular transaction that requires acknowledgement and recognition.

Giving: reaching out or being reached?

We know from personal experience that giving, or not giving, is always of social importance. Consequently, we can say that giving is a meaningful and very powerful human activity which unifies and bonds people within a very precise process. The act of giving was one of the major research themes of the sociologist Marcel Mauss at the beginning of the twentieth century. His renowned work on giving in traditional societies (Mauss 1923), demonstrates that the logic of giving involves three successive obligations: giving, receiving/accepting, and returning.

The first obligation, giving, initiates the process. According to Mauss, giving must be a voluntary and personal action that creates a social connection between the giver and the receiver. This action could be interpreted as one of solidarity because the donor shares a part of their identity when they reach out to the recipient. In spite of this apparent gracious gesture, the gift is, in fact, a restraining action because of the recipient's implicated and programmed response: the second obligation of the Maussian cycle, receiving.

This second obligation calls for the recipient's acceptance of the gift. By doing so, the receiver also accepts the connection with the giver. This situation establishes a double relation of status inequity between giver and receiver. Although the gift brings together giver and receiver in an act of human bonding, at the same time, the authority of the donor firmly restrains the receiver. In debt to the donor, the receiver bears the responsibility of the last obligation of the cycle: returning.

Mauss calls this third obligation the 'counter-gift', since it requires the debt to the giver to be recognised with symbolic or concrete action. However, it does not completely clear the original debt. Indeed, Mauss asks how a gift could be acknowledged, recognised, and its social connection be totally wiped out by a receiver subordinated, in authority, to the donor? The connection established by the gift ends up in perpetual debt. Mauss proposes that the gift carries literally a part of the donor, justifying the perennial state of the debt. Maurice Godelier (1996) discusses the enigmatic debt of the gift. He comes to the conclusion that the paradoxical asymmetry between gift and counter-gift, generating the debt, can be solved by admitting that one can give and keep an object at the same time. His explanation is that the counter-gift cannot wipe a debt if the given object has not totally been given, since it is always connected to the first owner, by means of social bond. Even separated from the donor, the gift is never truly alienated. Then, it carries the giver's presence and authority. Of course, this perpetual ownership is possible only if we accept the symbolic functions and effects of gift circulation in a social structure. Since the gift is never truly alienated and is invested with the donor's identity, it implies the receiver is more a keeper than a new owner. The act of giving is essentially a process that creates and recreates connections in society helping the reproduction of certain accepted social frameworks and, in the end, participates in the structuration of society. Gift exchange is, therefore, the search for structuration and social connection, but a social connection that can never truly be complete, as it is always open-ended.

A collection of artefacts is intended to materialise a discourse or express personal views considered to be important by its author; at least, important enough to be passed on through time and generations for those who wish to give their collection to a museum. A particular collector seeks to build a legacy and intends their collection to acquire heritage status. After a series of exploratory interviews with collectors intending to donate their collections, it seems possible to argue that since the collector thinks about a time-distant addressee, the museum is often seen as a vehicle for legitimising and taking custody of the collection. Nevertheless, the collector-donor has to interact with the museum and its representatives to achieve this communicational activity of transmitting their discourse, and giving is among the strategies to reach this goal.

Giving to the museum

What form does gift exchange take in the museal context? Let us return to the first pair in the sequence: giving and receiving. These two acts frequently occur simultaneously and, in the case of gifts between collectors and museums, they are often sealed by a legal agreement signed by both partners. In that document, it is generally recognised that the transaction is without compensation or that it is made in exchange for a tax-deductible receipt, according to the country's tax legislation. The contract bears witness to a transfer of property that is free of ties, implying that the need for return is absolved. To the donor's benefit, the fiscal tax-deductible receipt is made out for the same amount as the object's fair market value. If we are tempted to see this benefit as the counter-gift of the Maussian logic, we must keep in mind that the fiscal incentive comes from the fiscal system and not from the recipient of the gift. Thus, lack of compensation cannot be reconciled with the notion of gift-exchange. Without return, the 'sacred' connection sought by the donor and which must culminate in a counter-gift is eclipsed and impossible to reach.

This issue might be resolved by initiatives of symbolic recognition given by the museum for the gift. Taking many forms, these initiatives can be seen as the counter-gift in the process and often take the form of the representation of the collector-donor in the museum. Naming a room after the collector-donor, putting their name beside the artefact donated or providing media exposure are some of the possible ways to credit the collector-donor, give them a presence within the institution and acknowledge them for the gift.

The presence of a collector-donor in the museum space

Observations on museum sites and interviews have led to the identification of three forms of collector-donor presence. The first, which shall be termed the 'toponymic' presence, is usually unattached to the artwork but rather to physical place in relation with the museum. A toponymic presence in the museum can be achieved by naming a section after, or giving an honorary mention to the donor. The second form of presence, here termed 'intellectual' presence, is directly related to the artwork or collection previously owned by the collector. The 'intellectual' presence can be actualised by identifying the name and intentions of the collector alongside the donated piece of art, or by keeping together a set of donated objects to stress the meaning of the collected *ensemble*. Finally, a privilege-based presence was observed, that I like to think of as a 'political' presence. It is given to the collector-donor through unwritten privileges such as honorary status or media publicity regarding the collector themselves. It might also be a presence in the museum's collective memory, in its annals or historical archives.

Interviews carried out with collector-donors have revealed a major issue: while the collector-donors' appreciate the museum's acts of recognition and these acts help them fulfil their presence within the institution, those same acts also leave them hungry for more. Although they may be pleased to have given one or more works from their collection, collector-donors still wish to be connected to that work once it has been donated. For the donor, this desire might take the form of a need to foresee for the future display, interpretation or development of the given collection (Koltun 1998). This might make museum curators and staff uncomfortable, or even embarrassed, if they feel an obligation to be constantly accountable to the donor. This situation may arise from a disjunction between the collector's reasons for donation and the museum's reasons for acceptance. Museum professionals may attach a quite different significance and value to the given artefacts, as Koltun argues:

The donor's attitude is often based on a sense of worth, not just of the collection, but of himself or herself. There is a sense of '*I am important, even unique*' in possessing this historically or artistically important collection or object. The donor may assume that the institution being approached shares this attitude. Sometime it does. But more likely, because the percentage of material rejected by an institution is frequently so high (it is not atypical to reject about three/quarters or more of everything offered), the usual assumption is that the material is overrated both artistically and historically, unless it has been sought out by the curator.

(Koltun 1998: 125)

A specific case: collectors and Montréalers exposed

The exhibit *All for Art! Our Great Private Collectors Share Their Works*, held at the Montréal Museum of Fine Arts (MMFA) from December 2007 to February 2008, can be used to examine the manifestation of collector-donor presence in the museal space. This case is an example that reveals the difficult interactions between the two constituencies. The exhibit was intended as a stepping stone between the collectors and the museum. The museum sought collectors, both known and anonymous, donors and non-donors, in the Montréal art scene. The goal was simple: to bring together selected objects belonging to these collectors and present them to the public. The exhibit featured some 70 collectors, and nearly 300 artefacts. A book entitled *In Conversation with Collectors* was published to complement the event. Although the participants were not all usual donors to the MMFA, they were all collectors who had shaped their own specific worldview, with the help of their collection. The design choices for the exhibit space were very clear. A private setting was recreated to make visitors feel as if they were in the collector's home, thus allowing them to appreciate the works as their owners had done (Figure 17.1). The goal was neither to invade collectors' privacy nor to transform visitors into voyeurs, the curator said, but rather to make them feel like the collector in order that they might better enjoy his or her artworks.

Despite this desire for connection between the museum and collectors, the concomitance of the museum and the collector's presence in the same sphere, regardless of whether they were donors or non-donors, remained difficult. Indeed, where the discourse of one began, the discourse of the other would often yield. For instance, before entering the exhibit, visitors were invited to read a statement signed by the curator explaining the concept behind it. This statement was an introduction as well as the final word and the frame for the embedded exhibition. As soon as visitors entered the exhibit space, it was the works that made the connection. These works were presented with the name of their owner or the appellation of 'private collection' for those collectors who wished to remain anonymous. These mentions were a light 'intellectual' presence. Pleasantly hung, the works followed a chronological trajectory without explanation of style nor provenance. They were not framed any differently than they would have been in the collectors' homes.

Figure 17.1 The design of the exhibition *All for Art!* recreated the collector's home, allowing the visitor to appreciate the artworks as their owners did. © MBAM, Christine Guest.

The collectors themselves were not given any visibility in the exhibition space. There were no individual portraits, collection profiles or descriptions of the collections from which the works had been selected. Instead, it was a simple space where visitors could appreciate the artwork according to their personal knowledge, tastes and sensibilities. Only the overall context was commented on by the museum; the collector's voice was silent in the exhibit space and present only in the publication that accompanied the exhibition.

Acknowledging the difficulty of bringing the collector's presence and discourse into the visitor's awareness, the publication takes the form of questions and answers, where the reader can consult the verbatim of the interview of each collector. When the reader browses through interviews, they can get in touch with the collector's own discourse on their collection, outside the legitimacy of the museum.

Conclusions

Presentation and representation are links through which the back and forth interactions between subjects and objects take place. When engaged in exchange, the '*museum–collector–donor*' relationship raises important issues. I began my reflection with the question of how the museum makes the visitor aware of the collector-donor's presence and whether the collector-donor is absent or present. Professional experience, exploratory interviews with collectors and exploratory on-site observations have suggested the following interpretations. Far from resolving the nature of the relationships between collector-donor and museum-recipient, those interpretations will, nevertheless, be useful to progress the comprehension of the phenomenon of giving and receiving in the museum context.

The first observation is that museums and museum representatives often seem uncomfortable in the gift-exchange relationship, particularly with regard to the Maussian concept of the counter-gift which recognises a debt to the collector. This immaterial situation can be rationally solved by circumscribing the gift with a contract that leaves no interpretation for the counter-gift and that, legally, frees the museum from any relationship with the donor. This, in effect, removes the museum from this unfulfilled obligation, which would otherwise be difficult to manage for an institution.

Nevertheless, I observed that the expected counter-gift finally exists, taking the form of a series of recognition-based privileges that are established according to the economical value of the works donated. However, those privileges barely include the collector's worldview in the official or scientific museum discourse towards the public. The history of the piece of art is often silenced to leave room for the collector and vice versa.

My second observation is that it would appear that one of the two discourses – the collector's, or the museum's – often make way for the other. On-site observations have revealed that the presence of the collector-donor is often obscured in museums or restricted to highly defined zones.

This presence or absence logic leads towards other avenues of reflection that also consider the notion of dissimulation or silencing. Could it be that the museum or the collector-donor were judging the value of the other's discourse, despite sharing the objects of these discourses?

In conclusion, I note my first query, whether the discourse intended by the collector can be a part of the artefact donated and on display, is more complex than I thought because it includes both material and immaterial issues depending on constituencies difficult to conciliate should it be in their motivations, in the goals they wish to achieve, or in the performance of the ritual of giving itself. However, emerging clearly is the complexity of the relation between donor and museum, a field that existing literature reveals to be under-theorised although an important mean of acquisition and development of collections.[2]

Notes

1 The author is currently working for the development service of a large Canadian university. Among her duties, one aspect involves negotiating gifts in kind for the library.
2 Documented statistics for 2001–2008 show that museums in province of Quebec (Canada) rely on gifts at the rate of 80% for acquisition and collection development. (Source: http://www.stat.gouv.qc.ca/donstat/societe/culture_comnc/arts_visuel_media_metiers/oeuvre_art/tab3_07_08.htm, accessed 1 March 2011.)

Bibliography

Baudrillard, J. (2007 [1968]) *Le Système des objets*, Paris: Éditions Tel/Gallimard.
Baudrillard, J. (1994) 'The system of collecting', in J. Elsner and R. Cardinal (eds) *The Cultures of Collecting*, Carlton: Melbourne University Press, pp. 7–24.
Bal, M. (1994) 'Telling objects: a narrative perspective on collecting', in J. Elsner and R. Cardinal (eds) *The Cultures of Collecting*, Carlton: Melbourne University Press, pp. 97–115.

Belk, R.W. (1988) 'Possessions and the extended self', *Journal of Consumer Research*, 15: 139–68.

Bourdieu, P. (1987) *Choses dites*, Paris: Éditions de Minuit.

Godelier, M. (1996) *L'Énigme du don*, Paris: Editions Fayard.

Koltun, L. (1998) 'Two porcupines dancing: issues that arise when donor gives and the institution receives', in S.D. Campbell (ed.) *The Private Collector and The Public Institution*, Toronto: University of Toronto Centre, pp. 124–37.

Mauss, M. (1923–1924) 'Essai sur le don', *L'Année Sociologique*, Paris.

Schiffer, M.B. (1999) *The Material Life of Human Beings: artifacts, behavior, and communication*, New York: Routledge.

18 Exhibiting absence in the museum

Helen Rees Leahy

Within the material world of the museum, a fantasy of completion is constantly replayed in the intersection of collections and spaces. Objects are marshalled to fill the entire gallery, to tell the whole story, and to satiate the visitor's hunger for knowledge and distraction. Barbara Kirshenblatt-Gimblett writes:

> When envisioned in terms of its collection, the ideal museum was a Noah's Ark, with a complete set of specimens providing the entire DNA needed to regenerate the world in its entirety, or a Temple of Solomon, imagined as a miniature world, a complete archive of knowledge, and a treasure house.
>
> (Kirshenblatt-Gimblett 2004: 1)

Even in today's discursive museum (Noever 2008), gaps, whether physical or symbolic, are rarely allowed to break the seamless narrative of the collection. It is not surprising, therefore, that the experience of absence in the museum can be both novel and unsettling. There are, of course, instances of museums that have opened to the public before their collections were installed in order to show off their programmatic architecture: in these cases it is the museum building that is being presented as the object of attention. For example, when the Altes Museum in Berlin, designed by Karl Friedrich Schinkel, was finished in 1830, it was first shown without any works of art in place (Giebelhausen 2003: 4). In the same city, the empty shell of Daniel Libeskind's Jewish Museum was completed in 1999 and was visited by over 350,000 people before it was filled with exhibits and formally opened in 2001. For two years, the bare museum stood as an eloquent statement of the narrative power of Libeskind's architecture, as well as the histories of erasure and diaspora experienced by Berlin's Jews that the new museum would recall. However, both the Altes Museum and the Jewish Museum were designed to be filled: their blank walls and empty showcases were a temporary measure, pending the installation of the collections that would render the museums complete. The experience of absence in the museum is rather different, although not necessarily less spectacular, when it is unplanned and unexpected. In August 1911, the Mona Lisa was stolen from the Louvre; when the museum reopened a week later, the empty wall where the painting had hung became an immediate sensation. By the end of 1911, the trail of the missing picture had gone cold and the space previously occupied by the Mona Lisa was quietly filled by Raphael's portrait of Baldassare Castiglione (Scotti 2009: 160). Although the gap left by Mona Lisa was no longer visible, visitors remained aware of its troubling absence until it was finally restored to the museum in 1913. As these brief examples suggest, absence in the museum hovers between memory (of objects lost, forgotten or beyond reach) and anticipation (of objects that will be found, returned or acquired).

At a time when the sustainability of collections and the ethics of disposal are topics of concern for museum staff, audiences and critics alike, the meaning of absence in the museum has received less attention than the issues associated with having too much (rather than too little) stuff. Although this chapter can only make tentative inroads into this rich terrain, my aim is to explore the problematic of absence in the museum, in both theory and practice. As well as discussing how its paradoxical presence has been managed by the institution, I am interested in how absence has been understood by such diverse observers of the museum scene as William Hazlitt, Andre Malraux and Bruno Latour. Although this seems an unlikely trio, they have each addressed absence as an important dynamic in the history and meaning of museum collections in general and of art museums in particular, where, as Duncan and Wallach (1980) have argued, the work of art is transformed into a link in the chain of art history. Despite their very different experiences of the time, space and politics of the museum, the conditions of access to, and visibility of, works of art emerges as a critical theme for, successively, Hazlitt, Malraux and Latour. And, in turn, all three lead us to discussion of the use of reproductions in enabling us to know the absent object. If, as I argue in this chapter, the acknowledgement of absence produces a crisis of signification in the museum, does the use of reproductions (such as digital scans and plaster casts) either resolve or exacerbate that crisis? To begin to answer that question, let us re-enter a world of plenitude and order.

The museum's *horror vacui*

The *horror vacui* of the museum was vividly predicted by Giovanni Paolo Panini in his *Views of Ancient Rome* (painted in 1757) in which an idealised assemblage completely fills the space of display: monuments and buildings are captured in paint and conveniently resized to fit alongside each other for the purposes of visual comparison (Figure 18.1). In the words of Jonah Siegel, the aim is to depict 'the elegant conceit of an abundance of beauty elegantly displayed' (2005: 3). The painting is, of course, a *capriccio*: a fanciful ensemble of sculpture and architecture laid out for the pleasure and edification of an élite viewer. Within the imaginary gallery, images and objects are locked into a unified visual schema which can be appreciated both en masse and close up, as demonstrated by the exemplary connoisseurs who complete the scene for us.

Panini's gallery is a fantasy, yet it is one that mirrors depictions of early modern collections, such as David Teniers's views of Archduke Leopold Wilhelm's celebrated picture gallery in Brussels (Figure 18.2). Here too the pictures are

Figure 18.1 Giovanni Paolo Panini, *Views of Ancient Rome* (1757). Metropolitan Museum of Art, New York. © Photo SCALA, Florence. Metropolitan Museum of Art New York.

Figure 18.2 David Teniers the Younger, *Archduke Leopold's Gallery* (1651), Petworth House, The Egremont Collection (acquired in lieu of tax by H.M. Treasury in 1957 and subsequently transferred to the National Trust). © NTPL/Matthew Hollow.

either stacked on the walls from floor to ceiling or presented for closer inspection by a handful of cultivated viewers. Unlike the wandering visitors in a public museum, the Archduke's guests do not need to pace around the gallery: the paintings are brought to them. In fact, although the pictures of pictures in Teniers's painting are remarkable for their detailed fidelity, they too have been subtly resized to fit his scheme of showing them in serried ranks 'the better to convey the impression of a magnificent collection' (Van Claerbergen 2006: 72). Even if the walls of (most) public museums are less densely filled today, the curatorial urge to fashion a collection into a seamless and structured narrative remains unabated. In order to maintain the art museum's fiction of completion and coherence, institutional narratives are woven around the raw materials at hand and diverse objects are arranged so as to display their art historical or aesthetic affinities. In order to keep up appearances, the contingencies of acquisition are rarely acknowledged: lacunae in collections are glossed and lists of desiderata remain locked in the curator's desk. It is only when a new work of art enters the museum that previous absences are briefly recognised: as soon as the symbolic gap is revealed, it is immediately filled by the new acquisition (Rees Leahy 2007). Losses and omissions are conventionally occluded in museum displays and rarely is a collection publicly revealed as a work in progress. There are, of course, exceptions to this rule, such as the New Acropolis Museum in Athens which has been described as an 'argument in concrete' (Kimmelman 2009) for the return of the Parthenon Marbles. Whether or not absence is deliberately staged within museum displays (as it is in Athens), its relationship to the museum is paradoxical: it is the source of acquisitive desire that fuels the process of collecting while simultaneously destabilising the appearance of completion to which the collection aspires.

If Panini's *Views of Ancient Rome* reflects the dense hanging styles of early modern picture galleries, it also predicts Andre Malraux's formulation of the *musée imaginaire* in which disparate works of art are made available in a boundless play of juxtaposition and reassembly through the medium of photography (1953). The endless possibilities of the *musée imaginaire* contrast with the contingencies and limitations of its real world counterpart:

> Inevitably in a place where the work of art has no longer any function other than that of being a work of art . . . the assemblage of so many masterpieces – from which, nevertheless, so many are missing – conjures up in the mind's eye *all* the world's masterpieces. How indeed could this mutilated possible fail to evoke the whole gamut of the possible?
>
> (Malraux 1953: 15)

Just as Panini marshalled the monuments of Ancient Rome on the walls of his imagined gallery, so Malraux laid out a museum of masterpieces in black and white photographs on his office floor. In practice, the *musée imaginaire* mimics the operation of the real museum via its processes of dislocation, fragmentation and systemisation. As Malraux says, the infinite possibilities promised by the *musée imaginaire* haunt the contingent histories and holdings of every concrete museum. Siegel points out that, in reality, museums are never as satisfying as Panini's *capricci* because we know that:

> [T]hey are not perfect, they cannot show us all we want to see, that we do not want to see everything that they hold. Even in the most well-lit gallery

each component part on display, as much as the ensemble those parts constitute, is shadowed by ghosts of promise or of disappointment.

(Siegel 2005: 4)

For every work of art in the museum, the *musée imaginaire* recalls its absent companions and competitors; these are the objects that eluded the museum's grasp, that it failed to appreciate or forgot to remember. They are the ones that got away (Gould 1974). However, the *musée imaginaire* also holds a reservoir of possibilities (Rees Leahy 2007), comprising those objects that have yet to enter the condition of what Igor Kopytoff (1986) calls 'terminal commoditization' within a museum collection. Their existence also haunts the institution, holding out the prospect of successful acquisitions in the future, which may additionally compensate for past omissions (Gould 1974, Rees Leahy 2009).

The space between

In some museums, the spectres of absence and loss are palpable. The Sigmund Freud Museum in Vienna, housed in the Freud family's abandoned apartment at Berggasse 19, is suffused with memories, but holds few objects. Its melancholy atmosphere as the place from which Freud was forced into exile in 1938 is countered by the material plenitude of the 'other' Freud Museum at 20 Maresfield Gardens, London, where his family subsequently fashioned a new home with the possessions that they had been able to bring from Austria. The well-read library, beloved antiquities, pictures, rugs and furniture in the London house still cast the shadow of exile over the Vienna flat. The profound fracture in the lives of Freud and his family is preserved in the division of his material legacy between Vienna and London: each museum acts as the other's *musée imaginaire* of unrealised possibilities. Yet, the doubling effect of the two institutions is not made evident to the casual visitor: each maintains the conventional museum appearance of internal coherence and institutional autonomy.

How is absence experienced in the museum, especially when it is not explicitly signalled? Kirshenblatt-Gimblett argues that it can be a subtle and disquieting encounter. She quotes the Russian political theorist, Ivan Chtcheglov, who observed that:

> We know that an object that is not consciously noticed at the time of a first visit can, by its absence during subsequent visits, provoke an indefinable impression: as a result of this sighting backward in time, the absence of the object becomes a presence one can feel.
>
> (Kirshenblatt-Gimblett 2004: 3)

Chtcheglov describes this awareness of absence as an 'indefinable' feeling of something not being quite right, not quite there. Paradoxically, the object that was previous overlooked becomes more palpable in its absence – or perhaps more accurately, through an awareness of its non-presence. This awareness is triggered through a knowledge of the museum over a period of time, rather than in a single visit. It is only on successive visits that you become aware of what has been either lost or added since you were last there. Absence unsettles the stasis of the collection, as well as the composure of the visitor; it is a reminder of the contingencies of acquisition and of the constant threat of loss, whether by force, accident or design.

Recording and comparing his impressions of diverse art collections at the beginning of the nineteenth century, William Hazlitt nurtured memories of paintings that he had previously seen and admired; in effect, stocking his own *musée imaginaire* with those works that he most cherished. Here he describes how he cultivated the capacity to recall pictures in his mind's eye, in the hope of seeing them again one day:

> We sometimes, in viewing a celebrated Collection, meet with an old favourite, a first love in such matters, that we have not seen for many years, which greatly enhances the delight. We have, perhaps, pampered our imaginations with it all that time . . . we wish to see it once more, that we may confirm our judgement and renew our vows.
>
> (Hazlitt 1856: 4f)

However, the pleasurable anticipation of meeting a 'first love' again could also be tinged with anxiety: what if a picture no longer resembled its fondly remembered image or, worse, if it was no longer on display? When Hazlitt visited the Louvre in 1826, the recollection of a previous visit over twenty years before was still vivid in his mind: he wrote that 'there were one or two pictures (old favourites) that I wished to see again, and that I was told still remained. I longed to know whether they were there, and whether they would look the same' (1826: 38). Having first visited the museum during the Peace of Amiens (1802–3) when its holdings had been temporarily swelled with artistic loot from Napoleon's military conquests, Hazlitt knew that many of these treasures had since been repatriated following the French defeat at the Battle of Waterloo (Gould 1965). In the event, he was relieved to discover that much of what he remembered remained intact: 'One finds no considerable gap until one comes to the Antwerp pictures' (1826: 42). Gone were the great religious paintings by Rubens, including *The Descent from the Cross*, described by Gould as then one of the most famous pictures in the world (1965: 34); now restored to Antwerp cathedral. However, overall, Hazlitt reflected that there were still 'so many of those select and favourite pictures left, that one does not all at once feel the loss of others which are more common in prints and in the mouth of fame' (1826: 47). The nineteenth century *musée imaginaire* of print reproductions was valuable as an aide memoire, but it could not compensate for the unpredictability of gaining access to the greatest works.

For Hazlitt, the reduction in the size of the Louvre following the defeat of Napoleon was a source of both nostalgia and regret. There was, he wrote, 'a want of larger pictures to answer to the magnitude of the Collection' (1826: 47).

Unlike the majority of visitors who complained that the museum and its contents were simply too vast to apprehend, Hazlitt believed that the 'largest Collection in the world ought to be colossal' (1826: 48). Others felt differently. In 1855, the English 'biographer' of the Louvre, St John Bayle commented sardonically: 'What a wonderful place, after all, that Louvre is! How few visitors really appreciate it!' (1855: 6). According to Bayle, the sheer size of the museum defeated many visitors, while others simply did not know where or how to look. Then, as now, the performance of attentive visuality within the museum was continuously destabilised by the accumulation of so many diverse objects (Valéry 1960, Haskell 1985). Considered in this light, is the paradoxical allure of the museum's empty wall so surprising?

Invisible masterpieces

Hans Belting describes how, as soon as the Louvre reopened after the theft of the Mona Lisa, 'thousands made the pilgrimage . . . to gaze, overcome with emotion, at the blank space and the three nails from which the picture had formally hung' (2002: 274). Among those who stood in front of the blank wall in the Salon Carré were Max Brod and his friend, Franz Kafka, who later commented ironically in his diary: 'Crowd in the Salon Carré, the excitement and the knots of people, as if the Mona Lisa had just been stolen' (Brod 1988: 457). According to one newspaper, the crowds 'contemplated at length the dusty space where the divine Mona Lisa had smiled only the week before . . . It was even more interesting for them than if the Giaconda had been in its place' (Leader 2002: 66). This was an understatement: the blank wall was the sensation of Paris, and the museum colluded in staging the drama: 'A cordon of four gendarmes and six museum guards stood at attention as the mourners and the merely curious filed past the blank wall and paid their respects to the emptiness . . . The mourners left flowers and notes, wept and set new attendance records' (Scotti 2009: 74). As soon as the space where the Mona Lisa had hung was filled with the portrait by Raphael, visitors' attention drifted once more: the scene of the crime lost its thrall as soon as it was, literally, covered up. Even when the picture eventually returned to the Louvre in 1913, the excitement turned to anti-climax. Only two years later, reflecting on the 'squalid tale' of the picture's recent 'ravishment', the art critic, Lionel Cust, speculated that there are 'surely many persons who have at first felt some disappointment when they first came before Mona Lisa in the Salon Carré at the Louvre' (1915: 29). Meanwhile, the missing picture had acquired unprecedented visibility outside the museum via its frantic reproduction in every available outlet: 'She was nowhere in the Louvre, but she was everywhere else, smiling from kiosks, advertisements and magazine covers' (Scotti 2009: 75). Within the *musée imaginaire* of an expanding mediascape, the Mona Lisa was installed as the star exhibit: as Belting notes '. . . the original's loss of visibility increased its fame' (2002: 275).

Recently, Bruno Latour has further pursued the relationship between the singularity of the work and its incessant visibility via reproductions:

If no copies of the Mona Lisa existed would we pursue it with such energy . . . In other words, the intensity of the search for the original depends on the amount of passion and the number of interests triggered by its copies. No copies, no original. In order to stamp a piece with the mark of originality you need to apply to its surface the huge pressure that only a great number of reproductions can provide.

(Latour and Lowe 2008: np)

Latour is not alone in arguing that the flood of reproductions of the Mona Lisa (initially triggered by its theft) has turned the picture into a symbol of painting itself (Leader 2002: 4). It has become what Belting calls the 'invisible masterpiece': a metaphor for an ideal of art which can never be realised (2002: 11). But it is also invisible in the sense that the actual painting in the Louvre is impossible to see, not only because of the number of tourists that it attracts (Carrier 2006: 35), but because we already know it too well. Unlike Hazlitt, we do not have to train our visual memory to recall an image that saturates the contemporary museum-mediascape.

Latour's interest in the dialectics of presence/absence, visibility/invisibility and reproduction/originality has focused on a project to install a sophisticated digital reproduction of Veronese's painting *The Marriage at Cana* (1562–63) in the monastery of San Giorgio Maggiore in Venice in 2007 (Figure 18.3). For over two hundred years, this massive painting occupied an entire wall of the monastery refectory designed by Andrea Palladio, for which it was specifically created (Pavenello 2007). Then, in 1797, Napoleon's invading troops carried off to Paris

Figure 18.3 Reproduction of Paolo Veronese's *The Marriage at Cana* installed in the refectory of San Giorgio Maggiore, Venice. Factum Arte.

twenty of the most celebrated artworks in the city, including seven by Veronese (Gould 1965: 7). In order to facilitate the transportation to Paris of *The Marriage at Cana*, the canvas was cut into two pieces and then subsequently relined when it arrived in the Louvre. When the time came for the restitution of the looted artworks from France, the practical difficulties presented by the return journey to Venice were deemed insurmountable, and so the Veronese stayed in Paris. Diplomatic, if not artistic, honour was satisfied by its symbolic exchange for a picture by Charles Lebrun, whose value was considered by John Ruskin to be the equivalent of a 'dirty, torn rag' compared with the 'most perfect representation possible of colour, and light, and shade' of the Veronese (Pavenello 2007: 90f, see also Gould 1965: 126).

Today, the Veronese hangs in the same room as the Mona Lisa; yet despite its size and drama, it too has become invisible within the museum. Latour describes how both paintings are 'seen' within the Louvre today:

> To finally get at this cult icon of the Da Vinci code, hundreds of thousands of visitors have to enter through two doors that are separated by a huge framed painting, Veronese's Nozze di Cana, a rather dark giant of a piece that directly faces the tiny Mona Lisa barely visible through her thick anti-fanatic glass.
>
> (Latour and Lowe 2008: np)

Compared with the *in situ* installation of the facsimile in Venice, Latour suggests that the display of the original in the Louvre actually obscures the meaning of the work:

> Why such a huge gilt frame? Why the doors on both sides? . . . Why this ugly zenithal light? Why this air conditioned room with its dung brown polished plaster walls? . . . And, anyway, the visitors could not move in and out of the painting to ponder those questions without bumping on the crowds momentarily glued (queued) to the *Joconde* turning their back to the Veronese.
>
> (Latour and Lowe 2008: np)

Rethinking authenticity

Meanwhile, a very different viewing experience has been created by the installation of the picture's facsimile (made by Factum Arte in Madrid) in the refectory of San Giorgio Maggiore (Pavenello 2007). Once again, visitors can see the picture within its architectural context, at the 'right' height, unframed and without surrounding visual distractions. It took three months to scan the original painting in order to create an exact replica in every detail, including the raised seams of the rejoined sections after it was cut into pieces by Napoleon's troops. Latour argues that, in light of such sophisticated technologies of reproduction, the 'aura' of the artwork is no longer fixed and confined to the original. Instead, it has the potential to migrate beyond the original, via processes of reproduction that vary enormously in terms of quality and intention. And when the creation and use of a facsimile is as precise as this, it may be the reproduction, rather than the original, that enables us to appreciate and explore the meaning of the work as it was first intended and experienced:

> There it was . . . a painting on canvas, so thick and deep that you could still see the brush marks of Veronese and feel the sharp cuts that Napoleon's orderlies had to make in order to tear the painting from the wall, strip by strip, before rolling it like a carpet and sending it as a war booty to Paris in 1797 – a cultural rape very much in the mind of all Venetians, up to this day.
>
> (Latour and Lowe 2008: np)

Not surprisingly, the Factum Arte facsimile project has divided press opinion in Venice itself (Povoledo 2007). However, much of this debate overlooks the critical capacity of the project. There is no question of the Louvre returning the original picture to Venice, but the re-opening refectory of San Giorgio Maggiore as a space of display calls attention to the topography of blank walls and empty niches in both sacred and secular sites that constitutes a counter narrative to the museum's work of fragmentation and removal. It is also an apt reminder that the presence of (even the facsimile of) a work of art may resonate more powerfully outside the museum's walls.

Finally, the same issues of reproduction, restitution and display *in situ* lead us to the opening of the New Acropolis Museum in Athens in June 2009. The museum is, of course, an intensely political project, designed to assert both the right and the ability of Greece to preserve and interpret its national heritage and, by extension, the case for the restitution of its material culture. Absence fills the symbolic core of the museum: its agency is fuelled by the continuing diaspora of the Parthenon Marbles, in particular the refusal of the British Museum to repatriate the so-called 'Elgin Marbles' in London.

One of the most difficult questions facing the designers and curators of the new museum was how should those sculptures that are still located in other cities be represented? The initial proposal was to build a niche for the display of each extant piece of sculpture, whether in Greece or overseas; those niches allocated to the diasporic fragments would simply remain empty until they are returned to Athens. Such a stark exhibition of absence would have made an eloquent case for the restitution of the scattered marbles, but the scheme was eventually rejected on the grounds that blank niches would be too shocking for visitors. According to the museum chairman, Dimitrios Pantermalis, the display of voids would also fail to explain fully the historical and artistic contexts of the surviving fragments, both present and absent (Dorment 2009). A subsequent plan to install plaster casts of the missing sculptures shrouded in scrims was also abandoned as the netting could not be satisfactorily attached to the displays. Eventually, it was decided to integrate both plaster casts and original marbles in a continuous display, with the copies clearly distinguished by their pale surface which contrasts with the amber hue of the Pantelic marble. Blank spaces mark the position of fragments that are now lost.

Ironically, the display scheme in the New Acropolis Museum, designed to evoke absence and the desire for reparation, echoes a much earlier integration of casts and original marbles in the so-called Elgin Room in the British Museum. In 1869, the then Keeper of Greek and Roman Antiquities had envisaged a new display with the objective of 'for the first time of arranging all the existing parts of the frieze in their original sequence' (quoted by Jenkins 1990: 96). This would involve the integration of the original sculptures owned by the British Museum with casts of all the fragments that had been, and were still being, discovered, including those housed in other European museums and private collections. Ian Jenkins describes the process:

> As each new fragment found on the Acropolis or elsewhere was identified as belonging to the Parthenon, British agents would arrange for it to be moulded, and a cast was then added to the collection in the Elgin Room.
> (Jenkins 1990: 89)

An international network of exchange was established: the British Museum received gifts of casts from other museums, including the Acropolis Museum and the National Museum in Athens, while casts of the marbles in London were made and despatched across Europe on request. As if assembling a massive and complex puzzle, the British Museum staff tried to fit every newly arrived piece (cast or original) into the existing ensemble. According to Jenkins, the Keeper responsible for the early twentieth century display, Cecil Harcourt Smith, 'could not conceive of the Parthenon sculptures other than as parts of a whole, and was strongly opposed to the view that they should be presented in isolated form. He . . . believed that the Parthenon sculptures should be displayed, as far as possible, as architectural sculpture rather than as art' (1990: 101). Before its eventual dismantlement, the Parthenon frieze as displayed in the old Elgin Room consisted of 60 per cent original and 40 per cent cast pieces; it was not until the creation of the Duveen Gallery in the 1930s, that Smith's scheme was replaced with the highly fragmented display consisting only of the original marbles which remains intact today.

There is, however, a crucial distinction between the former display in the British Museum and its counterpart in the New Acropolis Museum. In the former, the bright tone of the casts was modified to blend in with the (then rather dirty) appearance of the original marbles (Jenkins 1990: 99), so as to present a seamless unity, comprising both originals and copies. In the New Acropolis Museum, the white colour of the casts deliberately contrasts with the amber hue of the Pantelic marble. Whereas the desired effect in London was one of continuity and completion, in Athens it is one of discontinuity and rupture. But despite the current stalemate between the two museums over the ownership and location of the marbles, they remain locked together within a *museé imaginaire* of physical reproductions (the casts in the New Acropolis Museum were made by the British Museum) and virtual reconstruction.[1]

The examples of the New Acropolis Museum and the monastery of San Giorgio Maggiore in Venice are very different in terms of governance and politics. Yet both have deployed curatorial strategies in which absence is evoked, rather than erased, via the use of reproductions in order to instantiate the missing object and, by extension, the argument for restitution. There is no pretence in either case: the use of reproductions is not intended to fool the visitor, but to convey the longing that the absent object inspires. In both spaces, absence is acutely present.

Note

1 See: http://projects.ict.usc.edu/graphics/parthenongallery/ (Accessed 14 January 2011).

Bibliography

Bayle, S-J. (1855) *The Louvre, or Biography of a Museum*, London: Chapman and Hall.

Belting, H. (2002) *The Invisible Masterpiece*, London: Reaktion.

Brod, M. (ed.) (1988) *The Diaries of Franz Kafka*, New York: Schocken.

Carrier, D. (2006) *Museum Skepticism*, Durham, NC and London: Duke University Press.

Cust, L. (1915) 'Mona Lisa', *The Burlington Magazine*, 28 (151): 29–31.

Dorment, R. (2009) 'Acropolis Museum: Athens unveils its bid for the Marbles', *The Daily Telegraph*, 30 June 2009. Available online at: http://www.telegraph.co.uk/culture/art/5699833/Acropolis-Museum-Athens-unveils-its-bid-for-the-Marbles.html (Accessed 14 January 2011).

Duncan, C. and A. Wallach (1980) 'The universal survey museum', *Art History*, 3: 448–69.

Giebelhausen, M. (2003) *The Architecture of the Museum*, Manchester: Manchester University Press.

Gould, C. (1965) *Trophy of Conquest*, London: Faber and Faber.

Gould, C. (1974) *Failure and Success: 150 years of the National Gallery 1824–1974*, London: National Gallery.

Haskell, F. (1985) 'Museums and their enemies', *Journal of Aesthetic Education*, 19: 13–22.

Hazlitt, W. (1826) *Notes of a Journey through France and Italy*, London: Hunt and Clarke.

Hazlitt, W. (1856) *Criticisms on Art and Sketches of the Picture Galleries of England* (2nd edn), London: C. Templeman.

Jenkins, I. (1990) 'Acquisition and supply of casts of the Parthenon sculptures by the British Museum, 1835–1939', *The Annual of the British School at Athens*, 85: 89–114.

Kimmelman, M. (2009) 'Elgin Marble argument in a new light', *New York Times*, 23 June 2009. Available online at: http://www.nytimes.com/2009/06/24/arts/design/24abroad.html?_r=1 (Accessed 14 January 2011).

Kirshenblatt-Gimblett, B. (2004) 'The museum: a refuge for Utopian thought'. Available online at: http://www.nyu.edu/classes/bkg/web/museutopia.pdf (Accessed 14 January 2011). [Appeared in German translation in Jörn Rüsen, Michael Fehr and Annelie Ramsbrock (eds) *Die Unruhe der Kultur: Potentiale des Utopischen*, Seiten: Velbrück Wissenschaft.]

Kopytoff, I. (1986) 'The cultural biography of things: commoditisation as process', in A. Appadurai (ed.) *The Social Life of Things: commodities in cultural perspective*, Cambridge: Cambridge University Press, pp. 64–91.

Latour, B. and A. Lowe (2008) 'The migration of the aura, or how to explore the original through its facsimiles'. Available online at: http://www.bruno-latour.fr/articles/article/108-ADAM-FACSIMILES-AL-BL.pdf (Accessed 10 December 2009).

Leader, D. (2002) *Stealing the Mona Lisa: what art stops us from seeing*, London: Faber and Faber.

Malraux, A. (1953) *The Voices of Silence*, London: Doubleday & Co.

Noever, P. (ed) (2008) *The Discursive Museum*, Ostfildern: Hatje Cantz.

Pavenello, G. (2007) *Il Miracolo di Cana: l'originalità della ri-produzione*. Verona: Cierre Edizioni.

Povoledo, E. (2007) 'A painting comes home (or at least a facsimile)', *New York Times*, 29 September 2007. Available online at: http://query.nytimes.com/gst/fullpage.html?res=9C05EFD7103FF93AA1575AC0A9619C8B63 (Accessed 14 January 2011).

Rees Leahy, H. (2007) 'Desiring Holbein: presence and absence in the National Gallery', *Journal of the History of Collections*, 19: 75–87.

Rees Leahy, H. (2009) 'Assembling art, constructing heritage', *Journal of Cultural Economy*, 2: 135–49.

Scotti, R.A. (2009) *The Lost Mona Lisa*, London: Bantam Press.

Siegel, J. (2005) *The Haunted Museum*, Princeton: Princeton University Press.

Valéry, P. (1960) 'The problems of museums', in J. Matthews (ed.) *The Collected Works of Paul Valéry*, Princeton: Princeton University Press, pp. 202–6.

Van Claerbergen, E.V. (ed.) (2006) *David Teniers and the Theatre of Painting*, London: Courtauld Institute of Arts.

19 Arctic 'relics'

The construction of history, memory and narratives at the National Maritime Museum

Claire Warrior

This chapter analyses the Polar collections of the National Maritime Museum (henceforth the NMM), Greenwich,[1] and examines their contribution to notions of national identity, as well as to personal histories. It aims, through an investigation of the movements through the museum of a particular set of artefacts, to ask questions about the nature of the institution, the relationship between objects and people and how meanings relating to both personal and wider social narratives are constructed around things. It connects the history of exploration and empire with that of the museum, and thereby demonstrates how each has played its part in constructions of Britishness over time.

Histories of the cultures of exploration, such as Felix Driver's *Geography Militant* (2000), have clearly demonstrated the ways in which geographical knowledge, exploration and empire are inextricably linked, showing both how knowledge is constructed in the field from a multiplicity of sources and how this knowledge is then utilised in public contexts to support and shape ideas and perceptions of empire. The historiography of Arctic exploration, in particular, has become especially strong in relation to the region's imaginative impact on the British public. Spufford (1996), in his history of polar exploration, examines 'an intangible history of assumptions, responses to landscape, cultural fascinations, [and] aesthetic attraction to the cold regions', demonstrating the layers of meaning built upon around practices of exploration in the Arctic and, later, the Antarctic. David's (2000) analysis of nearly a century of Arctic exploration focuses upon the different institutions and media which conveyed notions about the region to the British public, including museums and exhibitions, although its conclusion in 1914 is prior to the founding of the NMM. Other more recent works have tended to focus on literary representations of the Arctic (Hill 2008), and its perception in print media (Cavell 2008).

In terms of exploration histories and material culture, the collections made on Cook's voyages have been subject to close scholarly attention, particularly in the work of Adrienne Kaeppler (1978), although it is the Pacific artefacts that have sustained the greatest interest, particularly within ethnographic collections such as the Pitt Rivers Museum.[2] Artefacts have not been the focus of sustained attention in Arctic historiography, nor have collections of specific artefacts been traced through their museum life. The work of Janet Owen (2006), looking at

Inupiat artefacts in the collection of Sir John Lubbock, has demonstrated the links between collecting, scientific understanding and imperialism, but their subsequent museum history is not covered. It is unusual to find any analyses of collections relating to specific voyages of geographical exploration that are not solely focused on ethnographic material and that cover their meanings in the twentieth century and beyond. This work aims to help redress that imbalance.

Subjects and objects, identity and the museum

The museum, as an institution, is predicated upon, and helps to perpetuate, a fundamental separation of people and things. Objects – artefacts, specimens – are collected, preserved, catalogued, stored and displayed within the museum setting. They may have particularly close links to individual subjects: indeed, they may be associated with people, such as collectors or donors, through museum classificatory systems, or used in exhibitions to illustrate specific life-histories of which they are perceived to belong. However, despite these overlapping biographies, subjects and objects are generally held to be distinct and separate entities.

Yet this separation is clearly not straightforward, as much recent scholarship has shown. Studies of collectors and collecting (e.g. Pearce 1995) have made manifest the ways in which objects are closely implicated in people's identity, playing an active part in constructing a sense of self, and helping people to construct meaning throughout their life. The importance of material culture in the process of creating a sense of who we are, both individually and within a wider society, has thus been clearly demonstrated. Work in anthropology, such as that of Miller (2005) and Henare (2005), further suggests a close interdependence in which 'people are shaped by things as much as artefacts are crafted by people' (Miller 2005: 6). Here, objects help to create social relations that can be sustained across vast expanses of time and space, and the museum becomes a vibrant hub in which the social lives of objects, and their connections to people, are sustained. Such a position is radically different from the traditional view of the museum as a relatively static institution, of things past rather than relationships present, and of objects as passive and highly distinct from those who make and own them.

This intermingling of subject and object can also be clearly seen in relation to the NMM's Polar collections, many of which have been classified in the category of 'Polar equipment and relics'. The category of the relic, and its presence in the museum, deserves some unpacking. As Geary (1986: 169) notes, the notion of the relic is an unusual one in Western society, for it encapsulates objects that are both persons and things. Relics are seemingly imbued with the potency of an individual, their presence allowing an increased proximity to the person and memorialising them in a tangible form. Whilst this is literally true for religious relics – those connected to the remains of figures such as saints and embedded within, for example, the Christian tradition – secular relics can also be seen to share this close sense of connection between subject and object. The relics in the NMM's Polar collections have been understood as encapsulating individual experiences of exploration in these regions. They have been seen to be important for their associations with particular explorers and expeditions, rather than for the multiplicity of relationships that they potentially embody. Those connected to the final tragic Franklin expedition of 1845,[3] in particular, are held up both as the only evidence of the expedition's fate in general and as very personal links to the men that were lost. It is perhaps unsurprising that, with their close links to men and their deaths, these objects have attained relic status. Yet, interestingly, the material culture of other expeditions also carries these associations.

So, can this classification as relics tell us even more? And what is its significance within a museum context? Are there other meanings of these artefacts that have hitherto been either suppressed or ignored, and what can this tell us? In order to explore these questions further, I will use a particular case study – a collection of Arctic artefacts belonging to Admiral Sir George Back (1796–1878), a nineteenth century Naval explorer. The categorisation and display of artefacts within a museum is not a neutral act, and understanding the different contexts in which these objects have been collected and understood will enable us to examine the wider social and cultural ideas in which they are embedded. Links – and sometimes schisms – will be revealed between personal biographies of exploration and the wider imperial tropes of heroism and discovery that have played their part in British national identity, demonstrating which values have been held to be important, how they have been seen to contribute to the national character, and the role of certain individuals therein. There are political ramifications here: constructions of the past within any public context are crucial to the creation of identities within the present, whilst definitions of Britishness inevitably also include understandings of what it is not, 'the Other', and foreground whose histories have been considered to be important. Furthermore, as power relations change, so ideas about the nation and national identity also shift. The museum may be an arena in which such shifts can be identified.

Setting the scene: the Arctic, the nation and museums

Before beginning an analysis of the artefacts and their placement in the NMM in more detail, certain scenes need to be set. First, we need to understand both the significance, or otherwise, of the Arctic, and of displays of the region, to Britain. British interest in the Arctic began in the sixteenth century, with the search for the North-West Passage, a putative route through North America to the East, where lucrative commodities such as spices could be obtained. Whaling and fur-trading had become prevalent and profitable in the region by the seventeenth century, whilst official British Naval expeditions joined the hunt for the Passage, now thought to exist across the top of the American continent, in the following century. A period of intensive warfare in the late eighteenth century saw a hiatus in these government-sponsored expeditions, and it was not until 1818 that they began again with increased vigour, spurred on by the efforts of John Barrow, Second Secretary to the Admiralty. Initial exploration of the region had been founded upon the hope that it would provide commercial and economic advantages to Britain, but it was never settled or colonised, and, although whale products and beaver furs were important commodities, the economic benefits were not as great as originally hoped. The Arctic was, we might say, on the periphery of empire. Yet, particularly from the nineteenth century onwards, the Polar regions were highly visible to Britons as key sites for exploration and scientific endeavour, and as a focus for patriotic feeling (David 2000: 2). Navy-sponsored expeditions, commanded by men such as John Ross, William Parry, John Franklin, Frederick Beechey and George Back, were subject to much comment in the press, reports of their progress and expedition narratives reaching a wide and enthusiastic audience (Cavell 2008), whilst the Arctic was also highly visible in literature and other art-forms (Spufford 1996). As David (2000: 6) puts it, 'for most of the [nineteenth] century the Arctic was part of the collective imagination, no less significant to that era than the exoticism of the Orient or the darkness at the heart of Africa'. Thus, although displays of the Arctic and its material culture may not seem the most obvious source material with which to begin an investigation into national identity, the region was significant to constructions of British identity during a time in which, it has been argued, the nation was forged and in which an expanding British empire sought to re-imagine itself (Colley 1996). Furthermore, some of the individuals involved in Arctic exploration can be seen to be 'heroes of empire' (Cubitt and Warren 2000: 83), their lives perceived, or even constructed, to encapsulate particular values and used for ideological purposes. John Franklin, in particular, was a well-known heroic figure, whose iconography as a national martyr was connected to imaginings of nation and narratives of empire. The worship of national heroes has been identified as part of a potent ideological cluster in the later Victorian era and beyond (MacKenzie 1984: 2), contributing to patriotic ideas about the empire and creating a critically important worldview that sustained British identity for nearly one hundred years.

Secondly, we need to see how museums can be conceived to contribute to formulations of national identity, and how the NMM is positioned as a national institution. As Mason (2007: 1) demonstrates, national museums may have an important role in the creation and confirmation of particular version of national cultures, constituting as well as reflecting identity and actively choosing which histories and cultures to foreground. For Britain, the sea has had a crucial role in facilitating trading relationships, in imperial expansion and in discouraging invasion. It has, as a consequence, been important to notions of British identity, with the notion of Britannia ruling the waves a particularly predominant one in the late eighteenth and nineteenth centuries and the sense of an 'island nation', with a proud maritime heritage, still present today.[4] The NMM has preserved and displayed this heritage since 1937, and it has been called 'perhaps the closest we have to a national museum of history' (Aronsson, Bugge and Knell 2007). Founded, after lengthy negotiations, prior to the Second World War, its original paradigm could be characterised as one of salvage – preserving something uniquely British that was perceived to be vanishing, at a time just before the Empire which had originally been created by maritime means, and which had been so crucial to the British worldview (MacKenzie 1984: 2), began to disintegrate. The museum now has an important role in determining which elements of Britain's maritime history are visible to the general public through its displays, learning programmes and research, and remains an important institution in sustaining notions of Britishness and, by extension, in defining relationships with 'the Other'. For example, one of the most recent permanent galleries to open, *Atlantic Worlds* (2007), focuses on the connections between Britain, North America and the Caribbean from the seventeenth century onwards. It foregrounds the historic nature of global movements of people, goods and ideas, demonstrating that Britain has long been implicated in worldwide systems of exchange, and that such movements have had a profound impact on British society which still resonate today. One of the next permanent galleries scheduled to open will examine Britain's trade with Asia, again suggesting far-reaching and long-lasting connections between two continents. These galleries intimate that Britishness is a complex notion to untangle, that globalisation is perhaps no recent thing and foreground the importance of maritime activities in creating the world we live in today.

Constructing objects and collections: classifications and meanings

Both museums and the objects within them have been described as palimpsests, upon which successive layers of meaning and thought are inscribed (Ames 1992, quoted in Cruikshank 1995: 36). How, then, have objects associated with Arctic exploration been understood, and have these understandings changed over time and with changing contexts? And how do these understandings relate to the context in which the objects were originally collected? The main emphasis of most of the voyages in this period was scientific. Mapping, charting and surveying were key tasks; other important duties included keeping records of latitude and longitude, magnetic variation and weather, and making observations of the aurora borealis, mineral resources and natural history. It is unsurprising, then, that scientific instruments are commonplace within the NMM's Polar collections, representing the kinds of work that expedition members carried out in the region. They reinforce the idea of the Arctic as a barren and unpeopled landscape, in which British explorers and scientists were the active agents, and represent what has been called 'the explorer's Arctic' (David 2000: 158).

But there are other artefacts that, with deeper digging, indicate more complex encounters and experiences, and it is to those that I now turn. Donated to the Royal Naval Museum, a precursor of the NMM,[5] in 1900, Admiral Sir George Back's collection includes 'snow shoes, a model of a canoe given to Sir George Back by an Indian chief . . . bows and arrows, Esquimaux needlework, gloves etc.'.[6] They were left to the Admiralty as part of the bequest of Mrs Eliza Back, Admiral Sir George Back's nephew's widow, and were described by her solicitors, Frere & Company, as 'certain Arctic relics' (David 2000). Provenance information is sparse, but it is assumed that Back collected these objects from Subarctic and

Arctic Canada between 1819 and 1834, the main period of his naval career. Back was known primarily for his role on the two Arctic overland expeditions led by John Franklin (1819–22 and 1825–7), although he made two further trips to the region in the early 1830s, and was an active member of the Arctic Council, convened to search for Franklin's missing 1845 expedition. It is hard to locate where many of the artefacts he collected were actually made. This confusion reflects the rich ethnic mixture of northern Canada where, by the early nineteenth century, European fur traders had been interacting with Native peoples for nearly two hundred years. Native women, in particular, acted as mediators between groups and distinct Métis, or mixed-blood, communities grew up as a result of the relationships between Europeans and First Nations peoples. Stylistic analysis suggests that pouches such as the one illustrated in Figure 19.1 are probably Métis,[7] rather than being 'Esquimaux needlework' as they were originally described. The apparent assumption that anything connected with Arctic exploration could only have come from the 'Esquimaux' demonstrates a misunderstanding of both the realities of exploration in the region and the area's ethnic make-up. What is certain, and what was not understood at the time, is that most of the artefacts

Figure 19.1 Quillwork pouch, probably made by an unknown Métis maker, AAA2626, © National Maritime Museum, Greenwich, UK.

that Back collected were of types common to the material culture of fur-trade society, and many of them were made by women. Women prepared and treated skins, embroidered and quilled, and made clothing. A key meaning, then, lies in the making: these objects demonstrate the artistry of Native women, their skill in incorporating new materials and motifs, and their central role within fur-trade society in the early nineteenth century. What we do not know is the relationship – if any – between these makers and George Back. But the importance of an indigenous presence in northern Canada and in the task of Arctic exploration can be seen through a history of these artefacts, even if this has not been clear in museum records or displays.

Simply wearing and owning such things was symbolic of participation in fur-trade society. As Peers (1999: 294) argues in relation to a similar embroidered bag, now in the Pitt Rivers Museum, Oxford, having such artefacts may have been 'a statement of identity, a declaration of experience'. Perhaps Back acquired and kept these objects to demonstrate his participation in a society far removed from the one he grew up in – they may be both exotic souvenirs and proof of the hardships he endured. They were not heavily used, and despite the gruelling nature of Arctic exploration, they were important enough to him to ensure their safe transit back to England. He kept them in his possession until his death in 1878. Interestingly, his descendants still own some material, including the pairs to some of the moccasins and mittens now held at the NMM, suggesting that these artefacts have continued to contribute to Back's life-history, at least within a family context, even after his death. They can be seen as contributions to his own biography and identity as an Arctic explorer – and in this way, their cat-egorisation as 'relics' within a museum context may be particularly appropriate. In the context of Arctic exploration, the bodies of explorers have been shown to be particularly important sites for the validation and valorisation of experience in the field (Schimanski and Spring 2009), demonstrating the hardships that the men had suffered. Just as the objects that were associated with saints came to perform the same relic functions as their actual human remains, so perhaps artefacts associated with being in the Arctic came to act as confirmation of an explorer's bodily presence in what was perceived to be an almost otherworldly environment. In relation to John Franklin, perhaps, it may be that artefacts/relics were particularly significant *because* his body has never been found: they are the last material traces of his and his crew's presence in the Arctic. With both religious and secular relics, too, issues of provenance and the actual histories of objects are relatively unimportant or are, at least, often overlooked. Their significance lies not in their detailed provenance – although this may bolster their importance – but rather in their very existence. They are thus easily subsumed into other grand narratives, such as that of explorers, heroes, nation and empire. This is true for the material collected by George Back.

However, the objects that Back collected have not remained defined as 'relics'. Many of them were redefined as 'ethnographic' in the early twenty-first century. From their association with a named individual and with a very British set of exploration practices in the nineteenth and twentieth centuries, they had become

'Other'. This redefinition was part of a collections management project that ranked artefacts by their importance to the NMM's self-defined mission, 'to illustrate for everyone the importance of sea, ships, time and the stars and their relationship with people' (National Maritime Museum 2009). The NMM's collections are generally dominated by European-made objects. The underlying intention of this reclassification was laudable: the recognition of the 'otherness' of these artefacts was seen as a way of highlighting their importance and uniqueness, suggesting that they were 'about' other cultures rather than continuing to subsume them in the European narratives of exploration and heroic male explorers with which they had been so closely associated. Yet it also had the effect of isolating artefacts from their complicated histories, much of which was related to contexts of exchange and contact with Europeans. Perhaps this is an illustration of the limitations of museum classification systems, and their inability to straightforwardly encompass the multivalency of objects, whose lives of manufacture, exchange and ownership, just like the lives of human beings, cannot easily be encapsulated on paper or computer databases.

Displaying the Arctic

Exhibitions and display are the most visible functions of the museum, although they are closely linked to other activities such as research, conservation and collections management. In the nineteenth century, displays of the Arctic demonstrated Britain's global supremacy, scientific pre-eminence and the individual heroism and sacrifice of explorers such as Franklin (David 2000: 158). Many of the artefacts in the NMM's collections, including those belonging to George Back, were part of earlier displays, such as those of the Royal Naval Museum. The Royal Naval Museum was founded in Greenwich in 1873. Its displays emphasised the personal histories of naval heroes (Littlewood and Butler 1998: 13), making the objects in them relics indeed. When the objects associated with Back were donated and first displayed there, no mention was made of their makers. In the masculine worlds of the Royal Navy and Polar exploration, women did not have a recognised role, and there was little room for First Nations and Inuit people. Their presence might have defied preconceptions of the Arctic as a harsh and empty space in which (male) humans were to struggle and nature was pre-eminent. In 1913, Back's artefacts were displayed in the museum's Franklin room as the 'relics and records of the Arctic Expedition under Sir John Franklin, 1845–6, and of subsequent expeditions'. This was despite the fact that they must have been collected prior to this, between 1819 and 1834, if Back himself had collected them, as the expeditions in which he participated took places between those dates. The space focused on Franklin, who had become the archetypal 'explorer-hero' (Lewis-Jones 2005: 196) by this time. The Franklin story, important to British patriotic sentiment and national identity (Lewis-Jones 2005: 200) subsumed all others and Back's own earlier contributions to British Arctic exploration were all but forgotten. The overwhelming emphasis was on Franklin as a national hero, as MacKenzie's (1984) work suggests we might expect.

When the NMM opened to the public in 1937, no material associated with Polar exploration was on display. The first permanent galleries followed a chronological sequence, stretching in time from the Tudor dynasty, 'the foundation of British maritime greatness' (National Maritime Museum 1937), to the end of the Napoleonic Wars in 1815. The emphasis was on illustrating historical events in a grand continuous historical narrative, with conflicts particularly prominent as framing devices, and fine art favoured as a medium for display, as the first catalogue demonstrates (National Maritime Museum 1937). As Littlewood and Butler (1998: 90) put it, 'aesthetics dominated', and there was little room in two-dimensionally dominant displays for the artefact-rich Polar collections. The Second World War halted early plans for future galleries, but by the early 1950s, a Polar Gallery had opened in the basement of the Museum's East Wing, combining a narrative of British Arctic and Antarctic expeditions. This gallery was refurbished in the early 1970s, to focus purely on Arctic exploration (Savours 1977). Chronologically arranged, the exhibition briefly touched upon early sixteenth and seventeenth century voyages and exploration in the twentieth century, the latter mainly using photographs. However, its main focus, the 'great glory of the gallery' (Savours 1977: 358), was the nineteenth century. This part of the display was divided into three main sections: 1818–45 (covering the revival of the Royal Navy's attempts to locate the North-West Passage), 1845–8 (the lost Franklin expedition and subsequent searches) and 1875–6 (the British Arctic Expedition led by Sir George Nares). Franklin's presence was less overwhelming by this time, although still a significant part of the gallery, and voyages before his lost 1845 expedition were also considered. George Back had his own portion of the display – 'Eskimo' artefacts and all – placed next to a portrait of Qalasirssuaq, a Greenlandic Inuit man who accompanied one of the Franklin search expeditions in the 1850s. By this time, then, the potent heroes of the Victorian and Edwardian eras were becoming less important to narratives of nation and empire. Indeed, as MacKenzie (1984: 12) suggests, the worship of national heroes, part of a potent ideological cluster from the later Victorian period onwards, declined from the mid-twentieth century onwards, and it is unsurprising that this became apparent in the NMM's displays. What contributed to a sense of the British nation seems to have been shifting.

In the more recent past, Arctic exploration has continued to occupy a small space in the NMM's permanent galleries. The refurbishment of the NMM at the end of the twentieth century, when the central court of the museum was roofed over to produce the new Neptune Court, offered an opportunity to rethink the arrangement of what was on display. This time, a thematic approach was taken. Material relating to the Arctic was placed in the two *Explorers* galleries, and any sense of a narrative chronology of Polar exploration was interrupted. The first *Explorers* gallery, seen in Figure 19.2, is theatrical in style and with relatively few objects, and identifies explorers and their achievements. The main thrust of the display concerned with the Arctic is devoted to the 1845 Franklin expedition, its disappearance and subsequent search expeditions. This very much reflects the numerical strength of the NMM's collections and demonstrates

Figure 19.2 Explorers gallery, part of the 1999 Neptune Court redevelopment. © National
Maritime Museum, Greenwich, UK.

continued interest in the mystery of Franklin and his men's disappearance,
although the actual display space is relatively small. There is some sense of an
Inuit presence, particularly with regard to discovering Franklin's fate. The second
Explorers gallery, which is no longer in existence, considered exploration from a
wider perspective, asking questions about why humans were driven to explore.
It used material mainly from the now less well-known 1875–6 British Arctic
Expedition to illustrate the conditions within which explorers were active. Between
them, the two galleries told a story that was more self-consciously global than
British, again reflecting the changing political context within which the nation
was situated, and sought reflexively to ask questions about the practice of exploration. Finally, in November 2007, the NMM opened a new permanent gallery,
Atlantic Worlds. Its aims were ambitious: to display some 300 hundred years of
history, exploring, according to the gallery text, 'the interrelationships, connections
and exchanges created between Britain, Africa and the Americas' (Figure 19.3).
Here, the material culture of Back's Arctic expeditions is once more embedded
in its original fur-trade context, in which exchanges between European and First
Nations people were crucial. At one level, cultural interaction is more explicit than
it has ever been in the NMM. However, the gallery's focus on broad historical
sweeps gives a sense of impersonality, and there is little sense of the individuals
involved. Back's relics are no longer 'Esquimaux' but his own personal narrative
does not have a significant role. The relationship with Arctic exploration is more
or less absent, but rather, the objects are used to discuss one of the significant
trades that Britain was involved in. This gallery can be seen to follow on from
the more global narratives of the 1990s, but takes them a stage further by firmly
embedding the indigenous presence in North America and by emphasising the
importance of economic motivations to the expansion of empire.

Figure 19.3 Atlantic Worlds gallery, opened in November 2007. © National Maritime Museum, Greenwich, UK.

Displays of material culture associated with Arctic exploration have thus shifted their focus over time, emphasising individuals, then imperial tropes of heroism and discovery and now specific histories within a global context. Categorisations and understandings of artefacts such as Back's have also changed. The late nineteenth century emphasis was on the person in the service of empire, publicly representing 'the heroic deeds performed . . . by those who have done so much to build up this great Empire' (Markham, quoted in Lewis-Jones 2005: 200). Franklin came to dominate this narrative, his tragedy overwhelming the stories of others. Thus, Back's artefacts came to represent a generic experience of Arctic endeavour rather than a specific life-history; although they remained as 'relics', they were related less to the individual than to narratives of Polar exploration more generally. Others – Inuit and First Nations people – were largely absent or reduced to stereotypes. As British imperial and sea power waned in the twentieth century, the Arctic became ever less important, but displays have gradually come to incorporate other explorers and to recognise the agency of Inuit and First Nations people, and classifications have, for better or worse, moved towards the 'ethnographic'.

In an era of climate change, the Arctic is arguably more important than it has been for over a hundred years.[8] The NMM now has the opportunity to use its historic collections to suggest that the links between past and present are robust and long-lasting – the perceived economic significance of the region spurring on its exploration both in the nineteenth century and today, for example. Rather than solely representing the efforts of a once mighty imperial power, exploration in the Arctic can be viewed as part of a longer historical continuum, creating ideas of identity and relationships between the British, Canada and the indigenous groups of the area that should not be forgotten. The region, perhaps because of its climatic extremes, has always fostered an interdependence between those who live there and more transient visitors, even if this has not always been explicitly acknowledged. As the Arctic becomes the focus of the world's attention, the NMM may represent a new form of transnational identity and global citizenship, demonstrating the motivations behind interest in the region, which have often been economic, yet which have drawn together diverse cultures. If the past of the Arctic has been crucial to Britain's understanding of itself, its future will almost certainly be equally, if not more, important.

Notes

1 This research is supported by the Arts and Humanities Research Council. The work presented here is part of an ongoing collaborative PhD between the Scott Polar Research Institute, University of Cambridge, and the National Maritime Museum, Greenwich.
2 See, for example, the Forster Collection (Pitt Rivers Museum 2010a) and Pacific Pathways (Pitt Rivers Museum 2010b) projects online (http://projects.prm.ox.ac.uk/forster/home.html and http://projects.prm.ox.ac.uk/forster/pathways.html).
3 This is perhaps the best-known of all the British expeditions to the Arctic of the nineteenth century. Sir John Franklin and his crew of 128 men left England in 1845 in search of the North-West Passage, on what was the biggest and best-equipped voyage of its time. The men were never to return. Numerous search expeditions were sent to discover what had happened to them. Although fragments of material culture and some bodies have been recovered, the ships, and Franklin himself, have not yet been found.
4 For example, the continuing intimate relationship between Britain and the sea was celebrated in the 2005 SeaBritain festival, in more than 2000 different events held throughout the country (National Maritime Museum 2010). The success of BBC Television's *Coast* series has also been linked to notions of British identity, and the place of the sea within this (Moss 2005).
5 The Royal Naval Museum's collections were incorporated into those of the NMM on its foundation. They, along with material from the former Royal United Services Institution, form the major constituent of the Arctic collections.
6 Letter from Frere and Company, Solicitors, to Admiral Sir Richard E. Tracey, President of the Royal Naval College, Greenwich, 29 June 1900 (The National Archives, Kew, Admiralty Papers (Pensions – Benefits – Bequests – Trusts) ADM 169/267).
7 This attribution is derived from a stylistic analysis of the artefacts and the materials and techniques used to create them. I am grateful to Professor Kate Duncan (Arizona State University), Dr Sherry Farrell Racette (University of Regina), Judy Hall (Canadian Museum of Civilization), Dr Jonathan King (The British Museum), Dr Cath Oberholtzer (Trent University), Dr Laura Peers (the Pitt Rivers Museum) and Professor Ruth Phillips (Carleton University) for examining the artefacts and providing provenance information.
8 See, for example, a recent article in *The Observer* newspaper. This states that 'the region looks fated to determine the outcomes of many vital 21st-century concerns, including the vexed issue of global warming' (McKie 2010), whilst 'Its vast deposits of oil, gas and ores will soon be freed of the ice covering that has limited their exploitation, a point that has not escaped the attention of major powers.'

Bibliography

Aronsson, P., A. Bugge and S. Knell (2007) 'National museum narratives', NaMu: Making National Museums Workshop 2, Leicester, June 2007.
Cavell, J. (2008) *Tracing the Connected Narrative: Arctic exploration in British print culture, 1818–1860*, Toronto: University of Toronto Press.

Colley, L. (1996) *Britons: forging the nation 1707–1837*, London: Vintage.

Cruikshank, J. (1995) 'Imperfect translations: rethinking objects of ethnographic collection', *Museum Anthropology*, 19: 25–38.

Cubitt, G. and A. Warren (eds) (2000) *Heroic Reputations and Exemplary Lives*, Manchester and New York: Manchester University Press.

David, R.G. (2000) *The Arctic in the British Imagination 1818–1914*, Manchester and New York: Manchester University Press.

Driver, F. (2000) *Geography Militant: cultures of exploration and empire*, Oxford: Blackwell Publishers.

Geary, P. (1986) 'Sacred commodities: the circulation of medieval relics', in A. Appadurai (ed.) *The Social Life of Things: commodities in cultural perspective*, Cambridge: Cambridge University Press, pp. 169–94.

Henare, A. (2005) *Museums, Anthropology and Imperial Exchange*, Cambridge: Cambridge University Press.

Hill, J. (2008) *White Horizon: the Arctic in the nineteenth-century British imagination*, Albany: State University of New York Press.

Kaeppler, A.L. (1978) *'Artificial Curiosities': being an exposition of native manufactures collected on the three Pacific voyages of Captain James Cook, R.N. at the Bernice Pauahi Bishop Museum, January 18, 1978–August 31, 1978 on the occasion of the bicentennial of the European discovery of the Hawaiian islands by Captain Cook, January 18, 1778* (Bernice P. Bishop Museum Special Publication 65), Honolulu: Bishop Museum Press.

Lewis-Jones, H. (2005) ' "Heroism displayed": revisiting the Franklin Gallery at the Royal Naval Exhibition, 1891', *Polar Record*, 41 (218): 185–203.

Littlewood, K. and B. Butler (1998) *Of Ships and Stars: maritime heritage and the founding of the National Maritime Museum, Greenwich*, London and New Brunswick, NJ: The Athlone Press and the National Maritime Museum.

MacKenzie, J.M. (1984) *Propaganda and Empire: the manipulation of British public opinion 1880–1960*, Manchester and Dover, NH: Manchester University Press.

McKie, R. (2010) 'It's getting grimmer up north', *The Observer*, 18 April, p. 41.

Mason, R. (2007) *Museums, Nations, Identities: Wales and its national museums*, Cardiff: University of Wales Press.

Miller, D. (ed.) (2005) *Materiality*, Durham, NC and London: Duke University Press.

Moss, S. (2005) 'Tribal television', *The Guardian*, 19 August. Available online at: http://www.guardian.co.uk/media/2005/aug/19/britishidentityandsociety.ruralaffairs (Accessed 19 July 2010).

National Maritime Museum (1937) *Catalogue, National Maritime Museum (Greenwich)*. Greenwich: National Maritime Museum.

National Maritime Museum (2009) 'Mission statement'. Available online at: http://www.nmm.ac.uk/about/the-organization/mission-statement/ (Accessed 30 August 2009).

National Maritime Museum (2010) 'SeaBritain'. Available online at: http://www.nmm.ac.uk/about/partnerships-and-initiatives/seabritain/ (Accessed 19 July 2010).

Owen, J. (2006) 'Collecting artefacts, acquiring empire: exploring the relationship between Enlightenment and Darwinist collecting and late-nineteenth century British imperialism', *Journal of the History of Collections*, 18: 9–25.

Pearce, S.M. (1995) *On Collecting: an investigation into collecting in the European tradition*, London and New York: Routledge.

Peers, L. (1999) ' "Many tender ties": the shifting contexts and meanings of the S BLACK bag', *World Archaeology*, 31: 288–302.

Pitt Rivers Museum (2010a) 'The Forster Collection'. Available online at: http://projects.prm.ox.ac.uk/forster/home.html (Accessed 28 July 2010).

Pitt Rivers Museum (2010b) 'Pacific Pathways'. Available online at: http://projects.prm. ox.ac.uk/forster/pathways.html (Accessed 28 July 2010).

Savours, A. (1977) 'The Arctic Gallery of the National Maritime Museum, Greenwich', *Polar Record* 18 (115): 388–90.

Schimanski, J. and U. Spring (2009) 'Explorers' bodies in Arctic mediascapes: celebrating the return of the Austro-Hungarian Polar Expedition in 1874', *Acta Borealia*, 26: 50–76.

Spufford, F. (1996) *I May Be Some Time: ice and the English imagination*, London and Boston: Faber and Faber.

Part IV

Objects and difficult subjects

Introduction

Julia Petrov

This final part of the book moves on neatly from the political contexts introduced by Warrior's chapter at the end of Part III, to present a range of perspectives on challenges or contestations in museum representations and, ultimately, in the notion of 'heritage' itself. While many visitors may not enter museums expecting to be made to feel uncomfortable, the range of experiences and traditions within any audience may mean that the museum represents a story different to the one they know, and this can lead to cognitive and interpretive conflict. Since the rise of the 'New Museology', writers on museums have increasingly recognised the need for a sharing of power between the authority of the museum and its communities; the authors in this part of the book each in their own ways reflect on how this democratisation can be materially manifested. The section ends with a reflective critique of the very notion that 'heritage' is in some way 'good for us'.

The first three chapters in this final part of the volume deal with museums and the construction of social identity through the material objects on display. Through an analysis of a visitor's complaint about the attribution of *kente* cloth in the collection of Leicester's New Walk Museum, Malika Kraamer considers the ways in which a Ghanaian art-historical tradition is locally understood, constructed and contested. Kraamer persuasively argues for museums to be aware of the pressures on them to interpret this material 'correctly', and contends that behind every simple representation in the museum we can probably find competing claims. The museum may never be able to do justice to all competing interpretations of an object, but it can highlight in more general ways the contestation of the past and the fluidity of meanings, especially in post-Colonial contexts.

The following chapter, by Marzia Varutti, also deals with museum objects with competing geopolitical significance. It explores the representation of the fifty-six officially recognised Chinese minorities in Chinese museums within a political rhetoric of national unity. In many, the minorities are represented side-by-side as plastic figurines, mannequins or wax models, forming a materialised rendition of the 'colourful' cultures of the Chinese nation. This discussion reflects on the significance of this method of representation, and investigates the agency of museums in shaping the image of collective subjectivities. Calling for a critical assessment of the political and social roles of museums in China, Varutti endeavours to enhance our understanding of the political and intellectual implications of specific representations of ethnic minorities.

An exploration of the representation of modern Chinese identity abroad is undertaken in the chapter by Amy Jane Barnes. This chapter brings Pearce's collecting theories to bear on the display of the propagandist visual culture Chinese Cultural Revolution (1966–76), with particular reference to its treatment in British museums – the V&A, the British Museum and the University of Westminster. Ultimately, the chapter explores whether the spike in contemporary sinophilia might be suggestive of the disintegration of modernism, or simply the continuation of a long pattern of connoisseurial collecting from China, and concludes that the increasing desire to challenge official Chinese history may well represent a challenge to the hegemonic character of the museum.

Barnes's meditation into the significance of Maoist Utopian representations for a Western audience segues in the final three chapters in this section, which focus on the uses of museums in constructing visions of the past and present, as well as challenging the notion that this is a straightforward process that arises directly out of the material remains of history. In her chapter, Meighen Katz re-evaluates the uses of photography as a means of knowing and constructing history. Drawing on Pearce's call for a re-evaluation of old collections, Edwards' arguments on the materiality of photographs and Poole's theory of visual economy, and focusing on the Farm Security Administration's photographs of poverty in the American Great Depression, this chapter makes the case for a reconsideration of the inclusion of images in historical exhibitions, as material, rather than visual, culture. Katz argues that an understanding of the material life of these images – their construction, alteration and distribution – problematises not only the aestheticised nature of these images as well as the public vision of the period that they depict, but also challenges the role of the museum in producing this aspect of the visual economy.

The role of representations of trauma and dislocation in creating community identity is also addressed by Alice Semedo. Her chapter takes as its case study a museum in the Portuguese village of Luz, which was relocated to make way for an artificial lake. Here, immaterial narratives of loss and nostalgia are examined within the museum, which serves not only to memorialise the disappeared village, but also to create a new sense of community in its new setting. The importance, roles, perspectives and methods for recovering the past of 'experts', such as the archaeologist and anthropologist who oversaw the development of the museum, are compared with those of the locals. An examination of the links between this and the museum's architecture and exhibition design, shows the museum as a space where private and the public intertwine, and where sightseeing and therapy go hand in hand. Semedo theorises the Luz museum as a healing place that mediates past, present and future identities.

The final chapter, by Beverley Butler, also discusses the role of memory-work in constructing shared social heritage. This chapter seeks to redefine cultural heritage according to the Greek notion of '*pharmakon*', or 'poison-cure'. Drawing heavily on the inspiration provided by Susan Pearce's theories, Butler addresses conceptual intimacies between heritage, well-being and memory-work and uses alternative perspectives to problematise the canonical, grand narrative projections of cultural heritage as symptom, cure or healing (a trajectory still dominant in heritage discourses, bound up with post-conflict therapeutics of healing, recovery, economic revitalisation and historical and contemporary reparation). The chapter argues that we need to recognise and take responsibility for how heritage has been and continues to be not only a symptom or cure, but the very *cause* of human suffering, dislocation and disinheritance.

Taken as a whole, the chapters in this final part of the book each highlight the power of objects to subvert hegemony – that of the museum, of historical narrative or of political power. Whether in their presence or absence, the objects represented in museum collections challenge their custodians to represent different perspectives on the past and on social experience. To be true to the material, demands the necessity of highlighting contested meanings of an object on display.

20 Challenged pasts and the museum

The case of Ghanaian *kente*

Malika Kraamer

As Curator of World Culture in New Walk Museum and Art Gallery, Leicester, I received a complaint about the label for a colourful cloth on display in the World Arts Gallery:[1]

> I think the info given about the *kente* cloth is wrong. It is made in Ghana (Bonwire) in West Africa from the spider's web. I am actually a royal from Bonwire village.
>
> (Complaints, comments and compliments form,
> Leicester City Council, 29 May 2008)

The museum's label described the cloth as Nigerian.[2] The writer of the comment card, however, asserts in plain language that it is a cloth from Ghana, and that it was made by the Asante people, who invented this type of textile. Bonwire is one of the main weaving villages in the Asante region of Ghana, and the description 'from the spider's web' refers to one of the Asante origin myths about the invention of weaving.

The museum's label fails to recognise that most cloth of this kind is woven in Ghana, although Ghanaian (Ewe) weavers have been weaving in Nigeria since the 1930s.[3] As such, it might be interpreted as incomplete and misleading. This is not, however, the reason why I refer to the complaint. Clearly, this lady, who moved a few years ago from Ghana to Leicester, felt misrepresented and felt strongly about it. In her complaint, she indirectly refers to a fierce debate on the origin of these hand-woven textiles in Ghana, and seeks to make sure that should the museum change the label, it will get the story right.

This example highlights some of the wider issues associated with the display of objects from all over the world, one aspect of which I want to focus on in particular: how to represent objects when their histories are fiercely contested by their source communities.

Museum representation and local communities

Many museums, including several regional museums in the UK, have objects from different parts of the world. Although large parts of these so-called ethnographic collections were gathered in colonial times, additions have been made through donations and ongoing active collecting, especially in response to, and sometimes in collaboration with, migrant communities. Two examples from the 1980s are the transcultural collections in Bradford and the Gujurat collections in Leicester (Nicholson 1988, Poovaya-Smith 2006). The display and contextualisation of these objects has shifted dramatically in the last two decades: critiques on museum representations (e.g. Karp, Kreamer and Lavine 1992, Coombes 1994, Clifford 1997, Barringer and Flynn 1998); responses and protests from source communities on ethnographic museum practice and particular exhibitions (e.g. Handler and Gable 1997, Frank 2000, Tapsell 2000); and 'shifts in attitude towards museums by external funders' (Watson 2007a: 1) in promoting diversity and accountability in museums, have led to new ways of thinking about curatorial practice (e.g. Hooper-Greenhill 2000, Peers and Brown 2003, Watson 2007b).[4]

Many museums worldwide have attempted to become more responsive to community groups and individuals through, for example, community consultation panels, and (community-led) exhibitions and partnerships with source communities. They have become much more open to recording the perspectives of source communities on the continuing relevance and local knowledge of these objects. They increasingly consider how museum representations are perceived by and affect source community members. Some museums now also see source communities as an important audience for exhibitions (Peers and Brown 2007: 519). However, research and museum practice over the last decade have shown that changing the relationship between communities and museums, and the incorporation of local and source community voices in curatorial practice is challenging (e.g. Karp *et al.* 1992, Butler 1999, Davis 2007, Knell, Macleod and Watson 2007, Mason 2007, Peers and Brown 2007, Watson 2007b).

So, let us return to the example of *kente* cloth and its contested origin history. I studied this debate as part of my doctoral research on southern Ghanaian textiles.[5] When I arrived in Ghana at the end of the 1990s, this heated debate was at its peak, and framed mainly in ethnic terms; it predominantly focused on the primacy of Asante versus Ewe weaving.[6] The Asante are part of the Akan, the largest ethnic group in Ghana. From the seventeenth to nineteenth century, the Asante kingdom, with Kumasi as its capital in the middle of Ghana, was one of the most powerful states in West Africa. In contrast, the Ewe-speaking region, in south-east Ghana and southern Togo, consisted of many small states, some comprising just a few villages. This area has a complicated German, British and French colonial past.

Local art histories of *kente*[7]

Kente is the common name for hand-woven textiles in southern Ghana and Togo, produced predominantly by Ewe and Asante weavers for a number of centuries.[8] These textiles, like many other types of cloth produced in West Africa, are composed of narrow strips with a width of approximately three inches sewn edge to edge and woven on a double-heddle loom (Picton and Mack 1989: 45–54). A

Figure 20.1 Mama Sebeso II (left), Queen Mother, at the 1999 Agbamevorza, 'hand-woven or *kente* festival' in Agotime (Ewe-speaking region), wearing a rayon *kente*, also called *adanudo* (creative textile) with a design created by Agotime weavers in the 1990s. Photograph by author, Agotime-Kpetoe (Ghana), 1999.

particular characteristic of many *kente* cloths made during the last 200 years is the alternation of warp-faced and weft-faced blocks and the weaving of many weft-float patterns (Figure 20.1).[9]

Kente is mainly produced in three weaving centres and in some workshops in Ghanaian and Togolese cities. One centre is comprised of several villages located around Kumasi, including Bonwire, the village the complainant referred to as the centre of *kente* weaving.[10] The other two weaving centres are located in the Ewe-speaking area in south-east Ghana and adjacent Togo: Agotime in the middle of this area, and the villages of Anlo and Somé on the upper eastern part of the Keta lagoon. Historically, Asante weavers were more restricted as to what to weave for whom than Ewe weavers, as the latter were not controlled by a centralised court. This is one of the reasons why the greatest variety of cloth types can be found in these two Ewe weaving centres, although all three centres have a long history of interrelation (Kraamer 2006b: 36–53, 93–5).

The best-known *kente* today, colourful rayon textiles decorated with non-figurative motifs, stem from the Asante tradition and are invariably classified and displayed in museum collections as Asante cloth (Figures 20.2 and 20.3). Textiles classified in museums as Ewe cloth are mainly one type of the many made in the Ewe-speaking region: cotton textiles decorated with figurative motifs (Figure 20.4). However, the Asante-attributed rayon cloths have been woven and developed in Asante

Figure 20.2 Nana Addai Yeboah, Kentehene, at the 1999 Kente Festival in Bonwire (Asante region), in a rayon textile woven with three pairs of heddles. Photograph by author, Bonwire (Ghana), 1999.

Figure 20.3 Nene Nuer Keteku III, paramount chief of the Agotime Traditional Area (Ewe-speaking region), in a 'modern' *kente* at the 1999 Agbamevorza, 'hand-woven textile or *kente* festival'. Photograph by author, Agotime-Kpetoe, 1999.

Figure 20.4 Adanudo (creative textile), textile decorated with figurative motifs woven in the 1950s in Agotime (Ewe-speaking region). Photograph by author, Agotime, 1999.

and Ewe weaving centres throughout southern Ghana since the 1950s, as they became increasingly associated with a national Ghanaian, and even a pan-African identity (Fosu 1996: 12–13, Ross 1998: 166, Kraamer 2005a: 194–5).

In discussions about the true origin of *kente*, the Asante perspective often asserts the premise that *kente*, thought of as these rayon textiles, is an invention of the Asante, and it is reasoned, therefore, that Asante weavers taught the Ewe people their weaving skills. Reference is often made to the following oral history account: the art of weaving was invented when one or two hunters went to the bush and learned weaving skills from a spider making a web. The complainant's remarks made an explicit reference to this origin myth and, by extension, reasserted the Asante claim that they are the originators of *kente*.

In contrast, the Ewe origin of *kente* mainly focuses on the word itself, which is thought to be a corruption of the more proper Ewe word *kete* for hand-woven textiles. Through the process of Ewe weavers teaching the Asante how to weave, it is said, the word changed into *kente*, as Asante people do not speak Ewe. Many Ewe also give an etymology of *kete* as: *ke* 'to open' and *te* 'to press'. Often, weavers will accompany the word with bodily movements which express the making of a shed and pressing of the imagined weft with the beater.[11]

These origin claims are especially pronounced in the new *kente* festivals in Bonwire and Agotime-Kpetoe which have developed since the second half of the 1990s, and in the printed media. For example, in the 1997 article 'Another story about *kente*', published in Ghana's state-owned and widely-distributed newspaper the *Daily Graphic*, an Akan origin of the word *kente* was openly contested. Furthermore, other commonly used 'evidence' for the Ewe weaving primacy was discussed in this and other articles: weaving has always been an Ewe activity since their migration to their current abode. The growing of cotton in the Ewe area facilitated the widespread practice of weaving, in contrast to the forested Asante area, where cotton had to be imported from the north (Apaa 27 August 1997). The transfer of weaving knowledge is pinpointed to the time when the Asante took many Ewes into captivity during the Asante wars between 1869 and 1873. These claims were fiercely contested at the first Bonwire *Kente* Festival. The subtitle of the festival, '300 Years of Kente Evolution (1697–1997)', was clearly intended to stress the historical depth of Asante weaving (Ross 1998: 23) and emphasis was placed on Bonwire as the centre and home of *kente* weaving (Oteng 1998: 2, Bonwire Festival programme). At the Agotime festival in 1998, the guest of honour, Nana Konadu Agyamang Rawlings, the First Lady – herself of Asante origin – confirmed this version of the origin myth, after which the debate reached its peak, particularly in the print and other media of Ghana (e.g. Agboyo 1998, Damson 1998, Kodua 1998, Noretti 1998, Safo Kantanka 1998a–d).[12] Those opposing the 'Kpetoe school' and supporting the 'Bonwire school' (categories introduced by O.B. Safo Kantanka who became one of the most vocal advocates of the Bonwire School) reacted mainly to the Agotime assertions. They gave different claims for the word *kente* and often stated that Bonwire people invented the art of weaving independently of Ewe people and developed *kente* under the reign of Osei Tutu at the end of the seventeenth century. References were made to the publications of Rømer (1965 [1760]) and Bowdich (1966 [1819]) as supporting evidence for the existence of Ashante weaving before the Asante wars of the mid-nineteenth century.

This public origin discourse fuelled negative ethnic sentiments with remarks such as 'from those people who have just recently woken up to the realisation of wanting to write, or re-write their history and, in the process, audaciously claiming, as their own, what has persisted through the centuries as inventions or creations of civilised Ashantis' (Damson 1998).

One of the main reasons for this ongoing debate is the fact that three different claims became conflated, and all kinds of evidence used to support one claim were taken to support other claims as well: first, the origin of the term *kente*; secondly, the origin of weaving in Ghana in general; and, thirdly, the origin of rayon non-figurative textiles. Investigation of each claim indicates that semantic fields have shifted, that these different textile centres have a long history of inter-relationships, and that weaving likely came independently to these weaving centres from outside Ghana.[13] Furthermore, it is apparent that there are different understandings of what the term *kente* embodies. Today, many Asante and other Ghanaians understand *kente* as a rayon textile, while a Ewe understanding is much more inclusive of all kinds of hand-woven cloth produced in southern Ghana and Togo. To reach a better understanding of this discrepancy, and why Ewe people have continued to wear and produce a style of textile acknowledged locally to have first developed in the Asante region, I will now focus on the ways knowledge is produced in these discussions of origin. As hinted briefly before, the building of the nation state was the main initial stimulus to produce and use rayon textiles on a larger scale throughout Ghana in this particular style, which was then further developed in the different weaving centres.

The particular time that this debate captured public attention can be understood by looking at the wider political and economic context. Roots tourism, mainly by African-Americans, meant an increase in the market for *kente* but, for several historical reasons, this mainly benefited the Asante region.[14] Ethnicity increased as a political factor and seeing history through an ethnic lens became more acceptable, but at the same time Ghanaians became more concerned with the marking of social position, status and personal taste, within a context of conspicuous display, than the marking of an ethnic identity in the wearing of cloth.[15]

Even though this gives a clear context as to why alternative interpretations, from an Ewe perspective of the history of *kente* were given at this specific point in time, the most important reason has been the way this shift to rayon textiles was perceived and experienced in the Ewe-speaking region: it was not experienced as a radical change from previous practice. This also explains why it was not felt problematic to use primarily these rayon non-figurative motif textiles on all kinds of ceremonial and civil occasions. Another indication of this continuity lies in the way men and women wrap these textiles around the body. In an area encompassing Togo, southern Ghana and parts of the Ivory Coast, the wrapping of the textiles has hardly changed in the last few centuries (Figures 20.1–20.3).[16]

Furthermore, for many Ewe, these specific rayon textiles have been considered just an addition to a larger repertoire. Ewe textiles are characterised by a bewildering diversity of colours and patterns. The invention of new textile types and the incorporation of new elements, such as imported yarns and characteristics from other textile traditions, together with further incremental and innovative changes within a textile type, have been ongoing characteristics of Ewe textile traditions (Kraamer 2005a: 107–87, 257–79, Kraamer 2005b, 2006b).[17] Ewe weavers continually restate details of specific designs. They experiment with new colour combinations. They augment the design possibilities made available by the wide range of existing techniques through the use of an increasing range of threads.

Perceived continuities of practice can also be traced when we look at local terminology, and the organisation of textiles and technology. For example, textiles throughout the twentieth century, either cotton textiles decorated with figurative motifs or rayon textiles with non-figurative motifs, are generally called *adanuvor* (creative textiles) (Figure 20.4). They are subdivided into two main groups, depending on the organisation of weft-blocks over the entire cloth. The same two basic types of block juxtaposition can be found in both rayon and cotton textiles.

Many Ewe weavers, including Nene Nuer Keteku III, paramount chief of Agotime, Fred and Albert Gbadago, Gator Gbogbo, Komla Akotey and John Alada, all from the main weaving villages in the Agotime area, have specifically commented that, in terms of technology, there has hardly been any shift in the older and newer types of 'creative textiles': weavers continue to use the same technology to make these weft-blocks and motifs.[18] Appropriation of this newer type of textile meant, therefore, no major alterations in weaving technology. The principal new elements were the shift to rayon and a new aesthetic colour framework.

Finding the authoritative voice

What we see, therefore, are differences in understandings of an art-historical tradition, and these differences can only be grasped by the way people relate to the material world around them through many different lived-through practices. The understanding of the past is further shaped in their fierce contests over control and authority in interpreting the past 'correctly'. In the comment made on the museum label, not only was it pointed out that the country attribution was wrong, but direction was also given to the correct origin of this kind of cloth, with the affirmation that they – the complainant – had authoritative knowledge.

The case of *kente* cloth does not stand alone, although the highly vocal contestation of the art-historical narrative is uncommon. Wrong or incomplete attributions of African objects in Western scholarship and museums are as old as the institution of the museum itself. For instance, one section of the 2010 British Museum exhibition *Kingdom of Ife: Sculptures from West Africa* discussed changing attributions (see also Drewal and Schildkrout 2009). Much misunderstanding and misrepresentation in museums, increasingly contested by migrant and source communities, is brought about by colonial and biased views in museum ledgers,[19] and insufficient (allocation of) funds to access up-to-date knowledge of world histories of art and museological practice.[20] Furthermore, even when a critical stance towards past museum representation is the theme of an exhibition, such as the 1989 Royal Ontario Museum exhibition *In the Heart of Darkness*, or the 1996 South African National Gallery exhibition *Miscast: Negotiating the Presence of Khoi and San History and Material Culture*, huge controversy among stakeholders and within local and source communities can arise (for in-depth discussion of these exhibitions see Butler 1999, Coombes 2003: 230–42).

However, I would suggest that the most important issue is that even when representation is based on the latest research and in consultation with community groups, real barriers may be experienced: for instance, who has the authority to speak on behalf of a community?[21] This issue is very clear in the case of *kente*, but there are many other examples. When I curatorially supported the community-led Sikh exhibition *The Living Guru – The Holy Sikh Scripture* held at New Walk Museum and Art Gallery, Leicester, in 2008, within the community group with which we were working, there were extensive discussions around exhibition texts and particularly about the inclusive phrase 'Sikh ways of living', as opposed to the exclusive 'Sikh way of living'; and whether the exhibition should show images of Sikh men with short hair (see also Kaur 2008).[22] Representation is, of course, not only about the community to which an object belongs, and which groups are represented, but also the most appropriate way to discuss its relevance and its importance to different groups within the same community, and how to capture its main uses and possibly debated historical and artistic importance as understood by source and other communities. These are very complicated issues to address, as curators typically have responsibility for a range of objects, from different parts of the world. Keeping on top of relevant literature and good practice, let alone carrying out new, intensive research, is time and resource-consuming and often an impossible option for many curators.

Conclusions

Many museum professionals think about new curatorial praxis and are open to consultation with different communities.[23] There is a long history of museum institutions and their staff, especially social history curators, developing consultation procedures with local, including diaspora, communities (Watson 2007b). But collaborative projects with geographically distant source communities are very sporadic and 'curatorial and institutional procedures have not shifted much at all as far as overseas communities are concerned' (Peers and Brown 2007: 522; see also Karp *et al.* 1992, Clifford 1997: 208, Ames 2003, Watson 2007b).[24] When collections comprise objects from hundreds of different source communities, which one should have priority? Furthermore, which voices within those communities should be taken as the authority? How can we be faithful to source communities and negotiate that with the demands of many audiences, including those from source communities, who demand clear, uncomplicated representations? These are challenging and exciting questions for contemporary curatorial staff. Much work still needs to be done, but it seems important that, in the meantime, museum staff became more aware of these contestations. Behind every simple representation in the museum we can probably find competing claims. In recent memory studies, it is well-established that the past is always contested, and that conflicts are as much about which version of the past is evoked through memorials, museums displays, texts and so on, as about who is entitled to speak for that past in the present (Hodgkin and Radstone 2005: 1). Even though a museum will never be able to do justice to all the potential interpretations of a particular object, it can try to highlight, in more general ways, that pasts are contested and interpretations informed by present concerns; that meanings are always in flux, and identities always in the making.[25] A museum display that evokes questions, challenges presupposed ideas and provides an opportunity for visitors to relate to other people, near and far, is a display that I would enjoy visiting.

Notes

1 The World Arts Gallery was opened in July 2005. The ledger for some of the objects on display, including this cloth, was not available to the staff working on this gallery at the time, but became available in 2008. The information on the label was, therefore, produced on the judgement of those working on the gallery. I joined Leicester Arts and Museums Service, Leicester City Council, of which this museum is part, in July 2007.

2 The original label reads: 'Strip-woven textile, sometimes called a *kente* cloth. Viscose and lurex, made in Nigeria, 1975–1985.'

3 It turned out, in the case of this particular cloth, that it was indeed woven in Bonwire, Ghana as stated in the ledger that we managed to access in 2008.

4 The term 'source communities', sometimes referred to as 'originating communities', refers both to the groups from which these objects were collected, and to their descendants today. Although the term has been mainly used for indigenous peoples in the Americas and the Pacific, they apply to local people, diaspora and migrant communities, religious groups, settlers and indigenous peoples (Peers and Brown 2007: 520). No difference is made in the literature, and often in practice, between descendants living in the same place as the makers of these objects, or descendants migrated to other parts of the world (a distinction which I think should be made in most cases).

5 I finished my PhD dissertation on Ewe *kente* at the School of Oriental and African Studies, University of London, under supervision of Professor John Picton in 2005, which involved one and a half years of field work in Ghana and Togo and intensive research into museum and archive collections in West Africa, Europe and the USA. I also wrote my (equivalent to Masters) thesis on economic and social aspects of *kente* at the Erasmus University Rotterdam, the Netherlands, for which I conducted five months of fieldwork in Ghana.

6 In my PhD dissertation (Kraamer 2005a) and especially in my article in *Afrique: Archéologie et Arts* (Kraamer 2006a) I discuss the different claims made for either an Asante or Ewe primacy in the origin of *kente*. The term primacy was first used by Ross (1998: 21).

7 This section is a reworking of an article I published in *Afrique: Archéologie et Arts* (Kraamer 2006a).

8 At present, *kente* is one of the best known of all African textiles. Since the second half of the twentieth century, *kente* figures prominently in the 'worlds of design, fashion, and politics' (Ross 1998: 21; see also Kraamer 1996). It appears both in sacred and profane contexts, and has 'come to evoke and to celebrate a shared cultural heritage, bridging two continents' (Ross 1998: 19). In Ghana, the demand is especially high for textiles that are recently developed or that incorporate new patterns, often called locally 'modern' cloth (Kraamer 2005a: 196–7).

9 The structure of a plain weave textile (whereby the interlacing of the warp and weft is over-one/under-one) is composed of one set each of warp and weft elements and can be either warp-faced (the warp elements are greater in number relative to the number of wefts and more closely packed together so that the warp will dominate and tend to hide the weft) or weft-faced (the reverse process). Uncommonly, *kente* cloth often combines the alternation of warp-faced and weft-faced plain weave in one length of strip. These areas are referred as weft-faced and warp-faced blocks. Compound weaves have more than one set of either warps or wefts or both. Weft-float patterns, more precisely supplementary weft floats, are patterns formed by additional supplementary wefts that float over or under more than one warp. In Asante and Ewe weaving, supplementary wefts are used to form patterns of floats on both faces of the fabric. For an accessible introduction to weaving technology focused on African textiles, see Picton and Mack (1989: 17–18, 45–54).

10 The claim that Bonwire is the main locality of Asante weaving does not go unchallenged even within the Asante heartland. There are over forty Asante towns and villages where weaving forms a substantial occupation for many of the (male) inhabitants and the Asantehene's official weavers reside not only in Bonwire, but also in Adanwomase (Ross 1998: 23). Furthermore, Bonwire is not mentioned in Bowdich's nineteenth century account of Asante life and culture, although he discusses weaving and royal regalia (Bowdich 1966 [1819]). However, Rattray states that Bonwire was the main weaving centre for the Asante royalty in the olden days (Rattray 1927: 234). Outside Ghana, Bonwire is the most famous Asante weaving town; attracting busloads of tourists.

11 Weaving a textile requires that two sets of elements, the warp and the weft, are interlaced with each other at right angles. The interlacing of these two elements is made

easier if one set, called the warp, is held in tension. The interlacing can be made still by a mechanical device, called the shedding device, to separate alternate warp elements into two groups, called the shed, between which the elements of the other set, the weft, can pass. A loom gives both tension to the warp and provides a shedding device (Picton and Mack 1989: 45).

12 I would like to thank Nana Addae Yeboah, Kentehene to the Otumfua Asantehene and Nene Nuer Keteku, Kronor of Agotime Traditional Area, for their discussions with me and sharing their material (including a collection of newspapers and a taped interview with the BBC) on this issue.

13 A lengthy discussion of the origin of *kente* and *kete*, the origin of weaving and the origin of rayon non-figurative textiles can be found in Kraamer (2006a: 63–7, 2006b).

14 Ghana, with the two largest slave forts on the West African coast, has become the top destination of African-American tourists searching for their 'roots'. This diaspora tourism is often called Rootstourism, as the 1977 hit mini-series *Roots*, based on the book by Alex Hailey, has been largely responsible for the popularity of diaspora tourism (Holsey 2004: 170). *Kente* has become the textile of choice for African-Americans on many occasions that foreground issues of heritage and achievement and it was a potent marker in the context of many of the most important African and African-American ideologies in the twentieth century (Ross 1998: 21; see also the extensive literature on Black Power ideologies such as Penniel 2006). The physical history of *kente* cloth in the USA began in the 1950s, but the ideological history that anticipated its arrival started in the 1920s (Ross 1998: 120). *Kente* has not only been bought by African-Americans visiting Ghana, but has also been imported in large quantities since the 1980s. Sales of African and African-style fabrics, of which *kente* is definitely the hottest, reached fourteen billion dollars in the USA in 1991 (Quarcoopome 1998: 193).

15 Furthermore, the wide distribution of many textiles in West Africa (also historically) far beyond their production centres indicates that ethnicity is not a strong issue in the choice of what to wear (Aronson 1982: 43–7, Eicher and Erekosima 1995: 41, Kraamer 2005a: 235–43). Only under very particular circumstances is there a need to define ethnic identities through textiles or dress, for instance in the construction of such an identity, or in a process of commodification as part of a cultural strategy to attract tourists (Hansen 2004: 374).

16 *Kente* also has a long history of being used in ways other than as a garment. In the beautiful illustrated catalogue *Wrapped in Pride* edited by Doran Ross in 1998, many other contexts in and beyond Ghana at various times are explored.

17 An eclectic mix of local and imported elements are ongoing characteristics of several West African flourishing and developing textile traditions (Picton 2004: 26), but the variety of textiles woven in the Ewe-speaking region is unique in the whole West African region, including Asante and Yoruba cloth.

18 I conducted interviews with many weavers in the Agotime and coastal Anlo-Somé area, and conducted group interviews in forty main villages all over the Ewe-speaking region in Ghana and Togo between 1998 and 2000. Many weavers started to explain to me, even before I asked, that *kente* originated from their ancestors, and many pointed out the continuity in technology. As the usage of local terminology to refer to the what weavers often called the 'older type' and 'modern type' is in the great part the same, this suggests that this is a wide-spread experience of art-historical understanding of what constitutes Ewe textiles, beyond mere rhetoric to prove their claim (see also Kraamer 2005a: chapter 8).

19 A museum ledger is either an accession book, listing only those objects accessioned in the permanent collection, or a daybook, listing all objects that have come into the museum, including loans, objects for enquiry and objects for consideration to be accessioned. In some museums, like the Leicester Art and Museum Service, the

educational handling collections do not form part of the permanent collection. Ledgers created for those objects than take the form of an inventory list.

20 Access to up-to-date knowledge (especially access to journals and e-journals) is especially difficult in non-national or university museums as subscription to these journals is often beyond the capacity of museums, and curators are not automatically affiliated with research institutions. Fortunately, in time, many core articles are published in edited books, and initiatives like the University of Leicester Research Archive and other open access archives and websites help.

21 Also, when curators have access to the latest research, this can be very limited, as there is still enormous imbalance in art-historical research undertaken and funded in different parts of the world.

22 This is common in many community-involved exhibitions on Sikh religion and identity, although there are exceptions, such as the exhibition *A Sikh Face in Ireland: Photographic and Life History Project*, 7 May–26 September 2010, Chester Beatty Library, Dublin, Ireland (see http://www.cbl.ie/getdoc/950b834a-6386-4334-b992-0307eab82e70/A-Sikh-Face-in-Ireland.aspx, accessed 18 October 2010).

23 The literature also gives many examples of the willingness of museum staff to take community involvement seriously (see, for instance, Watson 2007b). Also in talks about community involvement with colleagues taking care of world arts collections (in Nottingham, Leeds, Bradford, London, Brighton and Birmingham), I have come across many examples. At New Walk Museum, I have worked on a community-led Sikh exhibition and currently work with four youth and four community curators and a youth panel together making a new exhibition *Suits and Saris* about global fashion connections.

24 Museums in North America and the Pacific have a much longer tradition of collaborative projects with source communities than those of the UK and the rest of Europe. This is partially because of the higher cost and more difficult logistics for Europeans, as source communities are often far more geographically distant, and they have 'a sense of political distance from source communities that such situations lead to' (Peers and Brown 2007: 520). In the UK, the most common approach has been to invite a 'representative' of the source community to the UK, and often an indigenous artist has been asked to create a work in public in the museum, especially when an exhibition is one of the collaborative outcomes (Heywood 2009: 25). A recent conference 'Contact and context, working with source communities' (London, 12 February 2009) looked at good practices and ways forward.

25 One of the hindrances in the representation of many 'ethnographic' objects, for instance, is the ongoing equation of ethnic group with art style (embedded in the museum, for example, in the classification system), even though it has been shown in many art-historical and anthropological studies that this is very problematic (Kasfir 1984, Vansina 1984: 29–33).

Bibliography

Ames, M.M. (2003) 'How to decorate a house: the renegotiation of cultural representations at the University of British Columbia Museum of Anthropology', in L.L. Peers and A.K. Brown (eds) *Museums and Source Communities: a Routledge reader*, London and New York: Routledge, pp. 171–80.

Aronson, L. (1982) 'Popo weaving: the dynamics of trade in Southeastern Nigeria', *African Arts*, 15 (3): 43–7, 90–1.

Barringer, T. and T. Flynn (1998) *Colonialism and the Object: empire, material culture and the museum*, London: Routledge.

Bowdich, T.E. (1966) *Mission from Cape Coast Castle to Ashantee*, 3rd edn. (1st edn. 1819), London: Cass.

Butler, S.R. (1999) *Contested Representations: revisiting into the heart of Africa*, London: Gordon and Breach.

Clifford, J. (1997) *Routes: travel and translation in the late twentieth century*, Cambridge, MA: Harvard University Press.

Coombes, A.E. (1994) *Reinventing Africa: museums, material culture, and popular imagination in late Victorian and Edwardian England*, New Haven and London: Yale University Press.

Coombes, A.E. (2003) *Visual Culture and Public Memory in a Democratic South Africa*, Durham, NC and London: Duke University Press.

Davis, P. (2007) 'Place exploration: museum, identity, community', in S. Watson (ed.) *Museums and their Communities*, London and New York: Routledge, pp. 53–75.

Drewal, H. and E. Schildkrout (2009) *Kingdom of Ife: sculptures from West Africa*, London: British Museum Press.

Eicher, J.B. and T.V. Erekosima (1995) 'Why do they call it Kalabari?: cultural authentication and the demarcation of ethnic identity', in J.B. Eicher (ed.) *Dress and Ethnicity: change across space and time*, Oxford and Washington, DC: Berg, pp. 162–4.

Frank, G. (2000) ' "That's my dinner on display": a First Nation's reflection on museum culture', *B.C. Studies*, 125 (6): 163–78.

Fosu, K. (1993) *20th Century Art of Africa*, 2nd edn, Accra: Artists Alliance.

Handler, R. and E. Gable (1997) *The New History in an Old Museum: creating the past at Colonial Williamsburg*, Durham, NC: Duke University Press.

Hansen, K.T. (2004) 'The world in dress: anthropological perspectives on clothing, fashion, and culture', *Annual Review of Anthropology*, 33: 369–92.

Heywood, F. (2009) 'Source materials', *Museum Journal*, 109 (2): 22–7.

Hodgkin, K. and S. Radstone (2005) *Memory, History, Nation: contested pasts*, New Brunswick, NJ: Transaction Publishers.

Holsey, B. (2004) 'Transatlantic dreaming: slavery, tourism, and diasporic encounters', in F. Markovitz and A.F. Stefansson (eds) *Homecomings: unsettling paths of return*, Lanham, MD: Lexington Books, pp. 166–82.

Hooper-Greenhill, E. (2000) *Museums and the Interpretation of Visual Culture*, London: Routledge.

Karp, I., C.M. Kreamer and S. Lavine (eds) (1992) *Museums and Communities: the politics of public culture*, Washington, DC: Smithsonian Institution Press.

Kasfir, S.L. (1984) 'One tribe, one style?: paradigms in the historiography of African art', *History in Africa*, 11: 163–93.

Kaur, S. (2008) 'The politics of self definition: the monitoring of Sikh identity and culture', *Museological Review*, 13: 29–43.

Knell, J., S. Macleod and S. Watson (2007) *Museum Revolutions: how museums change and are changed*, London: Routledge.

Kraamer, M. (1996) 'Kleurrijke veranderingen: de dynamiek van de kentekunstwereld in Ghana', unpublished MA thesis, Erasmus University Rotterdam.

Kraamer, M. (2005a) 'Colourful changes: two hundred years of social and design history in the hand-woven textiles of the Ewe-speaking regions of Ghana and Togo (1800–2000)', unpublished thesis, School of Oriental and African Studies, University of London.

Kraamer, M. (2005b) 'Contemporary visual arts in the Ewe-speaking region', in B.N. Lawrence (ed.) *A Handbook of Eweland*, vol. 3, *The Ewe of Togo and Benin*, Accra: Woeli Publishing Service, pp. 293–310.

Kraamer, M. (2006a) 'Origin disputed: the making, use and evaluation of Ghanaian textiles', *Afrique: Archéologie et Arts*, 4: 53–76.

Kraamer, M. (2006b) 'Ghanaian interweaving in the 19th century: a new perspective on Ewe and Asante textile history', *African Arts*, 39 (4): 36–53.

Mason, R. (2007) *Museums, Nations, Identities: Wales and its national museums*, Cardiff: University of Wales Press.

Nicholson, J. (1988) *Traditional Indian Arts of Gujarat*, Leicester: Leicestershire County Council.

Peers, L.L. and A.K. Brown (eds) (2003) *Museums and Source Communities: a Routledge reader*, London: Routledge.

Peers, L.L. and A.K. Brown (2007) 'Museums and source communities', in S. Watson (ed.) *Museums and their Communities*, London and New York: Routledge, pp. 519–37.

Penniel, E.J. (ed.) (2006) *The Black Power Movement: rethinking the civil rights-Black power era*, New York and London: Routledge.

Picton, J. (2004) 'What to wear in West Africa: textile design, dress and self-represenation', in C. Tulloch (ed.) *Black Style*, London: V&A Publications, pp. 22–47.

Picton, J. and J. Mack (1989) *African Textiles*, 2nd edn, London: British Museum Press.

Poovaya-Smith, N. (2006) 'Keys to the magic kingdom: the new transcultural collections of Bradford Art Galleries and Museums', in T. Barringer and T. Flynn (eds) *Colonialism and the Object: empire, material culture and the museum*, London: Routledge, pp. 111–28.

Quarcoopome, N.O. (1998) 'Pride and avarice: kente and advertising', in D. Ross (ed.) *Wrapped in Pride: Ghanaian kente and African American identity*, Los Angeles: UCLA Fowler Museum of Cultural History, pp. 193–202.

Rattray, R.S. (1927) *Religion and Art in Ashanti*, Oxford: Clarendon Press.

Rømer, L.F. (1965, 1st edn. 1760) *The Coast of Guinea*, Legon: Institute of African Studies.

Ross, D.H. (ed.) (1998) *Wrapped in Pride: Ghanaian kente and African American identity*, Los Angeles: UCLA Fowler Museum of Cultural History.

Tapsell, P. (2000) 'The flight of Pareraututu: an investigation of *Taonga* from a tribal perspective', *Journal of the Polynesian Society*, 106 (4): 323–74.

Vansina, J. (1984) *Art History in Africa: an introduction to method*, London: Longman.

Watson, S. (2007a) 'Museums and their communities', in S. Watson (ed.) *Museums and their Communities*, London and New York: Routledge, pp. 1–24.

Watson, S. (ed.) (2007b) *Museums and their Communities*, London and New York: Routledge.

Newspaper articles

Agboyo, J. (1998) 'Kente came from Volta – Nana Konadu', *The Ghanaian Chronicle*, 23–24 September 1998, Accra.

Apaa (1997) 'Another story about kente', *Daily Graphic*, 27 August 1997, Accra.

Damson, I.B. (1998) 'Nana Konadu and Anlo Kente', *The Ghanaian Chronicle*, 30 October–1 November 1998, Accra.

Kodua, C. (1998) 'Bonwire responds to Kente controversy: Nana Konadu challenged', *The Ghanaian Chronicle*, 2–3 November 1998, Accra.

Noretti, A.M. (1998) 'Time to form co-ops to claim copyright: Nana advises kente weavers', *Ghanaian Times*, 14 September 1998, Accra.

Safo Kantanka, O.B. (1998a) 'Who started Kente weaving: Ewes or Ashantis?' *Ghanaian Voice*, 11–14 June 1998, Accra.

Safo Kantanka, O.B. (1998b) 'The evolution of Kente: Part 1', *Ghanaian Voice*, 3–8 August 1998, Accra.

Safo Kantanka, O.B. (1998c) 'Evolution of Kente: Part 2', *Ghanaian Voice*, 17–23 August 1998.

Safo Kantanka, O.B. (1998d) 'Anthropological significance of some Kente designs and patterns', *Ghanaian Voice*, 31 August–2 September 1998.

Brochures

Festival programme, Agotime Traditional Area 1997.
Oteng, Festival programme, Bonwire Kente Festival 1998.

21 Standardising difference

The materiality of ethnic minorities in the museums of the People's Republic of China

Marzia Varutti

How do museums negotiate cultural difference in contexts where they are urged to represent national identity? What role do museum exhibitions have in such processes? And how is the material culture on display engaged with in such contexts? This chapter aims to address these broad questions through the analysis of the museum representation of ethnic minorities in China and its articulation with the definition of Chinese national identity. China is formally defined as a 'unified, multinational state', where the Han majority cohabits with some fifty-five officially recognised ethnic minorities.[1] It follows that the dilemma inherent in the representation of cultural difference – given the tension between uniqueness and resistance to overarching unifying definitions of identity – is especially acute in China. Here, museums are challenged to represent the cultural diversity of fifty-five ethnic minorities and, at the same time, to closely adhere to the official rhetoric predicating the unity of all Chinese people on the basis of their allegedly shared 'Chineseness'.

Building on a comparative analysis of museum narratives and display techniques in a number of museums of various scale – national, provincial and local – and location – museums of major coastal urban centres (such as Beijing and Shanghai) and of the south-western inland (Yunnan and Sichuan Provinces), this analysis sets out to explore the place and role of the material culture of ethnic minorities, and of their museum representation, in the formulation of narratives of the Chinese nation. Museum displays can be approached as a tool through which to analyse the politics of ethnic difference in China, since the displays of the materiality of ethnic minorities operate as a counterfoil that makes visible and apprehensible the relationship between Chinese museums, ethnic minorities and the Chinese nation.

The problem I wish to address through this case study is one that many national museums displaying cultural difference (and of course, specifically, anthropology museums) are faced with: how to create displays and narratives of identity that are both cohesive at national level and inclusive and respectful of ethnic communities and their cultures? These questions prompt a reflection on the challenge to reconcile the idealised cultural homogeneity of the nation-state with the reality of increasingly multicultural societies. The parts that museums – and especially national museums – could or should play in these contexts have been the object of much debate in museum studies and cognate disciplines (see Karp, Kreamer and Lavine 1992, Chakrabarty 2002, Macdonald 2003, Karp *et al.* 2007, Watson 2007, Knell, Aronsson and Amundsen 2010, among others).

In the post-colonial era, a self-reflective museology has emerged from the critique of hegemonic practices of cultural representation. Whilst critically engaging with the capacity of museums to objectify and commercialise cultures (see Stanley 1998, Price 2001), these works have also pointed at the potential of museums to foster social inclusion and intercultural dialogue, notably by putting less emphasis on the exoticism of other cultures to the benefit of the valorisation and explanation of cultural difference. This new paradigm set the intellectual and material conditions for ethnic groups and source communities to participate and, increasingly, collaborate in the representation and re-interpretation of their own cultural heritage both in national museums (Simpson 2001, Peers and Brown 2003, Golding 2009) and at a local level through experiments in self-representation and autonomous management of local cultural resources (Brown and Sant 1999, Hendry 2005, Witcomb and Healy 2006, Stanley 2007).

Acting both as 'differentiating machines' and as a 'facilitators of cross-cultural exchange', as Tony Bennett put it (2006: 59), museums bear the potential to transform cultural difference from issue into resource, from barrier into a link that makes cultures mutually intelligible. However, to this end the prior recognition of cultural difference is essential: the non-denial of difference is a necessary condition to engage with it. As we shall see, this is not quite the case in Chinese museums. Here, through specific narratives and display techniques, museums contribute to the objectification of ethnic minority cultures and to their subordination to the Han Chinese majority. Through a sapient threading of exhibits, *ad hoc* texts and exhibitionary techniques, museums construct ethnic minorities as passive, inert objects which can be arbitrarily interpreted and 'narrated'. It could be argued that museum displays mirror the position of ethnic minorities in official rhetoric: likewise their materiality in museums, in the official rhetoric ethnic minorities are treated as objects to be manipulated for nationalistic purposes. In this sense, this chapter contributes a counter-example of how museums, though fully engaged in a process of modernisation as in the case of China, may actually resist change, and deepen rather than erase existing patterns of social exclusion. This finding bears the potential to question received ideas about the benefits of modernisation and economic development, re-instating the centrality of political choices and asserting their full responsibility in the evolution of museums' social roles.

Chinese cultural nationalism and the 'ethnic question'

The museum representation of ethnic minorities in China can be fully appreciated in the light of the priorities and concerns that shape the political discourse on Chinese national identity and, notably, on the role of ethnic minorities in the process of nation-building. In 1953, the Chinese government initiated a census of ethnic groups (*minzu shibie*); this led to the identification and official recognition of fifty-five ethnic minorities. Ethnic groups were identified and classified on the basis of the Marxist–Leninist theory of human social evolution (drawing from Lewis H. Morgan, 1985 [1877]). Among the rest, the theory postulates that human societies can be classified according to their stage of development in primitive, slave, feudal or capitalist societies. In accordance with these principles, Chinese ethnic groups were classified and located in a precise position along an idealised path of development. This attained the twofold result of collectively subordinating ethnic minorities to the Han majority, and of scaling them according to their proximity or distance to Han – implicitly located at the apex of civilisation. In this perspective, ethnic minorities are seen as 'in need of civilisation', of 'modernisation' and socioeconomic development. The construction of the ethnic minority as 'backward' crucially entails the production of the cultural, historical, civic discourses that call for a state intervention (and the related arguments for cultural backwardness, lack of development, need for moral guidance and so on). In this respect, museums have provided the conceptual space, moral justification and the logic of 'civilising missions' for state policies to unfold.

Although central to communist ideology since the creation of the People's Republic of China in 1949, the issue of the status of ethnic minorities within the Chinese nation has become critical over the last two decades in reaction to the crisis of legitimacy experienced by the communist regime. Starting from the late 1980s, and following the disintegration of communist regimes at international level in 1989, the Chinese government has experienced an ideological crisis challenging the very foundations of its political authority (Friedman 1995). Although the official political philosophy is still imbued with communist values, these arguably fail to provoke a real emotional resonance (Schwarcz 1991, Tu 1993: xiv). As the efficacy of communist ideology is fading, the Chinese government is turning to other tools to justify its authority. Nationalism, and notably cultural nationalism, has provided a new source of political legitimation (Friedman 1994, Suresh 2002).

The phenomenon of Chinese cultural nationalism is multifaceted and complex, and cannot be comprehensively discussed here. Specific aspects of nationalist ideology are nevertheless worthy of consideration as they cast light on the position of Chinese ethnic minorities vis-à-vis the Han majority. For instance, Hsiau A-Chin (2000: 14) argues that 'the ultimate object of cultural nationalism is to create a "new man" by instilling a distinctive culture into those who are regarded as members of the nation'. Dikotter, drawing on Hutchinson, explains that:

> [C]ultural nationalism [. . .] imagines the nation to have a distinctive civilization based on a unique history, culture and territory. [. . .] Cultural nationalists seek to integrate and harmonize notions of tradition and modernity in an evolutionary vision of the community. [. . .] Although the idea of 'nation-race' was officially extended to include all the so-called 'national minorities' living within the political boundaries of the country, in practice it has remained confined to the 'Han' only. Similar to the racial taxonomies used by the reformers at the end of the nineteenth century, 'national minorities'

are represented as less evolved branches of people who need the moral and political guidance of the 'Han' in order to ascend on the scales of civilization.

(1996: 590)

The problematic integration of Chinese ethnic minorities in the national framework reveals all the difficulties inherent in China's transition from the multicultural dimension of a millenarian empire, to the logic of a modern nation-state in need of strong social and political bounds to cement its citizenship basis. This process is not exempt from inconsistencies: as the scholar Prasenjit Duara (2002: xiv) has noted, 'ironically enough, it is China as a modern nation-state that undertook the most unprecedented measures to homogenize and standardize the population'. Yet, it is important to point out that the communist government chose not to fully assimilate its ethnic minorities, nor to grant them the right to self determination. Rather, the politics of cultural difference took a third approach, based on a temporary 'tolerance' and a selective celebration of ethnic minorities' cultural difference.

In an effort to make sense of this move, some scholars have suggested that the ethnic policies of communist China retrieved and renewed the ideological basis of the empire. Magnus Fiskesjö for instance holds that:

[N]ew China is also a new formulation of the imperial Chinese model, which resurrects the corollary idea of civilisation as a transformative force that requires a primitive, backward periphery as its object. [. . .] Imperial tradition favoured the explicit recognition of 'ethnic minorities', formulated as 'barbarians' (that is, as a limit figure which simultaneously represents the threat which justifies imperial power, and serves as its favourite object of benevolent tutelage and civilising).

(2006: 15, 28)

In this perspective then, the construction of the ethnic minority as 'backward' and peripheral is instrumental to the production of the Han as 'central' and 'modern'. In museum displays of ethnic minorities, it is possible to locate a tension between China-the nation-state, and China-the empire – and, by extension, a tension between the unity and the cultural diversity of the Chinese nation. Ambivalent about its status as empire or nation-state, and unwilling to move away from a paradigmatic national unity resting on the cultural and historical centrality of Han civilisation, China is today compelled to negotiate its idealised national unity, against the undeniable cultural diversity of the populations inhabiting its territory. Such negotiation, as the repeated clashes between members of ethnic minorities and the Han majority show, is a difficult and thorny process. Crucially, as the scholar Stevan Harrell points out, the implementation of the Chinese government 'civilising project' entails that 'the civilising center, in its formulation of its project, needs to develop formal knowledge of the other and of itself' (1995: 7). It is precisely in the light of this need that one can fully appreciate the role of museums as privileged loci for the interpretation of ethnic minorities' cultures, and the dissemination of images and narratives aiming to objectify and standardise the 'ethnic Other'.

Narratives of ethnic minorities' inclusion and subordination in Chinese museums

Mieke Bal (1996: 3) notes that the act of display creates a subject–object dichotomy that 'enables the subject to make a statement about the object'. This observation is a valuable starting point for the analysis of the museum representation of ethnic minorities in China. Here, in fact, the voices of ethnic groups tend to be marginal if not absent from museum displays – their cultural alterity being staged to suit the needs of specific political agendas (Varutti 2008). How then are ethnic minorities represented in Chinese museums? Because ethnic minorities' voices are absent, and because of the marginal place of the intangible cultural heritage in museum displays, this question could be rephrased to read 'How is the *material culture* of ethnic minorities represented *by* museums'? This rephrasing highlights the arbitrariness of museums' representative and interpretative choices, and cautions that one pay attention to the implications of the over-emphasis on a selected range of ethnic minorities' objects.

The analysis of museum displays suggests that objects are interpolated by at least two major, interconnected narratives: of inclusion and subordination. In line with the official discourse that postulates the formal equality of all ethnic minorities, museum exhibitions assert ethnic minorities' status as Chinese citizens through a discourse that conflates historical and civic inclusion. Historical inclusion is attained through the inscription of ethnic minorities onto Chinese history. This strategy is pursued through the representation of harmonious relations between government officials and members of ethnic minorities. For instance, at the Yunnan Museum of Nationalities the visitor could see[2] life-size sculptures depicting officials from the People's Liberation Army (the military arm of the Communist Party) being warmly greeted by members of ethnic minorities during the Long March – the series of battles initiated in 1934 between supporters of the Communist Party and the Chinese Nationalist Party (Guomintang) and leading to the establishment of the Communist Party as the main political force under the leadership of a young Mao Zedong. Similarly, at the Museum of the University of Ethnic Minorities, a large wall painting depicts members of the People's Liberation Army welcomed by an exultant crowd in a village in Southern Yunnan. By materialising the positive role of ethnic minorities in the revolutionary cause and in the making of the Chinese nation, these fictional scenes aim to solder the civic bond between ethnic minorities and the Chinese government. At the same time, by providing a visual representation of harmonious inter-ethnic relations, they also ease the imagination – in Benedict Anderson's (1983) sense – of the multicultural Chinese nation.

The rhetoric of inclusion, however, is not confined to the past, it also unfolds in the present through the theme of civic inclusion expressed by the notion of 'nationalities unity' (*minzu tuanjie*). This is epitomised by the metaphor of the 'Chinese big family' whereby ethnic minorities allegedly 'consider themselves as descendants of common ancestors and members of the same big community' (Fei 1979: 3). The opening panels at the Museum of the Central University of Nationalities in Beijing eloquently illustrate this idea: 'China is a unified multi-ethnic country. Its fifty-six nationalities and their forebears are of one great cultural tradition, and they have formed a diligent, intelligent and peace-loving Chinese nation' [*sic*].[3] One of the most visually powerful ways in which museum displays communicate the ideas of unity and equality of all ethnic minorities is by juxtaposing similar items of ethnic minorities' material culture in a way that invites comparison, whilst at the same time, possessing the potential for variation. For example, at the Museum of Anthropology of the Yunnan University, the Nationalities Museum of Yunnan, the Museum of the Central University of Ethnic Minorities in Beijing, the Sichuan University Museum in Chengdu and the Museum of the University of South-Western Nationalities in Kunming, visitors are consistently presented with arrays of mannequins showing ethnic minorities' costumes, juxtapositions of musical instruments and of cooking vessels.

The metaphor of the 'Chinese big family' – central to Chinese nationalism – is also being translated in museum displays through the medium of wall paintings and murals. Large wall paintings including different ethnic groups can be seen in the Museum of the Central University of Nationalities in Beijing, the Yunnan Museum of Nationalities, the Museum of the University of Ethnic Minorities in Kunming and the Mengle Museum in Jinghong. These paintings usually depict members of ethnic groups (mostly female) immersed in lush natural environments in the context of creation myths, or happily tending to everyday activities such as agriculture, embroidery or paper-making. These depictions suggest the idea of an assemblage. Here, I concur with the scholar Tony Bennett, who suggests that museums operate as:

> [S]ites of assemblage, bringing together varied objects, practices and persons [. . .] [*thanks to their*] capacity, through the studied manipulation of the relations between people and things in a custom-built environment, to produce new entities that can be mobilized – both within the museum and outside it – in social and civic programmes of varied kinds.
>
> (2008: 7, 5)

How is this made possible? Following on Bennett (2008), by eradicating objects from their original context and locating them in an artificial, *ad hoc* environment – the wall painting, in our case – museums alter the perception of objects, their meanings, as well as the interrelations *among* objects and *between* objects and persons. Moving along the lines of this metaphor, the collective depictions of ethnic minorities through the medium of wall paintings contribute to modify both the identity of the ethnic group represented (objectified and essentialised in the painting), and the relations that ethnic groups entertain among themselves and with the Han majority (depicted as friendly and harmonious).

As a corollary of the theme of inclusion, one can identify in Chinese museums the theme of the subordination of ethnic minorities to the Han majority (see also Gladney 2004). In spite of the official discourse on the equal status of ethnic minorities, it is significant that whilst some ethnic groups are patently absent from museum displays (such as the Muslim Hui from the north-western provinces of Ningxia and Xinjiang), others are over-represented. For instance, no museum display of ethnic minorities would fail to include exhibits from the Naxi, the Dai or the Miao.[4] The Miao in particular, embody the iconographic ethnic minority: their spectacular silver headdress and body ornaments have become a trademark of displays of ethnic minorities' material culture in Chinese museums.[5]

The non-equal status of ethnic minorities one in relation to the other, and their collective subordination to the Han majority, emerges from a system of related narratives which, taken together, are meant to reveal the degree of 'backwardness' of each ethnic group. Such narratives revolve around the disruption of temporalities, specific gender construction and the infantilisation of ethnic minorities.

Museum representations of ethnic groups are framed by the notion of development and, more precisely, by developmental stage. This notion is a by-product of the evolutionist theories of social development embraced by the Communist Party. In this perspective, each ethnic group is constructed as more or less 'primitive' or 'modern'. This results in the hierarchisation of ethnic groups based on cultural and social features. For instance, in the Yunnan Nationalities Museum, agricultural methods employing 'slash and burn' techniques are described as 'primitive'; shamanistic practices are labelled as 'superstitious'; specific marriage rituals or funerary practices are described as 'backward'.[6] In order to ease the comparison of the developmental stage of each ethnic group, displays are consistently organised around the same object categories, including textiles and costumes, musical instruments, religious items, everyday tools and implements. One can find this taxonomy reproduced in a range of museums at various levels, including the Nationalities Gallery of the Shanghai Museum, the Nationalities Museum of Yunnan in Kunming, the Mengle Museum near Jinghong in Southern Yunnan and the remote Nanjian Village Museum in the mountains of central Yunnan.

The assumption that ethnic minorities are ageless – museum texts often describe ethnic groups as 'living fossils' (cf. Harrell 1995: 16) – that their culture delves its roots in an undetermined, remote past, is particularly intriguing when set against the fact that ethnic minorities are actually denied an historicity of their own: their non-Han, pre-communist past being simply omitted. For instance, the development of independent scriptural systems among ethnic groups is downplayed and presented as ancillary to Han Chinese culture in the permanent exhibition *Memories of Mankind: Exhibition of Ancient Documents of the Yunnan Ethnic Groups* at the Nationalities Museum of Yunnan. Here, museum panels explain that the ancient scriptural systems of the Yao, Zhuang, Bai and Sui ethnic groups of Yunnan were derived from Chinese characters ('by adding or cutting strokes from a Chinese character') as a result of the 'strong influence' of Han Chinese nationality. Moreover, the visitor is reminded of the benevolent salvaging role of government authorities, as museum texts emphasise that 'the Chinese Communist Party and Government have paid a lot of attention to the ancient documents of ethnic peoples since the People's Republic of China was founded in 1949'.[7]

In the same vein, the artistic and craft traditions originally developed by ethnic groups are not acknowledged as cultural features specific to the group in question. Rather, they tend to be described as 'rough' and 'primitive' versions of crafts ascribed to the Chinese civilisation. So, for instance, in the permanent exhibition of ethnic groups at the Nationalities Museum of Yunnan, the paper-making techniques developed by the Bai and Naxi ethnic groups are described as 'comparatively primitive ones [. . .] which can serve as living materials for the study of the start of paper making in Ancient China'.[8] Similarly, the panels in the Nationalities Gallery of the Shanghai Museum explain that 'the pottery made by the Dai nationality, through the use of traditional clay slip-strip forming techniques, has shapes of ancient simplicity' [*sic*].[9] In these displays, the recollection of ethnic minorities' past is only conceded to the extent and the condition that it upholds the argument of ethnic minorities' antiquity and 'backwardness', or serves the argument of their historical subordination to the culture of the Han majority. But it is denied in its main conceptual implication: the recognition that most ethnic groups have historically enjoyed a cultural independence from the Han Chinese (Harrell 1995).

The denial of historicity to ethnic minorities is coupled with a correspondent denial of modernity. Ethnic minorities can at best emulate the modernity of the Han; hardly ever is modernity ascribed directly to them. In a striking installation at the Museum of the Sichuan University of South-Western Nationalities, fifty-six ethnic groups are represented as small-scale plastic figurines; all ethnic groups except the Han are depicted in traditional ethnic costume, the Han figurine wearing blue, working style overalls. As James Clifford (2002: 161, emphasis in the original) has noted: 'what's different about peoples seen to be moving out of "tradition" into "the modern world" remains tied to inherited structures that either resist or yield to the new but cannot *produce* it'. Whilst ethnic minorities' cultures are repeatedly described as 'ancient' and 'traditional', assumptions of modernity and superiority of Han culture are implicit in museum texts such as the following 'in the past, some ethnic groups in Yunnan Province, paid a lot of attention to learning advanced Chinese Han culture'.[10] In these instances, the representation of ethnic minorities as backward, locked in a 'traditional' world is meant to provide a stark contrast to the modernity of the Han majority.

As Louisa Schein puts it with reference to China, 'in the official regime of representation, that which was excluded from state-defined modernity (i.e. local tradition) was not "disappeared", but rather rendered hyper-visible in order to highlight, by contrast, the civilized character of the state' (1997: 90). In this sense, museum displays instantiate the argument that the peripheral, backward minority is instrumental to the construction of the modern Han political and cultural core. More precisely, the above mentioned narrative constructions that museums unfold about ethnic minorities' 'backwardness' and 'antiquity', bear the effect of disrupting temporalities at two levels: first, they establish an 'internal temporality' for each ethnic group (through the attribution of a more or less 'backward' position), and, secondly, they transform the 'backwardness' of ethnic minorities into a backdrop for the expression of the modernity of the Han-centred State.

Narratives of subordination of ethnic minorities to the Han majority also develop around ethnic minorities' gender, and more precisely the construction of ethnic groups as female. The privileged subject of museum pictorial representations of ethnic minorities, in photos, paintings or sculptures, are young, smiling, attractive women wearing colourful ethnic costumes. These kinds of representations aim to crystallise a close association between a set of features considered female prerogatives – such as acquiescence, submission, docility, exoticism, simple-mindedness, inarticulateness, 'closeness to nature' – and the 'character' of ethnic groups, thus contributing to the construction of the ethnic minority as female, as opposed to the Han male (cf. Gladney 1994).

The narratives of subordination also adopt the metaphor of life stages to construct the ethnic minority as a child, with its corollary of condescending and paternalistic approaches (in this sense see also Schein 1997: 75). For instance, panels at the Yunnan Nationalities Museum describe members of ethnic groups in these terms: 'brave, intelligent and unsophisticated people [. . .] working together with diligence and intelligence'. Here again, the life stage metaphor is a discursive device that enables the transposition of the ethnic group to a different temporal framework and its simultaneous subordination to the Han. It is also worth noting that the strategy of infantilisation bears intriguing Confucianist undertones. By portraying the ethnic minority as a child, the Han set for themselves the role of the knowledgeable, wise, guiding adult. The relationship so established between the ethnic group and the Han is not simply one of generational disparity, but a typically Confucian relation of the kind father–child, master–student or emperor–subject, calling into play the Confucian moral imperatives of respect for the elderly and for ritual, which would confer moral and philosophical legitimacy to the Han's claim of superiority.

Conclusions: standardising difference

In closing this analysis of the representation of ethnic minorities in Chinese museums, one is reminded of the words of Sally Price commenting on Western approaches to 'primitive art':

> [O]nce having determined that the arts of Africa and Oceania are produced by anonymous artists who are expressing communal concerns through instinctual processes based in the lower part of the brain, it is but a quick step to the assertion that they are characterized by an absence of historical change.
>
> (2001: 61)

The similarities with the treatment reserved for ethnic minorities in Chinese museums are striking, and lead one to wonder whether, to a certain extent, ethnic minorities are for the Han Chinese what the societies from which 'primitive art' emanates are for Western art connoisseurship: an object to be appropriated in its material, conceptual, artistic, political, emotional and symbolic properties.

By focusing on a set of fixed object categories and by displaying side by side the material culture of each ethnic group, displays of ethnic minorities in Chinese museums tend to reduce cultural difference to its minimum terms, to folklorise it, to make it comparable (hence scalable) and ultimately suitable for integration into the Chinese nation. The rich intangible heritage of Chinese ethnic minorities does not find expression in museum displays, which conversely focus on a limited range of objects. Quite paradoxically, the tangible expression of the cultural diversity of ethnic minorities – their extraordinarily varied material culture – is interpreted and displayed in museums in a fashion that contains variation within a pre-established matrix in order to produce a sense of seriality and homogeneity. Through the manipulation of the material culture of ethnic minorities, their cultural diversity is being 'standardised' in order to produce similarity and, consequently, a sense of national unity.

The inclusion of ethnic minorities in the visual ethnoscape of the Chinese nation (to which museums are tributaries) is instrumental to the validation of the master narrative of the nation (see Harrell 1995, Schein 2000, Blum 2001). Yet, such inclusion is partial and conditional. Extolling ethnic minorities' folklore, and in the same breath describing them as culturally and technologically in need of modernisation, museum representations of ethnic minorities succeed in obviating any expression of substantial cultural difference. Conversely, the expressions of cultural difference that do find their way in museums consistently focus on ethnic minorities' materiality – ethnic costumes, musical instruments, personal adornments, food vessels and so on. This kind of display significantly contributes to the folklorisation of ethnic minorities' cultures. Also, and most importantly, these displays are non-menacing since they do not call into question the links of ethnic minorities' cultures to Han Chinese culture, as would, for instance, a comprehensive representation of the historical trajectories of ethnic groups, of ethnic scriptural and language systems, or religious cosmologies. The cultural difference of ethnic minorities is thus embraced only to the extent that it does not threaten the unity and the 'harmony' of the Chinese nation. To this effect, it could be said that museums contribute to the production of an array of similar forms of difference. Almost ironically, as a result, cultural diversity is expressed as an unequal relation among equivalent forms of difference.

The choice to downplay cultural difference and to emphasise the idea that ethnic minorities are simply 'lagging behind' the Han, bears the important conceptual implication to construct the cultural difference of the ethnic minority as temporary, transient, bound to disappear over time, as the ethnic minority 'evolves' along the path of development to reach the level of the Han. This discourse enables the transposition of cultural difference on a temporal rather than substantial level. In a move not too dissimilar from the one described by Joannes Fabian (1983) in *Time and the Other* – whereby anthropological accounts transpose the object of study to a different temporal level by spatialising time (*there* is the past, *here* is the present) – the Chinese government is constructing the Otherness of ethnic minorities as a temporary category. The ethnic minority lives far away, in a *there* that is past, whereas the Han live in a *here* that is present and modern.

As a result, the representation of the Other in Chinese museums does not involve a process of construction or translation of cultural difference, but of *denial* of alterity. Such a strategy entails not so much assimilation or integration, as internalisation of difference *via* its standardisation. Whilst assimilation requires the prior existence of some form of difference and its recognition (the process of Othering is also, in a way, constitutive of the Other), in the Chinese case we are confronted with a process of internal 'neutralisation' of difference. China defines itself as a 'container' of nationalities, but crucially these are constructed as differing not in their cultural substance but in their degree of 'Han-ness', defined as a temporal variable. Through their displays, Chinese museums are ultimately agents in implementing a political agenda aimed at containing and standardising difference by reducing it to its minimal terms and by transforming it into a temporal category.

The full representation of cultural difference may become problematic in those countries, like China, that need to enforce their unity. The weaker the civic, political and moral bonds between the government and its citizens (as is the case with several of China's ethnic groups, notably the Tibetan and the Hui), the stronger the need for narrative and visual representations of national unity. This should lead to a rethinking of the assumption that the ongoing processes of modernisation and socioeconomic development are bound to improve museums' potential for social inclusion. The Chinese case study shows that modernisation can actually leave untouched, if not contribute to deteriorate, engrained configurations of the relations between the nation, museums and their communities.

Acknowledgements

Fieldresearch in China was made possible thanks to the support of the Swiss National Science Foundation (SNSF) and the Swiss Agency for Development and Cooperation (SDC-KFPE), which I gratefully acknowledge. I would also like to thank the volume's editors and reviews for their comments. Of course, any misinterpretations or inaccuracies are my own.

Notes

1 The fifty-five officially recognised Chinese ethnic minorities only account for less than 10 per cent of the population (Wang 2004: 6).
2 This gallery, which I visited in Spring 2006, was being refurbished in occasion of my second visit in Spring 2008.
3 Museum panels, Museum of the Central University of Nationalities, Beijing, last visited May 2006.
4 Members of the Naxi ethnic group mostly inhabit the area of Lijiang, in northern Yunnan. A matrilinear society, the Naxi developed an independent pictographic script, mainly used for religious texts. Naxi women are known for their elaborate costume including a sheepskin cape embroidered with seven stars, which often features in

museum displays. The Dai ethnic group is mostly located in the southern areas of Yunnan. The influence of Thai culture from Thailand – to which the Dai culture is closely related – is present in Dai language, architecture, food, clothing and religion (most Dai people are Theravada Buddhists). Over the last decade, Xishuanbanna, the area of Yunnan inhabited by the Dai, has become a major tourist attraction for the wealthy Chinese of the coast. The Miao are an ethnic group mainly inhabiting the mountainous province of Guizhou, in southern China. The Miao are immediately recognisable for their extraordinarily rich costumes, including complex embroideries and elaborate silver headdresses and personal adornments. In contrast to the Naxi, Dai and Miao, the Hui ethnic group is less visually prominent – members of the Hui are hardly distinguishable from the Han majority – and much less 'exotic'. Over the last years, members of Hui ethnic group have been involved in violent clashes with Han Chinese due to social discrimination and demands for autonomous rule in Hui areas. For an overview on Chinese ethnic minorities see Mackerras (2006).

5 On the diverse images of the Dai, Hui and Naxi ethnic groups, see Blum (2001), especially 'Part II: Prototypes of Otherness'.
6 Museum panels, Nationalities Museum of Yunnan, last visited April 2008.
7 Museum panels, Nationalities Museum of Yunnan, last visited April 2008.
8 Museum panels, Nationalities Museum of Yunnan, last visited April 2008.
9 Museum panels, Shanghai Museum, last visited February 2008.
10 Museum panels, Nationalities Museum of Yunnan, last visited April 2008.

Bibliography

Anderson, B. (1983) *Imagined Communities: reflections on the origin and spread of nationalism*, London: Verso.

Bal, M. (1996) *Double Exposures: the subject of cultural analysis*, London: Routledge.

Bennett, T. (2006) 'Exhibition, difference and the logic of culture', in I. Karp *et al.* (eds) *Museum Frictions: public cultures/global transformations*, Durham, NC: Duke University Press.

Bennett, T. (2008) 'Anthropological assemblages: producing culture as a surface of government', *CRESC Working Paper Series*, no. 52. Available online at: http://www.cresc.ac.uk/publications/documents/wp52.pdf (Accessed September 2010).

Blum, S.D. (2001) *Portraits of 'Primitives': ordering human kinds in the Chinese nation*, Lanham, MD: Rowman & Littlefield Publishers.

Brown, J.N. and P.M. Sant (eds) (1999) *Indigeneity: construction and re/presentation*, Commack, NY: Nova Science Publishers.

Chakrabarty, D. (2002) 'Museums in late democracies', *Humanities Research*, IX (1).

Clifford, J. (2002) 'The others: beyond the salvage paradigm', in R. Araeen and S. Cubitt (eds) *Third Text Reader on Art, Culture and Theory*, New York: Continuum International Publishing Group.

Dikotter, F. (1996) 'Culture, "race" and nation: the formation of national identity in twentieth century China', *Journal of International Affairs*, 49 (2): 590–606.

Duara, P. (2002) 'Foreword', in S.D. Blum and L.M. Jensen (eds) *China Off Center: mapping the margins of the middle kingdom*, Honolulu: University of Hawaii Press.

Fabian, J. (1983) *Time and the Other: how anthropology makes its object*, New York: Columbia University Press.

Fei, X. (1979) *Modernisation and National Minorities in China*, Occasional Papers of the Centre for East Asian Studies 6, Montreal: McGill University.

Fiskesjö, M. (2006) 'Rescuing the empire: Chinese nation-building in the twentieth century', *European Journal of East Asian Studies*, 5: 15–44.

Friedman, E. (1994) 'Reconstructing China's national identity', *Journal of Asian Studies* 53: 67–91.

Friedman, E. (1995) *National Identity and Democratic Prospects in Socialist China*, New York: M.E. Sharpe.

Gladney, D. (1994) 'Representing nationality in China: reconfiguring majority/minority identities', *Journal of Asian Studies*, 53: 92–123.

Gladney, D. (2004) *Dislocating China: reflections on Muslims, minorities, and other subaltern subjects*, Chicago: University of Chicago Press.

Golding, V. (2009) *Learning at the Museum Frontiers: identity, race and power*. London: Ashgate.

Harrell, S. (ed.) (1995) *Cultural Encounters on China's Ethnic Frontiers*, Seattle: University of Washington Press.

Hendry, J. (2005) *Reclaiming Culture: indigenous people and self-representation*, New York: Palgrave Macmillan.

Hsiau, A. (2000) *Contemporary Taiwanese Cultural Nationalism*, London: Routledge.

Karp, I., C.M. Kreamer and S.D. Lavine (eds) (1992) *Museums and Communities: the politics of public culture*, Washington, DC: Smithsonian Institution Press.

Karp, I. *et al.* (eds) (2007) *Museum Frictions: public cultures/global transformations*, Durham, NC: Duke University Press.

Knell, S., P. Aronsson and A.B. Amundsen (eds) (2010) *National Museums: new studies from around the world*. London: Routledge.

Macdonald, S. (2003) 'Museums, national, postnational and transcultural identities', *Museum and Society*, 1: 1–16.

Mackerras, C. (2006) *China's Ethnic Minorities and Globalisation*, New York: Routledge Curzon.

Morgan, L.H. (1985 [1877]) *Ancient Society*, Tucson: University of Arizona Press.

Peers, L.L. and A.K. Brown (eds) (2003) *Museums and Source Communities*, London: Routledge.

Price, S. (2001) *Primitive Art in Civilized Places*, Chicago: University of Chicago Press.

Schein, L. (1997) 'Gender and internal orientalism', *Modern China*, 23: 69–98.

Schein, L. (2000) *Minority Rules: the Miao and the feminine in China's cultural politics*, London: Duke University Press.

Schwarcz, V. (1991) 'No solace from Lethe: history, memory and cultural identity in twentieth century China', *Daedalus* 120: 85–111.

Simpson, M.G. (2001) *Making Representations: museums in the post-colonial era*, Durham, NC and London: Routledge.

Stanley, N. (1998) *Being Ourselves for You: the global display of cultures*, London: Middlesex University Press.

Stanley, N. (ed.) (2007) *The Future of Indigenous Museums: perspectives from the Southwest Pacific*, Oxford: Berghahn Books.

Suresh, T. (2002) 'Rediscovering nationalism in contemporary China', *China Report* 38: 11–24.

Tu, W.M. (1993) 'Introduction: cultural perspectives', *Daedalus* 122 (2): vii–xxiii.

Varutti, M. (2008) 'A Chinese puzzle: the representation of Chinese ethnic minorities in the Museums of Kunming, Yunnan Province of China', *International Journal of the Inclusive Museum*, 1 (3): 35–42.

Wang, C. (2004) *Ethnic Groups in China*, Beijing: China Intercontinental Press.

Watson, S. (ed.) 2007 *Museums and their Communities*, London: Routledge.

Witcomb, A. and C. Healy (eds) (2006) *South Pacific Museums: an experiment in culture*, Clayton, VA: Monash University ePress.

22 Displaying the Communist Other

Perspectives on the exhibition and interpretation of Communist visual culture

Amy Jane Barnes

Introduction

The visual culture of the Great Proletarian Cultural Revolution (1966–76), upon which this chapter focuses – has been, I would argue, an active agent in the development of Western perceptions of the People's Republic of China (PRC).[1] Its interpretation may be problematic. Three aspects are key: the tensions inherent in its display (especially outside the temporal, ideological and geographical context of its creation); its role in mediating (sometimes subverting) official and unofficial histories of the Cultural Revolution; and what it represents (both visually and symbolically), challenging the image of contemporary China promoted in the West by the PRC and received images of China and 'Chineseness' in the West. With these issues in mind, this chapter takes a critical look at two contemporary British examples of institutions with collections of Cultural Revolution-era visual culture, using aspects of collecting theory theorised by Susan Pearce. I will delimit the extent of contemporary collecting practice within this subject area, and begin to reveal the tension between material of an explicitly propagandist nature, and representations of Chinese art and culture within an orientalising discourse. While recognising that there are highly practical (and pragmatic) influences upon the collection, interpretation and display of this material, among them the challenges of presenting to audiences the Cultural Revolution as a sociopolitical and ideological phenomenon, and the macro political considerations that collecting and displaying institutions have to take into account when entering into high profile and potentially lucrative (in both terms of financial and intellectual return) relationships with the Chinese cultural authorities (for a closer examination of these aspects see Barnes 2009). After a description of the focal collections, this chapter turns to a particular, theoretical aspect: the challenge that the visual culture of the Cultural Revolution presents to deeply entrenched museal representations of China and the traditional Western canon of art.

However, I am aware that many of us[2] in the West have little more than a cursory knowledge of Maoist China. The cultural productions of the Cultural Revolution are, I would argue, inextricably tied to the ideological ambitions of the communist state. In order to 'see' beyond their superficial aesthetic qualities and to gain a more complete sense of their sociopolitical meaning and their inherent power as propaganda tools, it is necessary to begin with a brief overview of the historical context.

The Cultural Revolution: politics and art

The decade 1966–76, which we now call the Great Proletarian Cultural Revolution, began with Mao Zedong's struggle to regain power after the failure of the 'Great Leap Forward': an ambitious and ultimately flawed programme of socialist development.[3] It ended with his death on 9 September 1976. Although portrayed somewhat erroneously in the West as a period of perpetual ultra-repressive state control and political terror, the influence of radical Maoist elements in the Party waxed and waned after the initial years of the Cultural Revolution: the so-called manic phase of the Red Guard movement and the political ascendancy of the People's Liberation Army (PLA). After the death of Mao's erstwhile heir apparent, Marshal Lin Biao, apparently following an abortive coup, the armed services over whom Lin had held command were relieved of their power and the martial character of the Cultural Revolution abated. The rest of the period was characterised by a struggle for Mao's favour, with Jiang Qing and Premier Zhou Enlai the principal players. Zhou was a relative moderate and under his aegis the restrictive controls placed upon art and culture were somewhat loosened, catalysed in no small part by the visit of US President Richard Nixon to the PRC in 1972.

Art was central to the dissemination of Maoist ideology, and the promotion of the cult of Mao was integral to the movement. Borrowing from Lenin, the Chairman proclaimed that proletarian literature and art were the 'cogs and wheels in the whole revolutionary machine' (Mao 1967, speech given in 1942). As such, the cultural sphere was rigidly controlled by Mao's appointed cultural supremo and fourth wife, Jiang Qing and her radical clique. For her part, Jiang was clear that paintings 'must serve the workers, peasants, and soldiers' (Jiang 1968, cited by Schoenhals 1996: 197). Culture was to become a battlefield.

By the mid-1960s a peculiarly Chinese version of Soviet Socialist Realism,[4] one that fused hyper-realism with traditional Chinese *guohua*[5] and *nianhua*,[6] had emerged. It was this genre that was to become the sanctioned art of the Cultural Revolution.

It was predominantly figurative, with the revolutionary trinity of worker, peasants and soldier as its subject, depicted in dynamic poses heavily influenced by the performing arts (a field over which Jiang exerted total control).[7] Colours were brilliant and borderline gauche (Johnston Laing 1998: 64). Red predominated, the liberal use of which was used to indicate revolutionary spirit and loyalty to Mao and the Party. Accompanying slogans were bombastic and their meaning unambiguous. Largely anonymous and sometimes collective, works of art were instilled with the spirit of the commune. Opportunities for personal interpretation (for both producers and audiences alike) were excised. Thus, as an educational or propagandist weapon, the message was assured. It is not for nothing that the decade has been described as a 'big blank' (Andrews 1994: 314) by those artists who were active during the period.

'New China' displayed

With the scene thus set, the attention of this chapter is now drawn towards a consideration of Cultural Revolution-era visual culture in Britain and the exhibitionary genesis of collections held by British institutions. One outcome of the re-opening of diplomatic relations between East and West was increased contact with, and availability of information from the PRC in Britain. Cultural exchange resulted in *Genius of China* (29 September 1973–23 January 1974), a blockbuster exhibition of new archaeological finds shown at the Royal Academy, which helped to challenge and salve contemporary Western concerns about the fate and conservation of Chinese cultural heritage.[8] The exhibition presented little of Mao's China, being comprised of dynastic bronzes, ceramics, jades, metalware and textiles, which reflected deeply entrenched ideas about Chinese art in the West.

The visual culture of 'New China' made its first, in-gallery appearance in Britain during the summer of 1974. A small, low-key display of woodcut prints, predominantly on political themes, were displayed at the then Gulbenkian Museum of Oriental Art in Durham, far from Britain's cultural epicentre. It was not until 1976, during a period which straddled Mao's death and the final death throes of the Cultural Revolution, that the first *official* exhibition (jointly arranged by the British and Chinese cultural authorities) of post-1949 Chinese art was mounted in the UK: *Peasant Paintings from Hu County*.

The exhibition grew from an ambitious initial plan of the Arts Council of Great Britain which aimed to represent contemporary China alongside a more traditional exhibition on the subject of Daoism. Concurrently, the Chinese cultural authorities offered a touring exhibition of peasant paintings[9] from Jiang Qing's pet project, the model artist commune at Huxian in Shaanxi province, to the Great Britain–China Centre (GBCC). The GBCC was a not-for-profit organisation set up after *Genius of China*. It subsequently deferred to the Arts Council as 'the best qualified' organisation to host the paintings.[10] A deal was struck and the exhibition replaced the larger proposed show on Daoism. Between 1976 and 1977, it went on tour to seven locations in Britain – London, Cardiff, Edinburgh, Birmingham, Nottingham, Stockton-on-Tees and Bromsgrove. The full exhibition comprised seventy-eight original paintings and two woodblock prints. The majority of the works, a selection made by the Chinese authorities, were painted circa 1973 by sixty amateur artists. It featured several works that were to become contemporaneously well known in the West, among them *Our Commune's Fishpond* by Dong Zhengyi (Figure 22.1) and Liu Zhide's *A Veteran Party Secretary*.

A range of diverse reasons, such as availability, value-for-money, individual interest and institutional policy, were responsible for the development of collections of Cultural Revolution-era visual culture in Britain, not to mention the wider popular and ideological context of British society during the late 1960s and 1970s, which are impossible to examine fully here. But one can view these early examples of contemporaneous Chinese art displayed in Britain as laying the foundations for the recognition of and attribution of museum-value upon the genre. The following section of this chapter introduces and offers an exploration

Figure 22.1 Dong Zhengyi. *Our Commune's Fishpond (Gong she yu tang)*. June 1974. Chinese Poster Collection, University of Westminster.

of three particular extant examples. While several museums count amongst their holdings small numbers of visual culture specifically pertaining to the Cultural Revolution,[11] the two most significant collections in public hands – and the foci of this chapter – are held by the Victoria and Albert Museum (V&A) and the British Museum.

Contemporary collections

Victoria and Albert Museum

The V&A's collection comprises one of the largest assemblages of post-1949 and Cultural Revolution-era material culture in Britain today.[12] Particularly notable for ceramics and paper-cuts on socialist themes, the collection is augmented by a diverse range of objects – textiles, badges, mugs, works-on-paper, posters, desk plaques, portrait busts and figures – for the most part dated to the decade 1966–76. Many of the ceramics are high quality pieces and were not produced for mass market consumption. Instead, they were destined for the collections of high-ranking officials, visiting dignitaries and foreign guests. This somewhat belies one of the key stereotypes of the visual culture of the Cultural Revolution; that it was produced by, and destined solely for consumption by the masses. However, other objects in the collection are more representative of quotidian material culture, among them propaganda posters with impeccable provenance purchased direct from the factory at which they were printed, and Mao badges acquired during the latter half of the Cultural Revolution by future members of V&A staff studying in China under the aegis of the British Council. The collection developed from a combination of private donation, collecting in the field on behalf of the museum, and direct purchases. The bulk was acquired throughout the 1990s, although objects entered the museum as early as the late-1970s, and acquisitions continued to be made throughout the last decade.

To date, objects from the collection have been sparingly displayed. From 1992, until the exhibition was re-installed, in a slightly altered format, in an adjacent gallery space in 2008–09, a selection of ceramic Mao badges and covered mugs were displayed in a design-focused exhibition, located in the Twentieth Century Design Galleries, alongside a group of objects pertaining to youth culture from across the Cold War ideological divide and interpreted as relics of Western socio-political activism.[13] The turn of the millennium saw the first and, to date, only substantial exhibition of this material: the temporary exhibition, *Mao: From Icon to Irony* (October 1999–April 2000), which ran alongside *Fashioning Mao*, another temporary display which examined the contemporary commodification of the Mao image by fashion designers Vivienne Tam and Flora Cheong-Leen. The display featured eighteen pieces from the V&A collection, supplemented by an additional eighteen objects, or groups of objects, lent by private collectors. Contemporary Mao memorabilia and political kitsch – original art, mugs, a watch and a Shanghai Tang t-shirt, amongst other items – were juxtaposed with Cultural Revolution-era objects, including badges in various media, desk plaques, a silk picture and a porcelain figure of Mao. Interpretively, these objects were explored from a design history perspective. The exhibition sought to chart the development of the iconic use of the image of Mao Zedong from 1949 to the present day, with a particular focus on how revolutionary themes had been iconoclastically recycled by contemporary Chinese artists.

More recently, the twentieth century has invaded the T.T. Tsui Gallery, the principal display space for Chinese objects at the V&A. A subtly political Cultural Revolution-era ceramic is now displayed in the main body of the gallery: a high-quality, polychrome figure of Li Tiemei (dated to 1969), heroine of the model opera *The Red Lantern*. The inclusion of this figure in a gallery space more usually reserved for dynastic China was a significant gesture, which went some way towards closing the gap between the typical museological separation of pre- and post-revolutionary China (examined in closer depth in the following section).

This concession to the twentieth century, albeit small, reflects the V&A's recent efforts to throw off the shackles of its modernist, predominantly aesthetic approach. A cogent example, which partially deconstructed this tradition, was the temporary exhibition *Cold War Modern* (25 September 2008–11 January 2009), which explored European and North American art and design during the years 1945–70. The central premise of the exhibition was that 'Art and design were not peripheral symptoms of politics during the Cold War: they played a central role in representing and sometimes challenging the dominant political and social ideas of the age' (Anon. 2008). It reflected the material manifestations of 'anxiety and hope' (Anon. 2008) that characterised the period on both sides of the ideological divide, highlighting the sometimes symbiotic relationship between East and West. This was an exhibition that explored sociopolitical history as much as it presented an image of mid-twentieth century design.

The Cultural Revolution appeared in a corner of 'Revolution', the sixth section of the exhibition, and was interpreted from the perspective of late-1960s political activism in Europe and the attendant romanticisation of 'the exploits and ideals of revolutionaries in China and Cuba and liberation movements in Africa, Asia and Latin America' (Anon. 2008). Accompanied by excerpts, on continuous loop, from Jean-Luc Godard's *La Chinoise* (1967) – Godard was a prominent French Maoist – the Cultural Revolution section featured just two objects, both from private collections:[14] a 1967 woodblock printed propaganda poster, emblazoned with the typical slogan 'Down with US Imperialism. Down with Soviet revisionism', and a Mao suit.

British Museum

In comparison, the British Museum came late to post-1949 and Cultural Revolution-era material, but its holdings now rival the V&A's collection. The museum holds a modest number of badges and a growing collection of propaganda posters (and original artwork) based upon a single donation made in 2002, and since augmented by a significant purchase (of around seventy posters) at auction in 2006 (see Barnes 2009: 275). Curators have also acquired artists' prints, textiles, ceramics, nianhua and paper-cuts.

Little of the collection has been displayed until recently. A standing sculpture of Mao and a Cultural Revolution-era polychrome figure featured in the inaugural exhibition held in the Great Court gallery from December 2000, but the collection otherwise remained in storage (admittedly like the vast proportion of most institutions' collections) until the opening of the temporary exhibition *Icons of Revolution* (10 April–14 September 2008), in which the museum's Mao badges (and related material) were interpreted predominantly as historical artefacts (much more so than the V&A's approach, which was, despite the thematic ordering of the exhibition, predominantly focused on aesthetic aspects). The exhibition was intended by its curator, Helen Wang, to present the key visual iconography of the Cultural Revolution: to reveal its antecedents and development, and the perpetuation of its symbolic value into the twenty-first century. She has commented that 'everyday life [in Cultural Revolution-era China] was saturated with symbolic imagery' (Wang 2008: ix), and therefore one cannot begin to comprehend the Cultural Revolution without an awareness of the *meaning* behind the iconography. The link between image and text in revolutionary visual culture is key to this understanding, but while some of the more oblique slogans and allusions would be clear to their original intended audience, contemporary visitors generally require additional background information to engage fully with the objects on display. Wang (personal communication 2008) was keen to explore through the medium of display, how the Cultural Revolution material fitted with the rest of the China collection in the British Museum. The exhibition would, she planned, go some way towards explaining what contemporary China *is* and how the Cultural Revolution fits into the development of the PRC. These objectives – the situation of the visual culture of the Cultural Revolution within a broader discussion of Chinese art *and* political history – made the exhibition unique in Britain.

China as Other, China as counter-cultural icon

The historical Othering and Otherness of China in European imaginings is well documented (Pagani 1998, Spence 1999, Mackerras 1999, Hung 2003, Barnes 2010). While the historical relationship between East and West has been far from consistent and highly contingent upon the political aspirations of both parties, a general theme characterises Western imaginings of China since the earliest known contact during the Roman Empire: at times a utopian ideal, at others, a dystopian nightmare, but always exotic (in that it is strange and different), mysterious and unknown (unknowable). To paraphrase Said (1995), the imagined China has functioned throughout history as a mirror, reflecting back at us what we believe we are, and what we believe we are not.

Perceptions of communist China cannot be separated from China per se. Despite the radical political, social and cultural changes the Chinese people have witnessed over the last century, the PRC is still China: the thought of which triggers similar, often dichotomous images to those that have characterised the popular British consciousness of China since the eighteenth century, if not before: inscrutable, irrational, cruel, exploitable, spiritual, visionary, reactionary, threatening. These images need not have a definite footing in reality. In many ways the *reality* of China and the *idea* of China have long been divorced in popular imaginings. As Cohen has put it: 'China and its people might have been a series of ink-blots, a Rorschach test, to which responses revealed more about the responder than about China' (1993: 272). China, in the Western consciousness, has always been more than empirical knowledge can boast. Mackerras reminds us: 'Images are not . . . the same as reality. At all times there is an infinity of realities' (1999: 1).

I would argue that Cultural Revolution-era China is, in particular, 'othered' to the power of three in Western discourse. Not only is it geographically and temporally removed from contemporary British experience, it represents an ideological Other. This aspect deserves further enquiry, especially with respect as to how ideological difference correlates with collecting practice. To these ends, Susan Pearce's discourse, as theorised in *On Collecting* (1995), may be illuminating.

The location of propagandist art (which communist art essentially is, to a greater or lesser degree) in the discourse of collecting, as theorised by Pearce, is of particular cogency to this chapter. Measured against modernist ideals (which one can detect in the legacy of Cold War imaginings) and conventions of normality, Pearce (1995) identifies communism *in Europe* as 'the Other within'. She asserts that from this perspective, the collection of objects pertaining to the Other within might be deemed 'improper', transgressive and irrational. It suggests an engagement (on the part of the collector) with a converse set of beliefs, a skewed mirror image of oneself, a tangible threat: such material offers 'inverted comment[aries] upon the normal' (Pearce 1995: 323). One might imagine that was exactly the effect that those members of the British counter-culture who displayed communist memorabilia in their homes (as posters) and upon their person (as badges) – the very subjects of 'Style as Statement' at the V&A – wished to broadcast about themselves to the wider community (indeed, Schrift 2001: 194 confirms this summation): difference, rebellion, ideological otherness. In this sense, Pearce's 'Other within' corresponds with the Orientalist Other in Saidian discourse: as a counterpoint to European rationality and/or a 'subversive commentary upon "normal" culture' (Pearce 1995: 323). Communist China is clearly without Europe, but a parallel surely exists. The utopian fantasy nominally offered by Maoism – its ideology of equality, the promise of a united workforce, shared ownership and communality – appealed to a left-wing counter-culture that sought to challenge the status quo.

Strangely, despite access to more accurate and balanced information about the realities of daily life under communism that the end of the Cold War and collapse of the Soviet Union facilitated and, perhaps, most influentially in the case of the Cultural Revolution, the mass of 'scar literature' which has found its way onto Western bookshelves,[15] Maoist China has remained just distant enough (spatially and ideologically) to develop a veneer of 'cool'. The iconography of the Cultural Revolution can be found in a diverse variety of contexts, from advertising to fashion (see Barnes 2009). Why have these images perpetuated in Western sub-cultural (and increasingly pop-cultural) contexts? Is it because those students and intellectuals who bought into Maoism in the 1960s and 1970s have gone on to work in the creative industries that promote and repackage sub-cultural coolness for a mass audience, the 'rebel sell' as Heath and Potter (2005) would put it? Or, is it simply because owning, displaying and wearing objects that pertain to communism are not exactly taboo, but just dangerously rebellious enough to produce 'an enjoyable emotional *frisson*' (Pearce 1995: 323)? The voidance of meaning facilitated by commodification has, in tandem with the passing of time, created a potent, yet malleable visual code which can, depending upon the needs of those making use of it, represent a two-dimensional utopian idealism, or dystopian nightmare: either way, discharged of its potentially 'dangerous' ideological content.

Simply put, the iconography of Chinese communism has been subsumed into the visual alphabet of contemporary Western popular culture. Used as little more than revolutionary kitsch, devoid of its original, albeit multiple, meanings (depending on the viewer's/consumer's – in the broadest possible sense – cultural background and personal ideologies), it has been thoroughly commodified, assimilated and appropriated. In skewed reflection of its earlier, counter-cultural application, it may represent a parody of the habitus, a commentary upon socially constructed systems of aesthetics and knowledge. To this category belong pop art and kitsch: 'copies begotten on the wrong side of the moral and aesthetic blanket' (Pearce 1995: 305). We now recognise the aura of subterfuge that hangs over propagandist art. We exploit, manipulate, subvert its contrary ideology to suit a new role: as capitalist commodity or a comment upon thereof. 'The reason why it [and not other mass-produced material] arouses us is because we don't always feel like being worshipful, [to our own 'Gods' as much as those of other times and regimes] even if it is at our shrine. Humans share a giggling, sniggering streak' (Pearce 1995: 305). Thus, what implications does this context – the Western consumption of Chinese communist visual culture – have for British museums?

To explore this question, one must consider the traditional and largely still omnipotent representation of China in British museums. This representation will reflect the modernist perspective that Chinese art history ended abruptly in 1911 with the nationalist revolution that ousted the Qing, the last dynasty, from power. It will, by association, decry the cultural productions of the preceding two centuries as sullied by Western influence and thus less authentically Chinese (read 'valid'). It will echo the preferences of 1930s scholars, who codified the Western history of Chinese art, and perceived the 'true' essence of China in ancient bronzes and ceramics. But it will also feature export ware and *chinoiserie*, lacquered furniture and silks, reflecting the passions of earlier donors. Thus, it will focus on dynastic China and, in so doing, perpetuate and consolidate images of 'old' China into the twenty-first century. What it will rarely do is engage with the twentieth and twenty-first century, the products of which – where displayed – will typically be displayed in a separate area, without the bounds of 'China' within the museum cosmology. Never the twain shall meet, because the cultural products of the twentieth and twenty-first centuries do not adequately reflect the 'proper' China as understood within the modernist paradigm.[16] The ruptured history of twentieth century China would undoubtedly require an engagement – on the part of curator and audience – with difficult and unsettling ideas and images that would challenge and disrupt the otherwise smooth, linear narrative: images that would cause 'us' to think as much about our own prejudices and self-identity, as those of revolutionary China.

Such tendencies (unconscious or otherwise) can be evidenced by the practice-based examples given in this chapter. At the V&A, the majority of objects pertaining to the Cultural Revolution are displayed in the Twentieth Century Design Gallery, in another part of the museum. This makes the inclusion of the Li Tiemei figure in the Tsui Gallery, at first glance so innocuous, in practice such a radical and noteworthy move. At the British Museum too, *Icons of Revolution* was situated in a position removed from the display of dynastic Chinese objects, in a gallery adjacent to the Department of Coins and Medals (which hosts the Mao badge collection), but otherwise in a section of the museum dealing with Roman and Greek artefacts.

The visual culture of the Cultural Revolution does not just have the potential to subvert conventional perceptions of Chinese art and culture. Its interpretation feeds into wider perceptions of what 'art' is understood to be. The modernist legacy places the art of other cultures in the realm of ethnography, itself borne out of evolutionary theory and the myth of scientific objectivity. Authentic art, so the traditional canon tells us, is rarefied, spiritual and singular. It reflects and consolidates ideas about ourselves. It confers intellectual and moral prestige upon its owner. It represents and supports the status quo, the cultural habitus. Thus, it is important enough to be preserved in a museum: a hegemonic institution closely associated with the development and expression of national identity. From this modernist perspective the development of a Western history of Chinese art per se was disruptive. It could not be dealt with in the same manner as the cultural productions of other, *Other* societies. It could not be classified as anthropological 'artefact'; China had a written history and theory of art that pre-empted the Western canon by centuries and its visual culture correlated, to a degree, with Western notions of art. 'A Chinese picture could be bad art, failed art, but it could not cease to be art at this point' (Clunas 1998: 45). A solution was to imply that Chinese art had already reached heights from which it was impossible to move on (King 1999: 1). Diversity and development were dealt with by being ignored. Innovation and imitation based upon Western art movements were decried as 'inauthentic'. This essentialisation of Chinese art was 'a way of reducing the threat . . . [it posed] to the single, linear history of art as a story that takes place above all in Europe' (Clunas 1999: 135). Even more so, communist Chinese visual culture does, in neither subject, form nor aesthetic value, conform to this received canon of art. Its fundamental fault, aside from its preoccupation with the political message, is its populist character.

Into the category of 'improper' collecting, Pearce (1995: 323) also places popular culture. The visual culture of communist China comprises – or is perceived to comprise – mass and popular cultural elements: its visual referents are often the 'masses', even if it has not been made – as was certainly the case with a proportion of the material held by the V&A, for example – with the mass consumer in mind. Thus, it is anathema to modernist Western canon with its emphasis upon 'high' art, lofty aesthetic ambitions and the artist-genius. Given this context, and the new, popular manifestations and associations of revolutionary iconography – its commercialisation in Western contexts (the ultimate irony), wrenched from its original ideological context and meaning – the visual culture of the Cultural Revolution is at odds with the canon. If we now perceive this material as, to use Kundera's term, 'communist kitsch' (1984: 248) and generally accept that kitsch is *not* art, nor culturally and historically valuable, one can appreciate the tensions at play in its selection and interpretation for display and the consequent confirmation upon it of museum-worthy status.[17]

Conclusions

This chapter has looked at several exhibitionary examples and considered the unique aspects of communist visual culture which challenge the hegemonic character of one of the bastions of modernism, the museum. At first glance, one might seem to contradict the other. I have directed a great deal of attention to the problems inherent in this material and the reasons why it might not be displayed but, on the other hand, have described several attempts at just that. However, these are the exceptions to the rule that while much to be lauded, have not been universally successful for the reasons I have identified as potential challenges. The achievements of the V&A, in particular, are stymied by a seeming reluctance in more recent years to engage with this material directly,[18] and a preference instead to interpret it from a partially emasculating Western perspective. It also remains profoundly bonded to the 'traditional' separation of dynastic and contemporary China (although recent practice evidenced in both temporary exhibitions and the Tsui Gallery, suggest that these boundaries might be permeable). For its part, the British Museum has taken only coy, small-scale and time-limited steps towards making its growing collection visible, again in separation from its more established and, perhaps, 'authentically' Chinese dynastic material (modernism still holds museums in its thrall).

Nevertheless, these collections have been made, in part, to redress the balance between representations of Old and New China. Can 'we', therefore, read these collections as intimations of a radical dismantling of museum modernism? Or, are they simply the continuation of a long-standing pattern of collecting from China? To address the latter first, the collection of this material frequently predates its display in the same institution by a number of years. It has thus been recognised as important to collect. But equally it is the only material available to collect from that period of twentieth century Chinese history, given the total saturation of Maoist ideology in the cultural sphere. At both the V&A and British Museum, the process of acquisition fits with earlier traditions. The V&A collects graphic art and contemporary design. The British Museum has a long tradition of acquiring contemporary prints and numismatics from around the world. It remains to be seen how these collections might develop and be interpreted in the future before we might come to some sort of conclusion as to their significance. However, it seems to me that the materiality of the Cultural Revolution is the key to the exploration of this period of history. While debate within China is stifled – the 'ugly past' thrown off (Gao 2008: 31) – Western museums, as potential sites of mediation between people and objects, and history and narrative, offer an opportunity to engage openly with the difficult legacy of the Cultural Revolution. The museum may operate as 'a public forum for discussion': it can offer a 'surrogate home . . . for debates that would otherwise be placeless' (Williams 2007: 130).

Objects, particularly those loaded with such a complexity of sociopolitical, cultural and historical meaning as those pertaining to the Cultural Revolution, fail to provide all the answers. They cannot, in themselves, provide any explanation for that decade. However, while the Cultural Revolution remains in living memory, individual voices may revitalise and advance new approaches to the interpretation of its visual culture. Techniques employed in dark tourism, such as the use of personal stories to drive the accompanying interpretation, may help to challenge the view that the visual culture of the Cultural Revolution is somehow distasteful, corrupt or invalid.

In the final assessment, why should British museums collect the visual culture of the Cultural Revolution? In China, a collective, official amnesia has hung over that decade. As *Icons of Revolution* at the British Museum attempted to show, the Cultural Revolution casts a shadow upon contemporary Chinese politics, society and culture, to which the West is economically so tied: to paraphrase David Crowley[19] this is our history too. The utilisation of objects, as media for the dissemination of knowledge, is familiar and comfortable, particularly with regards to information about China, with which the West has a centuries-old material engagement. The visual culture of the Cultural Revolution may challenge pervasive Orientalist ideas about China: a sense of 'Chinese-ness' that reveals more about ourselves and deeply rooted paternalistic attitudes towards art, than any reality of China in the twenty-first century.

Notes

1 I refer readers to my recent thesis 'From Revolution to Commie Kitsch: (re)-presenting China in contemporary British museums through the visual culture of the cultural revolution' (Barnes 2009) for a more complete discussion.
2 I take Torgovnick's view (1990: 4), which elaborates upon Malinowski's, that 'we' and 'us' refer to the 'narrative of the empowered' (Malinowksi cited by Torgovnick 1990: 4): white, literate, educated and middle class. 'We' imagines a primitive 'Them'. 'We' and 'us' are used 'strategically'; us-and-them thinking structures all discourse about Self and Other (Torgovnick 1990: 4). The direct use of these terms is intended to provoke a sense of discomfort in the reader and to expose the illusion of a representative Other, exposed and 'processed . . . through a variety of tropes' (Torgovnick 1990: 18).
3 I refer readers interested in the political context of the Cultural Revolution to Mac-Farquhar and Schoenhals' (2006) *Mao's Last Revolution*, widely accepted as the definitive work on the subject.
4 Based upon the nineteenth century European academic tradition, the genre is characterised by near photo-realist, large-scale oil painting, frequently depicting the Great Leader or an historic and politically significant event. Content is narrative and its message is intended to be read by the viewer. The key aspect of Socialist Realism is its pursuit of an indisputable truth. The emphasis on realism renders the interpretation of the subject – be it historical event or utopian pastoral scene – fact. These painterly truths are easily manipulated.
5 Traditional brush and ink painting.
6 'New Years' prints, a popular folk-art form.
7 The guiding principles of the reformed performing arts were that they should portray contemporary (communist) society and promote a positive view of the proletariat, free of bourgeois and feudal elements. Between 1961 and 1966, Jiang oversaw the reform of traditional Beijing opera, resulting in the creation of eleven 'model' works, comprised of revolutionary operas, ballets and a musical score. Each presented a particular incident from the revolutionary history of the PRC – largely related to war and resistance – and each featured highly stylised heroic characters inspired by Mao Zedong Thought. Landsberger (1998: 29) has observed that looking upon a propaganda poster dating from the Cultural Revolution is rather like observing a piece of theatre; subjects are portrayed realistically and are always flooded with light, at the centre of the 'action'.
8 Nevertheless, during the Cultural Revolution, 4,922 of Beijing's 6,843 officially designated places of cultural or historical interest were destroyed, by far the greatest number during the 'red terror' of August and September 1966 (MacFarquhar and Schoenhals 2006: 118).
9 Produced by ostensibly untutored amateur artists.
10 ACA: Ford, J.F. 1976. Letter to Joanna Drew, 10 March 1976.
11 Examples being the Ashmolean Museum, Oxford, the University of Westminster's China Poster Collection and the University of Hull's South-East Asia Museum.
12 My research has determined that there are some 200 objects in the collection, not including the individual leaves of paper-cut albums.

13 A section from the accompanying text panel read:

> Frequently the image has expressed an attitude to established society, which has sometimes been a reforming one. Ironically, in these instances the social role has become transposed from designer to consumer. These objects demonstrate the role of design both in the expression of aspiration and of social identity. In doing this they present design as an identifying uniform.

14 Rather surprising given the wealth of Cultural Revolution-era objects in the V&A's own collection.

15 As a literary genre, Scar Literature (*shanghen wenxue*) describes suffering under Mao, frequently with an autobiographical element. Among its best well-known authors are Jung Chang, Nien Cheng and Anchee Min.

16 Indeed, Clunas (1999: 135) has commented that, from the perspective of the modernist canon, the modern Chinese artist simply cannot exist; they are either 'Chinese artists' and work in a traditional genre, or 'modern artists', in which case their ethnicity is perceived to be irrelevant.

17 For a deeper analysis of kitsch see Greenberg (1939).

18 Particularly telling is the continued absence of a catalogue of this material, despite several decades of concerted effort to collect post-49 China (see Barnes 2009).

19 Crowley, David (2010), *Star City: The Futurological Congress*, 12 February, Nottingham.

Bibliography

ACA: Arts Council of Great Britain records, 1928–1997, held by Archive of Art and Design, Victoria & Albert Museum (Blythe House).

Andrews, J.F. (1994) *Painters and Politics in the People's Republic of China, 1949–1979*, Berkeley, Los Angeles and London: University of California Press.

Anon. (2008) *Cold War Modern* [Visitor Guide], London: Victoria & Albert Museum.

Barnes, A.J. (2009) 'From Revolution to Commie Kitsch: (re)-presenting China in contemporary British museums through the visual culture of the cultural revolution', unpublished doctoral thesis, University of Leicester.

Barnes, A.J. (2010) 'Exhibiting China in London', in S.J. Knell, P. Aronsson, A.B. Amundsen, A.J. Barnes, S. Burch, J. Carter, *et al.* (eds) *National Museums: new studies from around the world*, London and New York: Routledge, pp. 386–99.

Barringer, T. and T. Flynn (ed.) (1998) *Colonialism and the Object: empire, material culture and the museum*, London and New York: Routledge.

Clunas, C. (1998) 'China in Britain: the imperial collections', in T. Barringer and T. Flynn (eds) *Colonialism and the Object: empire, material culture and the museum*, London and New York: Routledge, pp. 41–51.

Clunas, C. (1999) 'What about Chinese art?', in C. King (ed.) *Views of Difference: different views of art*, New Haven and London: Yale University Press, pp. 121–41.

Cohen, W.I. (1993) 'Western images of China', *Pacific Affairs*, 66: 271–2.

Evans, H. and S. Donald (eds) (1999) *Picturing Power in the People's Republic of China: posters of the Cultural Revolution*, Lanham, Boulder, New York and Oxford: Rowman & Littlefield.

Gao, M. (2008) *The Battle for China's Past: Mao and the Cultural Revolution*, London and Ann Arbor: Pluto Press.

Greenberg, C. (1939) 'Avant-garde and kitsch', in C. Greenberg and J. O'Brian (1988) *The Collected Essays and Criticism: perceptions and judgments 1939–1944*, Chicago: University of Chicago Press, pp. 5–22.

Greenberg, C. and J. O'Brian (1988) *The Collected Essays and Criticism: perceptions and judgments 1939–1944*, Chicago: University of Chicago Press.

Heath, J. and A. Potter (2005) *The Rebel Sell: how the counterculture became consumer culture*, Chichester: Capstone Publishing.

Hung, Ho-Fung (2003) 'Orientalist knowledge and social theories: China and the European conceptions of East–West differences from 1600–1900', *Sociological Theory*, 21 (3): 254–80.

Johnston Laing, E. (1998) *The Winking Owl: art in the People's Republic of China*, Berkeley, Los Angeles and London: University of California Press.

King, C. (ed.) (1999) *Views of Difference: different views of art*, New Haven and London: Yale University Press.

Knell, S.J., P. Aronsson, A.B. Amundsen, A.J. Barnes, S. Burch, J. Carter *et al.* (eds) (2010) *National Museums: new studies from around the world*, London and New York: Routledge.

Kundera, M. (1984) *The Unbearable Lightness of Being*, London: Faber and Faber.

Landsberger, S. (1998) *Paint it Red*, Groningen: Groningen Museum.

MacFarquhar, R. and M. Schoenhals (2006) *Mao's Last Revolution*, Cambridge, MA and London: Harvard University Press.

Mackerras, C. (1999) *Western Images of China* (2nd edn), Oxford and New York: Oxford University Press.

Mao, T.T. (1967 [1942]) *On Literature and Art*, Peking: Foreign Languages Press.

Pagani, C. (1998) 'Chinese material culture and British perceptions of China in the mid-nineteenth century', in T. Barringer and T. Flynn (eds) *Colonialism and the Object: Empire, material culture and the museum*, London and New York: Routledge, pp. 28–40.

Pearce, S. (1995) *On Collecting: an investigation into collecting in the European tradition*, London and New York: Routledge.

Said, E.W. (1995) *Orientalism: Western conceptions of the Orient*, Harmondsworth: Penguin.

Schoenhals, M. (ed.) (1996) *China's Cultural Revolution, 1966–1969: not a dinner party*, New York: M.E. Sharpe, pp. 197–202.

Schrift, M. (2001) *Biography of a Chairman Mao Badge: the creation and mass consumption of a personality cult*, New Brunswick, NJ and London: Rutgers University Press.

Spence, J. (1999) *The Chan's Great Continent: China in Western minds*, New York: W.W. Norton & Company.

Torgovnick, M. (1990) *Gone Primitive: savage intellects, modern lives*, Berkeley, Los Angeles and London: University of California Press.

Wang, H. (2008) *Chairman Mao Badges: symbols and slogans of the cultural revolution*, London: British Museum Press.

Williams, P. (2007) *Memorial Museums: the global rush to commemorate atrocities*, Oxford and New York: Berg.

23 Reconsidering images

Using the Farm Security Administration photographs as objects in history exhibitions

Meighen S. Katz

> Too often museums have been content to rest with seductive appearances and forensic promise of photographs, as if this is all that photographs can do. Assumed to function didactically and unproblematically, photographs set the 'economy of truth' for a museum (Porter 1988) whatever their ideological and political nuances.
>
> (Edwards 2010: 27)

As Edwards has postulated, the interpretive potential of images remains under-utilised in museum exhibitions. Beginning with that premise, operating within the scope of history exhibitions, and using the Farm Security Administration photographs taken in the 1930s as an example, this chapter considers in practical terms the re-interpretation of photographic collections to engage more fully with their interpretive potential. Arguably, if photographs were more widely treated as objects within museums, if they were considered using the same criteria as three-dimensional objects, then aspects of their creation and use would be considered on par with their content. As will be discussed, to do so allows museums a great deal more scope for examining the ideas and debates of the eras from which these images emerge.

History exhibitions and use of photographs

Within the practice of history exhibitions, photographs have been most often used as a secondary level of interpretation, providing context and support for the physical objects (Edwards 2010: 27, citing Porter 1988). Images are employed as visual representations of things rather than interpreted as the thing itself. While this reflects a much larger cultural trend within photographic analysis (Edwards 2009: 36), within a museological context such practices do not reflect the full interpretive value of historical art, particularly photography. A telling example is to be found in (*significance*), an Australian publication by the Heritage Collections Council designed to aid museums in developing criteria for collection and deacquisition policies (Russell and Winkworth 2001). The book contains a great many photographs but amongst the many case studies there is not one example of a photograph as an object (though several paintings are included).

The closest is an *in situ* collection of swim club memorabilia that includes photographs, though they are not accorded specific discussion. The attraction of photographs as contextual tools is understandable. Within an exhibition, images add depth, both in meaning and literally in terms of light and shadow; photographs provide texture to the flat edges of an exhibition, the walls and plinths. That said, images have the potential to do much more when considered as objects.

History exhibitions as a form, have, for the most part, become narrative-driven largely a result of influence of social history on curatorial practice. As such, history museums and exhibitions have frequently featured in debates about the primacy of objects (Crewe and Sims 1991: 165, 171, Moore 1997: 50, Kavanagh 2000: 7, Trinca 2003: 88). Largely absent from these debates, however, is discussion of the use of any form of images within history exhibitions. Though particularly pronounced in the historical branch of curatorial practice, gaps in discourse with regards to use of images spans the breadth of the museology (Edwards 2010: 21, 27). Edwards has gone some way to rectifying this absence with regard to the materiality and the attendant sensory experiences of photographs (see Edwards 1999, 2006, 2009, 2010). In addition, Edwards, Janice Hart and Deborah Poole have all examined the use of images within anthropological exhibitions (Poole 1997, Edwards and Hart 2004). But historical and anthropological approaches to exhibitions, while related, are engaged with different processes, subjects and cultural parameters. Surprisingly little has been done to explore how photographs may be best incorporated into the specific practice of historical interpretation. Of the few writers who have examined history exhibitions with regard to the use of photographs, their greatest emphasis has been on those exhibitions concerned with the incidents of violent oppression, those of the Holocaust and apartheid in South Africa (Newbury 2005, Crownshaw 2007).

And yet we are consumers of photography; familiar with seeing images associated with a wide range of experiences, certainly those of war and oppression, but also of periods of celebration and rejoicing. From horse races to political races, we are conditioned to expect that an image will accompany and enhance any verbal or written information.

American photography during the Great Depression

Arguably, some of the aforementioned expectation of visual communication has its origins, at least within American culture, in the 1930s. This decade is most often defined in the USA by the Great Depression. However, as cultural historian Warren I. Susman noted, the 1930s also marked a profound shift in American culture, one that included a new a focus on image and sound. It was, in part, through the new technologies of radio and talking pictures, that Americans negotiated the crises of the era (Susman 1984: 160). In particular, the omnipresence of the photograph becomes a key component of this shift, and thus to the way the Depression era as a whole is remembered and interpreted.

Americans of the 1930s encountered photography in a number of ways; it was an era when existing periodicals began to reproduce high-quality photographs in large numbers and when new publications such as *US Camera*, *Life* and *Look* emerged to celebrate photographs as an art form, or to use photo essays as a new form of narrative. A range of subjects as diverse as Hollywood starlets and urban sociology came illustrated by well-produced images direct to the street-corner newsstand and, via subscription, to the American living room. Susman's sight culture was not just the result of visits to movie-palaces and museums; it was also part of the home-life.

When curators were planning the National Museum of American History's 1982 exhibition *FDR: The Intimate Presidency*, their planning notes indicate that they consciously included these publications, designating the illustrated periodicals as an essential element representing a medium as omnipresent as the radio in American life at that time (Smithsonian Institution Archives 1981). Readers turned to high-end magazines like *Vogue* and *Vanity Fair* for fashion photography and Edward Steichen's celebrated celebrity portraits (Raeburn 2006: 61–79). As photography became increasingly popular both as a hobby and as an art form, camera periodicals such as *US Camera* reproduced some of the finest works of the period. *Survey Graphic*, a Progressive, social-reform journal with an eye on a popular audience among intellectuals, began publication in 1921 with the express purpose of communicating the need for social change through visual methods (Finnegan 2003: 57–63). Less intellectual than *Survey Graphic* but still committed to visual communication were *Life*, published by media magnate Henry Luce (who already published *Time* and *Fortune*), *Look* which developed from the Sunday spread of the *Des Moines Register*, and *Midweek Pictorial*, an off-shoot of *The New York Times* which emerged during the First World War (Finnegan 2003: 171–2, 175–6). Though they emerged later than some of their competition, *Look* and *Life* were, according to Cara Finnegan, the most successful (2003: 175). So great was the interest in developing and formalising this new form of communication that the executive editor and the art director of *Look* taught a course at New York University in 'picture writing' and in 1945 published a book entitled *The Technique of the Picture Story: a practical guide to the production of visual articles* (Finnegan 2003: 179). In 1940, Farm Security Administration photographer Russell Lee credited *Life* and *Look* with making Americans, 'very photographic minded' (Finnegan 2003: 174–5).

The Farm Security Administration collection

However, what truly sets the 1930s apart in terms of American visual memory and experience are the massive photographic projects undertaken by the federal agencies of Franklin Delano Roosevelt's New Deal. Most famous are the photographs of the Resettlement Administration/Farm Security Administration/Office of War Information (RA/FSA/OWI).[1] But numerous agencies, including the US Department of Agriculture, the Civilian Conservation Corps and the National Youth Administration, used photographers to document their activities. The Works Progress Administration also supported a number of established photographers under the Federal Arts Project (Daniel *et al.* 1987). The result is a vast visual record of the decade. The Library of Congress file of the RA/FSA/OWI pictures number 164,000 separate black and white negatives and that is but a single agency, albeit a particularly prolific one (Library of Congress 1998).[2]

William Stott has argued that it is through the reproduction of these images that most Americans born after that period have come to know the Great Depression, but it was also through these images that many Americans in the 1930s came to understand the crisis (Stott 1986: 67). He cited the recollections of Frederick Lewis Allen and Caroline Bird, both of whom spoke of an absence – of people and of activity – so that while one could sense the problem, it was not instantly identifiable (Stott 1986: 67–8). As photography became more prevalent, particularly documentary photography, images began to fill the void. Photography became a way to negotiate the unseen but unnerving. Susan Sontag has argued there exists a relationship between photography, knowledge and the quest for an individual sense of security in uncertain times (Sontag 1977: 4–8). Pete Daniel, one of the curators of the Smithsonian Institute 1987 exhibition *Official Images*, speculated as to the desire for photographs on the part of Depression-era Americans:

> Maybe the answer is simple. Maybe people feeling deprived of material goods were attracted to those images that most closely resembled the look, surface, and solidity of *things*. Maybe, too, people feeling suddenly insecure about the future were comforted by photography's apparent matter-of-factness, even when the 'facts' were often distressing. Most likely, the appeal of photography contained contradictory impulses: to document *and* transform, to gain familiarity *and* distance.
>
> (Daniel *et al.* 1987: viii, emphasis in the original)

As Daniel's commentary indicates, photography of the 1930s is significant not only because of the sheer size of the collections, but because it reflects a particular approach towards obtaining knowledge and understanding that was prevalent in the USA in the inter-war years.

This period saw the emergence of the social sciences, which sought to combine the data collection of the hard sciences with studies of the human condition. *Middletown*, the Lynds' landmark study of Muncie, Indiana, was published in 1929 and set the standard for sociological methodology that was favoured by many Progressives of the period, including many in the Roosevelt administration. Roy Stryker, who led the Historical Section of the RA/FSA (as the photographic division was known), maintained a friendship with Robert Lynd and discussions with Lynd influenced Stryker's shooting scripts (Finnegan 2003: 42, Raeburn 2006: 161). The photography of the decade, therefore, provides both a visual and ideological insight into American society of the 1930s.

Great Depression photography in the museum

How then does a curator bring those ideological insights to the exhibition floor? It is true that the Great Depression shares some connections with the Holocaust or South African apartheid in terms of trauma and, for some, the experience of violence. However, the Depression experience is not as confined by violence or by the unmitigated malevolence of those in power. The images of the FSA are not of violence, and they are not, as are the family photographs in the tower space of the US Holocaust Museum and Memorial, defined by our knowledge of the tragic fate awaiting those pictured (Crownshaw 2007: 185). In exhibiting these images in a modern museum, another paradigm must be utilised, one that allows curators and visitors alike access to the many aspects of American Depression-era culture reflected by these images.

One possible approach lies in re-engaging with the specific materiality of these photographs. Daniel's observation suggests that in the 1930s there was a greater sense of photographs as material, a perception that has perhaps been lost in the intervening decades. Photographs, as Edwards and Hart asserted, 'are both images *and* physical objects that exist in time and space and thus in social and cultural experience' (2004: 1). Or, to put it another way, photographs are both representational and material (Edwards 2010: 21, 27).

Photographs and materiality

Materiality, as Dudley has argued, is a broad church, but for the purposes of this examination it can be understood as the intersection between meaning, physical form and sensory experience (2010: 8). For the purpose of this particular analysis, the sensory aspects are less central, with greater focus on incorporating the relationship between photographs' material form and meaning into history exhibitions. In this process of incorporation, Deborah Poole's theory of visual economy, though framed for anthropological discourse, is instructive. Poole argued that photographs need to be understood through three levels of organisation: the organisation of production, which includes both individuals and technology, the organisation of circulation, and the organisation of appraisal and assigning of worth (Poole 1997: 9–10). While the curator, the historian, the museum and the audience all, in a sense, continuously enact a process of appraisal, the first two processes should be considered alongside the content of an image as part of the history of any given photograph. In using the photography of the New Deal agencies for exhibition in an historical context, as opposed to an artistic one, who made them, why they were made and how they were disseminated should therefore be part of the formula.

Arguably, the FSA images are useful for interpreting three distinct but interrelated Depression-era experiences. Within the composition lies an experience of (predominantly) rural poverty. Within the production of the image, the creation, lies the experience of the photographer as the employee of a New Deal agency, as well as discussions of technology. Once that image has been taken, it takes on its own story, which invokes the history of circulation and the concepts of audience. The production and circulation of these images are widely discussed by photographic and cultural historians (see Curtis 1986, Stott 1986, Levine 1993, Starr 1996, Sandweiss 2002, 2007, Finnegan 2003). However, museums, with the exception of a few stand-out exhibitions, such as the ones here discussed, have largely overlooked this aspect.

This Great Nation Will Endure: Photographs of the Great Depression **exhibition**

The photographs taken by the Farm Security Administration (FSA) during the American Great Depression and New Deal have been exhibited many times, starting in the 1930s (Dixon 1983: 233–4, 247–9, Raeburn 2006: 102–5). They have been reproduced in textbooks and on postage stamps to the point where many Americans will recognise the more famous of the images such as Dorothea Lange's *Migrant Mother*. Given this familiarity, one might question why in 2004/2005 the Franklin D. Roosevelt Presidential Library and Museum chose to stage and then tour a major exhibition on these images. But their exhibition, *This Great Nation Will Endure: Photographs of the Great Depression*, made use of a number of interpretive techniques such that the photographs were re-interpreted and recontextualised, not along artistic grounds per se, but in order to better understand the society that experienced and created the New Deal. These interpretive strategies allowed the audience to engage with photographs in a manner that parallels the ways that museums often encourage them to engage with three-dimensional material culture.

Taking its name from a line within Roosevelt's first inaugural address, and curated by Herman Eberhardt, *This Great Nation Will Endure* included 200 photographs from the Library of Congress' RA/FSA/OWI file. One of the simplest methods employed in re-interpreting this collection of images lay in the way the exhibition was organised. The photographs were arranged by region rather than the more conventional grouping according to photographer. Providing a regional overlay to the exhibition allowed audiences to compare different photographers' approach to the similar regional experiences; for example, cotton sharecroppers in the South photographed by Ben Shahn were viewed alongside that same subject as photographed by Dorothea Lange, or photographs of the houses of the urban poor shot by Russell Lee juxtaposed with those by Arthur Rothstein. Organising by geography both encouraged consideration of the photographer's role in selection of images and worked against the mythology of a single visual narrative of poverty.

Re-introducing photographers as people

Another simple, inexpensive, highly accessible key to interpreting the images employed by the FDR Presidential Library and Museum was the provision of brief biographies of the photographers. Reminding the audiences that the photographs were taken by real people may seem to be stating the obvious, but it carries more weight than might first be apparent. One of the conclusions to be drawn from Rosenzweig and Thelen's landmark study of Americans' relationship to the past at the end of the twentieth century was that respondents put more faith in sources that they perceived to be unmediated. Thus, television was not a trusted source, not only because of its commercial connections, but because audiences worried about the ways in which it might impede their interaction with an 'impartial' account of the past. On the other hand, museums were seen as highly trustworthy because they were perceived as unmediated (arguably, a misconception since it does not account for curatorial choice) (Rosenzwieg and Thelen 1998: 90–1).[3]

Photographs, especially when presented as the collection of a government agency, run the risk of being perceived as a similarly unmediated source, which raises the question: does the camera lie? Australian historian Graeme Davison said of popular history that a 'just the facts ma'am' approach worked better for television detectives than it ever does for historians because, 'the "facts" are a response to questions, and one person's questions are never quite the same as another's' (Davison 2000: 6). The same may be said of the 'truth' in photographs, as they reflect the human beings who took them. Certainly, James C. Curtis has argued that Dorothea Lange's past work as a portrait artist is visible in the pictures that she took for the FSA (Curtis 1986: 14, 16–17). Similarly, it may be enlightening for the audience to know that Ben Shahn was, first and foremost, a painter and graphic artist, or that Gordon Parks was the only African-American photographer employed by the FSA, as all of these factors can influence the relationship between photographer and subject.

Advocating a re-evaluation of museum collections along similar lines, Susan M. Pearce has argued that refocusing on the collector or creator could serve to revitalise older museums. Pearce used the example of a nineteenth century butterfly collection from New Guinea, suggesting that the collection tells much more than just the story of butterflies; it also speaks, through the collector's life-story, to nineteenth century concepts about masculinity and the relationship to the natural world (Pearce 1999: 15–16). The FSA photographs do not necessarily cry out for revitalisation in the same manner as the collections of many natural history museums. Nevertheless, a broader collection of Depression-era experiences becomes accessible through curatorial engagement with the narratives of the images' creators. The photographers' stories provide points of entry for exploration of the experiences of New Deal employees and promoters, of African-Americans, of working women and of artists. Colleen McDannell has suggested that, 'by moving back and forth between what is in the photograph, who took it and why it was taken, historians can construct new narratives of old stories' (McDannell 2007: 114).

Reproduction and circulation of the FSA photographs

A discussion of FSA photographs is, almost exclusively, one about reproduced images. In this way they are set apart from other museum objects, in which the actual object rather than a reproduction is sought. It also distinguishes them from some other historical photographs. Edwards has discussed the way photographs assert their 'physical presence in the social world', that is to say, the way that they are physically handled, shared, damaged, preserved or hidden (Edwards 2010: 23). The FSA images, as they appear in exhibitions, have rarely undergone such experiences. Nevertheless, to engage with the FSA images as interpretive objects is to engage with the process of reproduction. Indeed, where, and how they were reproduced, and how those reproductions altered the image is one of the most crucial aspects about them. For the FSA photographs were not merely collected and kept in government files for future study.[4] Therefore, in answering McDannell's 'Why was the photo taken?' it is essential to factor in dissemination, the third plank of Poole's visual economy. These images are not the product of an individual creative impulse, but the work of government agency in the midst of a national crisis and they were reprinted and disseminated in numerous publications.

Dorothea Lange's *Migrant Mother*, for example, appeared initially in *The San Francisco News* (March 1936) in an article on the plight of starving pea-pickers, then in *Survey Graphic* (September, 1936) alongside an article by Paul Taylor entitled 'From the ground up' with the caption 'Dragging around people', in *Midweek Pictorial* (17 October 1936) with a headline that urged readers to 'Look into her eyes!' and then in the *US Camera Annual* (1936) (Levine 1993: 284, Starr 1996: 250, Finnegan 2003: 97–102, 140). In each case, depending on intended audience and message, the cropping, the exposure and the caption changed (Finnegan 2003: 97–102, 140–4). Part of the interpretive power of photographs is that they are materially malleable; that is to say, even as they change form they retain their historical authenticity. As such they become a powerful tool for unlocking the visual language and the driving informational discourses of a society in which they were created and used.

This Great Nation Will Endure included an audiovisual presentation on the use and reproduction of these images within various publications. In doing so, it provided audiences with a point of access to relationships of creation and reproduction. It also actively engaged with issues and debates surrounding use of the images, their recreation and circulation. For example, the exhibition illustrated how different cropping of images – that is, mutation of the object's physical parameters – changed their meaning. It explored this process through one of the most potent examples within the FSA collection, Lange's image *Plantation Owner: Mississippi near Clarksdale, Mississippi* (1936; Figures 23.1 and 23.2).[5]

This photograph features a white man, his foot resting on the bumper of his car, and African-American sharecroppers sitting on the steps behind him. When the image was included in poet Archie McLeish's 1938 book *Land of the Free*, the image was cut down to remove the sharecroppers, leaving only the man and his car, now reframed and reformatted from a position of power, alongside McLeish's poem, to that of an 'everyman' (Levine 1993: 270–1).[6] The image and its editing speak to debates about race and power and entitlement that were prolific throughout the New Deal era. The image becomes a powerful object for exploring those debates, but it is only through engagement with the physical aspects of the image, its dimensions and their mutations, and by treating the image as an object rather than just an illustration that those entanglements become transparent.

Figures 23.1   Dorothea Lange, *Plantation owner. Mississippi Delta, near Clarksdale, Mississippi* (1936),
and 23.2   original (L) and McLeish crop (R). Library of Congress, Prints and Photographs
Division, FSA-OWI Collection, LC-USZ62-103367 DLC.

By examining both where and how the FSA images were reproduced, museum
audiences are given insight into the aims of the creators, the photographers, the
FSA and the federal government. But they are also given the opportunity to
conceptualise their own counterparts within the historical period, the audience
of the 1930s for whom the images were initially intended. The images were taken
and reproduced with a specific target audience in mind, and the images that were
chosen, the different ways in which a same image was reproduced becomes
important in terms of that audience. The acknowledgement of an audience that
was present in the 1930s also allows for discussion of visual language of that period.

Migrant Mother and the visual language of the 1930s

Like many exhibitions, *This Great Nation Will Endure* included Dorothea Lange's
most famous picture, now known as *Migrant Mother* (Figures 23.3 and 23.4).[7]
Lange's portrait of a migrant Oklahoman pea-picker, Florence Owens Thompson,
and her children is arguably the most recognisable image from the USA in 1930s,
indeed one of the most recognisable photographic images within American history. It has been used as a synecdoche for the Depression experience by everyone
from textbook publishers to the Smithsonian to the US Postal Service. What is
less well known is that that the image is actually the last of six that Lange took
of the family.

This Great Nation Shall Endure employed a computer interactive which allowed
the visitor to access not just the familiar image, but Lange's full series.[8] By viewing
the lead-up photos the museum visitors were able to see the process of compositional framing and decisions that Lange made. Decisions which James C. Curtis
has argued were dictated as much by a sense of the audience in the 1930s, of
their social mores, prejudices and cultural reference as they were by any aesthetic
considerations (Curtis 1986). In his article, 'Dorothea Lange, *Migrant Mother*

Figures 23.3(a–d) Five of the six images from Dorothea Lange's *Migrant Mother* (1936) series
and 23.4 concluding with the last and most famous photograph. (NB: The first
photograph of the series was not included in the Library of Congress
file.) Library of Congress, Prints and Photographs Division, FSA-OWI
Collection, LC-USZ62-58355, LC-USF34-9097-C, LC-USF34-9093-C,
LC-USF34-9095, LC-USF34-9058-C.

and the culture of the Great Depression', Curtis (1986) traced the six shots that Lange took and which speak to the process by which the photographer sought to find the image that best suited the needs of her employer, the Resettlement Administration. The inclusion of a plate or a trunk becomes an allusion to the traditions of portraiture, for just as the rich were portrayed surrounded by artefacts of wealth, the poor are captured alongside those of migration and deprivation (Curtis 1986: 13–14). An older teenage daughter and piles of laundry visible in earlier shots are framed out in subsequent pictures as they may have lessened middle-class sympathy (Curtis 1986: 9, 13). Lange also positioned the trio in pose of familial affection, the child's head resting against her mother's shoulder. Curtis postulated that this provides a message that even in the midst of the crisis, there is still an intact family unit; these are people with values (Curtis 1986: 14, 16–17). This last allusion is particularly important as it serves to contradict what Kevin Starr has called the 'Tobacco Road canard', referring to Erskine Caldwell's popular novel that cast the Southern poor as morally degenerate (Starr 1996: 241). One of the goals of FSA photographers was to create a new vision of the migrant poor as people of good character who were victims of circumstance rather than corrupt lifestyles (Levine 1993: 283, Starr 1996: 252). All of Lange's visual allusions are considered yet subtle, and all become visible when the series is viewed one in conjunction with the other, accompanied by brief indicators. Together they illustrate, as Curtis has suggested, that '[Lange] created a portrait that incorporated elements she knew her contemporaries would understand and find worthy of support' (Curtis 1986: 2).

Martha Sandweiss argued that both intent and circumstances of creation are parts of the historiography of an image. To view an image in isolation of these factors reduces its usefulness as historical evidence and risks changing it into a convenient tool for the story the historian wants to tell, rather than the story actually evidenced by the image (Sandweiss 2002: 328–30, 2007: 194). If *Migrant Mother* is interpreted not just as a picture of the migrant agricultural poor, but as one in which Lange sought to find the image that would work best with visual language of the day, referencing existing markers within the society, then it becomes referential of a much broader history of the 1930s. *Migrant Mother* was taken with a specific audience in mind and it was constructed to be utilised in specific manner. As such, intent becomes part of the history of the image and acknowledging that intent leads to a greater understanding of how the image fits into the American social fabric of the Great Depression. To show it as a single decontextualised image obscures much of what is actually significant about it.

Conclusions

Through the recontextualisation of the FSA photographs, *This Great Nation Will Endure* succeeded on many levels. It provided a diverse narrative of agricultural poverty in the 1930s, the subject of the collection. It gave audiences a sense of real people with individual influences, backgrounds and experiences both as artists and also as employees of the New Deal. It created a sense of a 1930s audience alongside the modern one allowing for examination of the language of visual communication and how that communication fitted into the fabric of American culture at that time. In short, it provided a wealth of insight into multiple aspects of the 1930s. Granted, while a history exhibition rather than an art exhibition, it is not a fully integrated exhibition; photographs largely replaced three-dimensional objects, rather than being used in conjunction with them. Nevertheless, the techniques that were employed by the FDR Presidential Library and Museum are ones that could be integrated into broader exhibitions interpreting the Great Depression or the New Deal. Indeed, with some variation they are techniques that could be used to broaden the use of photographs in many history exhibitions. Certainly, these techniques will not work with every collection or every era. The high level of documentation, the skill of the photographers, the central role that visual culture played in the 1930s and the sheer number of photographs, make this a collection that is particularly well suited to recontexualisation. Not every exhibition is blessed with such useful material. However, the FSA photographs, their recent re-evaluation by some curators, and the potential for even greater re-engagement with elements of their materiality in the future, do illustrate the wider potential role for photographs as objects in integrated history exhibitions.

Notes

1 The RA/FSA is one agency that operated under different names during Roosevelt's presidency. It was initially the Resettlement Administration from 1935 to 1937. In 1937 it became the Farm Security Administration as its mission expanded. The photographic or historical section was then moved into the Office of War Information in 1942 and remained operational until 1944. As is the convention, this article will use the shorthand of 'FSA' to refer to the collection as a whole.
2 The site also lists approximately 1600 colour negatives, taken from 1939 on.
3 See also Katz (2005: 50–2) for a discussion on the misconception of museums as unmediated.
4 As the project went on the section head Roy Stryker became increasingly interested in creating a collection for posterity, however. This did not always sit well with his photographers who were interested in having their work published with more immediacy (see Curtis 1986: 3, Finnegan 2003: 38–42, 54–5).
5 Some labelling (including the Library of Congress file) substitutes 'Overseer' for 'Owner'.
6 To see both the original photograph and the McLeish crop on the Library of Congress website see: http://memory.loc.gov/cgi-bin/query/D?fsaall:34:./temp/~ammem_rnC2:
7 In the original file, Lange captioned the photograph, 'Destitute peapickers in California; a 32 year old mother of seven children. February 1936.'
8 To see the five of the six images on the Library of Congress website, see http://www.loc.gov/rr/print/list/128_migm.html

Bibliography

Crewe, S.R. and J.E. Sims (1991) 'Locating authenticity: fragments of a dialogue', in I. Karp and S.D. Lavine (eds) *Exhibiting Cultures: the poetics and politics of museum display*, Washington, DC: Smithsonian Institution Press, pp. 159–75.

Crownshaw, R. (2007) 'Photography and memory in Holocaust museums', *Mortality*, 12: 176–92.

Curtis, J.C. (1986) 'Dorothea Lange, *Migrant Mother* and the culture of the Great Depression', *Winterthur Portfolio*, 21: 1–20, accessed via JSTOR, 15 August 2008.

Daniel, P., M.A. Foresta, M. Stange and S. Stein (1987) *Official Images: New Deal photography*, Washington, DC: Smithsonian Institution Press.

Davison, G. (2000) *The Use and Abuse of Australian History*, St Leonards, NSW: Allen & Unwin.

Dixon, P. (1983) *Photographers of the Farm Security Administration: an annotated bibliography, 1930–1980*, New York: Garland.

Dudley, S. (2010) 'Museum materialities: objects, sense and feeling', in S. Dudley (ed.) *Museum Materialities: objects, engagements, interpretations*, London: Routledge, pp. 1–17.

Edwards, E. (1999) 'Photographs as objects of memory', in M. Kwint, C. Breward and J. Aynsley (eds) *Material Memories: design and evocation*, Oxford: Berg, pp. 221–36.

Edwards, E. (2006) 'Photographs and the sound of history', *Visual Anthropology Review*, 21: 27–46.

Edwards, E. (2009) 'Thinking photography beyond the visual', in J.J. Long, A. Noble and E. Welch (eds) *Photography: theoretical snapshots*, London: Routledge, pp. 31–48.

Edwards, E. (2010) 'Photographs and history: emotion and materiality', in S. Dudley (ed.) *Museum Materialities: objects, engagements, interpretations*, London: Routledge, pp. 21–38.

Edwards, E. and J. Hart (2004) 'Introduction: photographs as objects', in E. Edwards and J. Hart (eds) *Photographs, Objects, Histories: on the materiality of images*, London: Routledge, pp. 1–15.

Finnegan, C.A. (2003) *Picturing Poverty: print culture and FSA photographs*, Washington, DC: Smithsonian Books.

Katz, M. (2005) 'History under construction: curators and the experience of creating accessible public history', unpublished MA thesis, Monash University.

Kavanagh, G. (2000) *Dream Spaces: memory and the museum*, Leicester: Leicester University Press.

Levine, L. (1993) *The Unpredictable Past: explorations in American cultural history*, New York: Oxford University Press.

Library of Congress (1998) 'American memory: America from the Great Depression to WWII: black and white photographs from the FSA-OWI, 1935–1945'. http://memory.loc.gov/ammem/fsahtml/fahome.html (Accessed 1 July 2009).

McDannell, C. (2007) 'Religious history and visual culture', *Journal of American History*, 94: 112–21.

Moore, K. (1997) *Museums and Popular Culture*, London, Cassell.

Newbury, D. (2005) ' "Lest we forget": photography and the presentation of history at the Apartheid Museum, Gold Reef City, and the Hector Pieterson Museum, Soweto', *Visual Communication*, 4: 259–95.

Pearce, S.M. (1999) 'A new way of looking at old things', *Museum International*, 51: 12–17.

Poole, D. (1997) *Vision, Race and Modernity: a visual economy of the Andean World*, Princeton: Princeton University Press.

Raeburn, J. (2006) *A Staggering Revolution: a cultural history of thirties photography*, Champaign: University of Illinois Press.

Rosenzweig, R. and D. Thelen (1998) *The Presence of the Past: popular uses of history in American life*, New York: Columbia University Press.

Russell, R. and K. Winkworth (2001) *(significance): a guide to assessing the significance of cultural heritage objects and collections*, Canberra: Commonwealth of Australia on behalf of the Heritage Collections Council.

Sandweiss, M.A. (2002) *Print the Legend: photography and the American West*, New Haven: Yale University Press.

Sandweiss, M.A. (2007) 'Image and artifact: the photograph as evidence in the digital age', *Journal of American History*, 94: 193–202.

Smithsonian Institution (1981) 'Updating the immigrant home', Record Unit 376, Box 2/2, Folder: FDR Immigrant Home, Washington, DC: Smithsonian Institution Archives.

Sontag, S. (1977) *On Photography*, New York: Farrar, Straus and Giroux.

Starr, K. (1996) *Endangered Dreams: the Great Depression in California*, New York: Oxford University Press.

Stott, W. (1986) *Documentary Expression and Thirties America*, Chicago: University of Chicago Press.

Susman, W.I. (1984) *Culture as History: the transformation of American society in the twentieth century*, New York: Pantheon Books.

Trinca, M. (2003) 'Museums and the history wars', *History Australia*, 1: 85–97.

24 (Im)material practices in museums

Alice Semedo

Inventory

In 2002, once the Alqueva Dam is finished, what is announced as Europe's largest artificial lake will begin to appear. A possible inventory of what will be lost follows.

Inventory

Luz village
Estrela village (partially)
25 000 hectares of Alentejo land
14 000 hectares of National Agricultural Reserve
Our first kiss hidden by the night
　　　　your eyes remained closed
　　　　my body levitated
　　　　the stars alone smiled
360 archaeological sites
Vila Velha de Mourão
Several Roman bridges
　　　　We raced each other to dive into the river
　　　　we thrashed the waters
　　　　like a shoal of tuna fishes caught in the net
　　　　climbed out exultant – naked and shiny – like river gods
Xerês cromlech
Lousa's Roman castle
Cuncos' Roman settlement
On returning from school I would meet you in the yard
　　　　and on my request you would do a handstand
　　　　the white knickers – the contour of your legs
　　　　heavenly vision
　　　　gifts from a girl to a kid
Senhora do Alcance Convent
Outeiro do Castelinho's Roman villa

Xerês 12 Neolithic habitat
Do you remember
when we used to fill the stream with paper boats
a full crusade set on conquering the sea
Mercator 5 Calcolithic settlement
Monte do Tosco's Calcolithic settlement
Santo António Country House
Running away from home to Outeiro do Marôco
we returned in the evening dirty and scratched
we were beaten soundly – and never learned
The Watchtower of Portel's Port
80 Watermills
The largest heron colony in Portugal
Sitting on a bench in Rossio Square
all the time belonged to us
we would imagine bright futures for our children
Protected habitats of Black Storks
Egyptian Vultures
Bonelli's Eagles
Golden Eagles
Otters
Wildcats
13 kinds of rare or near extinct plants
Card-playing nights at the Sports Association – and all the dancing
I would glide my hands under your woollen jacket
press your thighs to make you feel my desire
your mother would crane her neck
the accordion accompanied our fugitive whirl
15 060 hectares of holm-oaks
951 hectares of cork-oaks
703 hectares of olive-groves
I would wake up frightened by the cracking of rockets
these were joyful days, the festivities of Our Lady of Luz
the mass – the procession – the bulls running
I would listen entranced to the night songs
and softly fall asleep on my mother's lap
245 hectares of grain
585 hectares of eucalyptuses
We would spend hours on end watching the storks
flying right above the river
we would lie on the castle's paving stones – and then turn around
and contemplate the clouds trying to guess their shapes
82 hectares of vine and orchard
28 hectares of stone pines
That day I saw you come by Rua da Igreja

carrying under your arm the confirmation of all our fears
your eyes were screaming in your silence
we clung to each other
25 000 *hectares of memory of water*

(Luís Campos, Luz Village, 3 July 2001)[1]

Introduction

The reworking of the museum concept during the past few decades, in relation to the theories and practices of the new museology, has offered us new and critical models for the representation of memories, pluralism and difference. The growing affirmation of local distinctiveness, changes in the styles of governance (which involved, for example, a move from centralised decision-making and funding to local support, from top-down to bottom-up organisations, from the undervaluing of local distinctiveness to its vigorous affirmation), of sensibility towards the nature and uses of heritage itself and a profound discussion about museum roles are essential contexts to understand the shift from a paradigm of aesthetics to a paradigm of representation in museums. New roles emerge as museums operate as central nodes in a network, bringing various elements, ideas, people and different types of interactions together in a border zone where different systems of representation meet. They are, indeed, shifting spaces of practice and cultural meaning.

Museums are also increasingly dealing with history in terms of memory, identity and its archives, producing critical museum spaces that use architecture, exhibitions, texts, new media, objects and people to reconfigure boundaries, intervene in the social world and assert new subjectivities. To some extent these approaches can be related to the value of heritage preservation as being associated with the meanings and interpretations of objects. Moreover, they propose a focus on the agency of objects in an attempt to play out the performed dimensions of cultural creation and transmission. But how do these museums consider and reconfigure the material conditions of these interactions; that is, how does materiality function, what does it do? What are its costs and who is included, excluded, given a voice or silenced? What conventions guide the displays, which subjects do they constitute and what are the implications for those who see and who are seen? What roles are they taking on within these discursive practices? What happens when different systems of representation meet?

In an attempt to explore some of these shifting and sometimes conflicting features I will look at a museum located at the village of Luz, in south Portugal, which I believe is a good example of these embodied and museological strategies. This is a memorial museum, commonly considered a bottom-up experience which was created in the course of very special circumstances. It is related to trauma and a particular moment of community grief: the loss of a village and its way of life. The poetics and politics of this museum's curation have often been associated with negotiation and mediation processes and, as we will see, collections, building and bodily practices both functioning as primary evidence and as incisive signifying devices. This is also a performative museum in a different sense:

the total physical environment itself, the building (and of course the story of the tragedy) has become the attraction. The public acknowledgement of this model and its symbolic power is apparent in the considerable attention it has received. In fact, this small museum has had more visitors than most ethnological museums in Portugal and has been awarded several important architectural and museological prizes.[2] After briefly presenting the museum and its contexts I explore the questions raised through the analysis of the exhibition spaces and its implications and offer a discussion of the terms involved.

Aldeia da Luz

Look up Aldeia da Luz on a map and you will find the plains of Alentejo, in south Portugal, one of the driest and hottest regions of Europe, which suffers from a recurring shortage of water supplies. Here summers are long and economic resources limited. Because of this a major water dam to produce hydroelectric power, irrigation for farms in the surrounding area and a large reservoir for *tourist recreation* came to be built in the river Guadiana during the 1990s and early 2000s. The water dam and its reservoir would swallow houses, archaeological sites, trees, bird nests and roads, changing the natural landscape and the way of life of the communities that lived in the region. Aldeia da Luz was a small village of 180 houses and some 300 inhabitants, located at a lower level in relation to the future reservoir, which meant that it would inevitably be submerged. The village inhabitants and their possessions had to be transferred to a different location. This was a very small village with predominantly rural characteristics at the end of a quiet road which gave access only to Castelo da Lousa, a Roman archaeological site which would also be submerged. Luz was suddenly catapulted to the first pages of national newspapers, capturing media and popular attention for a long time. The story of imminent tragedy and the demise of the village was most appealing for its human and social dimensions. Indeed, this was a highly mediated and disseminated process throughout the country which brought the village unprecedented numbers of visitors and supported a notion of tourism of urgency ('to see something that would soon disappear'). The outsiders went to Luz in search of living relics or souvenirs (Pearce 1994: 195–6), the tangible remains of the tragedy, of the dying village, looting the empty backyards, collecting abandoned artefacts, expecting to take back to their homes a piece of that moving and traumatic story and to participate in it.

Conscious of the profound changes the dam of Alqueva – 'the major European artificial lake' – would bring to local culture, studies regarding the impact upon heritage sites and landscapes were undertaken by various private and public entities, in an attempt to document and preserve all possible information. The announced death of the village was something the community learned to live with but its implications were only fully realised when the dam gates closed and the reservoir started to fill up in February 2002. In accordance with the community's wishes to stay on together and exchange 'house for house' and 'land for land' the new village, just two kilometres away from the old location, was almost finished and ready to receive everyone by that time. Between September 2002 and March the following year, the village was almost entirely removed. The whole planning process for the new village and abandonment of the old one was extremely painful and unsettling. The anthropologist Clara Saraiva studied and described in great detail the whole process (Saraiva 2005, 2007), offering an insightful discussion which allows for a better understanding of the role of cultural assets and of this museum. During this process the community took on the role both of victim and hero as they felt that theirs was a sacrifice for the entire country: victims of 'progress' and its entrepreneurs but also survivors and heroes; heroes that offered their sacrifice for the greater good of the development of the region and the whole country. In a way, the construction of the new village worked as a form of social emulation as it represented a new cycle in the life of the community. A new beginning.

A context of profound economic and social reordering which involved radical changes in the landscape, the loss of memorial cartographies and ways of living was, therefore, the starting point and working ground for the creation of this museum and the reordering of diverse community narratives. This context of a profound trauma informed community claims for a museum that was inaugurated in November 2003 when almost everyone was already living at the new site. The new village project included a church, a cemetery and the museum. The three would come to be placed almost next to each other and this is not just a functional occupation of space but, as Clara Saraiva (2007: 445) has pointed out, it is also a symbolic one. Or is this not a space of mediation par excellence? A space for the mediation of the sacred, the living and the afterlife, of memories and history, of celebration and mourning? In this monumental–ceremonial–mediation space, the museum seems to occupy a privileged space: half-buried in the landscape and in between land and sky, lake and village, church and cemetery, the museum reinforces its role as mediator between the prayers of the living and the memories of the lost ones. It is thus, fundamentally, as a mediator that the museum chooses to materialise itself.

Moreover, Benjamim Pereira, the museologist who, with Clara Saraiva, coordinated the team responsible for the constitution of the future museum collection, also envisaged the museum as an active and participative agent, a qualified mediator. In Pereira's words, the museum would act not only as a privileged space to re-encounter the common past, but also as a cultural locus which would actively participate in the development of the local community (Pereira 2003: 209). The team intended to document the ways of life of the community and the restructuring processes they were experiencing. This would prove to be a difficult proposal, not only to materialise in the museum but to be accepted by EDIA, the company responsible for the dam and the new village project. The acquisition processes are, in themselves, very interesting as objects and memories that were not seen as having memorial or museological value before, became during this process not only disputed by community members, but also by tourists, who raided the old site for mementos, relics or souvenirs, which were now invested with the attributes of tragedy.[3]

The community saw this invasion with mixed feelings: of course, they were proud of outside interest in their village, but the loss of private and intimate spaces was too great and fame also meant they were constantly in the public eye, and they began to feel observed, like 'museum objects or animals in a zoo' (Saraiva 2005: 188).

Clara Saraiva (2007) describes how objects often left behind in the old houses (as rubbish), were reclaimed by their owners to embellish gardens, creating, in reality, alternative narrative modes and commemoration sites. The relationship to the objects in question was altered through metacultural operations which involved not only the production of museum-value and the wider political context, but also engaged the representation of the community, the subject, as valuable and different. In this context the processes of patrimonialisation and museum making became more significant than the objects themselves. In any case, some 1,200 objects were collected during this troubled period and an extensive audio-visual campaign was also rather successful in documenting daily living, festivities and special moments of collective mourning.

The museum: representations of replacement and resonance

From its inception, the museum was thought of as a space for memory storage-archive that could also act as a catalyst to support community familiarisation with the new village. Furthermore, the destruction of the old village and its historical spaces led the team to think about the new village, and especially its 'monumental and historical part', as it came to be called, as a true act of replacement where the acts of destruction and of new foundation became part of the same equation. The old village would remain as the first, built during the centuries of territorial appropriation; however, its strong identity elements, the cemetery, the church and the museum, would support the foundation of a new place and in taking up the resemblances of the old, endow the new with representations of replacement (Pacheco and Clément 2003: 107–8) and resonance (Greenblatt 1991). In the case of the new church, a replica was even built to replace the old one in an attempt to maintain a certain historical linearity. Hence, also the concern of the design team in including elements of the old church and in using traditional building techniques, mud bricks and shale masonry extracted *in situ*, handmade vaults, mortars and lime plasters made by local artisans (Saraiva 2005: 272–3) embodying also intangible knowledges and meanings.

Once more, it is important to stress that Benjamim Pereira understood the museum at Luz to be a radical witness of a particular moment of this community's history, thus transcending the functions of other regional museums. In his vision, the museum took upon itself the mission of mediator, not only between EDIA and the community, but also as mediator of a memory now buried in the old village. Awareness of this mission is important for an understanding of how replacement and resonance act as key concepts. The museum has undeniably also been presented, over the past few years, as a site for relief, for comfort, which could help the community to rise above its pain, its loss of individual and social territories. In the words of Pereira, the displays even act, in some instances, as a practice of exorcism, implying a recent trauma, a loss or sense of deprivation that can only be healed through the drive towards closure through acts such as this. Heritage and the museum is here also constituted as 'a metaphor for the demand for justice and the resolution of a grief that remains a wound' (Rowlands 2002: 111). In fact, its location between cemetery and church assumes, accordingly, a ritual aura that materialises this transcendence (Pereira 2003: 209). The architectural options – the use of slate and the half-buried building – further underline this mediatory and memorial function. The polychromatic use of schist adds to the symbolic definition of spaces and to the very museum function: as a space between cemetery and church, which can be thought of as an element of the landscape instead of a building. Again, resonance is here an essential representation. For the effect of resonance, as Greenblatt says (1991: 45), can be achieved by awakening in the viewer a sense of the cultural and historically contingent constriction of objects, the negotiations, exchanges, exclusions by which certain representational practices come to be set apart from other representational practices that they partially resemble. Resonance often pulls the viewer away from the celebration of isolated objects and towards a series of implied, only half-visible relationships and questions, and this is precisely what happens here. Through their very reference to previous works the church and the museum physically embody memory and index past actions. The location of the building, the symbolic definition and occupation of space and the use of materials and traditional techniques (the use of architectural elements from the old church in the new building) are all endowed with representations of replacement and resonance.

In a way, this structure aims at giving an expressive form to the specific nature of this museum and, as such, it becomes evocative and resonant (Figure 24.1).

Figure 24.1 Museu da Luz. Photograph by Paulo Duarte.

In so doing it provides a symbolic and emotive expression of the museum's specific historical contents and display narratives, which are heavily charged with symbolic meaning, bringing out its memorial aspect (Giebelhausen 2006: 230–1). Its design and materiality evokes the memory of the surrounding schist enclosures and of Castelo da Lousa (Pacheco and Clément 2003: 110) in an overt reference to history and nature, and with culture as inscribed in the surrounding landscape. It takes on a symbiotic relationship between population and landscape. But this is also a fortress and one has to go round to find its entrance. This conquering move accentuates its memorial function and this may play against other envisaged functions, more related to the museum as instrument, where access and openness are fundamental characterisations. If we understand this museum and building as having an ongoing effect on the practices of performances, we might say that it produces a certain artefactuality – artefact effects with contingent social purpose: the 'factishes' of Latour (1999: 274), which acknowledge that the world is made up of entities, relations and processes that are at once real and constructed, in which objectivity and subjectivity (and, therefore, nature, culture, morality and politics) are entangled with each other in an indissoluble knot because 'facts' are both real and done – or, better, they are real because they are being done.

Besides being presented as a space of mediation, this museum is also presented as a space of memory and identity and as such, it may be understood as a *lieux de mémoire*, a mode of cultural production that gives the endangered or outmoded a second life as an exhibition itself. What is more, this museum lives – almost literally – on the remains of a community and it is, as such, a *lieux de mémoire*, the ultimate embodiment of a memorial consciousness that has barely survived in a historical age that calls out for memory because, as Pierre Nora (1989: 12) would say, it has abandoned it. These processes have occurred as an immense, and intimate, private fund of memory, disappeared, surviving only as a reconstituted object beneath the gaze of critical history and revisited by the museum and its makers. This museum of memory and identity also originated from a sense that without vigilance, the history of this community would soon be swept away and that one must intentionally create an archive, a storehouse for the preservation of the collective memory of the community. The identity of the community is, therefore, reinforced upon such strategies of preservation: in reality if it was not threatened, probably there would be no need to order, classify and display it in a museum. The less memory is experienced from the outside, the more it exists only through its exterior and superficial signs – and this is another reason for the obsession with the building of the museum, the archive and for the archival processes of this community's memories.

It is important to underline that, as in other cases (cf. Butler 2006), the whole process of creating this museum both produces and is produced by a category of cultural loss and redemption. The museum – and the display of, at one time, discarded objects, charged with memories of difficult times, but now loved and supportive of social strategies within the group – is constituted as a source of well-being through its capacity to cure a sense of loss and for its capacity of witnessing, acknowledging, the profound damage done to the community. The museum and its archive is the place of constant return, judgement and cure and is therefore the ideal locus for narrating this traumatic loss. Building, displays and performers are engaged in these acts of healing and are part of other ritual performances of memory work, which seek not only to celebrate the community's ways of life, but also to bring about cure, within strategies that have already been termed 'heritage magic' (Butler 2006: 474).

Exhibition spaces

The museum presents different metaphorical exhibition spaces which act as a framework for the discursive narrative options. The layout is marked by short axes: a first room (a passageway, in fact) acts as an introductory space and houses temporary exhibitions. As of September 2009 the temporary exhibition *Alqueva and Luz: The Territory and Change* occupies this opening space. A series of six display boards, using short texts and photographs, explains the reasons and impacts of the construction of Alqueva. At the end of it, a small distribution area with a bench in front of a large plasma screen also functions as a space of gathering and encounter in the exhibition: it plays the part of reference point in the spatial sequence and provides orientation. In the revised layout of the museum, this space was thought of as a concluding one and hence the film shows the new territory of the village: images of an aerial film show the immensity of the new territory, its beauty, unending possibilities and promises, filmed at a distance. The projection of the future, as seen by an all-encompassing eye, as a course of limitless development, is certainly an intended message here.

The Old Rural World room displays objects associated with working activities. Although the first panel of this room states, clearly, that what is shown here is a residue of ways of living mainly associated with rurality in the mid-twentieth century, the exhibition does not even attempt to show alternative modes of living at the time of abandonment of the village as comparison. Indeed, the display options are characterised by past temporal orientation and put forth strong, melancholic feelings of nostalgia, silencing other potentially more interesting approaches (Figure 24.2). Nostalgia is profoundly conservative and reflective and its set-ups restrict relationships among objects and viewers, and reproduce something already known. It follows that through the arrangement of spaces and objects the curator gains control over the information and reduces the exploratory aspect of the visit, both spatially and intellectually, and even emotionally. The displays are used in a conservative way so as to reflect something already known, to reproduce a set of relationships previously specified and restrict randomness in the experience of objects. As we all know, this is a mode of grouping that is marked by a high degree of conceptual intervention and non-interchangeability among objects within display. Furthermore, the messages to be communicated are well defined and by doing so decrease the potential for the unexpected (cf. Tzortzi 2007).

In fact, it seems that the place in which the least originality arises in the museum is precisely in its exhibition approaches. These display options use objects

Figure 24.2 Room *O Mundo Rural Arcaico*. Photograph by Alice Semedo.

(and here I include all kinds of materialisations) along historicist and techno-logical axes, to create representative images that reproduce a static, frozen picture of a lost and foreign rural countryside of the 1950s and 1960s. The change of the denomination of this room to *The Old Rural World* certainly acknowledges the nature of what is on display and the texts do attempt to create connections between the rudimentary objects, allowing something to appear as a whole even if only fragmented objects from the past are presented. But the fundamental intention expressed by the museum programme, of materialising the agency of objects, ways of life, processes and experiences, of displaying meanings and interpretations, is contradicted by the (re)production of highly structured and stereotyped cultural identity markers. What is (re)produced here, as in many other ethnographical displays in Portuguese museums, is an enshrined collective memory (Durand 2007: 377, Branco 2008: 54). Views and understandings about the world are profoundly subjective and depend very much on context and, therefore, different forms of display, perhaps more open and even ambiguous, courageous enough to abandon safe structures based on traditional discourses, are called for here. Besides, history always represents both past and present and that, indeed, seemed to be the first programmatic intention of both museologist and anthro-pologist: to represent social change that could only be understood as being about the present and as embedded in continuing cultural practice. Nevertheless, the way of seeing promoted here entails a detached observer, hovering about the different nucleus of the displays. The opportunity for the viewer to immerse themselves and become part of the ensemble comes, somewhat unexpectedly, from a different source than the objects themselves. The challenge to express one's perceptions, judgements and emotions is enacted, for the most part, both by the sometimes overwhelming and fragmented architectural options and by filmic voices and images. In reality, the glimpse through the window in the *Room*

Figure 24.3 Sala da Memória (Room of Memory). Photograph by Alice Semedo.

of Light of the surviving pine tree or stories told by the film, prompts the visitors to locate themselves and their identities in relation to what is displayed, and to see themselves as part of the performance, without denying their subjectivity and perceptions.

Memorialisation in museums is forcibly selective and necessarily accompanied by amnesia and this room does not escape these narrative configurations. On the other hand, these exhibition approaches reveal, perhaps, a weakness of the building. The relationship of content and container is always very complex and should be developed through constant dialogue between functional and aesthetical considerations. A solid – even if permanently debated – museological programme is always needed. If these framings are to be questioned, museum communicative devices will have to become more subversive, inspiring and relevant.

At *Sala da Memória (Room of Memory)* (Figure 24.3) we find the emotive film *A Minha Aldeia Já Não Mora Aqui (My village does not live here anymore)*. The room is organised around three thematic nuclei which refer to local traditional working skills: those of the blacksmith, the farm overseer and the potter. As well as using different implements associated with these activities and in an attempt to confer movement and open a space for the affirmation of different subjectivities (including the authors' and the visitors'), different voices, landscapes and stories are presented. But this film, even if the film-makers deny it, cannot escape the interpretation as a kind of collective family album, celebratory of a place already doomed and, therefore, a *lieux de mémoire* itself (cf. Mourão and Costa 2003).

Unexpectedly, a long and simple table with eight chairs is located at the very end of the room which opens up to the outside patio. This is not only an important symbolic space, but also a space where different systems of representation meet. Once more, the effect of light frames this composition. This is a space for communality. A meeting space. A mediation space (Figure 24.4). But this is also

Figure 24.4 Meeting spaces. Photograph by Alice Semedo.

a theatrical room, where the performative dimension of the museum gains a privileged space. Members from the community are invited to share their memories either through story telling or through more formal presentations and explorations of subjects and objects. In some instances, some of these performative acts are supported by small exhibition displays such as panels with photographs, texts and videos located currently at the entrance of the museum. During these sessions objects may be used by the community members as props and souvenirs of autobiographical tales; creating constantly shifting performances which set off personal meanings, memories and connections, triggered by the objects and stories told by self and others. It is performative and memorial gestures that are enhanced here. In a way, this exhibition-performance approach attempts to restore the agency of objects and to present personal memories. Indeed, by focusing on a few selected objects, some of these exhibitions are created around personal narratives, producing rich symbolic objects and embodiments. In this manner, memory takes the refuge in gestures and habits, in skills transmitted by unspoken tradition, in the body's inherent self-knowledge, in genuine reflexes and embedded memories, but at the same time, memory has also been transformed by its passage through history in the museum itself: intentionally and experienced as a duty, no longer spontaneous, no longer, even, a social practice (Nora 1989: 13). Telling the story becomes the social practice, and new subjectivities are facilitated or produced through this process (the storytellers). These intangible memories and processes are here, in fact, interiorised as limitations and, in reality, they work as effects of the materialising processes performed in and by the museum. The storytellers have gained a new public space in the pages of a book that prints their discussions with the museologist Benjamim Enes Pereira, and they became key memory markers of the community. All these stories are being intensively documented and archived. In this sense, objects may be here understood as souvenirs as they are an important attempt to make sense of personal histories, to create an essential social self centred in its own unique life story. Moreover, the collections relate to the constructions of a romantic integrated personal self in which objects are subordinated into a secondary role (Pearce 1994: 196). In this sense we might even say that material culture is treated here as knowledge, as objectified and as experienced and that the objects act, essentially, as aide-memoires.

These memorial gestures, performed in the museum-memory archive, pertain to the duty-memory and distance-memory fields, supported by these very museum practices: voluntary and deliberate, experienced as a duty and no longer spontaneous. Besides, the past is no longer perceived as being a retrospective continuity that can be entirely resuscitated by a simple effort of remembrance. It has become somehow invisible, unpredictable and fractured. Pierre Nora (1989: 17) argues that the 'return of the narrative' and the omnipresence of imagery and cinema in contemporary culture, for example, can well be understood within this modern metamorphosis of the distance-memory field referred to above. Informants, ordinary people, re-establish the flavour of things and lend a hand to the slowing of the rhythm of past times. The content-rich materiality of these memory gestures is, nevertheless, both functional and symbolic, since performances are crystallised and transmitted from one generation to the next and they describe, by referring to events or experiences shared by the group, the community itself, supporting the rewriting of its narratives. But these are also autobiographical tales, and as such, they are resources that produce a powerful subject's effect in its space. The performers, ritual specialists and artisans whose 'cultural assets' become heritage through this process, experience a new relationship to those resources; a metacultural relationship to what was once just 'habitus' (Bourdieu 1997: 4, Kirshenblatt-Gimblett 2006: 2). Once habitus becomes heritage in a museum, to whom does it belong? To each performer? To the community? To the museum? To us all? And what are, in reality, the effects of these performances? A crystallised archive or a creative repertoire?

The *Sala da Luz (Room of Light)* uses light in many different senses: as toponym and as a physical element, but also as ethereal and intangible; and as a result, light is the central character of this room: white walls, a skylight and a patio where a rose-bay is planted are all elements in this composition. All these different metonymic elements – with the effects of light and darkness they project – act as a strategy to materialise the atmosphere of the old village landscape; they act as a synthesis, an encapsulation of that memory. The sudden light of this museum space accentuates unexpectedness and surprise takes precedence over intelligibility (Figure 24.5). Furthermore, the surviving pine tree – already a fundamental reference point in the old personal cartographies – can be glimpsed from a small window, testifying to the endurance and the right to that land of the very community itself. This is both a space for introspection and catharsis. This room elicits both intellectual and emotional responses from the visitor, interpreting and framing any possible exhibition narrative. Its initial appearance is deceptive. It is not a discreet or objective room. Even if the constant sound of the voices of the film showed in the adjacent room were not always present, this would be a

Figure 24.5 Sala da Luz. Photograph by Alice Semedo.

room of 'noisy silence' (Lampugnani 2006: 257–8). Two display cases show some archaeological material referring us to the myths surrounding the creation of the village. The cases are set so as to emphasise and bring out the qualities of the architectural space. The structure of space and distribution of objects seem to work together so as to encourage space exploration, slow visitors' paths and delay the rhythm of perception. The experience of space is thus a critical discursive dimension particularly of this room and, as Tzortzi (2007: 13) would argue, in this room the informational function of the museum extends beyond the didactic aims and acts through its aesthetic quality. Moreover, the experience of space is here rendered more complex and information rich.

The museum instrument (and, certainly its instrumentalisation, towards the naturalisation of EDIA's actions) seems, nevertheless, to be reclaiming its territory. The layout of the exhibition on show in September 2009 intended to present two themes: *Changes to the Environment and the Heritage* and *Social Changes*. This exhibition follows the same lines of that shown in the introductory space by presenting the positive impacts, conservation actions and compensations developed during the past few years. A different section takes us to the construction and removal processes of village and population. The last panel presents the artificial lake as a mirror and the future of the new village.

Some further thoughts

This museum offers a space for the intertwining of public, exhibitionary space and private biographical space. It works not only as a collective archive but also as a therapeutic practice. It is both a place for sightseeing, which permanently displays the heroic role of the community and the souvenirs of the tragedy, and it is – perhaps more importantly – a site for cultural biography, in the sense that it enhances public recognition of the self and its stories. In this sense, it functions as a substitute heirloom that preserves the material culture of the past generations, thereby offering community members the pleasure of seeing their own personal realm displayed and confirmed in the museum. Even if memory, oral transmission and performance are put forward as ways for experiencing and comprehending the past, existing in the body's inherent self-knowledge and practices, this museum-memory archive of Aldeia da Luz is caught between freezing the practice and addressing the inherently processual nature of culture. The profound transformations lived by the community and the memory rituals it has developed have altered the fundamental conditions for cultural production and reproduction, changing the relationship of people to what they do and the way they understand their culture and themselves. As complex experiences become sedimented and tied into memories and these, in turn, are remixed and embodied through selective recall and repetition, what is left, perhaps, is the material which provides the common places of local histories: the nostalgic and well-rehearsed stories of particular places, reproducing mythical times of community and solidarity and re-enchanting the community's relationship to its past.

Notes

1 Campos, L. (2002) Inventário. Available online at: http://www.luiscampos.pt/IMAGES/ ZVARIOS/TEX_LUIS%20CAMPOS4.pdf (Accessed 15 September 2009).
2 In comparison with the National Museum of Ethnology, in Lisbon, for example, with 11,120 visitors (http://www.imc-ip.pt/Data/Documents/Recursos/Estatisticas/2009/ MuseusPalacios/Geral_2009.pdf, (Accessed 20 May 2010), the Museu da Luz had 12,435 visitors in the 2009 (Museu da Luz 2010: 5).
3 I use both the terms *relic* and *souvenir* since here objects take on different meanings depending on the subject's/collector's positioning (in fact, if we included the museologist and the anthropologist as a subject/collector we should, of course, also introduce a different mode of collecting more in accord to anthropological and museological theoretical frameworks, eventually more systematic).

Bibliography

Bourdieu, P. (1997) *Razões Práticas*, Oeiras: Celta Editora.
Branco, J.F. (2008) 'Significados esgotados: sobre museus e colecções etnográficas', in X. Roigé, E. Fernandéz and I. Arrieta (coords) *El futuro de los museos etnológicos: consideraciones introductorias para un debate*, San Sebastian: Ankulegi Antropologia Elkartea. Available online at: http://www.euskomedia.org/PDFAnlt/antropologia/11/03/03053068.pdf (Accessed 14 July 2010).
Butler, B. (2006) 'Heritage and the present past', in C. Tilley, W. Keane, S. Keuchler, M. Rowlands and P. Spyer (eds) *Handbook of Material Culture*, London: Sage Publications, pp. 463–79.
Durand, J.Y. (2007) 'Este obscuro objecto do desejo etnográfico: o museu', *Etnográfica*, XI (2): 373–86.
Giebelhausen, M. (2006) 'Museum architecture: a brief history', in S. Macdonald (ed.) *A Companion to Museum Studies*, Oxford: Blackwell Publishing, pp. 223–44.
Greenblatt, S. (1991) 'Resonance and wonder', in I. Karp and S. Lavine (eds) *Exhibiting Cultures: the poetics and politics of museum display*, Washington, DC: Smithsonian Press, pp. 42–56.

Kirshenblatt-Gimblett, B. (2006) 'World heritage and cultural economics', in I. Karp, C. Kratz, *et al.* (eds) *Museum Frictions: public cultures/global transformations*, Durham, NC and London: Duke University Press, pp. 161–202.

Lampugnani, V.M. (2006) 'Insight versus entertainment: untimely meditations on the architecture of twentieth century art museums', in S. Macdonald (ed.) *A Companion to Museum Studies*, Oxford: Blackwell Publishing, pp. 245–62.

Latour, B. (1999) *Pandora's Hope: essays on the reality of science studies*, Cambridge, MA: Harvard University Press.

Mourão, C. and C.A. Costa (2003) 'Imagens e sons para o Museu da Luz', in *Museu da Luz, Catálogo*, Luz: EDIA, pp. 99–103.

Museu da Luz (2010) 'Estatísticas de Públicos do Museu da Luz', unpublished document, Museu da Luz.

Nora, P. (1989) 'Between memory and history: les lieux de mémoire', *Representations*, 26: 7–24.

Pacheco, P. and Clément, M. (2003) 'Aldeia da Luz/Aldeias duplas', in *Museu da Luz, Catálogo*, Luz: EDIA.

Pearce, S. (1994) 'Collecting reconsidered', in S. Pearce (ed.) *Interpreting Objects and Collections*, London and New York: Routledge, pp. 193–204.

Pereira, B. (2003) 'O museu da Luz', *Etnográfica*, VII (1): 209–12.

Rowlands, M. (2002) 'Heritage and cultural property', in V. Buchli (ed.) *The Material Culture Reader*, Oxford and New York: Berg, pp. 105–14.

Saraiva, C. (2005) *Luz e Água: Etnografia de um Processo de Mudança*, Luz: EDIA.

Saraiva, C. (2007) 'Um museu debaixo de água: o caso da Luz', *Etnográfica*, XI (2): 441–70.

Tzortzi, K. (2007) 'Museum building design and exhibition: layout patterns of interaction', *Proceedings of the 6th International Space Syntax Symposium*, Istanbul, 07.1-16.

25 Heritage as pharmakon and the Muses as deconstruction

Problematising curative museologies and heritage healing

Beverley Butler

This pharmakon, this 'medicine', this philter, which acts as both remedy and poison, already introduces itself into the body of discourse with all its ambivalence. This charm, this spellbinding virtue, this power of fascination, can be – alternatively or simultaneously – beneficial or maleficent.

(Derrida 2004: 70)

They [heritage objects and places] have agency: they act on us as much as we act on them. A style of heritage conservation that transcends modernism's limitations would be amenable to the divine and in a dialogue with it.

(Byrne 2004: 19)

The very word museum (mouseion in Greek, museum in Latin) . . . applies to sanctuaries dedicated to the muses, to philosophical academies or to institutions of advanced learning or of scientific research, over which the muses quite naturally presided. Such is the case with the famous Mouseion of Alexandria, founded by Ptolemy Soter or Ptolemy Philadelphus.

(Bazin 1967: 16)

This point needs to be appreciated clearly, . . . because it has given rise to a large irritating shoal of what Hercule Poirot has called red kippers.

(Pearce 1995: 96)

In his opening address at the *Material Worlds* conference, Professor Simon Knell, in honouring the distinguished contribution of Professor Sue Pearce to the fields of material culture studies, archaeology and, perhaps most significant of all, museum studies, singled out her text *On Collecting* (1995) for particular praise. It is as a similar act of homage that I take Pearce's text as a point of inspiration from which to critically explore the phenomenon of 'heritage healing' and 'curative museologies' which marks the current intellectual and ethical drives of heritage studies. I argue, that just as Derrida's critical recovery of the 'pharmakon', made via a deconstruction of its ancient etymological roots and metaphysical origins, forms a central motif within the lexicon of deconstruction and as such is pivotal to his strategy of 'taking on the tradition' (Naas 2003), similarly, a strategic and critical recovery of the origins-etymology-mythologies-genealogies of the Muses and crucially of their efficacious – pharmakonic – qualities affords a potent deconstructive potential. Not least, positioning 'heritage as pharmakon' has the ability to distinguish the benevolent and malevolent agendas at play, the ambivalences and the overdetermined nature of discourses that institutionalise 'culture as cure' and as 'heritage healing'.

As Pearce, however, forewarns us (quoted above), a critical return to examine the origins of any discourse, especially when made via the analysis of ancient etymological roots, needs to be undertaken with extreme care. This pursuit of etymological origins, as Pearce continues – in her case with reference to that of the mouseion/museum – can lead to the encounters with a 'large irritating shoal . . . of red kippers' (Pearce 1995: 96). Pearce's purpose, quite rightly, like that of other critical, 'new' museologists after her, is to demystify the idealised pathway of 'old', canonical, museological-heritage histories, languages, fixities and orthodoxies. This critical, 'new' museological scholarship (notably Foucaultian critiques of 'nodal points' of museum 'history')[1] is evoked to re-frame the 'old' canonical (cf. uni-linear, developmental), museological-heritage genealogy as retrievalism, which relates it to early and late modernity's desire to 'cultivate the Muses' in order that they may preside – 'quite naturally', as Bazin (1967: 16) would have it – over modern institutions.

The 'new' criticism thus reveals the 'old' museological-heritage discourse as constructed within a robust and (within its own terms) resonant 'invented tradition' (cf. Hobsbawm and Ranger 1983). This affords the museum-heritage culture a longevity and legitimation which frames itself within a 'Euro-Western' epic vision of not only the Muses but also the ancient philosophical institutions synonymous with Plato, Aristotle and above all the legendary Alexandria Mouseion. What I find intriguing and particularly ripe for critical rethinking, however, is that just as the Muses have been variously knocked off their pedestals, silenced, exiled, abandoned or simply marginalised as 'ever increasing abstraction' (Spentzou 2002: 8), the motifs of 'heritage as cure' which were present in the 'old' Euro-Western (and distinctly colonial) grand narratives – notably as characterised in terms of its 'redemptive formulas' – are not only still dominant across 'new' and 'post', 'parallel', 'alternative' museologies and heritage discourses, but have taken on a renewed potency (Butler 2006, 2007).

These latter discourses continue to re-possess and valorise the efficacy of heritage, either as symptom of, as cure – and at times a diagnostic – for a varied set of contexts and concerns which range from modernity's literal and metaphysical conditions of alienation and rootlessness to post-colonial/late modern experiences of rupture and displacement. Similarly, an empowering 'politics of recognition' (Taylor 1994) has adopted 'culture as cure' as a resonant framework for the reparation of historical and contemporary social-culture justice. Not only is this turn to heritage and its redeployment as curative-redemptive languages synonymous with spiritual and psychodynamic enchantment but, in more grounded terms, is bound-up with a post-conflict therapeutics of healing and recovery. For example, as part of Truth and Reconciliation Commissions and with strategies for economic revitalisation, such as the 'Angel of the North' in north-east England, the Guggenheim Museum in Bilbao and the Bibliotheca Alexandrina in Egypt. The latter, a millennial project jointly managed by the Egyptian government in conjunction with UNESCO and costing over $220 million has revived the ancient Mouseion – *the* icon of the old museology-heritage paradigm – as mega-project and dubbed by *The Economist* as an exercise in 'urban shock therapy' (Butler 2007: 176).

As a timely critique of the growth of 'heritage healing' projects and their claims to efficacy, I want to draw upon Derrida's deconstruction of the concept of 'pharmakon' (Derrida 2004: 70). In particular, I focus upon his critical recovery of the complex and seemingly contradictory set of meanings in its original Greek etymological form. As Derrida iterates, 'pharmakon' is the origin of the term 'pharmaceutical' and therefore is synonymous with wellbeing in terms of medicine, cure, remedy and healing. However, it also translates as drug, charm, magic, talisman, amulet, poison, spell, and as such can mean: the cure, the illness or its cause. What is more, Derrida regards the 'pharmakon' as an overdetermined concept and as illustrative of the ways in which the very notion of signification becomes overloaded (Derrida 2004). Given the above historical and contemporary pressure on heritage and museology to redeem and cure, I argue that the heritage as healing-cure motif has become overdetermined. As such, heritage has been and continues to be, not only a symptom or cure but the very cause of human suffering, dislocation, disinheritance. As I will argue, this overdetermination is bound up in the production of new negative and racialised categories of difference.

My critical objective within this chapter is to give concrete examples of the diverse legacies of Muses. This is achieved, initially, in a critical return to and a Derridean 'taking on' of the myths of the Muses. Subsequently, I critically explore my own research projects as a means to understand museological-heritage efficacies at both elite and more popular level. This elite–popular shift is mirrored in my ethnographic studies of the revival of Bibliotheca Alexandrina and research on heritage and wellbeing in Jerusalem and the Occupied Palestinian Territories. This shift of focus takes me from a case study context synonymous with elite institutionalisation of the Muse to that of a popular engagement in which the person/community is in 'dialogue' with the Muse. This shift, in return, requires an alignment to the genre of 'enchanted heritage' (cf. Byrne 2004) in which the continuities of sacred, and magical, ideal and real discourses can be identified from North to South (see Parish 2007). It is also a movement that, I will argue, 'transcends modernism's limitations' (Byrne 2004: 19) and is capable of unfixing Occidental modernity's binarisms: notably those dichotomies of poetry–philosophy/ pre-modern–modern/rational–superstition/secularisation–religion. In my conclusions, therefore, I argue that the Muses' legacy is the capacity to 'speak to' the diversity of human cultural experience and to give recognition to strategies of wellbeing, and cultural transmission; many of which remain 'outside' dominant heritage, museums and therapeutic discourse. These need to be re-centred in future discussions and to do so is crucially important in terms of the recognition of more 'just' heritage-museological futures.

'Taking on the Muses'

> The Muse's truthful vision is 'efficacious' (Detienne 1996: 43) . . . and was able to affect the world of the audience for good or ill.
>
> (Lada-Richards 2002: 72–3)

Derrida's strategy of 'taking on a tradition' offers a critical framework capable of deconstructing the legacy of the Muses and their efficacious – pharmakonic – qualities. Derrida's strategy argues the need to select 'performative moments' in the 'the heritage of Western tradition' which he crucially locates as both the 'philosophical tradition' synonymous with Plato and Aristotle and the 'literary tradition that begins with the epic poetry of Homer' (Naas 2003: xxiii). As such, these 'performative moments' offer a means to reveal and reclaim the crucial role (currently undervalued) of the Muses as written into the origins of 'Western tradition' and their all important privileged intimacy with museum and heritage culture. In a double-movement Derrida thus advocates the need to address the 'testimony of memory' as 'fixed' within Greco-Roman origins and genealogies while also mobilising the 'openings' and 'fissures' that 'disrupt [traditional] memory' in order to unfix and remodel these as part of a fundamental reconceptualisation of 'tradition' (Derrida 2002: 9). Derrida's strategy also forms part of attempts 'to locate something within it that the tradition has itself never been able to make its own' – an 'othering' – and to apprehend heritage and tradition as a subversive memory-space in which 'performance' is bound up in action and in the 'unexpected' emergence of 'another event' (Naas 2003: xxx).

Here I align myself with the recent call for the recognition of 'enchanted heritage' as a popular and increasingly potent global faith. In taking on 'modernism's limitations' (Byrne 2004: 19), a growing number of critics have argued that diverse constituencies and global networks bear witness to an ongoing belief in the efficacy of heritage and museological forms. These forms are characterised by belief in and their engagement with spiritual forces that act ambivalently as both benevolent and malevolent agencies. What this popular search for the efficacy of heritage in spiritual forms promises is the fact that they are underpinned by a conviction that these modes of enchantment will reveal, 'explanations and answers for "the inexplicable"' (Parish 2007: 169). In what may be construed as a 'Romanticist turn' I could be accused of once again wanting to bring the aesthetics into the rational. However, I defend this move by stressing instead that both have to be judged in terms of the moral and ethical conditions in which the work of heritage is judged by its outcomes.

I return therefore to a key performative moment responsible for giving birth to Occidental modernity's insistence on binarisms. This also presents a means to engage more closely with a foundational 'fissure' within the museological-heritage genealogy. Significantly, this 'fissure' is also synonymous with what Plato referred to as the 'quarrel between poetry and philosophy' and is thus bound up with what Derrida dubbed the 'myth of the invention of writing' where pharmakon is more fully defined (Derrida 2004: 65–74). This shift from Archaic to Classical culture, emblemised by the shift from the Muses of Poetry to the Muses of Philosophy, is thus indicative of a period of categorical change and transformation of 'tradition'. As such, this can be understood as a competition or struggle for the custodianship of 'tradition' in which encounters between mythos and logos are powerful in disrupting and thereby redefining fundamental concepts. Moreover, these in turn disrupt and open up questions of textual performativity vis-à-vis the shift from oral to written text and the efficacy of various sensory registers: for example, that of the 'voice'[2] versus the eye. By taking on this 'quarrel' and the associated 'myth' of writing it is also possible to open up traditional orthodoxies of museological and heritage discourse.

In various myths the Muses occupy a privileged place as divine custodians of the dominant and powerful discourse: the poetic tradition. Thus, as wellsprings of inspiration the Muses give us an insight into magical, divinely inspired, archival museological-heritage imaginations in terms of their preoccupations with origins, foundations, curation, care and memory-work that also take on oracular, diagnostic, prescriptive and transformative agendas. The Archaic Muses are then liminal figures between the visible and invisible[3] and as such are conceived of as 'the infallible custodians of the ipisissima verba emanating from the Heroic age' (Lada-Richards 2002: 75). It is Hesiod's *Theogony* which not only names the nine Muses, but their origins are clarified by recounting how their father Zeus (king of the gods) created the goddesses in order to complete his 'cosmic design': as such, 'the world of the gods is thus seen as incomplete without the singing of the Muses' Chorus to celebrate its beauty and order' (Murray 2002: 38–9). The Muses' crucial association with origins and with the care and curation of divine and mortal worlds thus inspire Hesiod to articulate 'a genealogy of the Gods: a comprehensive record of their origins' (Murray 2002). Crucially, it is a 'useful history' that the Muses conserve, thus, '[w]hatever society has need for, the Muses are the means of remembering'. Homer is therefore empowered by the Muses (their mother being Mnemosyne, goddess of memory), to engage in strategic genres of memory-work that are both commemorative and hold symbolic meaning, in this sense he, 'transmits the genealogies of gods and men and the myths and legends that embody the existential and moral understanding of the culture' (Murray 2002).

It is the intimacy they establish between efficacy and memory-work and cultural-transmission that take the Muses further into the domain of wellbeing, care and cure. Therefore, as Hesiod argues, 'One of the greatest gifts they offer to human beings is forgetfulness from cares' (Murray 2002). Thus, 'in the case of mortals they [the Muses] provide solace for their sorrows, allowing them temporarily to forget the hardships and pains of life' (Murray 2002). It is then a particular secret recipe cooked up by the goddesses that associates wellbeing with a form of individual forgetting that simultaneously permits communal or collective 'memorability': as Lada-Richards details, '[j]ust as a-leithia vouched safe by the archaic muse co-operates with lesmosyne, that is the forgetting of one's own ills so that the hero's kleos can be kept constantly in mind' (2002: 75). Yet it is through their privileged control over alethia that what Hesiod's Muses claim for themselves should not be exclusively identified with 'our' concept of 'truth' as reality. Ambiguity also remains, in accounts of the Muses' more punitive pharmakonic acts, showing how the goddesses could be 'dangerous when provoked'. Examples, bound up in the Greek 'spirit of competition', see the Muses compete with the sirens in song only for them to pluck the sirens' feathers to wear 'as crowns'. Nine maidens from Piraeus were likewise turned into magpies for provoking the Muses' envy and engaging in the 'misuse of mousike' (Lada-Richards 2002).

Interestingly, it is both 'envy' and this spirit of competition that, it is argued, motivates Plato's 'propaganda' against the Archaic Muses and is thus staged as the 'quarrel' between poetry and philosophy. It is through creating binary positions between poetry and philosophy for the Archaic and Classical Muses that Plato seeks to variously civilise, domesticate, castrate and transform them for his own agendas of change. However, Plato cannot dispense with the Muses completely, for he is 'the philosopher who deals with the transition from the spoken word to the written text' (Murray 2002: 43). *Poesie* must be retained as the creative factor in both human and natural work. Therefore, amongst Plato's 'true Muses' – the Muses of Philosophy – are prioritised in the figures of Urania and Calliope, whose efficacies 'Plato wanted to claim for his emerging discourse of philosophy'. Henceforth, 'song and political discourse' would be 'parallel activities' as 'both depend on effective utterance' (Murray 2002: 41).

Plato's propaganda wars aggressively targeted the poet by recasting 'him' [*sic*] as inauthentic: a charlatan, trickster and imitator. It is the famous 'cave scene' in Plato's *Republic* that the aforementioned 'condemnation of the poet as *mimetes* is thus reinforced' (Cavarero 2002: 60). As such 'Plato's message is quite clear: the cave is Athens, the prisoners are the Athenians, and inside the projection room, next to the Sophists and the artists in general, is almost certainly Homer as well'. It is then as 'one of the prisoners manages to untie himself' and thus, 'ascend toward the real world of ideas, which is outside the cave' that he can take on the role of philosopher, thereby, 'Leaving the dark world of imitations and artifice, he goes on to contemplate (theorein) the brightness of being' and 'from this contemplation' can comprehend the 'criteria on which to build a city' (Cavarero 2002). There is, therefore, 'no room' for 'simulacra and charlatans' nor for the Muse of Poetry who is thus 'banished' from the emergent Republic (Cavarero 2002).

Plato's ultimate attack on the poet destroys confidence in the efficacious, pharmakonic qualities, notably that of healing and care. Thus, the poet 'speaks of medicine but isn't a doctor – he merely imitates doctors' talk', the implication being that poetry yields false knowledge, false wisdom, false cure. Similarly, 'divine inspiration' is devalued as 'the irrational flow of poetic song' (Cavarero 2002: 47–8). The final 'divorce' is 'made possible because Plato separates off the technical from the "musical" aspects of poetry, and appropriates for philosophy the higher functions of poetry which are traditionally associated with the divine' (Cavarero 2002). In sum, poetry is reduced to techne and philosophy is raised to the heights of authenticity and truth. The flow of transmission, synonymous with the Muses as rivers, springs and streams, is supplanted by the technology of the wax tablet, which perched upon the scholars knee emblemises the entry of writing within Classical philosophy and tradition.

Certainly, Bazin's *The Museum Age* (1967), credited as the canonical 'old' museological text, is crucial in further exposing how the Muses emblemise a transitional and tranformational 'moment' within 'the tradition'. The ancient 'birth' of the archival-museum space according to Bazin is a 'consolation' for, and a means to diagnose, manage, mediate and potentially redeem traumatic loss and reinstate or rehouse collective memory (Bazin 1967: 5). The epitome of this drive is located in the creation and importantly the destruction of the legendary Alexandrina Mouseion which is cast as the originary site of intellectual (rational) inspiration and as synonymous with 'universalising' knowledge and tradition. Efficacious, pharmakonic qualities, as Bazin insists, are internalised and continue to live within modernity's museological-historical discourse in a nostalgic ritual patterning that echoes the 'myth of the eternal return', i.e. a mourning for an explanatory system capable of giving meaning to 'the inexplicable' – however, it is also made clear that 'real' power and knowledge ultimately reside in the forward march of rationality into modernity (Bazin 1967).

From Old to New Alexandrinas

> The Muse animates, stirs up, excites, arouses. She keeps watch less over the form than the force. Or more precisely: she keeps watch forcefully over the form.
>
> (Nancy, in Spentzou and Fowler 2002: xi)

The rest of this chapter is given over to concrete examples of my engagement with legacy of Muses beginning with my research into the Old and New Alexandrinas. Here I want to use Derrida's fellow deconstructionist Nancy's alternative etymological excavations of the Muses (quoted above) and his articulation of a quarrel, struggle or competition between 'form' and 'force' as a starting point to critically recast 'heritage-museological' mega-projects including Alexandrinas, both old and new, as at risk to being categorised predominantly, if not exclusively, in terms of 'form': – as a architectural object – and not a 'force' in terms of inspiring popular and collective attachments vis-à-vis content and meaning.

The ancient Alexandrina is an institution that is perhaps best understood as an icon of Greek rationalism, secularism and imperialism, and has not been without its critics. A contemporary of the Ptolemaic institution, Timon of Phlius challenged its efficacy by infamously referring to the Alexandrina as 'the Birdcage of the Muses'. Nietzsche dubbed it a slave economy (Butler 2007: 53–4), while one modern historian of Ancient Greece called it the 'McDonalds of the ancient world' (Maehler, quoted in Butler 2007: 43): the elitism of the institution and inheritors of Alexander the Great's colonial project have further been accused of creating an apartheid culture of 'the Hellenes and the rest' (Butler 2007). The Ancient Alexandrian scholars are thus charged with transforming tradition via their translation of oral culture into fixed texts: Homer's *Iliad* and *Odyssey* being the first to suffer what has been couched as 'epistemological violence' (Spivak, quoted in Butler 2007: 81).

The Alexandrian moment also sees an elitism take hold as the popular force of tradition becomes polarised as the 'other' of the archival-museological orthodoxy. What is more the 'myth of return and redemption' (cf. Foucault, in Butler 2007: 39) is subsequently cultivated and templated to become the 'blueprint' for the resurfacing of the archival-museological project within the 'nodal points' of the Western tradition: the Renaissance, Enlightenment and into modernity. What is clear is that the legacy of the split between poetry and philosophy is not only still being felt but has given birth to the fixing of further binary positions. Modernity is thus located in dichotomies such as: superstition–rationalism/pre-modern–modern/nature–culture/enchantment–disenchantment/religion–secularism/popular–elite. As Byrne reiterates, modernity becomes synonymous with 'industrial capitalism, the nation-state, rapid economic development, and a sense of human mastery over the natural world' this saw 'science and rationality . . . elevated to a semi-religious status' (2004: 17).

This 'old model', as Byrne continues, was based upon the 'expectation that all cultures will eventually approach heritage objects and places from the rational-secular point of view' (Byrne 2004). This has also led to a situation in which the 'Non-west followed the west in using ancient monuments and sites as iconic emblems of the nation' and that these 'come to take precedence over their spirituality' (Byrne 2004). The outcome has been the fixing of a dominant 'vision of a world moving steadily in the direction of rationalism and secularism' and an insistence that 'all the societies of the world were seen to be at stages along the ladder leading to modern civilization (defined as the civilization of north-western Europe)' (Byrne 2004). Similarly, museums sanctified as modernity's 'secular shrines' and the 'sacralisation' of heritage sites have led to the univer-salising of the Western model as 'global model' and subsequently embedded in charters at international level, notably within UNESCO bureaucratic discourse.[4]

My ethnography of the New Alexandrina falls within this so-called 'global' template and within Nancy's form over force dichotomy. Thus, the 'Official stakeholders' – UNESCO and the Egyptian government – performed their own elite 'Sacred dramas' (cf. Cruise O'Brien, in Butler 2007: 104) in terms of creating a top-down, bureaucratised, diplomatic project which, initially at least, cast the revived Bibliotheca as an rhetoric filled model of return and redemption mirrored in its 'overdetermined' architectural style. The pharmakonic efficacy of the New Alexandrina was configured as 'urban shock therapy'. What became widely criticised, however, as a 'mound of metaphors' and as an 'alien architectural object' likewise alienated local Alexandrian elites and popular opinion which in turn led to the project being decried as merely 'cosmetic', a 'Las Vegasisation' of both Alexandria's ancient myth-history and the contemporary revivalist ethos, and thus ultimately a contentless 'form' (Butler 2007: 175).

What the Alexandrina project revealed is the fear that international global power networks (across 'old'/'new' nation states) continue to shelter elite colonising Western-centric rhetorics within the metaphorical mega-project mantra of 'culture as cure'. Moreover, 'we' – as global/local actors – may ask who or what is being cured? By whom, and with what intended and unintended outcomes? There is the accompanying realisation too that without the popular force of the Muses presiding over these ventures, these rhetorics – like other 'buzzwords' such as 'development', 'peace', 'cosmopolitanism' – are easily lost to 'overdetermination', and, as such, again are rendered meaningless and contentless. The risk here being that this top-down 'therapeutic turn' produces templated and therefore unresponsive models of cultural transmission and memory-work and healing which may be the cause of further traumatisation, illbeing and exclusion. It is here, too, that the limits of dominant memory discourse need to be brought into view.

Only after the emergence and ethnographic study of an alternative 'critical chorus', a hybrid network made up of Alexandrian cultural elites, international, local and regional NGOs, heritage, museum professionals and archaeological teams did the popular 'force' of ownership become empowered and initial criticism give way to the transformation (still ongoing) of the Bibliotheca as shared object across local–global, political, diplomatic and public worlds (Butler 2007: 93). Here actor-network theory offered a methodology by which to map the complex, animate and inanimate forces (both intentional and unintentional) exerted by 'actants', within the contemporary epic dramas of the revivalist context; also to critically apprehend the rhetorics of grand narrative redemptions that proved not only 'empty' but so destructive in terms of silencing local-popular voices and bringing violent transformations to the Alexandrian landscape. This ethnographic perspective was capable of giving voice to an alternative popular-collective struggle to construct more meaningful visions of Alexandrian revivalism based on contemporary desires for a better future for all.

As such, this raises questions concerning the need to apprehend specific cultural practices – in terms of performances and commemorative strategies – that address 'modernism's limitations' and have relevance in 'non-Western' contexts. It is also crucial to understand how critics of both the Left (e.g. Das 1996, Kleinman, Das and Lock 1997, Sontag 2004) and Right (infamously Furedi 2003) have cautioned the uncritical use of the projection of medical symptomologies onto cultural contexts. Thus, the 'therapeutic turn' and 'therapeutic ethos', and accompanying emotive languages and vocabularies, continue to establish new expectations and, I would argue, overdetermination: in such a context the Director of New York Metropolitan Museum, for example, claimed in the post-9/11 era – 'we are here to fix the soul' (Furedi 2003: 15). We should rather look to the alternative conceptualisation of 'critical events' and 'cataclysmic events', respectively, to explore local responses to experiences of violence (Das 1996, Feuchtwang 2000a,b). Rowlands and DeJong's (2007, 2008) work gives further case-study problematisation to the ethics-practice of 'heritage healing'. Questions of conflict and violence and attempts to recover 'meaning' also raise the question of the 'limits of the capacity to represent' (Das 2007: 79)[5] – a domain that our deconstructive Muses would do well to preside over. 'We' must also 'take on' Byrne's assertion that 'belief in modernity's disenchantment was not a 'universal' force and that everyday 'enchanted heritages' not only persist but are still popular, vital and efficacious.

Archival constellations – Palestine as Muse

> Jerusalem turned out to be one of those locations that 'worked' for Jews,
> Christians and Muslims because it seemed to introduce them to the divine.
>
> (Armstrong 1996: xv)

In order to chart further the legacy of the Muses I shift my focus to alternative
cultural, poetic and spiritual logics of efficacy and enchantment. Jerusalem as
spiritual mega-city couples its divine efficacy with 'wellbeing' by functioning as
the place to cure 'interior dis-ease'; moreover, the city's critical mass of spiritual
power has been monumentally objectified notably in terms of the form and force
of the three monotheistic religions (Armstrong 1996). However, as Nancy stresses
(in Spentzou and Fowler 2002: xi, with reference to the Muses) it is the 'multiple
origin' and plurality of faiths and of efficacious powers that should also concern
us. Jerusalem's pharmakonic aspect therefore, somewhat contradictorily, is bound
up in the drive to protect wellbeing on the basis of curing the self/selfgroup (cf.
Kohut 1978), a redemptive formula oft-expressed in real and bloody conflict.
Certainly, modern Israel as a 'return to origin-homeland' and the accompanying
manipulation of metaphorical to literal [re-]attachments has echoes of the
Alexandrina model and has been expressed as 'top-down' in every respect,
notably in the Israel State's use of archaeology (see El Haj 2001). While 'taking
on' Jerusalem's divine heritage my objective has been to foster ethnographic
research under the umbrella of 'heritage wellbeing' in journeys that took me
from Jerusalem's grand narrative sacred geographies (including future-visions of
'New Jerusalems') and into the West Bank, and to engage in alternative popular
networks of persons–objects efficacies. My key concern has been to understand
how persons establish their own 'Muse-like' or 'divine' self/selfgroup relationships
as a means to commune with that which offers efficacy and wellbeing. In doing
so I align my research with ethnographies that address persons as carers, guardians,
archivists, conservators and curators of their self/selfgroups' everyday lives and
environments (notably Byrne 2004, Parish 2007, Rowlands 2007, Miller 2009).

My stress is, however, on persons-as-Muse, in order to address the psychodynamic force of efficacy and its manifestations as, for example, inspiration, creativity,
animation, possession, mystery, divine-communion and pharmakon. As such, I
focus upon everyday practices of securing, restoring and sustaining wellbeing and
on performative interactions with past and present to create better futures. My
objective has been to understand these alternative logics and pathways to wellbeing via a multi-sited research context that draws together various institutions and
'archival constellations' (a term used by Doumani (2009) to highlight alternative
archival forms and networks in the Palestinian context) and engages directly with
heritage and health providers in a series of projects that provide layered insights[6]
into the reality of Israeli occupation. My stress is upon heritage in context and
thus on 'living', vital, popular, animate heritages of everyday life.

One such particular entry point into my research context which brought salience
to such themes was my visit to the Red Crescent Society in Ramallah for the

launch of the Order of St John Eye Hospital/The Rapid Assessment of Avoidable Blindness (OSJEH/RAAB) study report.[7] As I passed through the notorious Qalandia checkpoint which partitions Jerusalem from West Bank, I was confronted by another notorious monumental mega-form: the 'West Bank Barrier Wall'. Here, the Wall has been covered in graffiti, artwork and slogans and as such the form has been subverted by the force of popular opinion and transformed into a potent counter-cultural commentary of resistance. As an organic 'exhibition' or popular archival constellation one can witness here messages of international solidarity (e.g. 'Milton Keynes supports Palestine') and heritage-savvy slogans ranging from 'No More Wailing Walls' to the more prosaic 'Balls to walls'. Emotive comparisons are also made to the Berlin Wall and to the Warsaw Ghetto. The Wall thus not only took on an efficacy in bearing witness to current injustice and connecting this to past injustices, but also in articulating aspirations for a 'just' future (e.g. 'Free Palestine', 'Right to Return').

The graffiti or image-object that I took as being of particular resonance to my research is that of a tablet or pill bottle with a label that reads 'New! Israeli Brand – RACISM' (Figure 25.1). This particular ironic product placement used the motif of the medicine bottle – itself an icon of efficacy as synonymous with the restoration of health and thus with wellbeing, cure, care and protection from illbeing – subversively. Artistic licence was similarly used to satirically highlight that what has been prescribed by the Israeli state for the West Bank was not a cure but the poison of racism. Again, the popular force of opinion expressed in the genre of the 'weapons of the weak' (Scott 1985) reveals what is regarded by protesters as buried 'truth', and takes us to ethical domains.

The reframing of the tablet bottle, and by extension the Wall as pharmakonic object, is embedded in a binary-dichotomous format, here wellbeing/illbeing. It also exposes the underlying sense that there are those who [deserve to?] have access to wellbeing and those who do not. Depending on one's politics and (for many, literally) which side of the fence you are on in terms of the mega-structure, it is variously dubbed a 'security'/'separation' or 'apartheid' Wall: its efficacies (benevolent/malevolent) are for some regarded as a 'cure' for terrorist violence and thus as a security solution, while for others it is a violent separator of cultures, peoples, families and heritages: not only a destruction of heritage and audacious land grab, but a barrier to mobility, to life chances, medical aid and futures, synonymous with the theft of time (see Backmann 2010). The image not only highlights the perceived hubris of separation but also the racialisation of cultural identity accomplished by defining 'difference' as cultural possession – a key issue within museological-heritage discourse.[8]

Among the RAAB report findings presented at the Red Crescent Building was highlighted the need for further qualitative research into the 'cultural reasons' informing decision-making in terms of health-care and wellbeing in the Occupied Palestinian Territories. It was argued that the part played by local/traditional healers required particular investigation. This agenda was also reiterated by Al-Quds Health Institute's 'Health and Nutrition' report.[9] In response, I took local healers as a starting point to define a fieldwork context and as a movement

Figure 25.1 Pharmakonic graffiti – medicine bottle on the wall at the Qalandia checkpoint.
Photograph by Beverley Butler.

from the bio-medical world of ophthalmology to the invisible worlds of the 'evil eye' and the pharmakonic forces of good and bad. Moreover, whatever negative maladies were being diagnosed a more positive, vibrant force of 'archive fever [. . .] spreading among Palestinians' proved crucial to the research context (Doumani 2009: 3). It was here that the popular desire to create spaces and opportunities for remembrance and commemoration was clear. Interesting too is the shift of focus in terms of the 'archiving of the present, not just the past', due to the 'continued and accelerating erasure of the two greatest archives of all: the physical landscape and the bonds of daily life that constitute an organic social formation' (Doumani 2009). Here archival-heritage networks as living tradition, rather than as museal museum objects, emerged as a major concern.

Below is a brief sketch of my initial research findings[10] concerning the 'layering' of person-objects in terms of the potential pathways and routes to engaging with popular networks of heritage efficacies: healing, care, wellbeing and identity-work.

The healer as a holy man – and within Islam as Sheikh – is one particular figure of care, comfort and authority encountered in my fieldwork. One particular Sheikh spoke to me about his role in terms of offering 'a source of spiritual wellbeing'. Rejecting the use of amulets (the only objects he sanctioned were prayer beads), the efficacy of his healing came in the word of God through the recitation of the Quran. As efficacious voice and as a locally acknowledged moral authority, he offered prayers and spiritual guidance. He also complemented religious ritual with natural cures 'created by God': typically herbal substances. In an articulation of a spiritual world with its jinns[11] as invisible agents of good and evil, he saw his role as being to 'remind people of God's will' and to 'bring comfort' not only to the ill and suffering but their family and friends too. As such he saw himself as part of an effective popular support network.

The setting of Sheikh's simple surroundings was very different to those healers that fell into the category of 'magicians' and 'sorcerers'. I visited one magician in his 'magic room', the interior of which was all theatre, incense and drama. Here he called on the efficacies of astrology, horoscopes, various holy and magic texts and an array of substances to engage in a repertoire that included fortune-telling, the conjuring up and projection of visions and interventions that revolved around the promise of fertility, wealth, success at work, romance, etc. Here the pharmakonic aspect of spiritual worlds was accentuated further in the ambivalence of the magician working with not only good (as the Sheikh did) but bad jinn. This may have accentuated his magical power to dispossess people of the 'evil eye', curses and other misfortunes, but it was both valued and feared and gave rise to other informants fearing such efficacious powers and suspecting that some magicians work with not only 'bad' jinn but the devil. This particular magician's comment that bad jinns inhabit abject spaces – his examples included the 'WC' and 'ancient buildings' – help us to understand why official heritage spaces often lack popular appeal.

While not believing in jinn, the practices of astrology and numerology were taken further by the Samaritan healers I met. Of interest here is that their clients are typically from Muslim communities and many are women. The efficacy thus relies in part on the healer-as-other in terms of the repertoire of texts, figures, substances, liquids and signs used in the safeguarding of wellbeing. Clients were instructed to use (chant, ingest, pour, scatter, hide, position) such material in what often centred upon rituals of reconnection and/or disconnection with persons-objects. Again agendas of securing romantic attachments, family connectedness and restoring fertility and prosperity were uppermost. Pharmakonic traits can be found not only in the healer's power in counter-acting 'psychological pain' but there were clients who were seeking efficacy in the form of retribution. Elsewhere, for example in al-Khader outside Bethlehem, further inter-faith healing ceremonies could be found, notably at St George's Cathedral, where many from the nearby mosque sought efficacy in the ritual use of an icon alleged to be the bridle of St George's horse.

In meeting a number of herbalist healers, of significance was their shared vision that the very soil and unique plant-life of Palestine was efficacious. What was interesting too was that herbal medicine was effective in defining futures: not only in terms of clients use of herbs for future wellbeing but it connected many practitioners with the international networks in the growing fields of complementary, alternative and holistic medicine (for example, some Palestinian healers I met practised new and fashionable 'distance healing', massage, reflexology which took some well into 'New Age' efficacies) and to aspirations that the export of herbs would bring economic vitality for the future. The latter was aspiration of both local farmers' collectives and also of a bigger enterprise supported by US Aid.

My interest, however, is not only in designated or self-appointed healers but in the networks of efficacy they and their clients and the broader community engages in the promotion of wellbeing. Here Nancy's (1996) excavation of the Muses' efficacy proved useful in crystallising variants in which not only do persons aspire to commune with the 'moral authority' of the healer or divine (in same way poet communed with Muse) but also becoming the Muse in a context where healing, care and wellbeing is a matter of something transmitted – with the persons-muse not a stable binary of 'subject-object' but a spirit-force of efficacy and agency that could be 'cultivated' or experienced as a 'lent force' or as a form of 'possession' (Spentzou 2002). What is clear is that the popular drive to commune with that which is thought to be efficacious also offers recognition (to suffering, injustice) access to agency and explanatory systems, and is valued as a means of exposing power.

This was a topic explored in an interview with Professor Ziad Abdeen, Director of the Nutrition and Health Research Institute, Al Quds University, Jerusalem. Abdeen began with his own definition of wellbeing as 'feeling at harmony within yourself and your surroundings', another echo perhaps of the harmony located in the Muses' interconnectedness with the divine/cosmos. He continued to argue that at public policy level the 'health and wellbeing of society' must be seen to recognise not only 'bio-medical but psycho-social worlds'. The latter, Abdeen argued, was synonymous not only with 'the major role' played by healers in Palestine but with the 'driving force of religion', 'spiritual engagement' and what he termed as the value of 'folklore' and of 'traditional or cultural knowledge to strengthen family connectedness and community connectedness and thus wellbeing'. It was clear too that a certain return to 'traditional' efficacies was bound up in the pragmatics of the 'lack of finance' and other forces of illbeing wrought by occupation. Not only did many Palestinians fear the expense of visiting medical doctors, but there was also 'the popular fear of the figure in the "white coat" and the awareness of the "failure of doctors"'. Abdeen underlined his point that 'any thinking at public level requires thinking in terms of the psycho-social', which he reiterated was 'rooted and relevant', notably in 'poorer countries'.

The efficacies of the psycho-social were also called upon to imagine a 'better future', a crucial resource in an everyday life lacking normalcy, in which the future is unclear and thus uncontrollable. As Abdeen detailed, 'we do not have a vision of what is going to happen to us next', adding, 'As Palestinians we have never been in control of our destiny. The Ottomans, the British, the Israelis [issued] a series of mandates so to speak.' He highlighted the 'necessity for public health initiatives' to take on the 'pressures of occupation on mental status', the 'erosion of coping strategy', 'threats to pride' and 'lack of control to define futures'. He re-emphasised the psycho-social model as 'embedded' in the popular context through 'religion' and 'socio-economic necessity', and reiterated that the care of self/selfgroup was based upon creating harmony out of connectivities 'with environment, land, family and community' and with their ultimate 'rooted-ness' in 'traditional cultural knowledge and folklore' and 'religious faith'. Here Abdeen argued that 'anything that dissipates energy in a positive fashion is good for your health', and articulated a popular 'fatalism' also bound up in the 'optimism' that 'we [Palestinians] believe that justice will prevail'.

Conclusions – Keep 'taking on' the medicine

> Hercule Poirot: When she opened the cupboard, she tried to focus our attention on the wrong object, so she used the briefcase as a, what is it? A bloater? Kipper?
> Captain Hastings: Red herring.
> Hercule Poirot: Absolutely. And now, my friends, it is time for me to take you to lunch. . . .
>
> (Agatha Christie 1989: *Murder in the Mews*)[12]

Return of the Red Kippers

Finally, perhaps the best gift of goddesses when considering 'heritage as phar-makon' and the 'Muses as deconstruction' – as with ironic and poetic reception – is to invoke the capacity of heritage and museum places, objects and discourse to be 'self-performative', hybrid and transformative. Pearce's use of Poirot's 'red kippers' faux pas reveals how irony – like the Muse's poetic inspiration – invokes its own efficacy: it shows how something may be lost or obfuscated but also might be *gained* in translation/performance. One can also argue that like Christie's concluding scenario of the 'briefcase as red herring', heritage discourse has been focusing in many senses on the 'wrong object(s)' – cf. the overdetermined mega-project(s) and their grand narrative 'redemptive formulas' – and that attention needs to be strategically refocused on alternative foci outside the immediate, dominant frame. Heritage as deconstruction is similarly thus afforded the dynamic, strategic role as bearing witness to the plural pharmakonic worlds that both 'we' and our 'selfgroups' and 'others' inhabit. Here too is located the need to give recognition to the co-presence of hybridised forms of logos-mythos, rational and non-rational, divine and human-object efficacies bio-medical/psycho-social and old, new and alternative technologies of memory-work.

In her text *On Collecting*, Pearce similarly calls for an 'extended vocabulary'[13] (1995: 96) capable of articulating alternative museological-heritage discourses. In this spirit, there are, for example, further etymological links to the Muses to be pursued that confront contemporary contexts with resonant models of co-presence from which the coevality of diverse museologies-heritage and the recognition of pluralities of origins/traditions/preservational paradigms and cosmologies can be invoked: the deconstructive Muses' 'interweaving' of genealogies, forms and forces thus affords a means to re-envision a more 'just' cultural transmission 'after modernity' and a place to commune with, invoke and 'take on' 'an occasional truth of a kind'.[14] Recognition is also required that museology-heritage discourses like the Muses 'speak to' other traditions by invoking visions or perspectivisms (De Castro 1998) that are multi-sensory rather than ocularcentric, and which problematise canonical museological-heritage discourses on truth value, representation and wellbeing–illbeing. Further recognition is needed too in terms of the new and diverse engagements to be made with the custodians of popular museum-heritage discourse and in terms of critics taking forward the intellectual ethos initiated so successfully by Pearce and by so doing giving recognition in turn to the Muses, persons-objects and museology-heritage studies as heavy-weight philosophical, anthropological as well as popular operational discourses and practices.

Finally, if anyone should still doubt the Muses' efficacy, Simon Knell in his introduction to the *Material Worlds* conference highlighted his envy when Sue Pearce mentioned how *On Collecting* 'was the easiest book to write' and that the text just 'flowed from her pen'. Perhaps then the Muses were at work here too!

Acknowledgements

My thanks go to Dr Nick Sargent, Director of Medical Education, St John Eye Hospital, Jerusalem, and Professor Ziad Abdeen, Director, of the Nutrition and Health Research Institute, Al Quds University, Jerusalem. To Obaida and Samir Sawalha and their family for their help and hospitality during my fieldwork in West Bank. To Sandra Dudley and Mike Rowlands for commenting on my text. Finally to Sue Pearce.

Notes

1 See Hooper-Greenhill (1992), Crimp (1993), Bennett (1995).
2 Cf. 'A theology of sung speech' operating within a 'magico-religious system of utterance and thought' (Spentzou 2002: 2–3).
3 I.e. between human and divine worlds, the living and ancestors and the past, present and future.
4 As I demonstrate, UNESCO is in many senses a reincarnation of the Alexandrina model (Butler 2007).
5 As Das further comments, conflict, violence, catastrophe 'doesn't stay in the past' but such rupture brings with it the annihilation of real and psychic worlds and fear of social suffering and a recurrent possibility in the future. Thus, for many peoples – experiences and events, 'though of the past, it did not have a feeling of pastness about it' (Das 2007: 97). This in turn aligns itself to on-going grief and grievance in the present.
6 My research methods and networks are layered in the sense that I use the 'official' heritage and health providers as a means to access into popular networks of not only healers but efficacies within broader communities.
7 See http://www.plosone.org/article/info%3Adoi%2F10.1371%2Fjournal.pone.0011854 (Accessed 10 November 2010). The OSJEH is one of the key 'actors' within my research and my heritage-health networks. The OSJEH has its own pharmakonic edge.

Historically, the St John or Hospitaller Order famously established themselves as care-givers to pilgrims in Old City while also taking up military Crusader ethos. The modern OSJEH has reinvented itself as a humanitarian 'world' charity active within Palestinian communities in East Jerusalem and the West Bank.

8 For his analysis of museological cultural racisms see Bennett (2006).
9 See http://anahri.alquds.edu/index.php/drziad-abdeen.html (Accessed 12 May 2010).
10 The following interviews were undertaken in August 2010 the majority in the West Bank regions of Nablus and Jenin with the support of the OSJEH and the Institute of Nutrition and Health, Al Quds University, Jerusalem.
11 The Arabic word jinn comes from the verb 'janna' to hide or conceal. Jinns are thus understood as invisible forces existing within a parallel spirit world. Such spirits act as either good or bad forces in attempts to influence humanity: thus curing and/or causing human illbeing/wellbeing.
12 http://www.imdb.com/title/tt0676156/quotes (Accessed 24 January 2011).
13 Pearce makes this comment with respect to the historical and cultural specificities concerning etymology and the 'extended vocabulary of ideas and institutions (1995: 96).
14 For Spivak's discussion of reclaiming the efficacies of the 'forgotten', 'Tenth Muse' see Butler (2007: 79–80).

Bibliography

Armstrong, K. (1996) *A History of Jerusalem: one city, three faiths*, London: Harper Collins.
Backmann, D. (2010) *A Wall in Palestine*, New York: Picador.
Bazin, G. (1967) *The Museum Age* [trans. J. Cahill], New York: Universe Books.
Bennett, T. (1995) *The Birth of the Museum: history, theory, politics*, London and New York: Routledge.
Bennett, T. (2006) 'Exhibition, difference, and the logic of culture', in I. Karp, C.A. Kratz, L. Szwaja and T. Ybarra-Frausto (eds) *Museum Frictions: public cultures/global transformations*, Durham, NC: Duke University Press, pp. 46–70.
Butler, B. (2006) 'Heritage and the present past', in C. Tilley, S. Kuechler and M. Rowlands (eds) *The Handbook of Material Culture*, London: Sage Publications, pp. 463–79.
Butler, B. (2007) *Return to Alexandria: an ethnography of cultural heritage revivalism and museum memory*, Walnut Creek, CA: Left Coast Press.
Byrne, D. (2004) 'Chartering heritage in Asia's postmodern world', *The Getty Institute Newsletter*, 19 (2): 16–19.
Cavarero, A. (2002) 'The envied Muse: Plato versus Homer', in E. Spentzou and D. Fowler (eds) *Cultivating the Muse: struggles for power and inspiration in classical literature*, Oxford: Oxford University Press, pp. 47–68.
Crimp, D. (1993) *On the Museum's Ruins*, Cambridge, MA: MIT Press.
Das, V. (1996) *Critical Events: an anthropological perspective on contemporary India*, Oxford: Oxford University Press.
Das, V. (2007) *Life and Words: violence and the descent into the ordinary*, Berkeley and Los Angeles: University of California Press.
De Castro, E.V. (1998) 'Cosmological deixis and Amerindian perspectivism', *Journal of the Royal Anthropological Institute*, 4 (3): 469–88.
Derrida, J. (2002) *Ethics, Institutions and the Right to Philosophy* [trans. P. Pericles Trifonas], New York: Rowman and Littlefield.
Derrida, J. (2004) *Dissemination*, London: Continuum.
Detienne, M. (1996) *The Masters of Truth in Archaic Greece*, New York and Cambridge, MA: Zone Books.

Doumani, B. (2009) 'Archiving Palestine and the Palestinians: the patrimony of Ihsan Nimr', *The Jerusalem Quarterly*, 36: 3–12.

Feuchtwang, S. (2000a) 'Reinscriptions: commemorations, restoration and the interpersonal transmission of histories and memories under modern states in Asia and Europe', in S. Radstone (ed.) *Memory and Methodology*, Oxford: Berg, pp. 59–78.

Feuchtwang, S. (2000b) 'The avenging ghost: paradigm of a shameful past', in *Anthropology II: Beliefs and Everyday Life*, Third International Conference on Sinology, London: Academica Sinica, pp. 1–29.

Furedi, F. (2003) *Therapy Culture: cultivating vulnerability in an uncertain age*, London and New York: Routledge.

El Haj, N. (2001) *Facts on the Ground: archaeological practice and territorial self-fashioning in Israeli society*, Chicago: University of Chicago Press.

Hobsbawm, E. and T. Ranger (eds) (1983) *The Invention of Tradition*, Cambridge: Cambridge University Press.

Hooper-Greenhill, E. (1992) *Museums and the Shaping of Knowledge*, London and New York: Routledge.

Kohut, H. (1978) *The Search for the Self*, New York: International Universities Press.

Kleinman, A., V. Das and M. Lock (eds) (1997) *Social Suffering*, Berkeley and Los Angeles: University of California Press.

Lada-Richards, I. (2002) 'Reinscribing the Muse: Greek drama and the discourse of inspired creativity', in E. Spentzou and D. Fowler (eds) *Cultivating the Muse: struggles for power and inspiration in Classical literature*, Oxford: Oxford University Press, pp. 69–92.

Miller, D. (2009) *The Comfort of Things*, Cambridge: Polity Press.

Murray, P. (2002) 'Plato's Muses: the goddesses that endure', in E. Spentzou and D. Fowler (eds) *Cultivating the Muse: struggles for power and inspiration in Classical literature*, Oxford: Oxford University Press, pp. 29–46.

Naas, M. (2003) *Taking on the Tradition: Jacques Derrida and the legacies of deconstruction*, Stanford: Stanford University Press.

Nancy, J.-L. (1996) *The Muses*, Stanford: Stanford University Press.

Parish, J. (2007) 'Locality, luck and family ornaments', *Museum and Society*, 5 (3): 165–79.

Pearce, S. (1995) *On Collecting: an investigation into collecting in the European tradition*, London and New York: Routledge.

Rowlands, M. (2007) 'The elderly as curators in north London', in E. Pye (ed.) *The Power of Touch*, Walnut Creek, CA: Left Coast Press.

Rowlands, M. and F. DeJong (eds) (2007) *Reclaiming Heritage: alternative imaginaries of memory in West Africa*, Walnut Creek, CA: Left Coast Press.

Rowlands, M. and F. DeJong (2008) 'Postconflict heritage', *Journal of Material Culture*, 13 (2): 131–4.

Scott, J.C. (1985) *Weapons of the Weak: everyday forms of peasant resistance*, New Haven: Yale University Press.

Sontag, S. (2004) *Regarding the Pain of Others*, London: Penguin.

Spentzou, E. (2002) 'Introduction: secularising the Muse', in E. Spentzou and D. Fowler (eds) *Cultivating the Muse: struggles for power and inspiration in Classical literature*, Oxford: Oxford University Press, pp. 1–28.

Spentzou, E. and D. Fowler (2002) *Cultivating the Muse: struggles for power and inspiration in Classical literature*, Oxford: Oxford University Press.

Taylor, C. (1994) *Multiculturalism: examining the politics of recognition*, Princeton: Princeton University Press.

Afterword

A conversation with Sue Pearce

Amy Jane Barnes and Jennifer Walklate

In 2008, a conference entitled Material Worlds *was convened to honour the contributions of Professor Susan Pearce to the studies of material culture, museology and archaeology. This book is a product of that conference, made up of papers presented at, and inspired by, the event. The papers challenge convention, much as Pearce has done in her own life and work. Taking such unconventionality as inspiration, the editors chose to make this volume more than a simple Festschrift. Susan Pearce is not only the underlying theme of this work, but an active agent in its construction. Thus, it was deemed only appropriate to move away from an introductory linear biography, and so the following text is based upon an in-depth interview with the hope of giving our Emeritus Professor the final word.*

JW: Our first question for you is this – how do you feel about being put in the rather paradoxical position of being considered a theorist of the empirical world?

SP: Yes, my response to this is, I don't see any distinction. You expected that [laughing] but, truly, I don't see any distinction. For one thing, I think the neuroscientists are showing us the way to understand that everything we are is created by our brain's neuro-pathways and their memories of what went before, so at rock bottom thoughts and feelings are as material as the rest of the world, although this does not mean that we are 'programmed' and everything is deterministic. Also, you can argue that the medium is the message, and therefore how you're thinking about anything that's empirical is actually part of the empiricism of the thing you're thinking about. The thought is going to mould and construct how the empirical operates, and all the other words we use so much; theory and practice always feed off each other. They are going to inform each other in an endless cycle, and there's no way you can ever step off that roundabout, we're on it whether we want to be or not.

But I think there are a couple of other things that are worth saying. Firstly, our engagement with the world always is empirical, because both it and we are physical. Secondly, I have always seen the nature of theory as a proposition, the purpose of which is essentially to extend our understanding of the human condition. Scientists do this by looking at bits of the material world, don't they, and we do it by inter-reacting with either the material world as it now, or with the product that humans have made of it, like the arts or history or whatever it might be. And so that's what theory is, it's just a way of understanding our context and ourselves better.

Also, I don't think the fuel in the engine is actually thought at all, I think it's feeling, and I think it's feeling that drives the kind of theory that each of us turns to. I think most things are, at the end of the day, an emotional response, there's an emotional heart to what we do, rather than a rational one, whether we are talking about theory or the empirical, or the mixture of the two. So, theory and the empirical are really the same, and both emotionally driven.

JW: I think it's really interesting talking in a more informal way. I guess leading on from that is to ask you about the beginnings of your interest in material culture?

SP: I could see this coming, and this is where I tell my story of the Isle of Wight. When I was eight and nine and, this would be going back to around 1951, we went on holiday to the Isle of Wight, to Sandown; in those days people had family seaside holidays, with buckets and spades. At that time, I was passionate about collecting fossils, and then Sandown Museum was very near the beach, and it had a wonderful geology collection. I just spent the entire time in the museum. I don't think a great deal was happening in the museum; my recollection is that I was the only inhabitant apart from the man who was then curator, and I suppose for him having a dead-keen child there was better than nobody, even if she did get under foot. Anyway, I spent the first fortnight there, and he took me through the cabinets and everything in the drawers underneath and the stores, and he taught me how to identify fossils. I was delighted when we went back again the second year, people did that in those days, they went to the same place for years on end. And the curator remembered me, and we took up where we had left off. And that was it, I knew I was going to be a material culture student, and that I was going to be a museum person and I never deviated from it.

AJB: Sounds quite familiar [laughing].

SP: What happened with you?

AJB: I started with fossils . . .

SP: Yes, a lot of people do.

AJB: And hanging round museums all the time.

SP: Which one did you hang around in, chiefly?

AJB: We used to go to lots of museums, but my Mum and Dad were from Dorset and we used to go to the Dinosaur Museum in Dorchester and we spent a lot of time there.

SP: Yes, well, my home town did not have much in the museum line, but we did go up to London very often when I was a child, it was only a short train journey away, and so I knew the British Museum and the museums in Exhibition Road extremely well. My father worked in London so it was easy, and we haunted all of them, but it was the Isle of Wight thing that was the really crucial experience. After that, I knew.

AJB: And you started with archaeology?

SP: Well, I carried on with fossils through most of my teens, but by then I was also extremely interested in other things, like cycling all over Bucks and Oxford-shire rubbing brasses and looking at churches and graveyards; this was when I was doing my O-levels and A-levels. My degree is actually in history. By then, I was hooked on the idea of going to Oxford, I grew up quite near it, and I was absolutely dazzled by the place. In those days you couldn't do archaeology there as a first degree, but I was very happy to do history. And then I stayed on in my fourth year, and did a postgraduate thing with Christopher Hawkes in archaeology, 1963–4, that was. In those days Christopher was a major guru.

JW: That's a familiar name.

SP: Yes. But I should say that I don't draw any distinctions between one kind of material culture and another, whether it's natural history or anything loosely human history, because, as I have always argued and I think most material culture people would argue, that the moment you pick up a pebble it becomes a cultural object. Fossils are only truly natural history specimens while they're still sleeping safely in their sedimentary beds. I suspect that a lot of this is going to be about how I don't draw any distinctions, because I don't draw many, I don't see the world like that.

JW: I guess the combination of studying history and then doing your postgraduate year in archaeology was important. Did the different approaches that you find in history and archaeology have a great deal of impact on you, or is it again for you one of those things where you don't draw distinctions?

SP: I don't draw much distinction. To be honest, in those days, you must remember, archaeology was very much a way of doing history, or rather prehistory. You'd try and fit excavated evidence in to an existing historical scheme, drawn largely from what could be gleaned from classical documents. Archaeology was treated as if it was a rather dumb and brute kind of history.

JW: Yes, that is one of the things that I've read.

AJB: It was quite amateur as well, wasn't it, archaeology?

SP: Yes, viewed from the perspective of today, it certainly was.

AJB: It was your intention, though, to go towards archaeology?

SP: I still wanted to go into museums, I knew I wanted to do that, and as time wore on I realised that I didn't particularly want to be a social historian, I wanted to go further back than that in the past; that was really why I studied with Hawkes. In those days the first degree and then the postgraduate year, was perfectly adequate to get a job, and of course, it was all free, which is very different from what you guys are going through. My family income was below the lowest rung of the means test so I got the whole grant, and my four years at Oxford cost me absolutely nothing.

AJB: Did you go straight into museums, then, from that?

SP: Yes, I did. I went as the junior curator in the Department of Archaeology at National Museums on Merseyside. It was still City of Liverpool Museum, then.

AJB: And that was the route then?

SP: Yes. I suppose it was a more of a gentlemanly world in some ways. You wanted to do a particular kind of work and then you applied and they talked to you, and if you'd got vaguely relevant qualifications they took a decision on the spot. But it gives you an idea of the sort of thing that one had to put up with, when I tell you that in the interview I had in William Brown Street, one of the Liverpool City Councillors there said to me, "Now you're not wearing an engagement ring are you?" and I said "No", and he said "Oh, we'll find you a nice Liverpool lad for you while you're here." You had [laughing] to smile sweetly and swallow hard.

AJB: It's interesting how the whole process of getting museum work has changed.

SP: Yes. I made it clear that I did not want to excavate. I loathe excavation, I have to say. I'd done it once or twice in the vacs, and I hated it. For one thing, I was small and slight and I found it physically too hard. For another, I find excavations boring.

AJB: How long were you at the museum in Liverpool?

SP: About two years.

AJB: And what were you, sort of, responsible for?

SP: I was responsible for a section of the classical collection, accumulated by a man called Drope. I was working on the collector as much as the collection, so I suppose it was rather the shape of things to come. You have to remember that this was before the new Liverpool museum was built, and so the collections were all in a warehouse on Blundell Street, off the Dock Road, and that's where we worked. All the stuff had been sent hurriedly to north Wales when the war started, and it was still being sorted out.

AJB: So it was recovering and catching up I suppose?

SP: Yes, it was. It took museums an awful long time to recover from the war. Liverpool and Hull were the two main ones that were destroyed, but one branch of Exeter Museum was lost and one was badly damaged. And of course, the museums themselves were all requisitioned, as they had been in the First War, only twenty-odd years earlier. They had put their stuff in storage, but it was done hastily and not very professionally, labels lost, boxes mixed, things that belonged together found in separate buildings, that kind of thing, and so my generation had to retrieve it all and sort it out. It was all in pretty much of a pickle, and the history of individual collections had to be researched so that material could be identified. I remember one important Polynesian collection that I could only provenance because the wooden pieces had octagonal shadows where distinctive labels had once been.

AJB: I don't think anyone has looked at that particular period of museum history.

SP: It would be very interesting; it would be a good PhD for somebody.

AJB: It would, wouldn't it?

SP: I can't actually remember the war, but the whole of my childhood and early life was passed in its wreckage.

AJB: The same with my parents, my Mum grew up in North London so she played on the bomb sites. Where did you go after Liverpool Museums?

SP: I went to Exeter City Museums in 1965, where history repeated itself. The reason why they appointed a curator of archaeology when the Museums Service had never had one before was because since 1940 the collections had been stored in disused RSPCA kennels [laughs]. Not good enough for the dogs but good enough for the collections! It was my job to sort them out, and create a new display of archaeology in Rougemont House, which I did. In those days you did everything, you designed it, you did the labels with press-on letters, you chatted up the electrician and said I want the light here, it was very hands on. It was the age of hessian, so I covered everything with the stuff. It was a big exhibition with nine rooms altogether, displaying the archaeology of Devon.

And then, I became curator of antiquities, with responsibility for the ethnography collections as well. This meant that I had charge of some really very important collections of Inuit and Polynesian material, among much else. There was northern material from the Captain Cook voyages, and from Vancouver's, there were collections from the cruise of the *Blossom* in 1821, when she went up the Alaskan coast, and there was stuff connected with the search for Franklin. It was sorting all this out that triggered my thirst to go to the Arctic.

AJB: Yes, and I think that draws us neatly on to something.

JW: Yes, it does. You were suddenly confronted with the implications of an anthropological approach to collections. Has that really influenced you?

SP: Yes, this is hugely important, and personally pretty complicated. In 1975 I won a Churchill Fellowship to go to the Arctic, actually to the Central Arctic Research Centre at Igloolik, and I was there and in Baffin Island for nearly two months. I followed this up with time in Greenland, the Alaskan coast and Newfoundland, which used to have an Inuit population. In fact, the Inuit exhibition I had done in Exeter was transferred to Anchorage for a while. I was out there to gather information about the communities Exeter's collections had come from, and what they had developed into. While I was there I talked a lot to the Canadians and Americans, and to the Danes, as well as Inuit people. The 'new' anthropology was just beginning to influence the English-speaking world, translations from the French and Russian philosophers were being published, and the new kinds of literary criticism were being developed, which had great potential for interpreting material culture.

But meanwhile, I had put a lot of work into Bronze Age metalwork in the south-west, so ended up at Southampton University to do a part-time PhD. My supervisor was Arthur Apsimon, but in those days at Southampton you also had an advisor, and mine was Colin Renfrew, as I had hoped. The more intellectual approach to the past was just beginning, and this is what I applied to my thesis, which I finally finished in 1982.

AJB: Great.

SP: All of this made me brood a lot about the new thinking and how it could be applied to material culture in general, and to museum collections. There have been three moments in my life when a mixture of emotional excitement and theorising was a consuming passion and this was one of them (the others were when I first read *The Golden Bough* in my early teens, and when I discovered English poetry in the sixth form). So I was primed to come to Leicester and teach Material Culture Study.

AJB: When did you come to Leicester and what prompted that?

SP: 1984, I think. It was time to move on. Also, I was very lucky, the job was a Senior Lectureship, and to advertise one of those is very, very rare. I had done a great deal of teaching at Exeter University, both undergraduate and extramural, so I had learnt the lecturing trade. I did much trekking out to remote village halls to give courses, and if people didn't like it, they left. I had done a lot of Devon archaeological management by then, with the county Rescue Archaeology Committee and national bodies, and that experience came in handy, too. We had had large numbers of young graduates who worked on government-funded schemes for a year each, and this enabled us to get many projects, like rescue excavations and the Devon Sites and Monuments Register up and running. It enabled them to get proper jobs. There were about a dozen professional archaeologists in Devon then, we saw each other on a weekly basis, we all were in our thirties, and we were keen and eager and full of missionary zeal. I had also worked a good deal on the Early Christian period in Britain, and I wanted to develop this interest.

JW: So in many ways, then, coming to Leicester wasn't all that different?

SP: No. And though it was a wrench leaving Devon, I felt that I slipped pretty seamlessly into the department. I hardly noticed the difference, to be honest.

JW: You've had quite a role, then, in the department over the last thirty odd years.

SP: Is it that long? I suppose it is. Where shall we start?

JW: Well I suppose we would like to know about the role you had in changing the Department and the discipline?

SP: I had been recruited to teach a new Material Culture course, and over the first couple of years I developed my ideas, and the course itself, a lot, and I started publishing in the field. I found structuralist ideas quite intoxicating for a time, because they seemed to be a way of getting at the poetry of things, a way of understanding why we have feelings about white, or water, or tea leaves, or bacon. Working with the students was very exciting; indeed, working with the Masters and my doctoral students – I have had fifteen – has been one of the best things in my life.

However, the Department was going through a bad patch, and there was a good deal of student unrest. At that time we were teaching both Diploma students sent on short courses by the Museum Association and our own students, who mostly did the Certificate in Museum Studies. Student expectations had risen, and the framework had become inadequate. I became Head of the Department in the January of 1986 and I was to remain Head for nine years, which is a fair time.

The only full-time academic staff were Eilean Hooper-Greenhill, Gaynor Kavanagh and me, and we set up a completely new Masters degree, which everybody did, whether they were full-time, part-time, working in a museum or whatever; everybody did exactly the same work, and everybody got exactly the same university degree. All students received six or seven large packs of reading and work sheets, all completely new, and these were much pirated by other universities starting up their new courses. We had around a hundred students a year, a huge rise, and we had to teach everything twice for a while, because we had no space to get everybody together.

I also set up publishing programmes with Leicester University Press, Athlone Press and Routledge, publications poured out of the department in a way that Museum Studies had never seen before. We held yearly conferences, and steadily, we built up a strong body of doctoral students. It was all very fruitful, and one of the best times in my life. Eventually, we got the number of full-time lecturers up to six.

Simon Knell was one of the new appointments. Eilean became Head of the Department after me, and then Simon, and now Richard [Sandell]. The government of the day has run a Research Assessment programme for a long time now, which is done department by department, and involves giving each a score, on which funding is based. We had a hard row to hoe in the early stages because museum studies research was a new kid on the block. But we improved bit by bit, and in the last round, we came out top of the entire British university system, and we also got the highest possible score in the last government teaching assessment. Obviously, all this owes a huge amount to everybody in the Department, especially the recent Heads, but I think the ten-odd years I put in at the beginning can claim to have had some effect on it all.

JW: I think that's definitely the case. It was very important for me, because that last Research Assessment programme what gave me the money to be here. So you left the Department when?

SP: September 1996.

JW: Did you move on to something else?

SP: I still did my teaching. But at that stage, the University changed its management system totally, and devolved all the financial responsibility and spending power to Deans of Faculties. I was elected Dean of Arts, so I had six departments to manage in conjunction with their own Heads, where I had had just the one. The Faculty comprised Archaeology, English, Modern Languages, English Local History, Museum Studies and History of Art. I got the first Chair in Spanish established, the first Chair in American Studies and the start of Film Studies, and I also made sure that the Chair of English Local History continued.

JW: That's a lot of departments.

SP: One of the things that I am proudest of is that all the jobs I did I was elected to by my friends. I was elected Head of Museum Studies, and Dean of Arts, and later, Pro-Vice-Chancellor. I was elected President of the Museums Association around then, too.

JW: Yes, that must be very nice.

SP: One of the things I have always believed strongly is that in every sphere of life, actor managers are the best; those who become managers should always have done the jobs being done by the people they manage. Managers need to speak from real experience, because it is the only way to have real credibility.

JW: I think you may be right. You stopped being Dean in 2000. What happened after that?

SP: Yes, I did five years as Dean. And then I was elected Pro-Vice-Chancellor, one of three PVCs. I did not enjoy being a PVC. I was the first woman in the job at Leicester. Because of the generation I belong to, I was used to being the only woman in most positions, but there was a great deal of prejudice and unpleasantness at that time, from members of staff who had been around for a long time, and who could not, or would not, understand that a woman might do the job a little differently.

JW: What you have said about being the first woman is interesting, because when there were just three lecturers in the Department, they were all women.

SP: Yes, and I doubt if it helped us either. When I got my Chair in 1991, I was the only female professor in the University for a while. There had been a couple before, but they were retired. Senior University women were very few on the ground. There had been seven Deans, and I was the only woman. I was the first woman President of the Museums Association. And all the classic things did happen, I'm afraid. Once when I was a PVC at a drinks gathering, wearing black and white because it was a Degree Day but not my gown because it was social, a senior visitor mistook me for a waitress . . .

JW: Oh, nice.

SP: It's not just mythology, I have had these things happen to me, and I could go on but I won't. Do such things still happen?

JW: I suppose it is generally less overt now.

SP: Well, over the years, I have resisted a lot of pressure to enlist me in various feminist groups, chiefly partly because I thought being there and doing a job was as good a way of flying the flag as any. But there were huge problems. You see, it was a different world then. I was 18 in 1960, and my upbringing had been essentially somewhat-modified-Victorian, with social classes, fixed values, fixed gender roles, fixed personal relationships, steam technology and very low individual expectations. There have only been a few great shifts in human understanding, they happen once a millennium or so, and the last fifty years have seen one of them. Everything has changed, including what people think of as the English language. Much of it is an improvement, although naturally, there have been some casualties.

Anyway, by 2002 my husband, Mac, was seriously ill with Parkinson's disease, and I retired. He died in 2007.

JW: But you kept working.

SP: No. Somerville, my old college, gave me a Senior Research Fellowship, and this kept me at it. I have become interested in several groups of unpublished letters which survive from about 1790 to 1820, written home by men like Charles Tatham and Charles Cockerell, who were collecting antiquities in Italy and Greece. One of the things which fascinates me is the change which seems to come about around 1800 in how material from the past was perceived. Earlier, this material seems to have been significant for its surfaces, which could show what past things looked like, but later people looked into its substance, and saw the presence of the past within the present. It's tied up with the war, and developing romantic feelings, and the burgeoning of spectacle, and all that, but it had a huge impact on museums, historical painting, historical novels, historicism in general. The letters I've edited are a way into this, and I hope to write something eventually.

Also, I was working with the Society of Antiquaries for some time, on the Council and so on. They are at Burlington House in Piccadilly, next to the Royal Academy. The Society was founded in 1707, and so the three hundredth anniversary fell in 2007. I edited the volume that celebrated their Tercentenary, which was quite a big undertaking. And I became one of their Vice-Presidents.

JW: How do the antiquaries and museums and archaeologists, how do they kind of get along together I guess? Are there any kinds of political issues?

SP: I think that the university archaeologists, and I guess this is true of many disciplines, tended to be a bit patronising about museum archaeologists, for no reason, but they did. However, this is changing and I think that it is improving considerably. Many museum people have doctorates now, they publish a lot more, they're a lot more professional, and of course the whole rescue archaeology movement brought people closer together and created a real archaeological community. People now move back and forth between the various kinds of archaeology and museum work much more readily, and this is an excellent thing. This is partly because employment has changed and people have to construct their careers differently. There are fewer jobs for life these days, and one of the best changes has been the decline and fall of old-fashioned snobbery. I don't know which part of the country you come from?

JW: Birmingham. [laughs]

SP: Hmmm, well I expect it was just as rife there, if you ask your parents about it, as it was in the south, where I grew up. And it was just awful, quite frankly. It made it so difficult for people to move out of their sphere and that was the great thing about the post-war education system, it made this possible. I was born into the old working class, my grandparents had a corner shop. My father was a clerk in London and my mother didn't work, which was normal then. Education meant everything to me, and I'm grateful.

JW: Yes, it is one of the best things.

SP: The old system made for good novels, though!

JW: Speaking of good things and good writing, the post-war resurrection of museums and so forth, can you see areas that will be important for future museum studies research?

SP: Yes, I would like to mention a number of topics. Firstly, there is some historical research we would all benefit from. We have mentioned the upheavals to collections in the two wars, but nobody has yet studied how the World War II has affected museums in Europe. The Holocaust museums in the USA have been written about, but no sustained work has been done on those in Europe, nor upon how the Nazi and the Stalinist systems impacted upon the museum world.

JW: This may be because for many people these are still difficult subjects.

SP: Yes, indeed. But perhaps that is a good reason to research it. Another area is the detailed history of specific collections, in both the history of the pieces before collecting, and how they all have been discussed, labelled, exhibited and published once they were in a collection or a museum. Museums and the ways they treated people and things before, say, 1970, were much more various than we sometimes realise, and this has a lot to tell us about colonialism, and the relationship between local people and the educated elite both inside and outside Britain.

Another significant subject is the history of how the study of material culture has developed. The discipline is now sufficiently mature to generate its own reflective literature, and material culture study has been particularly conspicuous for its peaks and troughs. It had a huge peak in the later nineteenth century as a result of Pitt-Rivers' influence, that peak continued into the early twentieth century, then it had a major drop, and again over recent decades there has been another major peak, and it would be interesting to know why and how this has happened.

JW: That's a big one.

SP: Yes, it is, although it could be divided up in various ways, and approached from various perspectives.

JW: That's what's nice about the Department, there's that multiplicity of perspectives, whatever particular kind of background you yourself come from.

SP: Which discipline do you come from?

JW: I was a medieval historian.

SP: Oh, great. There aren't many of us.

JW: [laughs] No, there aren't, that's one of the reasons I did it.

SP: Another area where I would like to see work done, and this is very much a hobby horse of mine, revolves around the relationship between material culture (and museums and collecting) and novels, poems and films. To take just one obvious example off the wall, ever since the *Lord of the Rings* there's been a huge, enormous quest literature in which the hero generally seeks some object. It would be interesting to link all this with its medieval and Romantic antecedents, and to develop a better understanding of charismatic material. This is just one strand, novels and films often embrace museums, collections and objects in general as a way of explaining humans, and we have only just begun to explore all this.

There is also crime fiction and its connections in real life. Walter Benjamin says somewhere that detective fiction hangs on material culture in the sense that it always deals with physical evidence. And of course so does the legal system. There is huge scope for thinking about what actually constitutes the physical presence of a piece material culture. You are a medievalist like me, you know as well as I do that the medieval world wouldn't have taken it for granted, that if something seemed to be present at noon on Saturday, it was actually there at noon on Saturday, and nor would many of the world's cultures; so to the modernist concept of material culture as evidence that is hugely significant. I think that is a crucial critical hub, which remains unexplored.

JW: I think a lot of relationships can be drawn there. Part of what I'm studying is how literary writers and poets and novelists have used words in particular ways to create experiences in time, to give senses of speed or rhythm, so I have an interest in literature and literary practices.

SP: Oh, very interesting.

JW: I think there are a lot of links there that haven't yet been realised.

SP: Well, two thoughts come to me from this. One revolves around the fact that the act of creating a word is as much a material construction as anything else and, unless it's just going to be gobbledegook, the word has to twin with something that actually physically exists in one way or another. A verb, for example, has to twin with the thing you do when you say the verb. And linking up with this are the ways in which languages differ. For example, English does not assign genders to objects, but most other European languages do; what might this mean about relationships to the material world?

JW: What was the other thought?

SP: I've been wondering for some time if aesthetics, which is really about how we respond to the ways in which things look, and ethics, which is about how things seem right or wrong, have the same roots. I don't mean a reversal to the Victorian belief that viewing art will elevate the behaviour of the young person, however much this operated in the founding of museums. I'm thinking more about where our understandings of rightness come from. It is not necessarily true that beauty is in the eye of the beholder; a finely plaited cord is a finely plaited cord the world over, and there is an important conjunction between material fitness for purpose and its pleasing presence. But it is a notoriously difficult area.

JW: There are some big projects there.

SP: Yes. But the biggest project of all, the one which underpins a great deal, is to build a strong link between the new neuroscience and the growing understanding of how the brain brings together memory and immediate experience of the material world to create character, action, feeling, and everything else which makes a human. This has a fundamental bearing on why and how we, and material things operate together, and it is the next exciting frontier. Perhaps, eventually, it will be possible to have a neuroscientist working on the interaction of brain and objects in the Department. That would be hugely fruitful.

JW: So what are your immediate plans?

SP: There is work on the letters I mentioned. Also, I've just started a new book on the conversion of Britain, roughly AD 350–800, which is not going to be about the deeds of kings and bishops, but about how a pagan landscape, which had emerged by around 300, and was then re-worked, still as pagan, by Anglo-Saxon speakers, became a Christian one. I've been working on this for years, and it's high time I started getting it down on paper. So much to do, so little time!

JW: A good place to end. Thank you very much for talking to us.

SP: Thank you so much for taking the trouble to listen to me.

Susan Pearce bibliography

Monographs and edited volumes

(1974) *Redmen of North America: A Catalogue of the North American Indian Collections in Exeter City Museum and Art Gallery*, Exeter: Exeter Museums Publications no. 80.

(1975) *Towards the Pole: A Catalogue of the Eskimo Collections in Exeter City Museum and Art Gallery*, Exeter: Exeter Museums Publications no. 82.

(1976) *Arts of Polynesia: A Catalogue of the Polynesian Collections in Exeter City Museums and Art Gallery*, Exeter: Exeter Museums Publications no. 72.

(1978) *The Kingdom of Dumnonia: Studies in History and Tradition in South-Western Britain AD 350–1150*, Padstow: Lodenek Press.

(1982) (ed.) *The Early Church in Western Britain and Ireland: Studies Presented to C. A. Ralegh Radford*, Oxford: British Archaeological Reports.

(1981) *The Archaeology of South West Britain*, London: Collins Archaeology no. 5.

(1983) *The Bronze Age Metalwork of South-Western Britain*, Parts 1 and 2, Oxford: British Archaeological Reports.

(1985) *Eskimo Carving*, Princes Risborough: Shire Ethnography, Shire Publications.

(1989) (ed.) *Museum Studies in Material Culture*, London and Washington, DC: Leicester University Press and Smithsonian Institution Press.

(1990 and onwards) (series ed.) *New Research in Museum Studies: An International Series*, 7 vols, London: Athlone.

(1990 and onwards) (series ed.) *Leicester Museum Studies*, 8 vols, London: Leicester University Press.

(1990) *Archaeological Curatorship*, London: Leicester University Press.

(1992) *Museums, Objects and Collections: A Cultural Study*, London: Leicester University Press.

(1994) (founding series ed.) *Leicester Readers in Museum Studies*, 6 vols, London: Routledge.

(1994) (ed.) *Interpreting Objects and Collections: Leicester Readers in Museum Studies*, vol. 1, London: Routledge.

(1995 and onwards) (ed.) *Collecting Cultures: A Series*, 4 vols, London: Routledge.

(1995) *On Collecting: An Investigation into Collecting in the European Tradition*, London: Routledge.

(1997 and onwards) (series ed. with E. Gurian) *Contemporary Issues in Museum Culture*, 5 vols, London: Leicester University Press.

(1998) *Collecting in Contemporary Practice*, London: Sage.

(1999) (ed.) *Experiencing Material Culture in the Western World*, London: Leicester University Press.

(2002) (ed.) *The Collector's Voice*, 4 vols, Aldershot: Ashgate.

(2004) *South West Britain in the Early Middle Ages* (volume in *Studies in the Early History of Britain*, series ed. N. Brooks), London: Leicester University Press/Continuum.

(2007) (ed.) *Visions of Antiquity: Papers Celebrating the Tercentenary of the Society of Antiquaries of London 1707–2007*, London: Society of Antiquaries.

Principal papers

(1970) 'Late Roman Coinage in South Western Britain', *Transactions of the Devonshire Association*, 102: 19–33.

(1971) 'Traditions of the Royal King-list of Dumnonia', *Transactions of the Honourable Society of Cymmrodorion*, 154: 128–39.

(1970–1) 'A Late Bronze Age Hoard from Glentanar, Aberdeenshire', *Proceedings of the Society of Antiquaries of Scotland*, 103: 57–64.

(1973) 'Bronze Age Pottery from Berrynarbor, Nymet Tracey, and Lovehayne', *Proceedings of the Devon Archaeological Society*, 31: 45–51.

(1973) 'The Date of Some Celtic Dedications and Hagiographical Traditions on South Western Britain', *Transactions of the Devonshire Association*, 105: 95–120.

(1974) 'The Cornish Elements in the Arthurian Tradition', *Folklore*, 85: 145–63.

(1976–7) 'Amber Beads from the Late Bronze-Age Hoard from Glentanar, Aberdeenshire', *Proceedings of the Society of Antiquaries of Scotland*, 108: 124–9.

(1977) (with Tim Padley) 'The Bronze Age Find from Tredarvah, Penzance', *Cornish Archaeology*, 16: 25–41.

(1982) 'Estates and Church Sites in Dorset and Gloucestershire: the Emergence of a Christian Society', in *The Early Church in Western Britain and Ireland* (ed. Pearce), Oxford: British Archaeological Reports, pp. 117–38.

(1982) 'Presidential Address: Church and Society in South Devon, AD 350–700', *Proceedings of the Devon Archaeological Society*, 40: 1–18.

(1985) 'Early Medieval Land Use on Dartmoor and its Flanks', *Devon Archaeology*, 13–18.

(1985) 'Early Church in the Landscape: the Evidence from North Devon', *Archaeological Journal*, 142: 255–75.

(1987) 'Ivory, Antler, Feather and Wood: Material Culture and the Cosmology of the Cumberland South Inuit, Baffin Island, Canada', *Canadian Journal of Native Studies*, 7: 307–21.

(1987) 'Exhibiting Material Culture', *International Journal of Museum Management and Curatorship*, 6: 181–6.

(1990) 'Objects as Meaning; or Narrating the Past', in *Objects of Knowledge, New Research in Museum Studies*, vol. 1, London: Athlone Press, pp. 125–40.

(1993) 'Towards Modernist Collecting: Some European Practices of the Long Term', *Nordisk Museologi*, 2: 87–98.

(1993) 'Moon Man and Sea Woman: the Cosmology of the Central Inuit', *Archaeoastronomy in the 1990s* (ed. C. Ruggles), Loughborough: Group D Publications, pp. 59–68.

(1993) 'Artefacts as the Social Anthropologist Sees Them', in (J. Rhodes *et al.*, eds) *Social History in Museums*, HMSO, pp. 65–72.

(1995) 'Authority and Anarchy in a Museum Exhibition, or The Sacred Wood Revisited', *Cultural Dynamics*, 7 (1): 125–40.

(1998) 'The Construction of Heritage: the Domestic Context and its Implications', *International Journal of Heritage Studies*, 4 (2): 86–102.

(1998) 'Objects in the Contemporary Construction of Personal Culture: Perspectives Relating to Gender and Socio-Economic Class', *Museum Management and Curatorship*, 17 (3): 223–41.

(1999) 'Bronze Age Metalwork in the South West', in *Historical Atlas of South West England* (W. Ravenhill and R. Kaines, eds), Exeter University Press, pp. 69–73.

(1999) 'Material History as Cultural Transition: A la Ronde, Exmouth, Devon, England,' *Material History Review*, Fall 1999: 26–34.

(1999) 'Collections and Collecting', in S. Knell (ed.) *Museums and the Future of Collecting*, Aldershot: Ashgate, pp. 17–21.

(2000) 'The Making of Cultural Heritage', in M. de la Torre *et al.* (eds), *Research Report: Values and Heritage Conservation*, Los Angeles: Getty Conservation Institute, pp. 59–63.

(2000) 'Belzoni's Collecting and the Egyptian Taste,' in A. Yarrington (ed.) *The Lustrous Trade: Material Culture and the History of Sculpture in England and Italy c. 1700–1830*, London: Leicester University Press, pp. 54–73.

(2000) 'Giovanni Battista Belzoni's Exhibition of the Reconstructed Tomb of Pharaoh Seti I in 1821', *Journal of History of Collections*, 12 (1): 109–26.

(2002) 'Bodies in Exile: Egyptian Mummies in the early Nineteenth Century and their Cultural Implications', in S. Oudit (ed.) *Displaced Persons: Conditions of Exile in European Culture*, Aldershot: Ashgate, pp. 54–71.

(2003) 'Saintly Cults in South-Western Britain: A Review', in G. Jones and S. Tyas (eds), *Saints of Europe*, Donnington: Shaun Tyas and Paul Watkins Publishing, pp. 173–18.

(2003) 'Processes of Conversion in North-West Gaul', in M. Carver (ed.) *The Cross goes North*, Woodbridge: Boydell and Brewer, pp. 61–78.

(2005) (with F. Salmon) 'Charles Heathcote Tatham in Italy, 1794–96: Letters, Drawings and Fragments, and Part of an Autobiography', *Journal of the Walpole Society*, 67: 1–93 and 88 figs.

(2005) 'The *Matériel* of War: Waterloo and its Culture', in J. Bonehill and G. Quilley (eds) *Conflicting Visions: War and Visual Culture in Britain and France c. 1700–1830*, Aldershot: Ashgate, pp. 207–26.

(2007) 'The Strange Story of the Thing; or the Material World in the Contemporary Novel', *Museological Review*, 12: 33–41.

(2006) (with A. Catalani) ' "Particular Thanks and Obligations": The Communications Made by Women to the Society of Antiquaries, between 1786–1837, and their significance', *The Antiquities Journal*, 86: 254–78.

(2007) 'William Bullock and the Birth of the Object, 1802–1819', in S. Knell *et al.* (eds), *Museum Revolutions*, Abingdon: Routledge, pp. 27–41.

(2008) 'The Hinton St. Mary Mosaic Pavement: Christ or Emperor?' *Britannia*, XXXIX: 193–218.

(2008) 'William Bullock's Final Years at the Egyptian Hall, Piccadilly, 1819–1825', *Journal of the Histories of Collections*, 20 (1): 17–36.

(2009) 'Material Matters. Keynote Paper', in R. Amoeda, S. Lira *et al.* (eds) *Sharing Cultures*, Porto: Green Lines Institute, pp. 1–9.

Index